THE INNER MAN

THE INNER MAN

THE LIFE OF J. G. BALLARD

JOHN BAXTER

Weidenfeld & Nicolson
LONDON

First published in Great Britain in 2011
by Weidenfeld & Nicolson

1 3 5 7 9 10 8 6 4 2

A CIP catalogue record for this book
is available from the British Library.

ISBN: 978 02978 6352 6

Typeset by Input Data Services Ltd,
Bridgwater, Somerset

Printed and bound by
CPI Group (UK) Ltd, Croydon, CRO 4YY

The Orion Publishing Group's policy is to use papers that are natural, renewable and recyclable and made from wood grown in sustainable forests. The logging and manufacturing processes are expected to conform to environmental regulations of the country of origin.

Weidenfeld & Nicolson

Orion Publishing Group Ltd
Orion House
5 Upper Saint Martin's Lane
London, WC2H 9EA

www.orionbooks.co.uk

'To the insane. I owe them everything.'

J. G. Ballard

INTRODUCTION

LICENSED TO WARN

On 28 December 1970, J. G. Ballard, not yet well known for *Crash* and *Empire of the Sun*, wrote to his Danish translator Jannick Storm thanking him for a Christmas card and the letter that accompanied it, and complimenting him on the erotic illustrations that enlivened both. Encouraged by these, he solicited Storm's help in finding some examples of 'automobile pornography' – not as research, but for his private delectation. He outlined the type he preferred – no photographs of nude women sprawled over bonnets, but, rather, stories of a more secret sort: a beautiful Nordic blonde secretary services her boss in the back seat of a Mercedes; a honeymoon couple stranded in their car consummate their marriage in some pull-over or parking lot. The request was, he stressed, not lightly made. Such material, he said, was 'extremely important' to him.

Had any other British novelist of Ballard's stature written this letter, its exposure at the opening of his biography would have aroused controversy, conceivably even damaged his reputation. In the context of Jim Ballard's career, however, it will barely excite comment.

Is there *anything* he might have done to shock us? If, with equanimity, we enjoy creations called 'Why I Want to Fuck Ronald Reagan' and 'The Assassination of John Fitzgerald Kennedy Considered as a Downhill Motor Race', as well as speculations on the possibility of Queen Elizabeth and Princess Margaret undergoing cosmetic surgery, and fantasies of sexual fetishists who copulate with the wounds of car crash victims, what would we find unacceptable? With the exception of the US publisher who, in an act greeted with derision rather than applause, pulped the entire printing of a book that included an improvisation on the possible assassination of Jacqueline Kennedy, the public welcomed each product of his imagination with as little protest as the latest Hollywood horror film. Even his sadosexual 1973 novel *Crash* and David Cronenberg's film adaptation occasioned, by comparison with, for instance, the furore over Stanley Kubrick's *A Clockwork Orange*, only modest uproar.

In 1962, while still a minor writer of science fiction, Ballard staked his claim to a region of the imagination he labelled 'inner space'. His satisfaction with the phrase was unimpaired by the knowledge that both W. H. Auden and J. B. Priestley had used it first. Like an old blues number exhumed by a modern group, it instantly became his own. The space age had not only come, he announced, but had also gone, having lasted merely the few days during which we noticed men were walking on the moon. After that, we lost interest. Science fiction did it better, and had been doing so for a century or more. Blurry videos of USAF pilots dressed like Michelin Men, bounding over an ashy waste, thanking God and planting flags, could hardly compete with H. G. Wells's vision of a moon honeycombed with tunnels and inhabited by an eerie race of Selenites.

Moreover, Ballard suggested, our attempts to leave the planet might even be an offence against biology, an act contrary to our nature as creatures of earth. The same imperative that barred us from living in the sea prohibited us from going into space. If there was a *terra incognita* to be explored, he argued, it lay within us, in the imagination that could create fantasies of travel to other worlds.

Inspired by the surrealists, he evoked a succession of futurist landscapes roamed by the walking wounded of our hubris – lapsed technocrats and victims of technological blight. Grateful to be rid of responsibility for contemplating the horrors science created in our name, we leased inner space to him in perpetuity, and authorised him to behave, within that world, more or less as he chose. With the duty to document our bad conscience went an unconditional absolution – a *laissez-passer* that read 'The bearer has done what has been done for the good of the state'. Like another diligent civil servant, he was Agent 00∞: licensed to chill.

In the past, persons who exposed the secrets of our guilty imagination often paid with their reputation, their sanity, even their lives. Jim Ballard faced no such ostracism. He was no burning-eyed John the Baptist, preaching Armageddon from the bonnet of a Cadillac, but a reasoned, lucid voice, describing his visions with all the persuasiveness of a vicar sharing his opinions on 'Thought for the Day'. As he modestly put it, 'I see myself more as a kind of investigator, a scout who is sent on ahead to see if the water is drinkable or not.'

Stamped by the same die as T. E. Lawrence, another insider/outsider, he was capable, like Lawrence, of emerging dust-stained from the desert, discarding his native robes, and, after a wash and brush-up, standing a round in the officers' mess, during which he would quote Themistocles with an ease that showed he'd read him often, and in the original, too.

The voice was crucial. A resonant baritone, tirelessly emphatic, it embodied intelligence. Women melted in its flow, including this one:

> He wasn't handsome or beautiful or svelte or anything, but his voice! You could be seduced by that voice. It wrapped itself around you. It embraced you. It asked you questions. It lingered over your life. It sort of gobbled you up. Through the delightful interest this interesting man takes in you, through his wonderful melodious voice, you're sucked into his world. And before you know it, you're in bed with him.

One seldom disagreed with Ballard, and while he would politely hear one out, there was always the feeling that he was taking no notice anyway. 'You never had conversations,' says the writer Iain Sinclair. 'You listened to these monologues and hoped to hear something you hadn't heard before.' Though sometimes hesitant before an audience or reading a prepared text, Jim improvised fluently on radio and TV, or discoursed with a glass in his hand. He relished the act of speech, bearing down on key words, rolling the vowels, tasting each syllable.

An acquaintance complained, 'Ballard is one of those infuriating figures better at being themselves than at presentation through their work. Mel Brooks and John Landis are far funnier in person than their films have ever been. Likewise, Ballard is a better off-the-cuff commenter than he is a fantasy novelist.' This exaggerates, but it's also not entirely untrue.

With this fluency went the quality the Welsh call *hwyl* – 'a sudden ecstatic inspiration which carries the speaker away on its wings, supplying him with burning words of eloquence which in his calmer and normal state he could never have chosen for himself'. And since truth has no greater enemy than a smooth talker with a good story, Jim's accounts of his life needed to be seen as improvisations on a theme rather than trustworthy fact. He habitually revised his personal history, in particular backdating intellectual discoveries. Add to this his tinkering with the structure of narrative, subverting and condensing it, seeking to cram the maximum amount of meaning into the least number of words, and the verifiable truth was not only obscured but, over time, became indistinguishable from the imagined.

In Shanghai, where he was born, one could hear a dozen English-language radio stations, most broadcasting popular music and serials. Jim grew up with the theatrical voices of Orson Welles, Conrad Nagel and Franchot Tone as his models, and an understanding of the vividness of the spoken word. In a literal sense, he found his own voice in the mid-1970s when he learned that words flowed more freely if he read them aloud. As it had for Henry James and Ford Madox Ford, dictation became his preferred method of composition. His daughter Bea recalled: 'We had a pact, and would leave him alone for a few hours, but we could not resist slipping through his door to ask questions. He would be in the middle of composing a sentence, mouthing out the words as he wrote.'

Having completed a paragraph by hand, he would type a copy and read it to himself, making more corrections. Once he could afford them, he used audio typists, taping his texts and sending them out to be transcribed – anything to preserve that distinctive voice. The technique explains the simplicity of his sentences, their brevity and understatement, the lack of extraneous adjectives, and their special euphony. He isn't writing the story. He's telling it.

In person, Jim presented a veneer of good-fellowship, slick as Formica and just as impermeable. Author Neil Gaiman called him 'terrifying in his ordinariness, like the protagonists of his high-rises and drowned worlds, like the man on the motorway island'. To his editor Malcolm Edwards, he was 'a man who absolutely knew his own mind, and wasn't going to let anybody else in on the secret. He had a shell of good manners, and a way of deflecting people by over-praise, which was a definite technique. It was a way of closing off discussion. "The editing is superb" – therefore nothing more need be said, or would be said.'

This reflexive affability disguised a troubled personality that sometimes expressed itself in physical violence. Given his childhood in Shanghai and wartime internment, it could hardly have been otherwise. Novelist Diane Johnson compared him to 'an intelligent, idealistic child brought up in a bordello who sees things from an early age that no one should have to see'. Christopher Hitchens wrote:

> To see a once-thriving city reduced to beggary and emptiness, to live one day at a time in point of food and medicine, to see an old European order brutally and efficiently overturned, to notice the utterly casual way in which human life can be snuffed out, and to see war machines wheeling and diving in the overcast sky: such an education!

Jim never denied that his psychology bordered on the psychopathic. If anything, he took pride in it. While still a young child, he entertained deep hostilities and irrational impulses. The birth of his sister Margaret when he was six, threatening his relationship with his mother, planted a sense of grievance that wove through his writing. In *Concrete Island*, the most overtly self-analytical of his novels, the protagonist complains of how, as a child, his mother abandoned him in the empty bath while she attended to his baby sister. After bawling himself hoarse, he was left to climb out by himself, aware for the first time of a rival. Bizarrely, the young Jamie, as he was known during his childhood, manufactured a fretwork wooden screen and propped it between himself and his infant sister at the dining table, glaring at her occasionally through a sliding panel. Margaret was written out of his life story. Well into middle age, he never referred to her and many friends knew nothing of her existence.

Even before the war, Jim was harmed by the experience of living as a privileged outsider within a nation of the deprived. 'Shanghai' ran through him like 'Brighton' does through a stick of rock. To snap him anywhere was to expose something of that cruel and carnal city. We see it in his penchant for sleek cars and sleeker women, and a taste for sudden death and the machines that inflict it. His rationalisations echo in the snarl of the *films noirs* he enjoyed. 'Ordinary people of your class,' sneers the assassin Dancer in Don Siegel's *The Lineup*, 'you don't understand the criminal's need for violence.'

Condescending to ignore the *lèse-majesté* of 'Queen Elizabeth's Rhinoplasty' and 'Princess Margaret's Face Lift', HMQ offered him a CBE in 2003, which, as a lifelong anti-monarchist, he declined. He did, however, accept an accolade of more popular significance when he appeared on the BBC's *Desert Island Discs* in 1991 to present eight pieces of music that would, in theory, accompany him into involuntarily exile. It was a typically prankish act, since he disliked music intensely. 'I think I'm the only person I know who doesn't own a record player or a single record,' he said. 'That gene seems to have skipped me.' Four years earlier, he'd snapped, 'There's no music in my work. The most beautiful music in the world is the sound of machine guns.' But anyone alert for a darker Jim would have been warned by his choice of tunes. First was that children's favourite 'The Teddy Bears' Picnic', with its descending misterioso chords, like the tread of huge feet, and the ominous quatrain: 'If you go out in the woods today/You're sure of a big surprise.'

CHAPTER ONE

SHANGHAI JIM

Jim was always curt about his parents, even to relative strangers. There was none of the rueful humour with which some disguise a parental rift, nor anger, nor even hate; just distaste: 'I think I have to face the fact that I didn't really like them very much. I tried in my earlier fiction – and in my earlier life, I mean – to maintain a kind of neutral stance, particularly towards my mother. I mean it is perfectly possible she wasn't a very nice human being, I don't think she was.'

He assigned each of them a short, chilly profile in his memoir, *Miracles of Life*, written a year before his death. His indifference is implied in the fact that he didn't even check the dates of their births and deaths, which are a year out in both cases.

What was the problem? Superficially, his childhood appears tranquil, even pampered. James Graham Ballard was born on 15 November 1930 in the Shanghai General Hospital, in what was then the world's fifth most populous city. His parents were among its 70,000 non-Chinese residents, who included three thousand US citizens, and numerous Jews and White (that is, not Red) Russians who'd fled the Revolution: Jim remembered the women displaying their jewellery for sale on the steps of the Russian church.

Jim's father, also James, was born in Blackburn, Lancashire, in 1901. His son's descriptions, while never affectionate, are at least respectful, with the occasional humanising detail: he remained a Lancashireman to the end of his life, Jim recalled, loving tripe, Blackpool and Lancashire comedians. James graduated in chemistry from London University and joined the Calico Printers Association, which dominated the world production of cotton goods. After the First World War, new weavers in cotton-growing nations such as India, Japan and China flooded Britain and the Commonwealth with product, undermining the market. The CPA responded by starting manufacture in those countries. When it launched a Chinese subsidiary, the China Printing and Finishing Company, Ballard was sent out to work under its then managing director, Clive Hargreaves, at its factory in the Pudong area outside Shanghai.

Unless you were in the armed forces or the colonial service, going 'Out East' was an unusual way to make one's career, but plenty were ready to do it, particularly as the Great Depression bit. Also, a job in India, Africa or China was still regarded as a gesture of sacrifice; shouldering 'the white man's burden', as Kipling called it in his 1899 poem which urged sons of empire to use a firm hand with their 'new-caught, sullen peoples/Half-devil and half-child'. Shortly before leaving for Shanghai, James married Edna Johnstone, a schoolteacher from West Bromwich whom he'd met at a holiday hotel in the Lake District. Taking a wife before departing overseas was seen as prudent, insurance against the temptations of liaisons with the locals.

When Edna and James boarded the P&O liner for the five-week voyage, neither could have known what to expect, having never been further from England than a honeymoon week in Paris. They would have relied on popular fiction, which, for a century, had shown China as a nation of wise, gentle peasants, observed by philosophical sages quoting Confucius. Mark Twain wrote of the Chinese: 'They are quiet, peaceable, tractable, free from drunkenness, and as industrious as the day is long. A disorderly Chinaman is rare, and a lazy one does not exist.' It took a while for the reality to penetrate Western consciousness, but by the mid-1930s such films as *Shanghai Express*, *The General Died at Dawn* and *The Bitter Tea of General Yen* were more accurately reflecting a country in civil war. Split by the depredations of renegade generals leading private armies, and steady invasion by Japan, which coveted its minerals, China became associated with banditry, opium and seductresses, both Asian and white. By then, however, the

Ballards had been enfolded in the protective expatriate community of Shanghai's International Settlement.

Edna became pregnant shortly after they arrived. Jim's birth was difficult, and the slim-hipped Edna often complained about it within his earshot. As with many babies, his head was briefly squeezed out of shape during the delivery – which, she suggested, explained his later eccentric behaviour. It was an experience she didn't care to repeat, and when a daughter, Margaret, was born in 1937, it was by Caesarean section.

Shanghai owed its existence to foreigners. The International Settlement and the French Concession were cities within the city. Ceded to European and US governments by the Chinese in a *quid pro quo* for trade, they enjoyed the status of foreign territory, like embassies. Their architecture was predominantly Western, and any Chinese seen in the streets would be servants. Token contingents of British, French and US troops, backed up by a few gunboats, gave the illusion of military muscle, but the real power resided in the Bund, a cliff of high-rise banks, offices and hotels, including the Customs House and the English Club, running for two miles along the Huangpu River.

Jim speculated that his parents were shocked by Shanghai's chronic poverty, endemic disease and casual violence, but if they were they adjusted well, moving into the three-storey house at 31 Amherst Avenue which they occupied throughout the thirties. The avenue was itself a monument to Europe's commercial invasion of China, since it was named for Lord Amherst of the East India Company who opened up China to trade in 1832.

The Ballards enjoyed a level of luxury unimaginable in Depression England. Their house had double glazing, air conditioning and a modern kitchen, with every kind of electrical appliance. Jim had not only his own bedroom but a bathroom, too. Servants were plentiful and cheap. They kept ten, including a chauffeur for their large Packard, and a White Russian girl as Jim's nanny. The house had lawns and a garden, though not, as shown in Steven Spielberg's film of *Empire of the Sun*, a swimming pool; Shanghai was built on mudflats, and any excavation deeper than a metre struck water. Everyone swam at the Country Club, despite the bacteria that infested the unchlorinated pool, inducing earache.

In the late thirties, the Ballards, alarmed by the artillery shells passing over their house from the encamped Japanese, moved for a time to a different house, which did have a pool, though drained, like many others around the city where it was no longer so easy to find staff to keep them clean. Jim was drawn to such pools. He liked to walk on their floors and to take refuge in them, as in a bunker. In his writing, they are invariably empty, but often serve as sites of eccentric human activity: an ideogram is etched into the floor of a pool in his short story 'The Voices of Time', a family of nomads camp in one and roast a snake in *Hello America*, while in *Super-Cannes* he imagines men in the far future staring at a few surviving patches of tile, like Roman mosaics, and pondering their function.

One heritage of Jim's childhood was an enduring racism. James used Chinese workers, mostly teenage girls who supervised the spinning and weaving machines. Their low wages and willingness to work long hours were all that made the factory profitable. He was an enlightened employer, even setting up a school to teach them to read. However, the Ballards didn't socialise with the Chinese, nor, it seems, with anyone not European or, at the very least, American. Until he arrived in Britain, Jim never ate a Chinese meal. Their servants had no names – just 'Number 1 Coolie' or 'Number 2 Boy'. Knowledge of a Chinese language was regarded as the first step in 'going native'. Wallis Simpson, the future Duchess of Windsor who spent some time on the China Station with her first husband, knew only one phrase in Mandarin – 'Boy, bring more champagne.' Of pre-war Shanghai, Jim wrote, 'I thought it was exciting; a collision of all these different cultures. It's why I've always believed in multiracial societies and the hottest possible cultural mix.' If he did have such a belief, he didn't practise it. In adulthood, his few friends were Anglo-Saxon. He never learned any foreign language, aside from an adolescent flirtation with

Latin. His characters too, saving the occasional black or Eurasian villain, are entirely white.

Photographs of young Jim show a cheerful little boy, in one case mounted in equestrian costume on a pony. 'It is difficult to remember just how formal middle-class life was in the thirties and forties,' he wrote. 'I wore a suit and tie at home. One dressed for breakfast. One lived in a very formal way, and emotions were not paraded. And my childhood was not unusual.'

Adult indifference to children was axiomatic. With infant mortality high, it didn't pay to become too attached. Also, James and Edna were still young and enjoying their privileged life. They took little notice of Jim, meeting his numerous irritating questions with a blank stare and silence. His status, he wrote bitterly, was somewhere between a servant and the family Labrador, and even the servants never looked him in the eye. In *Concrete Island*, his protagonist sees his childhood embodied in the image of a boy playing by himself in a garden surrounded by a high fence. A street kid in the film of *Empire of the Sun* echoes this sense of isolation, shouting mockingly, 'No mama, no papa, no whisky soda!'

Not that his parents had time to waste on their children. Expat Shanghai offered an extensive and entirely British social network of schools, churches and clubs of all kinds for sport, drinking and business. Edna was preoccupied with bridge. When Jim saw Barbara Stanwyck as the seductive murderess Phyllis Dietrichson in *Double Indemnity*, all peroxide hair, lipstick and suggestive anklet, he could think only of his mother's friends who gathered at the house a couple of times a week to play. Jim sat on the stairs, listening to the gossip, picking up the rules and techniques of the game, of which he became a competent player. When he was twelve, he composed, by hand, writing in a school exercise book, a guide to the game, with hints on how to win, including 'psychic bidding' – his first literary effort.

An inveterate snoop, he used his parents' frequent absences to explore their possessions. He relished knowing his father kept an automatic pistol among his shirts. Edna and James can have had few secrets that he didn't uncover, and the knowledge, as is often the case with precocious children, created a sense of collusion, a belief that he was their equal. Young Jim in *Empire of the Sun* loiters around his mother's bedroom while she dresses for her bridge afternoons, and in *The Atrocity Exhibition*, the title of his collection of 'condensed novels', one of his alter egos refers enigmatically to the contours of his mother's body as a landscape which, in some unexplained fashion, was the site of 'psychic capitulations'.

CHAPTER TWO

NOTORIOUS WHITE FLOWER

From childhood, Jim was a reader and a writer, with an inclination towards fantasy. As a former schoolteacher, Edna taught him to read before he entered Shanghai's Cathedral School at five. He remembers starting with the boys' adventure paper *Chums* as well as the customary classics: *Alice in Wonderland*, *Winnie-The-Pooh*, *Robinson Crusoe*, *Treasure Island* and *Gulliver's Travels*. Since all his life he backdated his intellectual discoveries, it's unlikely he understood such difficult material so early. He was on surer ground with comics. He read *Flash Gordon*, *Buck Rogers*, *Superman* and in particular Milt Caniff's *Terry and the Pirates*, which takes place in China. As these ran daily in newspapers, he probably encountered them there. *Terry and the Pirates*, for instance, didn't appear in comic-book form, though he could have read stories based on the characters, and those of other strips, in the chunky Big Little Books series.

He dated his first experiences in writing from primary school:

> The whole form was given, for some reason, ten pages of lines to copy out. The masters didn't give a damn what we wrote out – all they wanted to see was all this paper covered. I was copying lines out of a thriller, and I found that it was easier if I didn't bother to transcribe, but just made up the story myself. That was the first time I realised it was exciting to invent things. That set me off. I was writing all through school.

He repeated this story frequently, with variations. In one version, the master says crossly, 'If you must copy from such a book, why not choose a better one?' In another, Jim copies pages of Charles Kingsley's Elizabethan adventure story *Westward Ho!*. Setting lines to write was a common penalty in British schools, but the text was seldom continuous. The punishment lay in being forced to repeat the same trite phrase, for example, 'All work and no play makes Jack a dull boy'. But it's conceivable that a school so far from Britain made its own rules.

Since there was little in the expat community to inspire him, Jim turned to the city. 'There were absolutely no restraints on life in Shanghai,' he said.

> I think that at one time there were four hundred night clubs in the city. It was described as the wickedest city in the world, the Paris of the Orient. [It was] almost a twenty-first-century city. Huge disparities of wealth and poverty, a multilingual media city with dozens of radio stations, dominated by advertising, befouled by disease and pollution, driven by money, populated by twenty different nations, the largest and most dynamic city of the Pacific Rim, an important political battleground. In short, a portent of the world we inhabit today. It was unlimited entrepreneurial venture capitalism carried to the nth point and I adored it.

In 1937, Japan's army reached the outskirts of Shanghai. Between 13 and 22 August, the Chinese forces under General Chiang Kai-shek battled the invaders, without success. The Western powers protested but didn't intervene. Having demonstrated their overwhelming superiority, the Japanese paused, digging in. They didn't enter the International or French Concessions, where life and business proceeded more or less as usual. At the same time, they selectively limited access to the city. Tourists dwindled as traffic on the usual sea route, via Japan, was reduced to a single rat-infested steamer that left from the remote port of Shimonoseki.

One tourist who did make the trip in 1937 was Josef von Sternberg. Though he'd helped shape the perception of China with his film *Shanghai Express*, starring Marlene Dietrich as 'Shanghai Lily, the notorious white flower of China', and Warner Oland as an Eurasian warlord, he made it without ever visiting Asia. Once he did so, the reality didn't disappoint him. In particular he admired, as did Jim, the Da Shi Jie, or Great World, an entertainment complex on the picturesquely named Yangjingbang West Street in the French Concession. As many as 20,000 people flooded through its multiple levels each day. Sternberg was exhilarated by its 'gambling tables, singsong girls, magicians, pickpockets, slot machines, fireworks, bird cages, fans, stick incense, acrobats, actors, jugglers, pimps, midwives, barbers, and earwax extractors'.

By August, he'd left for Manchuria and so escaped the disaster when a Chinese plane, attacking Japanese ships, accidentally dropped a bomb into the Great World, where thousands were sheltering. One thousand one hundred and twelve people died, establishing a grim record for the most casualties from a single explosion that stood until Hiroshima. In *The Kindness of Women*, Jim described the aftermath, with corpses littering the streets, as if he had seen it as first-hand, but, at less than seven years old, he could never have visited the site. Imagination told a better story.

The Ballards did take occasional family holidays. On excursions to the resort of Tsingtao, in northern China, they toured the First World War German naval base, a complex of forts and gun emplacements cut into the cliffs. Years later, Jim compared them to the labyrinthine cathedral-like prisons imagined by Piranesi. The navies of Britain and Japan, allies at that time, pounded the base in October and November 1914. Chinese guides pointed out where German gunners, driven mad by the bombardment, had left their handprints in blood on the concrete.

More rarely, the family made trips overseas. The first, in 1934, when Jim was only three, was to North America. The whole family sailed on the *Empress of Canada* and landed in Canada on 23 May. A longer trip took place in 1939. Edna, Jim and Margaret boarded the steamer *Ranchi* and arrived in Britain on 24 March. Edna and the children stayed for a few weeks with her parents in West Bromwich. When war threatened in the summer, the whole family headed back to China, crossing the US, and taking a ship from Vancouver, stopping off in Honolulu on the way. Years later, Jim still had happy memories of the Royal Hawaiian Hotel.

He was not so nostalgic for his grandparents' home, a three-storey house, always dark, filled with heavy, uncomfortable furniture and interior doors with stained-glass panels. Used to servants, he had been a troublesome house guest. Shown the house's only bathroom, he took it for granted that it was for his use alone. He resented his grandparents' insistence that little boys be seen and not heard. Since both taught music, the house reverberated all day to the sound of students picking their way through five-finger exercises on two practice pianos. For the rest of his life, Jim shunned music. It's been assumed he was tone deaf, but his aversion may have been psychological, triggered by this early experience.

Even in his memoirs, Jim never mentioned his pre-war visit to Britain, preferring to date his detestation from his permanent relocation in 1945. However, these weeks in England at his most impressionable age first prejudiced him against the country which was reflected with such pride and satisfaction in the magazines his mother read and the newsreels that preceded the movies he saw. After this visit, a suspicion of British adults coloured his perception of his parents, their life and their values, particularly their patriotic respect for the nation that James and Edna, like most expatriates of the time, still called 'Home'.

Through 1940 and the beginning of 1941, life in the International Concessions continued much as before, despite the Japanese army being dug in on the landward side and the imperial navy lying offshore. The defence of the city was left to one US and two British gunboats. Peggy Pemberton-Carter, another British expatriate, described the Concessions as 'a sort of "Never-Never Land of ExtraTerritoriality" where riots, rebellions, civil wars could (and did) rage within sight and sound of the city'. R. W. Jackman, in his introduction to her diaries, underlines the illusory sense of security:

> The British, French and American authorities, backed up by small naval and military establishments, ensured safety. Aside from the occasional inconvenience caused by a passing army under its war-lord, there was no possibility of real danger, no significant hardship, no likelihood of financial disaster and no chance of the loss of property. Nothing had ever happened to those blessed beings with 'Extra-territorial Rights', and as far as could be imagined, nothing ever would disturb the pace of their lives. Against such sanguine expectations, and despite the military activities and successes of the Japanese which increasingly threatened the survival of the Chinese Republic, people who were in Shanghai had no incentive to depart.

Edna continued to play bridge and James to run his factory, while Jim remained at school. He claimed that most of his spare time was spent cycling around the city.

> I'd tell my mother or my nanny that I was popping round the corner to see some friends of mine who lived further up Amherst Avenue, and instead I'd get on my bike – a small half-sized little bike – and set off for downtown Shanghai through this maelstrom of trams and trucks and huge American cars and thousands of rickshaws and pedestrians; a place full of gangsters and pickpockets and beggars on the sidewalk. Full of danger for the child of a rich man. There were lots of kidnappings.

Most of these excursions were imaginary. Any bike rides probably dated from 1941, shortly before he was interned, and from after his release in 1944. The scenes he evoked could just as easily have been seen from the safety of the chauffeured car, which is how he described them later in life. As he confessed in his autobiography, before the age of seven he had no clear memories of anything, and even after this, his recollection was coloured by a vivid imagination.

From whatever vantage point he saw the streets outside the foreign

Concessions, they confronted him with the cheapness of life. Homeless Chinese died by the hundreds every night of cold or starvation. Their corpses lay ignored until carts came round and gathered them up like so much garbage. With cemeteries rare in this waterlogged terrain and only the rich able to build a tomb above ground, their families put them in cheap coffins and consigned them to the river, where they were carried out to sea on the tide. Many of the dead had survived by begging, a Buddhist institution. An old man stationed himself at the Ballards' gate, where he was ignored by everyone, even the chauffeur, who once ran over his foot. Jim tried to get his parents to take an interest in the man, but Edna warned against encouraging the needy, since they would come to rely on one's charity and be even more demanding. In time, the lesson sank in. 'What Shanghai proved,' said Jim,

> was that kindness, which we place a huge value on . . . there, things were completely different. It's very hard to convey – a kind of terminal world where all human values really have ceased to function. Kindness didn't exist, and could be dangerous. I think that's something I learned very early on as a boy; to place too much reliance on kindness is a big error because it's such an intangible thing, and the supply of kindness is finite and can be switched off.

As an adult, Jim employed kindness as a barrier, to maintain his privacy. Attempts at contact or requests for assistance were seldom refused, just diverted with postcards and scribbled notes, prefaced by a jovial 'Happy to oblige', and often containing surprisingly personal details, since he knew he would never be required to live up to any promises made, nor express such feelings face to face. Instead of refusing to supply a letter of recommendation, he preferred to write one but then send a second to the intended recipient, telling him to take no notice.

Initially, Hitler's War brought few changes to Shanghai. Fascist sympathisers trickled back to Europe, and the Vichy government took over administration of the French Concession. Though each Dakota C-47 making the trip to Australia carried a few fleeing families, most US and British citizens remained – Americans because their country was neutral and Britons because theirs was at war. Their twin senses of security were shattered on 7 December 1941 when the Japanese bombed Pearl Harbor. Immediately, the besieging force seized Shanghai. Sinking the British gunboats after a hard fight, they captured the USS *Wake* almost without a struggle; most of the crew were on shore with Chinese girlfriends. Jim woke to the sound of tanks rumbling down Amherst Avenue.

The Astor House Hotel became the headquarters of the Japanese city government. It urged calm, but ordered foreigners to present themselves for registration, and to be issued a pass and an armband. After this, life settled down again, although the Japanese behaved in an increasingly heavy-handed manner, particularly towards the Chinese. On his way to school, Jim saw beatings and arrests. Streets were frequently blocked with barbed wire while the army conducted 'security checks', a pretext for looting.

Banks remained open, but withdrawals were limited to $500 per person. In 1942, the Japanese froze all accounts. Foreign currency was exchanged for worthless scrip, only usable in the city. Cars were confiscated. James Ballard had to cycle to the factory, which continued to operate with diminished staff. After that, the army began seizing anything else of value, even furniture. Some people were allowed to keep items, but with a label attached, indicating they belonged to the Emperor of Japan. The remainder, including automobiles, were stored in the stadium built by Madame Chiang Kai-shek when she hoped Shanghai might host the 1940 Olympic Games. The loot remained there, untouched, until the end of the war. In one of the strangest episodes of *Empire of the Sun*, Jim stumbles on the stadium, guarded only by a malevolent Eurasian who hopes to sell off the items as soon as the Americans arrive.

*

Life for James and Edna became increasingly dispiriting. Japanese officers took over the Country Club and stabled horses in its squash courts. Pinning up a map of Europe and Russia, James marked the German advances as reported by the BBC. In contrast, Jim's recollection of the time is almost happy-go-lucky. With no allegiance to Britain, and harbouring a growing admiration for the Japanese, he could be indifferent to the outcome of the war. He'd already made friends with other expatriate families more in tune with life outside the International Settlement, in particular their neighbours Arthur and Grace Kendal-Ward and their four sons. Arthur Kendal-Ward managed the Shanghai waterworks. Grace had lived in China since infancy. She spoke the Shanghaiese dialect, incomprehensible to outsiders, and addressed her servants by name, not just as 'Coolie Number 1'. Jim, who, even at eleven, had an instinct for survival, saw that his parents in particular and the British in general lacked the conviction to win what promised to be a long war against the fanatical Japanese, who would rather die than surrender.

CHAPTER THREE

LUNGHUA

After their defeat in the Battle of Midway in May 1942, the Japanese treated foreign nationals more harshly. In March 1943, they announced that all non-Chinese, including those from neutral countries such as Switzerland, would be 'relocated' in so-called Civilian Assembly Centres.

Shanghai's British Residents' Association canvassed all UK civilians and assigned them to appropriate CACs. Those in good health and with families were sent to Lunghua Middle School, a former teachers' college about ten miles outside the city. Damaged in earlier fighting, the complex, consisting of seven three storey concrete buildings, with three large wooden barracks, standing on an area of open ground, had been abandoned. The surrounding land, so flat you could see the distant towers of Shanghai, was paddy fields, infested with mosquitoes. The most visible landmark, a Buddhist pagoda, with a giant and threatening statue inside, bristled with anti-aircraft guns to protect the nearby airfield. In addition to installing a barbed-wire fence around the camp, the Japanese refurbished fifty-nine dormitories to house about a dozen individuals each, and 127 family rooms. Single women – 'loose women', as the Japanese categorised them – had a block to themselves.

To Jim, the move didn't so much signify a loss of his home as his introduction to an alarming but, at the same time, exciting new world. He viewed Lunghua in the way an animal raised in captivity might regard the wild into which it was being introduced.

> Our camp was a former university campus, occupying I suppose about one square mile. In fact, we occupied about two-thirds of the campus. There was a section of buildings which for some arbitrary reason – maybe the Japs were short of wire – they'd left out. Something like fifteen buildings were on the other side of the wire. You can imagine a little township of big, two- or three-storey buildings, the nearest of which was about twenty yards away. A complete silent world, which I looked out on every morning and all day from my block. After about a year, the Japs agreed to allow these buildings to be used as a school, so we used to enter this place every day, and walk through these abandoned rooms. Military equipment was lying around all over the place. I saw rifles being taken out of a well. All rifles were taken away, but spent ammunition, ammunition boxes and bayonets, all the debris of war, was lying around. We used to walk through this totally empty zone. It had been deserted for years.

The army managed and guarded the camp, but everything else, including cooking, was done by the internees. The commandant, a former diplomat named Hayashi, was chosen because he'd been a consul in Britain and spoke good, if stilted, English. Shortly after the camp filled, he issued an awkwardly worded proclamation urging inmates to behave well: 'The Civil Assembly Centre being the best home for those who live in it, must be loved and cherished by them. All persons shall take care of their health, and live in harmony with one another. There shall be no disputing, quarrelling, disturbing or other improper demeanours.'

Initially at least, life in Lunghua was endurable. Apart from a few suicides, death by anything but natural causes was uncommon. The sick usually succumbed to malaria or dysentery; Margaret became particularly ill with the latter, and suffered intermittent attacks for the rest of her life. Though Jim complained of having contracted malaria, this is suspect, since his 'attacks' often coincided with a troublesome commitment he wanted to avoid.

Getting enough food and, in particular, water became a major preoccupation. Water was delivered twice a day in trucks to distribution points, known as the Dewdrop Inn and Waterloo. Internees queued for their supply, which had to be boiled before it could be drunk. For washing, they used water from a pond in the compound. Food, cooked in a central kitchen, mostly consisted of stew, which contained whatever meat could be found. Breakfast was cracked wheat or congee: rice boiled to a paste with water, and invariably full of weevils. Occasionally, the Japanese distributed Red Cross food parcels or supplied vegetables or meat, which the internees cooked on 'chatties' – coal stoves improvised from petrol cans. As the war dragged on, the quality of ingredients declined. Everyone learned to hoard the weevils from rice and sweet potatoes as valuable protein. For a while, they subsisted on greyhounds from the dog track. Like other animals, these had been slaughtered when their owners could no longer feed them, but the more provident veterinarians froze the carcasses.

Food had almost run out when internment ended with the nuclear raids on the Japanese mainland. Unlike the apocalyptic finale of *Empire of the Sun*, the real-life residents of Lunghua woke to find that their guards had simply disappeared. Shortly after, US planes dropped canisters of food. Accustomed to rice and sweet potatoes, and not much of those, people became ill on the sugar and fat of candy bars, condensed milk and Spam.

When *Empire of the Sun* appeared, a number of people defended Lunghua against the novel's grim picture. They pointed out that, at least in the first years, theatrical shows were produced, school taught, church services held; couples even got married, with the correct ceremonial, down to a real wedding dress. Clandestine radios kept the inmates up to date on war news. There were almost no escapes, since the detainees were people of business, not soldiers. After the one successful escape, the liberal Hayashi was replaced by a tougher military man, and the Japanese guards were relieved by more brutal Koreans. Discipline became more strict, with a daily head count of the population. Asked to nominate the most embarrassing event of a long life, Jim recalled the morning when, late for this ritual, he had to run the entire length of the barracks to take his place, under the sneers of the guards and glared at by the other internees who'd been forced to wait. On the other hand, he counted as his greatest treasure a chess set from the camp, which he kept with him until he died.

Jim called his two and a half years in Lunghua 'largely happy', because his parents left him to himself. He agreed it was a slum, but it was *his* slum, and he flourished in it. Although the camp contained three or four hundred children, he made few friendships among them, preferring to play chess with older inmates or hang out with fifty American merchant seaman from freighters moored in the harbour when the Japanese invaded.

Reflecting this sense of independence, he used *Empire of the Sun* to rewrite his internment as a story of lone survival. In the novel, Jim doesn't enter the camp by bus with his family. Instead, he's separated from them as the Japanese march into the city. This moment, with refugees surrounding the family car and Jim being borne away on the human flood, became a high point of Spielberg's film. For a time, Jim lives like a castaway in his deserted home. After that, he wanders, dazed by the violence, trying without success to become a prisoner of the Japanese. Delirious with hunger, he's picked up by two renegade American sailors, Basie and Frank, who are scavenging corpses for loot, including pulling gold teeth. Failing to sell him to Chinese middlemen for ransom, they incorporate him into their plans when he offers to guide them to abandoned houses suitable for burglary, including his own.

Eventually, the Japanese sweep up all three, and they find themselves in Lunghua, but without James, Edna or Margaret. Though he's foisted on to a couple, the Victors, Jim prefers the company of Basie and the other Americans, who lead lives of glamorous indolence. He also makes friends with the guards, who allow him to watch their mock swordplay kendo, and even try on the light armour. At the nearby airfield, he's co-opted to help repair the runway so that kamikaze pilots can take off to sacrifice themselves for the Emperor. He's deeply impressed by this devotion to duty, and by the warrior creed of bushido. His experiences at the airfield instil a sense that flying represents a freedom from responsibility, a transcendence of earthly concerns.

When the war turns against the Japanese, the guards assemble the survivors, most of them ill and starving, and set out on a 'death march' inland, which threatens to end in slaughter. Jim, despite legs covered with pustular sores, and his rectum prolapsed from malnutrition, makes his escape, crossing paddy fields choked with dead, witnessing scenes of brutality perpetrated by the retreating Japanese. The internees survive because attacks by the US Air Force and the explosion of two atomic bombs on the Japanese mainland abruptly end the war. Jim visualises the flash of the Nagasaki blast as an image of revelation. Since the bomb, in a sense, was responsible for his survival it instilled in him an ambivalent view of post-war testing. He never supported the Campaign for Nuclear Disarmament, and even started to train as a pilot with the idea of becoming a crew member in a nuclear bomber.

Both in fiction and reality, Jim remained in thrall to the war, the central experience of his life. 'I lived in Shanghai until I was fifteen,' he said,

> went through the war and acquired a special 'language' – a set of images and rhythms, dreams and expectations that are probably the basic operating formulas that govern my life to this day. The significant thing for me was that all this was turned upside down by war. Friends suddenly vanished, leaving empty houses like the *Marie Celeste*, and everywhere I saw the strange surrealist spectacles that war produces.

He added, 'It taught me many lessons, above all that the unrestricted imagination was the best guide to reality.' The words are a tacit warning that we shouldn't assume everything in his accounts is necessarily true.

The Ballards moved back into Amherst Avenue, to find their home virtually untouched. American servicemen flooded the city, reviving some of the spirit of the pre-war days. Two US Marine officers occupied the house next door, formerly owned by Germans. They had a 16mm film projector and screened movies for Margaret and Jim, including a short of Bing Crosby singing 'Don't Fence Me In' that Jim recalled for his *Desert Island Discs* appearance (adding the participation of the Andrews Sisters, who don't appear in that particular film). One of the downtown cinemas even reopened, screening *The Fighting Lady*, a documentary about the aircraft carrier *Yorktown*. Once again, the bars and brothels lit up. It seemed impossible that this gaudy city would ever become the drab capital of Communist China, but the possibility was already looming as Mao Zedong's forces gathered and Chiang Kai-shek's Kuomintang army planned a retreat to Taiwan. Jim cycled out a few times to Lunghua, to find many former internees still in residence, hoarding the supplies parachuted in by the USAF. Mountains of canned food filled the dormitories, guarded by rifle-carrying former neighbours who looked suspiciously on anyone who seemed to expect a share.

At the end of 1945 it was decided that wives and children should be repatriated to Europe. Edna, Jim and Margaret sailed on the *Arawa* early in November. A pre-war New Zealand passenger steamer, it had been successively adapted to the transport of refrigerated meat, then, during the war, of troops. Jim believed he would return to China when things settled down. Instead, he remained in exile for the next half-century, clinging resentfully to the fantasy of a lost Shanghai.

CHAPTER FOUR

THE LOST BOY

The *Arawa* docked at Southampton on 14 December 1945. After Shanghai, Britain made a poor impression on the fifteen-year-old Jim. Having survived Lunghua, he found it doubly cruel to be consigned to a country barren of all comfort, with a capital described by Cyril Connolly as

> the largest, saddest and dirtiest of great cities. With its miles of unpainted half-inhabited houses, its chopless chop houses, its beerless pubs, its once vivid quarters losing all personality, its squares bereft of elegance, its dandies in exile, its antiquities in America, its shops full of junk, bunk and tomorrow; its crowds mooning around the stained green wicker of the cafeteria in their shabby raincoats, under a sky permanently dull and lowering like a metal dish-cover.

Jim claimed that, looking down on to the dock, he mistook British automobiles, small, drab and black, for machines used to carry coal – another embittered exaggeration. He would never cease to admire the gas guzzlers so popular with Shanghai's tycoons and gangsters. Sleek enamelled beasts in pastel and chrome, these insolent chariots glide through his fiction, doors yawning on leather-covered back seats where women recline, displaying curves that mirror those of tail fin, bumper and hood. Yet even when he became rich, he never bought such a car, always driving mid-level British saloons. Like Charles Foster Kane with his 'Rosebud' sled, he preferred to nurse a resentment of childhood loss rather than do something to redress it.

Exiled from Shanghai's Eden of streets noisy with life, and

swimming parties at the Country Club, Ballard became the poet of ruin, a geographer of decay. In exhibiting American sedans smashed, writing of swimming pools drained and of ruined cities empty of people, he laments his loss but also, in an orgy of recrimination, celebrates their destruction, the better to place the blame where he believed it belonged: with the culture of his parents.

> I'd been brought up to think of England as a land of rolling meadows and village greens, inhabited by a middle class living in only slightly scaled-down versions of Hampton Court Palace. I arrived here and found this small, grey, tired little island, very dark, where it drizzled perpetually, full of working-class people, whom I'd never met before, very badly treated, badly housed and very badly educated.

Far from softening with time, his dislike became more extreme. By 1987, he was drawing comparisons with the German jail that held Nazi war criminals. 'England was like Spandau, a huge rambling old prison full of mad people serving life sentences.' The accusation echoes 'Denmark's a prison!', that other outburst by a boy who nursed a grudge against his folks. England, in failing to live up to the promises made on its behalf, became a further proof of his parents' worthlessness. Yet, also like Hamlet with Denmark, he never seriously thought of living or dying anywhere else.

In July 1945, voters rejected Winston Churchill's wartime coalition and elected the Labour government of Clement Attlee, which left Edna's parents and her friends seething. 'It was impossible,' said Jim, 'to have any kind of dialogue about the rights and wrongs of the National Health Service, which was about to come in; they talked as if this Labour government was an occupying power; that the Bolsheviks had arrived and were to strip them of everything they owned.'

He never came to terms with the concept of class. Educated in private schools and brought up in relative luxury, he had the accent and manner of privilege. Yet his admiration for American brashness and Japanese bravado instilled conflicting values. Iain Sinclair intuited the contradiction in his character. 'When you meet him, he appears to be quite an Establishment person. He's got a very fruity voice and genial persona, and would fit into the colonial society in which he grew up. But he doesn't belong. He's completely an outsider.'

Edna Ballard, with Margaret, settled in Newton Ferrers, near Plymouth, close to friends from Shanghai. She never intended to stay in England. Her place was with her husband, who was struggling to get the factory working again in the face of increasing Communist interference. She and Margaret returned in 1947. Jim remained in England. In January 1946, he arrived at The Leys School in Cambridge, and was enrolled in the fifth form. The school was recommended to Jim's father by George Osborn, headmaster of the Lunghua camp school, who had been a pupil there himself.

A schoolmate of Ballard's wrote, 'I was one of the first to make my way into the daunting grandeur of the junior dormitory of North B, where a line of steel frame beds stretched seemingly forever from the doorway into the far distance. The huge room was empty, save for one earlier arrival, a boy who seemed to be much larger than me. The boy turned out to be Ballard – no first name use in those days.'

The Leys (pronounced 'Lees') was founded by liberal Methodists, and primarily served the Midlands, which had a long tradition of Methodism. Its secular curriculum and modern facilities almost persuaded Jim to suspend his detestation of Britain. He conceded that its science block was superior to that at King's College, where he later studied medicine, and it possessed the city's only covered swimming pool. Malcolm Lowry, author of *Under the Volcano*, had been a pupil there, as had James Hilton, who based the avuncular Mr Chipping of *Goodbye Mr Chips* on one of his masters, William Balgarnie. When Jim arrived, Balgarnie still lived in retirement in a cottage opposite the school gates. In 1946, he returned briefly to teach at the school, which was short-handed because of the war, during which its buildings had been requisitioned and the pupils relocated, improbably, in the Atholl Palace Hotel at Pitlochry, in the Highlands of Scotland.

The boys slept in high-ceilinged dormitories, each bed screened only partly from its neighbours by wooden partitions called 'horse boxes'. There was no running water and only two night lavatories for forty boys. Each cubicle contained a washbowl and jug, a soap dish and toothbrush holder, and a chamber pot which, because of the shiny waxed floors, was often used in impromptu games of curling. Accustomed to a lack of privacy, Jim accepted the arrangements with equanimity. He didn't resent the regimentation and petty rules. The Leys even reminded him, consolingly, of Lunghua – 'except,' he joked, 'that the food was worse'.

Most students strove to conform, whereas Jim, in the words of another contemporary,

> was *at* The Leys but not *of* it. He was coming among people who had already known one another for several years. In addition, the war created a chasm between those who had been through serious wartime experiences and those who hadn't. He kept aloof from our petty enthusiasms – sport, house competitions, prefectorial rank, ballroom dancing. He must have found The Leys community nauseating.

'Nauseating' may be an overstatement but Jim did shun organised activity, notably on Wednesday afternoons, which were reserved for sport and other improving pursuits. 'He might have been persuaded to play a bit of rough rugby,' says another student,

> but he was not by nature a joiner of anything organised. So he did not join the [Cadet] Corps, and certainly not the Scouts, which I suspect he would have regarded with considerable disdain. But even he had to do something on Wednesday afternoons, so he became a leading member of the Non-Cadets. I fancy I can see these fifteen or so conscientious objectors wandering around the Quad with shovels over their shoulders, carrying out badly organised maintenance tasks with barely concealed languor. They would then have plenty of time to slope off to distant parts of the grounds for a cigarette or three before returning to base.

Jim's skiving didn't stop with a smoke. Happiest in his own company, he took the bus into town, generally to see a film at the Arts Cinema, followed by tea and buns at the Copper Kettle on King's Parade, before returning to cottage pie and rice pudding in the school dining hall. His disdain for The Leys is telegraphed in the school photograph taken at the end of his first year. With arms folded and legs crossed, having placed himself at the far end of the front row, he regards the camera with the ghost of a smile. His pose suggests someone already halfway out of the door.

Academically, Jim did just enough to get by. His English master, while acknowledging his 'remarkable ability and general knowledge', suggested that 'with greater concentration, his work could be even better'. No such effort was forthcoming. He won the English prize at the end of his first year and was elected to the Essay Club, but never contributed to it, nor to the school magazine. He gave his greatest effort to Latin, which he called 'my first love'. He had learned some in Lunghua, absorbing it with more enthusiasm than the French that Peggy Pemberton-Carter struggled to inculcate. However, any enthusiasm for languages disappeared the moment he left The Leys, and he boasted in 1999 that he couldn't speak a word of French, Italian or Spanish.

Fellow outcasts made up his small circle of intimates. Brian Helliwell, an exchange student from the US, described by schoolmates as 'the school's bad boy', lived up to his reputation by returning to California after graduation, becoming a photo-journalist and dying in a 1959 motorcycle accident. Another outsider, Reinhard Frank, a German refugee, spoke little English and bore a tattooed concentration camp number on his arm. He had been in Theresienstadt, then Auschwitz, and escaped from the 'death march' when the latter was evacuated. 'I never mentioned that I had been an internee under the Japanese,' Jim said, 'because it seemed so trivial by comparison.' He also befriended Dhun Robin Chand, an Anglo-Indian one year ahead of him.

*

After Spielberg's film of *Empire of the Sun* was released, people mistakenly believed young Jim was as slight as Christian Bale, who played him. Far from it. By the time he got to The Leys he was husky and powerful, with a steady, threatening stare and what Martin Amis called 'hot eyes'. 'I was introverted but physically strong,' Jim confirmed, 'and knew from my wartime experience that most people will back away if faced with a determined threat. One of my classmates called me an "intellectual thug", not entirely a compliment. I was also prone to backing up an argument about existentialism with a raised fist.' Even the staff kept their distance. In his last weeks at school, he invaded the basement kitchen to boil the flesh off a rabbit, intending to wire the skeleton together as a decoration for his desk. The housemaster, coming to complain of the smell, retreated before Jim's glare.

That the superficially genial Jimmy possessed a violent streak will not surprise anyone who knew him, particularly during his periods of heavy drinking. It was an element of his character that he accepted, even relished. In contrast to the nerdy chatter of contemporaries such as Arthur C. Clarke, he spoke with natural authority and the peremptoriness of someone impatient with interruption. 'He talked in the cadences of extreme sarcasm,' noted Martin Amis, 'with very heavy stresses.' That voice and look inspired belief. Few figures in British public life could be depended on so confidently for a forceful opinion and a cogent quote. London journalist Jason Cowley recalled that 'a shout used to echo through the newsroom at moments of great national trauma, the death of Princess Diana, say, or a terrorist outrage – "Call J. G. Ballard"'.

CHAPTER FIVE

CIVILIZATION AND ITS DISCONTENTS

The winter of 1946 was made worse by a shortage of coal and Britain's draughty, uninsulated housing. Thousands accepted the offer from under-populated Canada and Australia and emigrated. Cyril Connolly's literary monthly *Horizon*, a Ballard favourite, published 'Where Shall John Go?', a series of articles in which writers discussed the attractions of various foreign bolt holes. The seed planted by Ian Fleming's vivid, though mostly invented picture of Jamaica germinated as *Doctor No*.

Having read little in Lunghua except *Reader's Digest* and *Popular Mechanics*, Jim used his time at The Leys to explore literature, mostly European. He claims to have sampled Freud, Dostoevsky, Kafka, Rimbaud, Hemingway and the philosophers of Europe's latest modish creed, existentialism, in particular Jean-Paul Sartre and Albert Camus. Not surprisingly, this smorgasbord of despair induced indigestion, and he conceded that trying to absorb so much so young was a mistake.

He probably exaggerated the width and depth of his reading. Paper shortages and the bombing of dockland warehouses meant books were as much 'on the ration' as food or clothing. With the possible exception of Hemingway, the school library contained nothing by the writers he mentions, and the public library and second-hand bookshops were little better. Sartre wasn't translated into English until 1948, when *Horizon* published some of his plays and stories, and Methuen issued *Existentialism and Humanism*. Jim may have read Camus's *L'Étranger*, as *The Outsider*, but while Kafka's *The Trial* and

The Castle did exist in English translations, he'd have struggled to find pre-war copies at a time when paperbacks were still uncommon enough for Jim to remember the first one he bought: a Raymond Chandler title from Penguin, which first appeared in 1948.

He almost certainly read Freud's *Civilization and Its Discontents* (*Das Unbehagen in der Kultur*) since Leonard Woolf's Hogarth Press had published the first English translation in 1946. In this 1929 essay, Freud argued that civilisation and the individual were in fundamental conflict. Each of us is born with tendencies towards violence and sexual gratification. Society seeks to limit these, since they threaten order. In doing so, it stifles the 'pleasure principle', our most potent motivation. In Freud, Jim found both an explanation and a justification of the lessons he'd learned in Lunghua. Impulsively he decided to become a psychoanalyst. He had the example of André Breton, who had also studied medicine with the same ambition. Breton dropped out of medical school, but experimented with Freud's methods as a hospital orderly during the First World War. The dreams and fantasies of traumatised soldiers revealed the creative potential of the unconscious, and inspired surrealism.

By rejecting religion, celebrating sex and endorsing violence, surrealism offered a species of anti-religion. It advocated the *acte gratuit*, a random, spontaneous action – 'The simplest surrealist act,' wrote Breton, 'consists of dashing down into the street, pistol in hand, and firing blindly, as fast as you can pull the trigger, into the crowd' – and revered *l'amour fou*: lust, undiluted by sentiment. (The only acceptable excuse for missing Breton's daily séance in the Café Cyrano on Place Blanche was that one had been having sex – an impulse beyond rational control.) Violently anti-clerical, Breton encouraged his followers to attack priests and nuns in the street. At the same time, he was himself fiercely authoritarian, on the pattern of any sect leader – some called him 'the Pope of surrealism'. He frequently led the group in disrupting exhibitions or theatrical performances that excited his displeasure, smashing furniture and brawling with both artists and audience.

By accepting, even revering violence as a fact of life, surrealism allowed Jim to rationalise his adulation of the pilots he'd watched take off from the airfield near Lunghua, as well as the revelation of Nagasaki. Hadn't the Marquis de Sade, a spiritual father of the movement, defined as the ultimate *acte gratuit* the destruction of the entire universe? Almost nothing by Sade, Breton, Georges Bataille or Louis Aragon existed in translation, but Jim's embrace of surrealism was intuitive. 'Existence precedes essence,' decreed Sartre. Belief occurs spontaneously; it's only later that we seek a rational explanation. Jim's conversion to surrealism marked him as a true existentialist, even before he knew the word or the concept it embodied.

It wasn't simply a shortage of books that limited Jim's adolescent reading. Literature interested him less than art. Among the attractions of surrealism was its emphasis on painting, which was easier to absorb than Breton's rhetoric. 'I always wanted to be a painter,' he said, 'but I simply lacked the technical ability; lacked the talent. People say my novels are tremendously visual. In a sense, I paint my novels. They're the life work of a frustrated painter.' He took art classes at The Leys, but had no facility for sketching and life drawing. As an adult, he asked artist friends to coach him, always without success. Though sculpture appealed more, his few attempts at school were failures. He made casts of friends' faces, but gave it up after the plaster almost suffocated one subject.

Post-war art historians regarded surrealism as a dead end. Only a few books bothered to reproduce its images, and primitive colour printing made them muddy and indistinct. But being forced to discover surrealist art through magazines such as *Horizon* and *Penguin New Writing* may have speeded Jim's absorption, since black and white emphasised the narrative element of the paintings: their story. The more abstract Yves Tanguy and Joan Miró appealed less, and, although Tanguy inspired the landscapes of his novel *The Drought*, his favourites were figurative. The bird-headed women of Max Ernst, the empty colonnades of Giorgio de Chirico, and in particular the moon-washed nudes of Paul Delvaux, all presented him with stories waiting to be told.

A creature of enthusiasms, Jim made bold claims for surrealism, suggesting that its artists anticipated all the horrors of the century, including Nazism. This would have startled the original members of the group. Poets, critics and journalists, they gathered around Breton and Aragon with conversation rather than revolution in mind. Politics were not high on their agenda. In fact, it was Breton's insistence on everyone joining the Communist Party, on pain of expulsion, that effectively destroyed the movement. But in surrealism, as in most things, Jim was drawn to the extremity, the dangerous edge, the abyss which, as H. G. Wells warned, will, if you stare into it long enough, stare back at you.

During the thirties, surrealist activity shifted from poetry and cultural criticism to visual arts, as Breton, having driven away many of the original members with his increasingly restrictive rules, was forced to admit more painters and film-makers. He was mortified when these newcomers, in his eyes at least, vulgarised and subverted the movement.

In particular, the public enjoyed the antics of Salvador Dalí, who declared, to the despair of Breton, 'I *am* surrealism.' By painting celebrity portraits, working with the Marx Brothers, Walt Disney and Alfred Hitchcock, and staging stunts such as the banquet at which guests including Bob Hope were served live frogs, Dalí associated the movement in the popular imagination with self-advertisement and eccentricity. Breton gave him the anagrammatic nickname 'Avida Dollars'. But it was Dalí's brand of surrealism that Jim embraced, not Breton's tortuous prose nor the Communist polemic of Louis Aragon. He supported the manic Catalan unreservedly. To him, *The Persistence of Memory*, the 1931 canvas that introduced his 'soft watches', was the greatest painting of the century.

Max Ernst was second only to Dalí in Jim's regard. A print of his *The Robing of the Bride* hung in his study for most of his life next to one of *The Persistence of Memory*, and an Ernst jungle hangs in Beatrice

Dahl's apartment in *The Drowned World*. Jonathan Cape, at Jim's urging, used Ernst's *The Eye of Silence* on the first edition of *The Crystal World*, though, as he told media critic Rick Poynor, 'the design department hadn't the faintest idea what I was on about'.

In retrospect, his allegiance to surrealism, while it helped focus Jim's talent, did so at a cost. As the critic Patrick Parrinder pointed out:

> His incessant, unashamed repetition of themes and settings suggests the work of a painter (such as one of his beloved surrealists) rather than a narrative artist. His stories stay in the mind like pictures at a grand retrospective, differing from one another in their superficial choice of colour or form but tenaciously exploring a small, interlocking set of artistic possibilities. The personal style is utterly distinctive, but the canvases when hung together look remarkably alike.

The Leys and the reading he did there completed the transformation begun in Lunghua, demolishing what remained of his skimpy moral education. His parents were already non-religious, but he ditched their patriotism as well, becoming a lifelong anti-royalist. In a typically truculent but not very precise metaphor, he compared his encounter with Freud and the surrealists to a stick of bombs that fell in front of him and destroyed the bridges he was hesitant to cross. He entered The Leys a lost boy. The Jim who emerged was somebody very different – a dangerous man.

CHAPTER SIX

DOCTOR IN THE MIND

Jim's family returned to Europe in 1947, and they took a driving holiday on the Continent. The Côte d'Azur, and Lake Como in Italy, made an impression on Jim, and he became a lifelong enthusiast for the warm south. They made another visit in 1948. A Pan American Airways passenger list of April 1948 shows James, Edna and Margaret Ballard leaving Hong Kong for the UK via San Francisco and Honolulu. Seeing his mother step out of her new Buick at The Leys in her trendy New York-bought clothes, Jim was embarrassed on her behalf. She appeared 'un-English' – something that, a few years earlier, he would have applauded.

The family returned to China, but Edna and Margaret were soon back in Britain, this time for good. The new Communist government had tolerated enterprises such as Calico Printers, islands of capitalism in a rising red tide, as long as their managers extracted foreign currency from parent companies and remitted the funds to Chinese banks. However, with the Allied armed forces no longer needing cotton clothing, factories cut back. James was arrested and put on trial for his perceived failure to cooperate. It grudgingly impressed Jim that his father, with superior negotiating skills and knowledge of socialist ideology, was able to talk his way out of the charge, then escape from China altogether, travelling across country to Canton and thence to Hong Kong.

Instead of rejoining CPA, James became a consultant in pharmaceutical textiles, and head of European operations for a large Boston-based company. Margaret studied Latin at university in Britain and became an art historian, which would lead to her becoming, as Margaret Richardson, the first female curator of Sir John Soane's Museum, in Lincoln's Inn Fields, in London. Jim told his parents he wished to follow Freud and Breton into psychiatry. Having passed his School Certificate and university entrance exams in the summer of 1949, he enrolled to study medicine at King's College, Cambridge.

Though he never admitted it to his parents, Jim didn't seriously consider a medical career, least of all as a psychiatrist. Later he joked that, had he ever become a therapist, it would be with one patient: himself. Many first-year students approached medical school with a similar lack of conviction. In *Doctor in the House*, the first of Richard Gordon's bestselling comic novels, published in 1952, the reasons for studying medicine are summarised by the veteran Grimsdyke, whom an aunt supports as long as he remains a student: a situation not unlike Jim's. To the newcomer's demand, 'Why have we all taken up medicine?' he replies:

> I've got a good reason; that I'm paid to do it. You've got a doctor as a father, and a leaning towards medicine in your case is simply a hereditary defect. Tony here took it up because he couldn't think of anything better that would allow him to play rugger three times a week. How many of our colleagues entered the noble profession through motives of humanity? Damn few, I bet. Humanitarian feelings draw more young fellows annually into the London Fire Brigade.

For as long as Jim continued at university, his father paid his fees and an allowance, albeit a skimpy one. Otherwise, his motives for remaining were muddled. Sometimes he believed his studies maintained him in the false childhood of Lunghua. At others, he speculated that confronting mortality promised catharsis and closure. War, he admitted, had been 'deeply corrupting'. Two years of dissecting bodies might restore a respect for life.

Since King's was just half a mile down Trumpington Street from The Leys, his routine changed hardly at all, although it was not so easy to play the truculent loner as it had been at school. Students had to live in college for the first two years, and meals were eaten communally. He kept his distance, advertising his separateness by hanging Dalí and Magritte prints in his rooms and reading Camus. He also tried to remain aloof at lectures, sitting well back, wreathed in tobacco smoke, until the professor told him to put out his cigarette, and, indicating the crowded front rows, ordered him to join the others, if only out of self-interest – progress, he suggested, depended on getting on with his colleagues.

Jim acquiesced, but never achieved much fellow feeling, having little in common with other students. As Richard Gordon joked, many were sons of provincial doctors, and 'rugger buggers' to a man – literally so in some cases, since King's had a long homosexual tradition. Notable gay graduates included economist John Maynard Keynes, computer pioneer Alan Turing, novelists E. M. Forster, Patrick White and Simon Raven, one of the few contemporaries Jim befriended. At a provost's sherry party, he even met Forster, but dismissed him as a bewhiskered dodderer who resembled, he said, a disappointed paedophile.

Any ambition to become a psychiatrist failed to survive his first months at King's. He learned quickly that a diploma in psychiatric medicine was hard won. Still regarded as a branch of neurology, psychiatry required a full medical degree even before one started training. Those not discouraged by this faced a further three years' learning and applying the crude therapies of the time, including electric shock, insulin coma and prefrontal lobotomy. The last involved penetrating the skull with ice pick and hammer, and scrambling the frontal lobes with an instrument like an electric drill.

Future psychiatrist and writer R. D. Laing went through his training just before Ballard entered King's. Not surprisingly, it made him an advocate of non-invasive treatments for mental illness, including LSD. Jim had no time for Laing, but in their telegenic skill and flair for self-promotion and popularisation, the two were alike. Laing even annexed some of his phraseology. Two years after Jim popularised the term 'inner space', Laing told an audience at the Institute for Contemporary Arts:

> I am a specialist, God help me, in events in inner space and time, in experiences called thoughts, images, reveries, memories, dreams, visions, hallucinations, dreams of memories, memories of dreams, memories of visions, dreams of hallucinations, refractions of refractions of refractions of that original Alpha and Omega of experience and reality, that Reality on whose repression, denial, splitting, projection, falsification, and general desecration and profanation our civilization as much as anything is based.

He concluded with a line that might have come straight from Ballard. 'We live equally out of our bodies and out of our minds.'

Disastrous as he would have been as an analyst, Jim was a promising subject *for* analysis, but always avoided submitting to treatment. Asked if he'd been tempted, he responded with a classic Freudian slip: 'I did appear in a film answering a questionnaire designed to expose psychopaths: "Do you love your mother?" "Are you ever cruel to animals?" They sat me down in front of a camera, and I answered randomly. Of course, any true psychopath would see through the leading questions instantly.'

Jim accepted with equanimity the likelihood that he harboured psychopathic tendencies induced by his childhood experiences. 'I'm sure [Lunghua] did affect me, probably in a rather corrupting way, in the sense of reducing the moral authority of the received world to nil, and placing an immense value on the power of the imagination to remake everything – rather psychotic, really.' As Ballard did, the psychopath embraces his lack of conscience as a badge of intelligence. Hervey M. Cleckley wrote in *The Mask of Sanity*, his pioneering study of the condition, that 'beauty and ugliness – except in a very superficial sense – goodness, evil, love, horror, and humor have no actual meaning, no power to move him'. Such a person talks entertainingly, can be brilliant and charming, yet 'carries disaster lightly in each hand'.

Like Breton, Jim saw psychopathy in its creative rather than socio-medical aspect, as a poisoned tree bearing toxic but toothsome fruit. In one of his last novels, *Cocaine Nights*, set in an apparently tranquil Mediterranean resort that's actually riddled with pornography, drugs and murder, one of its complaisant sybarites makes a direct comparison; they are lying under the tree of sin, he says, enjoying their fruit in company with the serpent. Vice and violence were tastes that Jim, as much as any Edenic tempter, believed his readers needed to share, for their own good. 'I think the future will be boredom,' he wrote, 'interrupted by totally unpredictable periods of volatility. I expect the world's great suburban sprawl to be constantly rippled by all kinds of outbursts of activity, like the tragedy at Waco. We won't be able to predict these and they may provide a necessary role, a little roughage in the social system.'

It would be decades before English literature learned to deal with an author whose work had no moral agenda – indeed, who presented an actively amoral one, and could, as Yeats urged, 'cast a cold eye/on life, on death'. As one would expect, the French, with the benefit of Sade, J.-K. Huysmans, Jules Barbey d'Aurevilly and the Comte de Lautréamont in their cultural history, caught up first. In a 1976 essay on *Crash*, the media philosopher Jean Baudrillard, a favourite of Jim, and vice versa, wrote of the novel:

> This mutating and commutating world of simulation and death, this violently sexualised world totally lacking in desire, full of violent and violated bodies but curiously neutered, this chromatic and intensely metallic world empty of the sensorial, a world of hyper-technology without finality – is it good or bad? We can't say. It is simply fascinating, without this fascination implying any kind of value judgment whatsoever. And this is the miracle of *Crash*. The moral gaze – the critical judgmentalism that is still a part of the old world's functionality – cannot touch it.

CHAPTER SEVEN

SHOT AT NOON

The cover copy for Ballard's collection *The Atrocity Exhibition*, published in 1970, reads like a profile of the writer himself:

> The central character is a doctor who is suffering from a nervous breakdown. His dreams are haunted by the figures of John F. Kennedy and Marilyn Monroe, dead astronauts and auto-disaster victims. Trying to find his sanity, he casts himself in a number of different roles – H-bomber pilot, presidential assassin, car-crash victim, psychopath.

The 'exhibition' takes place inside the brain of this man, which his life and imagination has furnished with images both erotic and terrible; sometimes both at the same time. The first printing of *The Atrocity Exhibition*, the Danish edition, was dedicated 'To the insane'. Jim never again added a dedication to any of his novels, and he removed this one for all other editions – a deletion he regretted. Those suffering from mental illness deserved his gratitude. 'I owe them everything,' he admitted.

It was this dream-haunted candidate for a nervous breakdown who stepped into the dissecting rooms at Addenbrooke's Hospital to start his second year of medical studies. Few fellow students shared his transcendental take on what confronted them. What induced a shudder in many held, for him, a glamorous familiarity. The greenish-yellow corpses on their tables, lit by overhead fluorescents, evoked both abattoir and nightclub. Many of the cadavers were those of doctors, the overwhelming majority male, who had willed their bodies to the college. As his dissection subject, Jim, perversely, chose a rare female cadaver. Jim's alter ego in the autobiographical novel *The Kindness of Women* christens her 'Dr Elizabeth Grant', and dreams of her as an ancient goddess ruling this outpost of the empire of death. Students worked on a corpse in pairs, but Jim never mentions his real-life colleague. Instead, he resuscitates 'Peggy Gardner', a composite of the girls in Lunghua. She becomes his dissecting partner and chaperone, a celibate presence who ensures that the intimate relationship with the late Dr Grant doesn't become too Oedipal.

Over the years, Jim's emotional, almost romantic evocation of the dissecting rooms seldom varied. Only once, in 1999, did he opt for simple description.

> There were 20 tables, each with a cadaver lying on it. At first it took one's breath away. It was quite unsettling. For dissection purposes a body is divided into five parts; leg, arm, abdomen, thorax, and head and neck. The whole dissection takes a full term, the head and neck take two terms. Once you had separated your part, you took it to a free table where you had more elbow room. And when you'd finished the afternoon's work, each part would be tagged with your name, and the identification number of the cadaver. You took the body parts down to huge lockers at the end of the room – and you'd open the locker and find it full of human legs or arms or heads. That was unsettling too. At the end of term, when all the body parts had been dissected, the bones would be gathered together for burial or cremation in the workrooms adjoining the dissecting room, where the laboratory assistants did their stuff. There were wooden tables and a lot of metal dishes, each with a pile of bones, and a name tag. It all looked like the remains of some huge cannibal feast.

Why this late abandonment of the former grisly glamour? Perhaps because his mother had died the year before, severing the emotional link to those weeks when he broke up the body of her surrogate as if it were a car being junked for parts.

*

Jim's two years at King's were not entirely academic. He played tennis, punted on the Cam and learned how to drink, shunning beer but developing a taste for whisky. He saw lots of movies, from *Sunset Boulevard* to *T-Men* and *Orphée* and *Open City*. He liked *The Third Man*, and in particular the subversive continental perspective of Michael Powell and Emeric Pressburger, who anatomised the sexual roots of religion in *Black Narcissus*, diagnosed British jingoism and xenophobia in *The Life and Death of Colonel Blimp* and extracted humour from brain surgery for *A Matter of Life and Death*: all themes close to Jim's heart. Once alcohol had dissolved his inhibitions, he also found sexual partners among the student nurses of Addenbrooke's Hospital, to which the medical school was attached. Discovering a recreational hypodermic in one nurse's 'fun drawer' alerted him that women could be as uninhibited and inventive as men. Their bohemianism effaced any lingering *pudeur*, and he became an erotic adventurer with a taste for sex in odd locations, with a variety of women, and often with a spice of violence.

He also began, seriously, to write. At The Leys, he'd sent stories to *Horizon*, but the magazine folded in 1949 without having shown any interest. For a while, James Joyce preoccupied him, but he acknowledged that the influence of *Ulysses* was almost entirely negative. More attractive were the experiments of thirties and forties modernism: Aldous Huxley's *Ape and Essence*, an apocalyptic fantasy told partly as a film script, Nigel Balchin's *Lord, I Was Afraid*, made up almost entirely of dialogue, and the plays of W. H. Auden and Christopher Isherwood, in particular *The Ascent of F6*, the name of whose main character, Ransom, became one of his favourites. He also fell under the spell of *The Exploits of Engelbrecht*, some relentlessly facetious surrealist adventures by Maurice Richardson. Appearing in *Lilliput*, they purported to be bulletins from the Proceedings of the Surrealist Sportsmen's Club, describing how dwarf boxer Engelbrecht shoots witches, plays football on Mars and enjoys rounds of surrealist golf that continue into infinity.

Starting a comic novel in the style of Joyce and Richardson, Jim found, like many before him, that such puns and wordplay demanded steely concentration and the scholarship of an encyclopaedist. He completed about sixty pages of *You and Me and the Continuum*, on the theme of Christ's second coming. 'I'd been bowled over,' he said, 'when I first read [Robert] Graves's *White Goddess* and Joseph Campbell's *The Hero With A Thousand Faces*, and also Graves's *King Jesus*, and I think my "novel" was trying to be an updating of the heroes of religious myth – but it was all totally mad as well as unpublishable, the product of too much scattershot reading.'

Max Beerbohm described the curse of Oxford as the belief that ideas alone are really worthwhile. Of Cambridge, Jim might have said that it proved ideas counted for little. One debate swirled around literary theorist F. R. Leavis. In 1948, Leavis's book *The Great Tradition* proposed a hierarchy of novelists for which authors qualified on the basis not only of skill but of moral worth. Initially, only Jane Austen, George Eliot, Henry James and Joseph Conrad attained his standards, though he did relent and admit Dickens. A friend took Jim to one of Leavis's lectures. It had a negative effect, and contributed to the decision that he was 'an old-fashioned story-teller at heart'. After that, he read as little fiction as possible. When his children studied Dickens at school, he confessed an ignorance of all his novels. He often cited *Moby-Dick* as a favourite book, but never finished it. Though many found *The Drowned World* 'Conradian', any similarities were, he insisted, accidental, since he hadn't read even *Heart of Darkness*, at least not at that time. And despite naming Percy Wyndham Lewis as a favourite author, what he knew of his work came entirely from BBC Radio's 1955 adaptation of *The Human Age* trilogy.

By far the largest part of Jim's reading took place in what he called his 'invisible library': books he knew from having dipped into them, heard radio programmes about, seen reviews of, or discussed with friends, but never actually read. In 1983, when the critic Peter Ronnov-Jensen asked about the possible influence of Georges Bataille and the

Marquis de Sade on his work, Jim said, 'I've got to make a terrible confession':

> I've never read a word by either writer, though I'm very familiar with their names. People have in fact, conversationally, referred to my connections with de Sade. I think that particular strand of my fiction, which began with *The Atrocity Exhibition* and culminated with *Crash*, grew spontaneously and wasn't directly influenced by anyone. As for Bataille, he crops up all over the place but I have never actually read any novels by him. He's one of the members of that invisible library, along with various other surrealist pioneers, that I have not read. I have read most of Rimbaud's poems in English. I've read Genet's novels: those two I'm happy to claim as powerful influences on me.

It would have mortified the young novelists of the nineties who rated him their spiritual father to discover he never read their books. This was less from indolence or ego than a superstition, shared with many authors, that, in reading one's competitors, one risked being influenced by them. To his publisher, Malcolm Edwards, he confessed he'd read only one contemporary novel: Iain Banks's *The Wasp Factory*. 'He did review some fiction,' concedes Edwards, 'and always praised it, since he said it was unfair to be critical if he hadn't actually read the book.' Novels sent to him in the hope of endorsement got short shrift. He enjoyed describing the satisfying thump of Salman Rushdie's *Midnight's Children* as it hit the bottom of the dustbin.

The handful of novels Jim read and genuinely respected dated from before the war. They included Nathanael West's *The Day of the Locust*, a picture of Hollywood as a graveyard of dreams, peopled by the maimed and despairing. Asked to list his ten favourite books, he put *Locust* at the top, followed by Hemingway's collected short stories, Coleridge's *Rime of the Ancient Mariner* (almost a surrealist painting in verse), Martin Gardner's annotated *Alice in Wonderland*, Patrick Trevor-Roper's *The World Through Blunted Sight*, about the effect of defective vision on painting, William Burroughs's *Naked Lunch*, *The Black Box*, a collection of aircraft-cockpit voice-recorder transcripts retrieved after crashes, the Los Angeles Yellow Pages telephone directory, Jean Baudrillard's *America*, and *The Secret Life of Salvador Dalí*. He liked the crime novels of Raymond Chandler and Lawrence Durrell's *Justine*, though he doesn't appear to have persisted with the other three novels of the *Alexandria Quartet*. Books earned his approval by the degree to which they ignited his imagination and stimulated his creative appetite – qualities he found less often in literature than in cinema, science, painting and popular culture. As he told the friend who took him to the Leavis lecture, the profundity of *Middlemarch* didn't make it superior to Anthony Mann's *film noir T-Men*.

He made a partial exception for short stories. Hemingway earned his respect, but his ideal and model was Ray Bradbury. Bradbury was a phenomenon: a stylist of natural gifts who, with no literary education and few obvious influences, created a form of fantasy fiction that transcended genre. One minute a minor writer for the pulp magazines, the next he was in the *Saturday Evening Post*. Established writers viewed Bradbury with anything from wary admiration to outright hostility, but nobody questioned his ability to evoke awe, wonder, fear, and the more subtle conditions critic Damon Knight isolated as 'the rage at being born; the will to be loved; the longing to communicate; the hatred of parents and siblings; the fear of things that are not self'. In Bradbury, Jim recognised a kindred soul, although, as with everyone who slipped through his emotional defences, he ultimately turned on him.

The most profound influence on his early work remains surrealist art. It taught him that the unreal was best conveyed by an almost photographic realism. In pursuit of that simplicity, he employed a writing style of brick-solid subject/verb/predicate sentences as unapologetically corporeal as Delvaux's women and Chirico's colonnades. In May 1951, this paid off when he shared first prize of £10 in the annual crime story competition run by the student magazine *Varsity*.

That year's theme was 'revenge'. His story, 'The Violent Noon', is set against the background of terrorism in Malaya. Planters Allison and Hargreaves are heading towards their plantations, with the former's wife and child, when they are ambushed on a jungle road. Before the attack, Hargreaves, lounging in the back seat, brandishes a machine pistol and laments Britain's retreat from empire. India, Burma, Ceylon have just been thrown away, he complains, leaving a formerly great Great Britain no more than a deflated balloon. Jim based Hargreaves on his parents' blowhard friends, middle-aged veterans not of combat but of rugger, golf, bluster and booze. (Hargreaves shares his surname with the managing director of the China Printing and Finishing Company, under whom Jim's father had worked.) But it's Hargreaves who repels the attackers, rescues Mrs Allison and colludes in her revenge for the death of her husband and child. When she unhesitatingly identifies some suspects produced by the police, Hargreaves, though he knows they're innocent, backs her up. Who is he, he muses, to thwart her traditional right of revenge, or to fail in his duty to oppose Communism? The judges who praised the rest of the story called these remarks 'preaching'.

Elements of 'The Violent Noon' point to the future Ballard, in particular the casual discarding of conventional morality and concepts of justice. The inheritance of South East Asia is evident in the jungle setting, with its fecundity and rot. In the smashed car and the helpless woman, Ballard for the first time links automobiles, violence and sex. That Hargreaves and Mrs Allison will become lovers is as foregone a conclusion as the coupling of James Ballard and Helen Remington in *Crash*.

In both cases, injury to the woman's mouth makes her less menacing and, in Ballardian terms, more alluring. Women with damaged mouths occur repeatedly in his work, reminding us that knocking out the front teeth to facilitate fellatio is an injury often inflicted on prostitutes, or newcomers to the prison system. The African girl (also called Noon) in *The Day of Creation* suffers from a damaged and infected mouth. In *Crash*, the fictional James Ballard refers to a whore nipping a piece of skin from his penis when it didn't promptly come erect. After he collides head-on with the car of Helen Remington, her husband's body is projected through both windscreens into the passenger seat beside him. Trapped and waiting for rescue, James and Helen stare at one another across the crumpled bonnets in a shared anomie that the writing depicts as almost post-orgasmic, while Ballard muses on her only visible injuries – a bruised upper jaw and loosened teeth.

Though Jim called 'The Violent Noon' a pastiche of Hemingway, the Hemingway who shunned adjectives would have blue-pencilled at least a quarter of the text. If there's a literary debt, it's more to Somerset Maugham, whom it recalls both in its setting and the theme of the White Man's Burden and an eagerness of many British colonials to lay it down. The judges called it 'the most mature story' of those submitted. 'It contains patches of high tension,' said their report, 'the characters come to life, and the ending is brilliant in its cynicism.' One of them, from London literary agency A. P. Watt, liked it well enough to invite Jim to call if he wrote anything else.

This was motive enough for him to abandon his studies at King's. His explanation for doing so, with its rambling free associations, goes some way to suggesting how unconventional a medico he might have become.

> I guess I learnt enough medicine to cure myself of wanting to be a doctor. That sounds pat, but I wanted to be a doctor for neurotic reasons and once I'd got over the neurosis, solved whatever problems I'd had, I found that medicine was a sort of fiction – all that anatomy and physiology. Grey's *Anatomy* is the greatest novel of the 20th century. By comparison with our ordinary experience of our bodies, to read Grey's *Anatomy* is to be presented with what appears to be a fantastic fiction, an epic vastly beyond *War and Peace* and about as difficult to read.

Satisfied in his own mind that medicine and literature were two sides of the same coin, he left Cambridge at the end of his second year of medicine and headed for London.

CHAPTER EIGHT

LONDON

Since Jim hadn't gained a medical degree, it was decided, in the light of his new literary ambitions, that he should graduate in English Literature. The decision was perverse. Better options existed. Other nascent novelists like Kingsley Amis, John Braine, John Wain and Philip Larkin became librarians – as would Jim, for a time – or teachers. Some entered broadcasting or publishing. But as long as he remained a student, his father would maintain his allowance, so he may simply have regarded university as a means to an end.

No British institution offered creative writing tuition of the sort that would proliferate in the seventies, so he enrolled in the London University four-year degree course in English Literature at Queen Mary College, with a subsidiary course in Latin. His father opposed the idea – not of getting a degree, since it was assumed anyone without letters after his name was crippled both socially and professionally – but, rather, the subject, and his son's ambitions to write. Literature was a precarious way of life. In 1946, *Horizon* surveyed British writers on what it cost them to live. Authors as various as George Orwell, John Betjeman and Robert Graves estimated anything from £500 to £3,500 a year, at a time when the average annual wage was less than £200.

Jim took up his place in October 1951 and rented a room on Onslow Gardens in South Kensington. The bedsit land of south-west London became his home, on and off, for a decade. His neighbours and fellow travellers on the Underground interested him in the same way as the cadavers he had dissected at King's. Through them, he gained some sense of how British society worked. It didn't make him feel any more at home in it. In China, he had seen the way most of the people of the world lived; in daily and often fatal contact with starvation, war and pestilence. England was an island of calm on which the English lived in ignorance of the potential disasters that lurked just over the horizon.

Central to his alienation was a discomfort with class, which he'd barely encountered before he arrived in Britain. With the election of a Labour government, the class system, already damaged by the war, came under further attack, particularly from the emerging popular culture. Cinema, photography, mass-market literature, jazz, and also, increasingly, art, required no pedigree. On the contrary, to be low-born conferred a reverse aristocracy. The best new writers, from Colin Wilson, John Braine, Alan Sillitoe and Stan Barstow to Philip Larkin and Ted Hughes, were provincial or working class, or both. The school of 'kitchen sink' drama and fiction, of scruffy photographers, typified by David Bailey, of painters from the Midlands and the North such as David Hockney, achieved its apotheosis in The Beatles.

Jim could have traded on his Mancunian parentage and foreign education to join this group. Instead he guarded his upper-class accent and manner, valuing the way they allowed him to 'pass' at the restaurants and nightclubs to which wealthier friends invited him. His most vivid memories of fifties London are not of literary insights but of a tutor who drove him home in her Allard convertible, the closest Britain could come to the Pontiacs and Cadillacs of pre-war Shanghai. As a writer, his characters were invariably such people – wealthy, professional, well-educated, white.

Studying English Literature proved as big a mistake as medicine. Such courses aimed to prepare students for an academic career teaching the same subject. They began with *Ralph Roister Doister* and *Gammer Gurton's Needle*, and took three years to reach Dickens, never mind Joyce. It was, Jim admitted, 'the worst possible preparation for a writer's career, which [my father] may well have suspected'. At the end of his first year, he dropped out, or, as he preferred to put it, was 'thrown out', presumably for failing to meet the requirements for essays, and seldom gave another thought to the history of English literature. This left dismaying gaps in his knowledge. Discussing Shakespeare, he claimed that *Macbeth*'s violence represented a refinement of the slaughters in *The Duchess of Malfi*. Michael Moorcock, the writer and editor who became his closest friend, had to explain that John Webster and the Jacobeans wrote after Shakespeare, not before.

Britain was emerging from wartime austerity. One symbol of rebirth, the Festival of Britain, ran from May to September 1951. Jim visited some of its attractions, but they didn't impress him. His memories of London in the early fifties contain nothing joyous. Asked why his first novel showed the city ground down to the bedrock by a hurricane, he said, '[You] should try living there for ten years. I'm only sorry that I couldn't call it "*Gone With the Wind*".'

His despair was subjective and continued for most of his life, its effects dulled by alcohol, sex and writing. Of these, writing was the most effective, but, as with all therapy, it never effected a cure: merely, in Freud's phrase, 'replaced unbearable misery with ordinary unhappiness'. Years later, Jim wrote that he always 'felt a complete outsider and never really integrated into English life until I got married in the mid-fifties, and had my children, and began to put down roots'.

The word 'outsider' reminds us that, while Jim struggled to find his voice, another nonconformist, Colin Wilson, was sleeping on Hampstead Heath and spending his days in the British Library, writing a book with that very title. Victor Gollancz published *The Outsider* in 1956, to enormous acclaim. An exercise in pop existentialism, it celebrated those figures in European art and literature who formulated their own schools of thought – in particular Camus, Sartre, Hemingway, Hesse, Dostoevsky, T. E. Lawrence, Nijinsky and Van Gogh.

A decade later, Jim would qualify for this group. He resembles no other British writer of his time. For comparisons, one must look to those contemporaries whom Kenneth Allsop labelled 'The Law

Givers' – science popularisers, social theorists and apostles of the alternative such as psychologists Edward de Bono and R. D. Laing, performance ideologue Peter Brook, media scholar Marshall McLuhan and computer scientist Christopher Evans, who became Jim's close friend.

Jim followed a career path closer to that of a scientist – a series of experiments, each occupying years, but always abandoned definitively for another, with almost never a backward glance. Reviewing his late novel *Millennium People*, the political theorist John Gray, a friend and admirer of Ballard, looked back on a discernable, almost systematic progress:

> In the course of his career, Ballard has used a series of genres to convey his unique vision. Experimenting with science-fiction, quasi-autobiographic realism and, more recently, the thriller, he has given us a rendition of the contemporary scene that is unsurpassed in its clairvoyant exactitude. In *Crash*, he announced the marriage of celebrity and sudden death that, more than a quarter-century later, was to give us the Diana cult. Seemingly a fable of the euthanasia of the bourgeoisie, *Millennium People* dissects the perverse psychology that links terrorists with their innocent victims. This is news from the near future, another despatch from one of the supreme chroniclers of our time.

The pattern of Ballard's development as a writer reflected surrealist principles. Its painters also shunned all sense of time, either historical or sidereal. Bathed in light as if from the flash of a camera or an explosion, their images exist in an eternal present, an effect Jim aimed for in his fiction. His work lacks any clear progression. He often appears like a man who, while remaining in the same room, opens a series of doors into adjacent spaces. After each exploration, he closes that door and returns to the room where he started. In the words of Iain Sinclair, 'every single book is a repetition, an extension of the same riff'.

CHAPTER NINE

AD MAN

In the spring of 1952, Eduardo Paolozzi, a burly Glaswegian of Italian extraction, nervously faced a handful of people in Lord Nelson's former mansion in Dover Street, Mayfair, then the home of the Institute of Contemporary Arts. Known, if at all, as a print-maker and teacher, Paolozzi explained little in advance of his presentation, called simply Bunk. Technically he was delivering a lecture to the first meeting of the ICA's Independent Group, a gathering of artists and critics, including Reyner Banham, Lawrence Alloway and Peter and Alison Smithson, interested in art that used 'found objects' and material discarded by others as junk. In 1947, Paolozzi had collaged a magazine cover and other items to create *I Was a Rich Man's Plaything*, the first British artwork to incorporate the word 'pop'.

Paolozzi disliked speaking in public, and said almost nothing. Instead, with the occasional mumbled 'I like this', he used an overhead projector to magnify a succession of collages created from magazine covers, advertisements and newspaper clippings, mostly scrounged from US servicemen between 1947 and 1949, when he lived in Paris. The material would form the basis of his *Bunk!* screenprint series of 1972 and the *Krazy Kat Archives*, now held at the V&A Museum, but at the time this was virgin territory. As image succeeded image, watchers gaped at the emerging face of pop art.

Jim wasn't in the audience at Bunk, except in spirit. It's significant that Paolozzi found his images in Paris, since both insisted France was the cradle of new ideas in communication. Paolozzi pointedly described himself as a European rather than a British artist, a lead Jim followed, emphasising that he found his intellectual stimulus on 'the European menu'. While this posed difficulties for someone who spoke only English, Jim recognised a fellowship that needed no language. Jean-Luc Godard, Michel Foucault, Alain Robbe-Grillet, Guy Debord and Roland Barthes shared his flair for the slogan. He also liked the French indifference to distinction; dream and reality, intellect and instinct – all swam together.

Godard, working in the Paris office of an American film company while awaiting his chance to direct, was detailed to write bios of Hollywood stars. Mostly he made them up. 'They were my first films,' he said proudly. No British intellectual would be so cavalier about the truth, but Jim thrived on such exhilarating lies. Nor were the British as ready as the French to express their enthusiasm for popular culture. Their snobbery was evident in the cover copy for Penguin's edition of John Wyndham's *The Day of the Triffids.* With a well-bred shudder, it called his early work 'a modified form of what is unhappily known as "science-fiction"'. While Kingsley Amis enjoyed SF, he was careful not to announce this in Britain, choosing instead the occasion of a visiting professorship at Princeton to lecture on the subject. Even then, he embraced mostly 'respectable' social satirists. He was just as cautious when invited to write a pastiche of Ian Fleming's James Bond, publishing the result, *Colonel Sun,* as 'Robert Markham'. In this, he took his cue from friends such as the composer Bruce Montgomery, who wrote crime stories and edited SF anthologies as 'Edmund Crispin'. As W. H. Auden once observed, in the brothel, both the prostitutes and the gentlemen use different names.

Jim had no such reservations. He took the road *more* travelled. For the rest of his life, he treated reality as a jazz musician deals with a 'standard' – respecting the chord structure, but otherwise improvising freely. London helped him perfect his flair for deceit, and make it the basis of a career. Recognising that, in a world driven by advertising, the writer is just another product, he repackaged himself repeatedly. 'Jimmy was torn between his self-invention and the truth,' says Michael Moorcock. 'He was highly perceptive on an ordinary human level but I suspect he talked himself into some of his "memories".' He had the natural ideologue's flair for the fable, the anecdote, the slogan, the image. Like Ernest Lehman, who made Cary Grant's character in Hitchcock's *North by Northwest* an ad man, Jim believed that 'in the world of advertising there's no such thing as a lie. There's only the expedient exaggeration.'

In June 1953, Jim joined the crowds that witnessed the coronation of Queen Elizabeth II. Already a confirmed anti-monarchist, he found the spectacle less than thrilling. Some of his ennui is conveyed in 'The Gentle Assassin', an otherwise mediocre story published in 1961. The inventor of time travel returns to London on the day of a coronation to forestall the assassination of the new monarch, and finds himself implicated in the plot. Jim makes no attempt to evoke the event. Instead, the visitor wanders behind the scenes, sitting in half-empty cafés, listening to the distant sounds of pomp and circumstance as he watches his younger self with the girl whose death by the assassin's bomb he hopes to avert. The story reminds us with what scepticism Jim viewed the possibility of enduring relationships. None of his characters walk, hand in hand, into the sunset. Instead, prefiguring his own unhappy future, one of them, almost always the woman, goes mad, disappears, or dies.

Even as Paolozzi presented Bunk, Jim was flirting with advertising as a profession. Early in 1953, a friend in the business recommended him to an agency recently launched by designer Digby Wills in two small rooms in High Holborn. Jim barely referred to this period of his life again, dismissing it as a wasted period of writing texts for booklets and manuals, and copy for ads for, among other products, lemon juice.

But this comment masks a key point in his development as a writer. Digby Wills specialised in print ads for magazines. A major client, the pharmaceutical giant Beecham's, asked for ideas to launch an unpromising new product, pure lemon juice, bottled as PLJ. Spotting its possible health and beauty value, Wills bought space in glossy women's magazines to inform weight-conscious readers that lemon juice 'shrank the stomach', reducing appetite. Jim worked on the copy for the six full-page ads that appeared in *Vogue* and *Harper's Bazaar.* The results were phenomenal. Sales of PLJ soared from £30,000 in 1954 to £1,300,000 in 1959.

The ads were still running in the early sixties. Their copy listed the health-giving merits of PLJ, then went on 'But forget these sound reasons! Just enjoy PLJ's natural tang . . . '. Forty years later, one hears the same voice in his writing about the Côte d'Azur for the *Mail on Sunday*. He urges visitors to forget travel writers who say 'Ignore the mythology of the Riviera', who advise us to forget Scott Fitzgerald, the Aga Khan and his private train, the Russian princes in their rented châteaux, the art of Picasso, Matisse and Renoir. Rather, he advises us to embrace it, along with the Cocteau chapel at Villefranche-sur-Mer and bouillabaisse eaten under the trees at Antibes.

The mark of the ad man runs through all Ballard's work. As he told Chris Evans in a 1989 *Penthouse* interview, 'the logical evolution of Western society of the fifties would have been a world in which the copywriter was king'. He had a flair for slogans. 'It is inner space, not outer, that needs to be explored' and 'the only alien planet is Earth' are as catchy (and as nebulous) as 'Put a tiger in your tank' or 'Coke – it's the real thing', and few book titles have the onomatopoeic force of *Crash*. The surrealists taught him well. Dalí's self-publicising and sloganeering could sound, he admitted, like 'an hallucinating speak-your-weight machine', but they kept him in the public eye. As for his other favourites, Delvaux was an ad man before his time. Borrowing the most obvious characteristics of Magritte and Chirico, he added that unfailing attention catcher, a nude woman. The mix was so successful that a generation of advertisements for foundation garments, perfume and cosmetics imitated it.

CHAPTER TEN

FEAR OF FLYING

Despite his success with PLJ, Jim wearied of office life. The proximity of Covent Garden's fruit and flower market suggested a better option, and he left to become a porter for a firm that sold chrysanthemums. But since work began before dawn and finished at noon, he was often too tired to write, or he would do so all night, and arrive at his day job exhausted. Abandoning London, he took a job selling books door-to-door. *The Waverley Encyclopedia: A Comprehensive Volume of Facts* was a one-volume condensation of a ten-volume work he'd enjoyed as a child. In exercising his selling skills on doorsteps across the Midlands, and sometimes waiving his commission or giving a discount if he felt the children needed the books, he learned he was no more a career salesman than he had been a porter.

By now, Jim had moved to a private hotel in Stanley Crescent, Notting Hill. It was not a particularly salubrious area. Mike Moorcock remembers when cabs wouldn't take you there, and policemen walked in twos, or even threes. This was also 'Christie-land'. John Reginald Christie, who lived in nearby Rillington Place, not only murdered a succession of prostitutes, but caused an innocent neighbour, Timothy Evans, to be hanged for one of his killings. In 1953, Jim, already drawn to the sites of celebrity crimes and their morbid onlookers, joined the crowd outside Ladbroke Grove police station as Christie was brought in under arrest. A red-coated woman, standing alone, watched in silence. She was Eileen, sister of the wrongly executed Evans.

At a party in the garden behind the hotel, he met another tenant, Helen Mary Matthews. Always called Mary, she was exactly his age and worked on the *Evening Standard* as secretary to Charles Wintour, later its editor. They began to spend time together in the pubs along the Portobello Road. Jim described her as tall, with an excellent figure, and instantly attractive, but Moorcock, one of the few people who met her, remembers her as short and plump, even a little dumpy. Jim tacitly confirmed this when he used her as the model for a woman in one of his early stories, 'The Watch Towers'. Her character, Mrs Osmond, is distinguished by her bulk and broad hips.

Class was both the basis of Jim's relationship with Mary and the barrier between them. Moorcock called her 'quite posh, with that quality you used to see in girls who'd been "finished". But there was absolutely no "side" to her. I feel she could have got on with anyone. She really was the most extraordinarily nice woman.'

All the same, Jim was daunted by her parents, landowners from Staffordshire, living in retirement in rural Wales. According to family legend, Mary was the great-niece of Cecil Rhodes, the turn-of-the-century South African adventurer and entrepreneur. While never quite denying the story, she always shrugged it off. Jim, however, occasionally joked about this with friends, and included it in a biographical note to the 1965 Penguin edition of *The Drowned World*.

He also characterised Mary's life before they met in terms of county high society as chronicled in *The Lady* and the *Tatler*, ignoring the fact that his own childhood had been just as privileged. Aware of the second-class-citizen status Britons accorded colonials, he hid his Shanghai childhood. His fears of disapproval were probably misplaced. His accent and manner would have permitted him to pass easily as Mary's social equal. However, he preferred to see her as a superior who condescended to him. As he would show again during his relationships with Claire Churchill and Emma Tennant, bedding women with aristocratic or 'county' backgrounds gave him an aphrodisiac thrill.

Having a girlfriend should have calmed Jim, but the prospect of a steady relationship, even marriage, had the opposite effect. As casually as he had taken up medicine and advertising, he decided to enlist in the Air Force. To build up its peacetime force and fulfil its commitments to NATO, the RAF offered commissions for periods of up to twelve years. He signed on for the shortest, three years, which would qualify him as a crew member in a Valiant, Victor or Vulcan bomber.

Superficially, the RAF move was baffling. In his memoirs, he was off-hand about his motives, suggesting that he felt a spell in Canada might inspire him and stimulate his imagination. This is rationalisation after the event, since he never expected to be sent to Canada for training, but to West Germany, NATO's newest member. The decision only makes sense if seen through the distorting lens of Jim's unsteady mental state. In *The Kindness of Women*, he acknowledges its roots in psychological disturbance and a desire to conserve what remained of his childhood. Fantasies of becoming a flyer are common in adolescence. The title of that chapter in *The Kindness of Women*, 'The NATO Boys', evokes the adventure series *The Hardy Boys* and *The Rover Boys*, and comics such as *The Wizard*, *Hotspur* and *Chums*, in which groups of English schoolboys, led by an intrepid master, cross the world to meddle in South American revolutions. Mike Moorcock remarked on Jim's debt to such stories. 'He'd read quite a lot of the same boys' fiction as me. Maybe the secret [of his skill] can be found in *Captain Justice* in *Boys Friend Library*, a serious rival to *Biggles*.'

As well, Freud believed that dreams of flight signified sexual release. These feelings in Jim were reinforced by memories of the Japanese pilots whose courage awed him. Moreover, aviation seemed pure and clean, the pilot transcending earthly concerns. He admired the visionary writers of flight, and quoted French philosopher/pilot Antoine de Saint-Exupéry, in particular *Wind, Sand and Stars*, the English translation of *Terre des Hommes*. Both in his fiction and in life, Jim associated flying with freedom from responsibility. In a 1987 letter to a woman who'd just won her pilot's licence, he described approvingly how the wife of a friend, with a child of four and a reputation as someone precise and self-controlled, had abruptly taken up flying, subsequently separated from her husband, and was even then heading for an air fair in the Czech Republic in her own plane. Learning to fly, he assured his correspondent, signified fundamental changes in the psyche, all of them positive.

While studying medicine, he would borrow a motorbike and visit the USAF bases at Mildenhall and Lakenheath, peering through the wire at the parked aircraft. In *The Kindness of Women*, he imagines slipping through the fence and actually sitting in an H-bomber, visualising himself as a crewman. For the novel, he invents David Hunter, an imaginary and unstable friend from Shanghai. It's Hunter who decides to join up, and Jim who volunteers with him. Almost as an afterthought, the Jim of the novel suggests an additional motive so outlandish that it probably approaches the truth. Having watched the airfields of Suffolk being refitted for NATO, he anticipates a nuclear war, and hungers to be part of it. It's his chance to experience the bushido of the Japanese pilots of Lunghua. As the fictional Jim and David stand outside the recruiting office, Hunter pats his shoulder and assures him that, as a crewman, he'll have a ringside seat at the Third World War. Jim silently admits that his friend has intuited his true reason for volunteering.

Expecting Mary to be impressed by his decision, Jim was disconcerted by her indifference. She'd been more intrigued by a rash lie about writing a novel. ('Are you almost finished?' she asked, and he jokingly replied, 'No – I've almost started.') In post-war London, flyers were ten a penny. One of the hit plays of 1952, Terence Rattigan's *The Deep Blue Sea*, explored the doomed relationship between a one-time RAF ace and the upper-class woman who leaves her husband to share his shabby Notting Hill flat. It begins with her failed attempt at suicide by gas – a poor advertisement for married life with an aviator.

The Kindness of Women introduces aspects of Mary in the character of Miriam, who also appears in his most sensuous and personal novel, *The Unlimited Dream Company*. Jim's fictional women are usually sleek, assured professionals, the equivalent of Detroit automobiles, but Miriam embodies their opposite. She's an anima figure, the apotheosis of female nurturing: the mother, some might say, that Edna never was. *The Kindness of Women* makes her a fellow Cambridge undergraduate of precocious sexuality. On weekends, she accompanies Jim on his motorbike tours of airfields. Miriam urges him to abandon medicine: carving cadavers just reminds him of Lunghua. As they watch a friend landing his Tiger Moth, he decides, quixotically, that he'll learn to fly, too. Miriam is instantly enthusiastic. Having committed himself, he reinforces the Freudian metaphor by taking her as his lover.

In the autumn of 1953, following three months of drill, weapons training and education in mess etiquette and sexual hygiene at Kirton-in-Lindsay, near Scunthorpe in Lincolnshire, his group, now officially officers and gentlemen, sailed for North America on the Canadian Pacific liner *Empress of Australia.* Their confidence would not have been bolstered by knowing that the ship had begun life as the French liner *De Grasse*, and had been raised and refitted after being sunk in 1944.

After four more weeks of orientation in North American manners at an RCAF base in London, Ontario, near Niagara Falls, Jim and his fellow recruits, a sullen and, in many cases, hung-over mixture of Turks, Norwegians, Frenchmen and Britons, moved to Moose Jaw, in the desolate tundra of Saskatchewan. The base had just been refurbished, so living conditions, compared to Britain, were luxurious, with a mess that resembled a four-star hotel. But with the average December temperature at minus 16° Fahrenheit, they did little flying. This left ample opportunity for trips into the US, at least as far as Detroit, and around the Great Lakes, but most of their time was spent staring at the snow that howled past the windows. Occasionally the hoot of a security alarm broke the gelid silence as a moose stumbled into the perimeter fence.

When they did fly, it was in two-seater Second World War Harvard trainers. The Jim of the novel decides to investigate the disappearance of a homesick Turk on a solo flight. He locates the Turk's plane submerged in a lake, but barely lands his own on a road before fuel runs out. The rest of the time, he and Hunter brawl with other trainees, or fornicate drunkenly in Moose Jaw's Iroquois Hotel. Jim invented the solo flying, but an Iroquois Hotel did exist in nearby Saskatoon, and conformed to the book's description. (Described as 'seedy, and the scene of many violent crimes', it subsequently became a halfway house for released federal offenders.) Jim and David, well liquored up, share Brigid and Yvette, shop-worn blue-collar housewives moonlighting as whores. Descriptions of vomiting, anal penetration, fellatio (with intrusive teeth) and the discovery that one woman is pregnant make the episode masochistically authentic.

CHAPTER ELEVEN

IT CAME FROM OUTER SPACE

Snow-bound in Moose Jaw, Jim read a great deal. Browsing newsstands in the town's bus station and drugstores, he discovered science fiction. It was a revelation. All ambition to be a pilot forgotten, he wrote to a friend that he couldn't wait to get back to England and start writing.

The post-war explosion in technology and the beginnings of the Cold War had sparked a new interest in the genre. As all but the most robust of the pre-war pulps expired in the wartime paper shortage, an avalanche of digest-size magazines replaced them. In 1950 alone, fifteen new titles appeared. Quality varied, but most flourished, for a time at least. Sales rose until 1953, then flattened out, to plummet at the end of the decade.

Astounding Science Fiction dominated the field. Its overbearing editor, John W. Campbell Jr, preached the gospel of Technology Transformative. Its stories demanded 'hard science', or at least the appearance of it. Each issue also contained a speculative article on some recent discovery or invention. Many promoted the claims of former pulp writer L. Ron Hubbard that we possess so-called psi mental powers which his system of self-therapy, Dianetics, 'the new science of the mind', could enhance. Previewed in a 1949 issue of *Astounding*, Dianetics evolved into the controversial religion Scientology.

Jim was angered by claims that, with its help, one could remember not only the moment of one's birth but the instant in which the cells of our primary zygote began to divide. For this, if for no other reason, he scorned *Astounding*, echoing Kingsley Amis's charge that Campbell was 'one of the cranks who seem bent on getting science-fiction a bad name'. He preferred *Galaxy* and *The Magazine of Fantasy and Science Fiction*. Stories in these magazines generally took place on earth, and favoured satire, fantasy and humour. As an ad man manqué, he particularly admired *The Space Merchants*, aka *Gravy Planet*, a novel by *Galaxy* stalwarts Frederik Pohl and Cyril Kornbluth in which the world of the future is run by advertising agencies. He would also have read their *Gladiator at Law*, serialised by *Galaxy* in 1954, about a society where government is in the hands of corporate lawyers.

In its issue of 5 December 1953, the *New Statesman* published an essay by J. B. Priestley entitled 'They Come From Inner Space'. It was inspired by Jack Arnold's film *They Came From Outer Space*, based, remotely, on an idea by Ray Bradbury. Priestley felt Arnold didn't do Bradbury justice, and took SF to task for being too concerned with UFOs and aliens. 'If such hack work could arouse thought,' he wrote of the film, 'then we should think what a pity it is that our idiotic species is shortly proposing to spread its dreary melodramatic doings from here to Sirius.' He urged writers to explore 'the hidden life of the psyche':

> Science-fiction and Flying Saucer legends seem to me important because they show us what is really happening in men's minds. Like the sexually sadistic thrillers now so popular, they are the myths and characteristic dreams of our age, and are psychologically far more important than our more rational accounts of ourselves. They take the lid off. They allow us a glimpse of what is boiling down below. They may be the first rumblings of the volcano that will overwhelm us. Behind all these topical tales, fables and legends, it seems to me, are deep feelings of anxiety, fear, and guilt. The Unconscious is protesting against the cheap conceit and false optimism of the conscious mind.

Jim never referred to this essay nor acknowledged that he had read it, but some of its ideas, rhetoric and even its phraseology resurfaced in 1962 as part of his manifesto 'Which Way to Inner Space?'.

Among short story writers, he admired Richard Matheson, who became famous for *The Incredible Shrinking Man*, *I Am Legend*, and the story on which Steven Spielberg based his film *Duel*, all of which describe strangeness and violence erupting out of the everyday. Of Matheson's stories, Jim said, 'They were probably a bit of an influence on me, because they showed that you could write a science-fiction set exclusively in the present day – which many of his short stories were. They were psychological stories set in the landscape of fifties America, owing nothing to time travel, interplanetary voyages and so forth.' One of the few books he took back to Britain with him was Matheson's first collection, *Third From the Sun*.

The book for which he reserved the greatest praise was *Limbo*, a 1952 novel by Bernard Wolfe. He may have read this in Canada, but as he always referred to it as *Limbo 90*, the title under which Secker & Warburg issued the 1953 British edition, it's possible he didn't encounter it until after he returned to Britain.

Wolfe and Ballard were two of a kind: mavericks who gravitated towards SF, only to find its conventions too confining. At one time bodyguard and secretary to the exiled Communist leader Leon Trotsky, assassinated in Mexico in 1940, Wolfe wrote fiction only sporadically, making his living mostly from science journalism. *Limbo* was his satiric take on the year he wrote it, but an Author's Note disclaimed any intention to forecast the future, and scorned those SF writers who claimed to do so.

> Anybody who 'paints a picture' of some coming year is kidding – he's only fancying up something in the present or past, not blueprinting the future. All such writing is essentially satiric (today-centered), not utopic (tomorrow-centered). This book, then, is a rather bilious rib on 1950 – on what 1950 might have been like if it had been allowed to fulfil itself, if it had gone on being 1950, only more and more so, for four more decades. But no year ever fulfils itself: the cow-path of History is littered with the corpses of years, their silly throats slit from ear to ear by the improbable.

The novel turns on two observations, one by Freud, the second by computer pioneer Norbert Weiner. In *Civilization and Its Discontents*, Freud spoke of machines – automobiles, aircraft, cameras: anything that replaced or supplanted a human function – as 'artificial limbs'. 'Man has become a god by means of "artificial limbs",' he wrote, 'but they do not grow on him, and still give him trouble at times.' Weiner's insight was more terse. He contended, in Wolfe's paraphrase, 'that, granted the technological savvy of the 1940s, an artificial limb superior in many ways to the real one could easily be created if society wanted to spend as much money on such a humanitarian project as it was willing to spend on developing an atom bomb'.

Limbo explores this idea of peace-through-surgery via the character of neurosurgeon Martine. Barely surviving the atomic war of 1972, he flees to an island where he uses the peaceful Mandunji people as lab rats in perfecting the prefrontal lobotomy. By inserting needles into those areas of the brain controlling sex and violence, he can render even psychopaths tractable, although at the cost of destroying their artistic powers.

In 1990, explorers arrive from a reborn America which has developed his pacifist ideas far beyond lobotomy. By creating the form of artificial limb foreseen by Weiner, Americans have made war physically impossible. Citizens compete to become voluntary amputees – 'vol-amps'. Depending on which prosthetic, or 'pros', they choose, the surgery, called 'Immob', makes them super athletes, Stakhanovite workers, even flyers, each person a private helicopter. As a bonus, they also become pacifists, since, at the first sign of aggression, their 'pros' are programmed to shut down.

The missing link in Jim's writing, *Limbo* connects the war, Lunghua, Freud, medical school, psychoanalysis, technology and sex. Scientists on the model of Martine, experimenting with human subjects to improve their lives, appear often in his work, but he was more attracted by Wolfe's style: 'the visual panache of the whole thing – the headings and diary inserts and the full-page "YES" and "NO".' Slogans pepper Wolfe's text: 'No demobilization without immobilization', 'War is on its last legs', 'Two legs shorter, a head taller', and 'Arms or the man'. They show the glee in paper propaganda that Jim shared.

Science fiction offered Jim a chance to create a new world from the ruins of his own. He also welcomed a form of fiction that didn't demand a knowledge of British social rituals, nor require him to examine and reveal his troubled personality. SF writers weren't interested in the Self. As Kingsley Amis wrote in *New Maps of Hell*, 'in science-fiction, the Plot is the hero'. But Jim's impatience with the technological present argues against him ever truly having been a science-fiction writer. He shared none of its faith in a future improved by technology or improvable by it. His acquaintance with his own century was polite but distant. Rather than belonging to our time, he was a tourist in it: that odd man who always lags behind the group and wanders off, but asks lots of questions and takes notes. And when he wrote of it, it was always as an outsider.

Early in 1955, Jim surrendered his commission. He implied that his new enthusiasm for writing was responsible, but evidence suggests he flopped as a flyer. According to James Salter, another novelist also training on prop planes around the same time, 'we were expected to solo in a few hours, not less than four or more than eight. If you were not able to take off and land by yourself after eight hours, you were washed out.' Jim flew twenty-two hours with an instructor and still wasn't proficient. Failure probably came as a relief. The boredom of Moose Jaw suggested that service in the peacetime RAF would be spent at similar remote bases, waiting for the balloon to go up. Writing was more inviting, and something for which he had talent.

The *Empress of France*, the ship bringing him back to Britain, docked at Liverpool on 26 April 1955. Britain that spring appeared as chill to Jim as Saskatchewan. For demobilisation, the RAF sent him to Booker, at High Wycombe in Buckinghamshire. A flying school during the war, it now formed part of a desolate sprawl of administrative offices, clustered round a disused airfield of the sort he would describe in his fiction. Even more appropriately, Booker housed the

United Kingdom Regional Air Operations Command, responsible for issuing a four-minute warning in the event of nuclear war. At the press of a button, broadcasts would be transmitted from 250 stations across Britain, and 17,000 sirens set wailing – the perfect premonitory setting for his re-introduction to Europe. Waiting for his papers to catch him up, Jim joined the floating population of miscreants, drop-outs and screw-ups huddled in Booker's unheated huts. Once demobilised, he headed for London. Checking into the Stanley Crescent Hotel, he confidently knocked on the door of Mary Matthews's old room – to be taken aback when it was opened by a middle-aged nursing sister in uniform. The lurch of panic was revelatory, alerting him to his true feelings about Mary. Fortunately, she had only moved to a better room in the hotel, and before long they were affectionately reunited.

CHAPTER TWELVE

WESTWAY

Ten years of peace had not changed much in Britain. Any benefits the welfare state coaxed from the depleted economy were spread so thin that the average citizen barely noticed. As the US welcomed CinemaScope movies, *Playboy* and the Beat Generation, Britons huddled around their two-bar electric fires and monochrome TVs for the debut of the UK's second channel, ITV. It doubled the number of choices but, as Kingsley Amis sourly observed of the expansion in higher education, 'more will mean worse'.

While Jim credited television with transforming Britain, he lamented its early feebleness, technical and intellectual. He remembered watching TV with his parents in Manchester around 1951, when there was still only one channel, and the screen appeared to him to be about the size of a light bulb. His first published story, 'Escapement', mocked a typical BBC TV programme, where three historians and a token glamour girl try to guess the origin of a Roman pot while the question master, another don, makes bad jokes about 'the bottom of the barrow'. Banality was no barrier to popularity, however, and Jim would later concede that 'sooner or later, everything turns into television'.

West London indelibly marked Jim and his work. The concept of 'inner space', in one sense grudging, in another recalling Christopher Marlowe's 'infinite riches in a little room', was born of the bedsit. Such images became part of the mental furniture he ceaselessly rearranged to create new fictions. As late as 1984, he told the *Paris Review*, 'A whole universe can be bounded in a nutshell', a partial quote which omits

its anguished corollary: 'O God,' cries Hamlet, 'I could be bounded in a nutshell, and count myself a king of infinite space, were it not that I have bad dreams.' The claustrophobia of Notting Hill and Ladbroke Grove and the bad dreams it engendered fed Jim's fantasies of cities devouring whole planets and people living in closets. Streets flooded after a rainstorm suggested the images he conjured in *The Drowned World*, and he used the London Planetarium on Marylebone Road as the setting for its most vivid episode, 'The Pool of Thanatos'.

In particular, he relished the Westway, the three-mile stretch of dual carriageway leading west out of London that opened in 1970. He spoke of the road and its forest of concrete supports in terms of sculpture and dream, but mostly as a fragment of futurism emblematic of frustration and disappointment, both in the way it foreshadowed the Americanised city that London never became and in its promise of an escape that petered out before it really began. *Concrete Island* begins with his protagonist crashing his car at the point where the Westway drops back to earth and plunges into a tunnel, a metaphor for the way Ballard viewed his life.

Notting Hill, Ladbroke Grove and Bayswater harboured a floating population of bohemians, emigrants, hermits, artists, whores and criminals. The laureate of this community was documentary film-maker Ken Russell, who flaunted his eccentricity by installing an Edwardian barber's chair on the first-floor balcony of his Ladbroke Grove home. His early films for the BBC anatomised fellow west Londoners, present and past, from painter and poet Dante Gabriel Rossetti to the tenants of a typical Victorian mansion, whose parlours and bedrooms slumlords such as Perec 'Peter' Rachman partitioned into a warren of bedsits. The six-storey hive in Russell's *A House in Bayswater* had no hot water and only a single telephone, guarded by the caretaker in her basement flat. Occupants included a painter, a photographer, a retired ladies' maid and an aged chorus girl-cum-dancing teacher, with a single gawky student. Russell coaxed the sexagenarian back into her jazz-age costume for a farewell performance before the house was demolished. His final image, worthy of the surrealists, shows teacher and pupil battling in slow motion against a phantom gale that seeks to thrust them back into the past.

This vision resonates with an incident from Jim's experience. A prostitute and her pre-teen daughter lived above Mary. When she was entertaining a client, the daughter would put on fancy dress of crinoline, parasol and hat, and accompany them into the room. Assuming the men had sex with the child, Mary urged Jim to intervene, but a neighbour assured him that this wasn't the case – she just watched. To Mary, this was almost as bad, and she pushed him to complain to the hotel's manager. After Jim threatened to call the police, the woman and her child disappeared. 'People say my films are strange,' mused Russell, 'but they pale beside reality.'

Ballard and Russell weren't alone in sensing a new Britain emerging without most of the population participating, or even being aware. So rich was the cultural medium that social structures grew like crystals, often in grotesque and threatening forms. *Look Back in Anger*, *The Outsider* and the novels of the 'Angry Young Men' reflected a suppressed hostility. Britain's new mass cult hero was James Bond, a licensed assassin, seductive, remorseless and amoral, a throwback to the pre-war vigilantism of Bulldog Drummond. In *Lord of the Flies*, published in 1954, William Golding captured the sense of things slipping out of control. The officer who rescues the survivors of the schoolboy choir can scarcely believe how quickly they reverted to savagery. 'I should have thought,' he says, 'that a pack of British boys – you're all British, aren't you? – would have been able to put up a better show than that.'

The sensation of Eduardo Paolozzi's 1952 Bunk had passed, but in 1956 a second and larger show, This Is Tomorrow, at the Whitechapel Gallery, ignited a revolution by repeating the lesson at greater volume and in more detail. Conceived by architectural critic Theo Crosby, it was inspired by a 1954 Paris congress on the convergence of 'fine' and popular art. One reviewer wrote:

> The exhibition consisted of a dozen stands, on each of which a different team of architect/painter/sculptor had collaborated. Richard Hamilton was teamed with John McHale and John Voelker; together they produced an environment which has been called the first genuine work of Pop. It combined a large scale use of popular imagery with an imaginative exploitation of perception techniques. Prominent were a 16 ft robot – with flashing eyes and teeth – making off with an unconscious starlet; a photo blow-up of Marilyn Monroe; a gigantic Guinness bottle. These large objects were placed at the rear of the exhibit. Another section of floor – part of a sci-fi capsule – was painted with fluorescent red paint. In a tall chamber some of Marcel Duchamp's rotor-reliefs spun in a setting which was itself compounded of optical illusion. Smells drifted about the whole exhibit; several movies were projected at once while a juke-box played in front of a huge collage of film posters which curved round like a Cinerama screen.

Though not in the show itself, the catalogue reproduced Richard Hamilton's collage *Just What Is It That Makes Today's Homes So Different, So Appealing?*, which combined magazine clippings of a body-builder and a pin-up with other consumerist objects in a stylised US interior. It was destined to become the first iconic piece of British pop art.

In the US, pop art was larky, playful; Europe turned it aspirational. The vision of plenty celebrated by American advertising and popular culture was real enough to taste. The public almost salivated over the clothes, cars and household gadgets, not to mention the sexuality and social mobility that Hollywood, Detroit and Madison Avenue dangled just out of reach. Andy Warhol painted only the Campbell can: Britons wanted the soup.

Ballard saw This Is Tomorrow, and recognised his own pre-occupations. In particular he was impressed by an installation by Nigel Henderson and Peter and Alison Smithson called 'The Patio and Pavilion', described in the catalogue as 'a habitat symbolic of human needs – space, shelter, and privacy'. It consisted of a hut on a patch of sand, and a display of the instruments man would need to survive a catastrophe: an electric drill, a bicycle wheel and a pistol. David Brittain believes 'it was this exhibition that convinced Ballard that writers were falling behind artists in their recognition of the impact of science on everyday life, and he resolved to write fiction along the same lines'.

Jim was primed for such a revelation. He scorned the new realist novelists and playwrights, particularly John Osborne and *Look Back in Anger*, the film of which, even fifty years later, he continued to nominate as one of the worst he'd ever seen. He had no time for relationships, class conflicts or feelings. He liked Things. His enthusiasms remained those of his Shanghai childhood: big cars, glossy women, gangsters, Hollywood films; the James Bond recipe of Snobbery with Violence. 'Hamilton and Paolozzi,' he wrote, 'were both very interested in science-fiction for the sort of reasons I was interested':

> But what that show did was to redefine the subject matter, the rightful subject matter of a painter or a sculptor or novelist. We were living in a world made up of advertising, supermarkets, the whole consumer landscape, and this didn't really enter the fiction of most novelists. I wanted, just as the pop artists wanted, Hamilton and Paolozzi and their American counterparts – [Claes] Oldenburg said he wanted a 7-Up art, a Coca-Cola art. It was a completely new subject matter. This Is Tomorrow confirmed me in my hopes. I felt, right, I'm not alone, there are others who also feel the same way.

CHAPTER THIRTEEN

NEW WORLDS

Since the war, American publishers, to protect the local industry, had been barred from selling in Britain. Magazines could only license often abbreviated and poorly produced British Reprint Editions, using local facilities. Thus sheltered, British short story monthlies such as *Argosy*, *The Strand* and *Lilliput* sold and paid well, though since they had their pick of established names competition was fierce. Even as late as March 1964, when Jim was well established, *Argosy*'s publication of his story 'The Lost Leonardo' was cause for celebration.

Determined to launch himself as a writer, Jim traded on his advertising background to compose ad copy and direct-mail letters, casual work he could do at home. Mary worked for Charles Wintour, and at night typed up the stories Jim had written by hand in Canada and while waiting for demobilisation.

It's possible that some of these were not science fiction at all but crime stories. In the early fifties, the detective and mystery genres were far more robust than SF. In addition to the well-established *London Mystery Magazine*, appearing erratically since 1953, there were British Reprint Editions of *The Saint Detective Magazine*, *Ellery Queen's Mystery Magazine* and *Alfred Hitchcock's Mystery Magazine.* Most ran only material from their US editions, but occasionally a British writer cracked that market. Stories that Jim later sold as SF, such as 'The Quiet Assassin', 'Mr F. is Mr F.', 'Now: Zero', 'The Man on the 99th Floor' and even 'Track 12' could have been intended for these magazines, or for *Argosy* and its sister publication, *Suspense*, which was devoted entirely to crime. It may only have been after he failed with these magazines that he turned to the science fiction monthlies.

The SF trade directory listed forty such titles, almost all published in the US. Their rates made UK writers salivate. Even minor magazines paid 1¢ or 2¢ a word. A few, including Jim's favourite, *Galaxy*, offered 3¢, and a minimum of $100 per story. With the average UK annual wage £180, the pound worth between $2 and $3, and rentals in Notting Hill standing at £5 ($10–15) a week, one such sale could support him for months. But cracking the US market meant toeing its party line, which held as a matter of faith the notion of mankind's perfectibility through technology. Editors mostly agreed on the specifics of this rosy future: world peace under benign US/UN control; cheap nuclear power; robots to do the work; the brain's telepathic and telekinetic powers harnessed; a longer lifespan, even immortality; then exploration and colonisation of the universe.

The magazine *Super Science Stories* was sufficiently confident of its writers' forecasting skill to advertise 'Read it today! Live it tomorrow!' However, most writers, pressed on details of how this agenda was to be achieved, ran for cover. Brian Aldiss, irritated by a reviewer's comment that his latest collection contained 'not one important new forecast', complained that critics expected 'a cross between Old Moore and the Air Ministry Roof'. Fantasist L. Sprague de Camp warned, 'It does not pay a prophet to be too specific.' He was right to be cautious. SF failed almost every attempt at prognosis, confidently forecasting humanoid robots, babies bred in bottles, food in pill form and telepathy, but unable to foresee the Cold War, personal computers or feminism.

This isn't surprising. Writers with real technical education were thin on the ground. Robert Heinlein, 'the Dean of Science Fiction', took only a few mathematics and physics classes at UCLA before turning to the typewriter. Exceptionally, space opera specialist Edward E. Smith possessed a doctorate. Always credited as 'E. E. Smith, PhD' and respectfully known as 'Doc' Smith, he was actually a food chemist, specialising in pastes to make doughnuts.

Over the next four decades, Jim revised his account of why he embraced science fiction. Initially he praised it for preferring the realities of technology over the self-absorbed analysis of social encounters. This view didn't survive his discovery of William Burroughs, who alerted him to the possibilities of a more visionary literature rooted in the everyday as seen through a mind disturbed by psychosis or drugs. Except in the most general way, science disappeared from Jim's writing. Later, when Kingsley Amis and Isaac Asimov, former supporters, accused him of apostasy, he pointed out that they were no better. 'Asimov, Heinlein, and the masters of American SF are not really writing of science at all,' he said.

> They're writing about a set of imaginary ideas which are conveniently labelled 'science'. They're writing about the future, they're writing a kind of fantasy-fiction about the future, closer to the western and the thriller, but it has nothing really to do with science. I studied medicine, chemistry, physiology, physics, and I worked for about five years on a scientific journal. The idea that [SF] has anything to do with the sciences is ludicrous.

For the first months of the summer of 1955, Jim sat in his room at Stanley Crescent and tapped out story after story, only to have US editors bounce them all. Other British SF writers could have warned him that US editors bought almost entirely from people they knew. Since many doubled as agents, the writers were also their clients, while the book publishers to whom they sold were also old pals.

A leading proprietor of this closed shop was Arthur Scott Feldman of the Scott Meredith Agency in New York. Hopefuls who asked him to represent them received a form letter suggesting they buy his book *Writing to Sell.* Any who persisted were funnelled into his mail-order writing school, where out-of-work clients of the agency, nicknamed by author/editor Judy Merril 'the Scotts', coached them in the formula for the Well-Made Story. It took a while for Jim to get the message, but within a few years, and partly on the advice of Merril, he'd also joined Scott Meredith, though his refusal to write 'hard science' stories ensured he would never achieve major success in the US.

In March 1955, the minor US magazine *Fantastic Universe* published 'Meet Miss Universe', a comic account of an intergalactic beauty contest by US writer Jack Vance. Vance's facetious fantasies, set in archaic and ritualistic cultures, demonstrated his admiration for P. G. Wodehouse and in particular James Branch Cabell, from whom he adopted a drily antique style of dialogue and a relish for exotic character and place names. Immediately inspired, Jim set out to write his own equivalent. One struggles to think of a less likely model for a writer of his seriousness. Imagine T. S. Eliot making his debut not with *Prufrock and Other Observations* but *Old Possum's Book of Practical Cats.*

Not for the last time, Jim was attracted less by content than form. For 'Passport to Eternity', he used a pastiche of Vance's style to describe a wealthy couple in the far future who, seeking an unusual vacation, are badgered by agencies offering a bewildering range of recreational opportunities: mind links with Venusian sexual athletes, Rhinosaur races on Betelgeuse, even command of an army in an interplanetary war. It's riddled with whimsical names, extravagant fantasy and literary allusions, including one to Orwell's *1984*, yet Jim insists that, after all this work, he never submitted the story. 'It didn't occur to me,' he said vaguely when pressed for a reason. 'I don't know why – I think I had other problems on my mind.'

The problem was a common one among young couples. Mary was pregnant. In an era when illegitimacy still retained a social stigma and abortion was illegal, marriage was the only option. In September 1955, Mary and Jim became the latest of the one-in-five British couples who married while the bride was expecting. 'Slightly disjointed' was Jim's summary of the ceremony which, as a concession to propriety, took place in church. Jim asked his father whether etiquette required he leave something in the offertory box 'for the poor of the parish'. The elder James joked tactlessly, '*You* are the poor of the parish.'

The Ballards' first child, and only son, Christopher James, was born early in 1956. Since neither wanted to raise a family in Notting Hill, they found a flat in suburban Chiswick, affordable only with parental handouts. Abandoning hopes of US sales for his fiction, Jim turned to the few British SF magazines. The most promising was *New Worlds*, edited by E. J. Carnell, who operated as Nova Publications from an address in Grape Street, near Covent Garden. He didn't list its rates, but Jim soon learned they were meagre – £2 2s. for a thousand words. However, Jim and Mary were elated when Carnell bought the first story he submitted, 'Escapement', and also his second, 'Prima Belladonna'. The pleasure was only slightly tempered by the amount paid – £8 8s. each: barely enough to buy the pram with which they rolled their baby son down Chiswick High Street.

Edward John Carnell signed his editorials 'John' Carnell but preferred 'Ted'. Stiff, thin and formal, with a small moustache, he was a working-class Londoner at heart. He lived in suburban Plumstead, and dined his guests at the down-at-heel Army and Navy Club, a souvenir of Second World War service in the desert, about which he seldom spoke. Before the war, he had launched an amateur quarterly version of *New Worlds*, and, with a consortium of friends, battled for more than a decade to take it professional. In the early 1950s, he persuaded Maclaren, publishers of trade magazines like *The British Baker*, to back a digest-format monthly. In time, he added two more titles, *Science Fantasy* and *Science Fiction Adventures*, to which he consigned 'softer' material. For as long as the SF boom lasted and US magazines were barred, *New Worlds* sold a modest five thousand copies a month, with the other titles lagging behind.

'Jim Ballard sent me a story, "Escapement", in the summer of 1956,' Carnell said. 'He then followed it up with a personal visit to my office, bringing with him a fantasy story called "Prima Belladonna", which I liked even better.' Jim's memory differed slightly. He remembered their first meeting taking place after Carnell had bought three or four stories. Nova's ground-floor office, which Jim misremembered as being in a basement, wasn't his idea of a science fiction editor's lair, although he soon learned that its framed movie posters and cover art gave an accurate impression of Carnell's conservative and somewhat prudish tastes, formed by his pre-war reading of Wells, Conan Doyle, Olaf Stapledon and the early pulps, and his continuing friendship with John Wyndham, E. C. Tubb, Arthur Clarke and other veterans.

'I liked him enormously,' Jim said. 'He struck me as a very likeable, sensitive and intelligent man, whose mind was above all the pettiness in the SF world. I think he recognised what I was on about from a very early stage and he encouraged me to go on writing in my own way.' Carnell, he said, urged him not to imitate writers like Jack Vance in the hope of US sales, but to continue his exploration of 'inner space' and surrealism. Anyone who knew Carnell will scarcely credit this. His interest in and knowledge of surrealism or any aspect of art was vanishingly small. If he urged writers not to model themselves on those from the US, it wasn't to encourage experiment but, rather, to suppress it. Experience had convinced him that the sophisticated content and occasional typographical experiments of magazines such as *Galaxy* scared new readers away. Simple was safer, and it sold.

Many of his writers fell out with Carnell at one time or another, usually over his shibboleth of accessibility that discouraged anything complex or obscure. But all took care not to offend him, since he controlled their best market and also, in many cases, acted as their agent. In hard times, he even lent them money, albeit at 10 per cent interest. Privately, however, some were less diplomatic. 'Ted had a singular talent as an editor,' said Brian Aldiss. 'He could go straight to the heart of a story – and cut it out.' To Michael Moorcock, Carnell 'had the manner of a slightly posh bookie. He was dapper, but it was that flash dapperness, a slightly spivvy look. I'm pretty sure he owned a camel-hair overcoat. You felt that, in different circumstances, he'd be the kind of bloke to send the men round with the hammers. You can hear him saying, "I'm really sorry about this. I hate to do it. But business is business."'

Jim was right to call 'Prima Belladonna' his first published story, though it qualifies only on a technicality. It appeared in *Science Fantasy* for December 1956, the same month *New Worlds* ran 'Escapement', but Carnell staggered the release of the two magazines, putting *Science Fantasy* on the stands two weeks earlier. Of 'Passport to Eternity', which preceded both, Jim said nothing more until it sold to the US magazine *Amazing* in 1962.

Few reading 'Escapement' would have sensed a major talent in the making. The story is timid, even banal. A London couple suffer from a time slip, induced by solar radiation, that causes events to repeat themselves in shorter and shorter episodes, an effect they first notice when scenes recur in the TV play they're watching. Carnell preferred 'Prima Belladonna', but regretted its lack of scientific credibility and so exiled it to *Science Fantasy*. He was startled when, in a hint at the way SF was widening its horizons, Judy Merril chose it for her prestigious US anthology *Year's Best SF.* It was a straw in the wind that was soon to sweep over science fiction, altering it fundamentally.

CHAPTER FOURTEEN

SAND

All popular writing is simple; that's what makes it difficult. Raymond Chandler called Sherlock Holmes 'mostly an attitude and a few dozen lines of unforgettable dialogue'. The same might be said of his own Philip Marlowe, or Ian Fleming's James Bond. Ray Bradbury, too, was considered simplistic by some. Damon Knight rated his imagination 'mediocre':

> He borrows nearly all his backgrounds and props, and distorts them badly; whenever he is required to invent anything – a planet, a Martian, a machine – the image is flat and unconvincing. Bradbury's Mars, where it is not as bare as a Chinese stage setting, is a mass of inconsistencies; his spaceships are a joke; his people have no faces.

All true, but of little interest to the public that made him the world's most successful visionary writer.

Each of Knight's criticisms of Bradbury, and more, could apply to Ballard's 'Prima Belladonna' and the seven other stories set in the future resort of Vermilion Sands. Written, Jim said, to celebrate the neglected pulp virtues of the glossy, lurid and bizarre, they use a landscape borrowed from Bradbury, who got it from the Martian pulp novels of Leigh Brackett, who in turn took it from Edgar Rice Burroughs. Despite typifying everything Jim affected to despise in the work of his US contemporaries – spurious 'dream' imagery, bogus futurism, pseudo-science – they remain the best-loved and most popular of his early work. They are love letters to the science fiction he was outgrowing, but with which he would keep up a correspondence for a few more years, returning periodically for a nostalgic reunion.

The narrator of 'Prima Belladonna' explains that the tales date from 'The Recess', a fallow decade in future history. Like Tennyson's land of the lotus eaters 'in which it seemed always afternoon', Vermilion Sands, in common with the surrealist paintings that inspired it, exists outside time and place. When Jannick Storm proposed an article on its geography, Jim denied all idea of its location. Later, when pressed, he invented some possible models, starting with the Californian desert community of Palm Springs, although he'd never been there and the resemblance is remote. In an introduction to the collected stories, he speculated that their inspiration lay along the Mediterranean, where many northern Europeans spent the summer soaking up the sun. If there was a physical state emblematic of Vermilion Sands, he said, it was that of a person like himself, sprawled on his back in one of the hundred resorts littering the Mediterranean from Gibraltar to Glyfada in Greece.

A few recluses loiter in the villas of the Sands, but the only year-round residents are fringe dwellers: glider pilots who shape clouds into sculptural forms, breeders of singing shrubbery, programmers of poetry machines that spew ribbons of taped verse across the dunes, and couturiers whose gowns respond to the moods of those wearing them. Like the potters, weavers and painters of Mykonos and Marbella, they scratch a living in summer and make do for the rest of the year. Atypically for Ballard, all the stories are told in the first person, which hints at his sense of himself in his early days as a Have-Not observing the Haves at play.

As part of exempting Vermilion Sands from the requirements of technology, many of the stories involve psi powers. The grander houses of the Sands respond to the personalities of their tenants, and retain memories of them. Statues, machines and even flowers come alive in the presence of human intelligence. 'Say Goodbye to the Wind' toys with the idea of clothing which, fed by fallen hair and sloughed skin cells, changes colour and texture with the wearer's mood, and even distils a liquor from their sweat. Jim calls such clothing 'psychotropic' – a misnomer, since psychotropic drugs are those that modify our emotions rather than being modified by them. But 'psycho-reactive' lacks lilt.

The narrator of 'Prima Belladonna' breeds semi-sentient singing plants, controlling their voices with chemicals in their nutrients, and tuning them into ensembles with the help of a Khan-Arachnid orchid, part spider, part flower, the voice of which spans fourteen octaves. Its song attracts Jane Ciraclydes, a beautiful newcomer to the colony. Both musically and in its action, the climax is operatic, but, this being Ballard, tantalisingly ambiguous. Jane's mere presence arouses the three-metre-tall Khan-Arachnid to furious tumescence. The narrator takes one look into his greenhouse, where Jane stands confronting the rampant flower, presumably as prelude to some lewd act of animal/vegetable sex, and slams the door. Next day, the flower is dead, and Jane has gone, though she survives to haunt other resorts, since he hears of her doing the rounds of nightclubs in Brazilian resorts like Pernambuco.

Jim returned periodically to the Sands, usually with the rueful nostalgia of someone squeezing into the bell bottoms they never had the heart to throw away. In 1967, the colony served as a device to rescue 'Mobile', a 1957 story that never quite found its level. Adapting the idea of sentient metal that spreads like rampant iron ivy, he endowed the material with musical ability, relocated it in the Sands, and sold the rewrite to *If* as 'Venus Smiles'.

Freud is present *passim* in all eight stories, generally in the female characters, whom one critic described as 'beautiful but insane'. Jim, while not denying the charge, just laughed, and said, 'They're more fun that way!' Surrealist art, in particular that of the Belgian Paul Delvaux, also plays an important role. A latecomer to the movement and not notably original, Delvaux enjoyed a vogue in the 1940s because of his nudes. Pale and heavy breasted, they loiter, expressionless, in moonlit landscapes reminiscent – too reminiscent – of

Chirico. But Jim embraced their pallor and lack of affect.

He disagreed with those who called the stories 'dreamlike', just as he rejected that label when applied to surrealist painting. Dreams are never as vivid as they appear in fiction or art. Rather, he compared them to a cross between Kafka and the radio soap opera *Mrs Dale's Diary*. He spoke with authority, since he dreamed prodigiously, and claimed to remember each dream. Only one story, 'The Watch Towers', from *Science Fantasy* in 1962, incorporates material from his own dreams, and the imagery is unglamorous. Every aspect of life in its society is scrutinised from inverted towers that depend from the sky, filled with alien scientists who observe the inhabitants in the way microscopes are used to observe bacteria, but never communicate with them.

'Hallucinatory' is a better adjective than 'dreamlike' for the visions of Vermilion Sands, which have the solidity of a delusion. To a psychotic, the voices in his head are real and the invaders of his world flesh and blood. It was the thinness of the membrane separating us from madness that the surrealists strove to document, to show to the supposedly sane, in Breton's words, 'how fragile their thoughts are, and on what unstable foundations, over what cellars they have erected their unsteady houses'.

Determined to find significance under their tinsel of the stories, the blurb writer for a 1971 US edition suggested Vermilion Sands represents 'the languid decay of a tawdry dream', continuing, 'A desert resort designed to fulfil the most exotic whims of the sated rich, it now moulders in sleazy dilapidation, a haven for the remittance men of the artistic and literary world and for the human lampreys that prey on them. It is a lair for malice and hate and envy – and the more cancerous forms of madness.' No reading supports so toxic an interpretation of the stories. Their mood is nostalgic, playful, self-consciously antique. We who read them are like visitors on holiday who, exploring a deserted beachside pier, find some dusty, shrouded coin-in-the-slot attractions. As our coins rattle in, the buildings light up with a desert glow, the singing flowers come to life, and, with a soft whirring of gears, the bare-breasted women turn to regard us with insect eyes.

Freud, surrealism and Ray Bradbury helped shape Vermilion Sands, but the strongest influence was Hollywood. One story, 'The Screen Game', even takes place during the production of a film. *Aphrodite '70*, a vanity project, stars a deranged aristo who spends her time embedding precious stones in the carapaces of spiders and scorpions. The narrator is hired to paint desert backdrops of the sort common to Technicolor musicals of the late forties.

Surrealism flourished in Hollywood during the forties, particularly at MGM. Its most accomplished director of musicals was Vincente Minnelli, a former Broadway designer who quoted from Tanguy, Chirico and Dalí in *Ziegfeld Follies*, *The Pirate* and *Yolanda and the Thief*. Another MGM employee, Albert Lewin, a producer turned director, collected surrealist art. In 1946, adapting Maupassant's *Bel Ami*, he needed a large painting on the theme of 'The Temptation of Saint Anthony', and invited ten surrealists, including Man Ray, Ernst, Dalí, Delvaux, Dorothea Tanning and Leonora Carrington, to compete for the $2,500 commission. Dalí's entry, featuring stilt-legged elephants, became one of his most popular images, but the judges – Marcel Duchamp, art dealer Sidney Janis and Alfred Barr of MoMA – chose a canvas by Ernst. Under a pale blue sky, a still, green lake is invaded by seething vegetation and a bestiary of apes, armadillos, staring birds, and a gaping devil-like beast, all entangled in a skein of orange fabric that imitates the contours of a female torso. The contest rated a tongue-in-cheek report in *Horizon*, and the film, called *The Private Affairs of Bel-Ami*, included a scene where speechless ladies and gentlemen stare bemused at 'Saint Anthony'. Defying Hollywood practice, he accorded the painting the single colour shot in an otherwise monochrome film.

Two years later, Lewin chose Man Ray to create the paintings supposedly executed by James Mason in *Pandora and the Flying Dutchman*, which Jim admired for its frank debt to surrealism. In a Spanish seaside resort, car racers and matadors cluster round Ava Gardner's wilful, self-destructive Pandora. A key scene in the film brings Delvaux to life as a nude white-skinned Gardner swims out by moonlight to the newly arrived yacht of Mason's Flying Dutchman, doomed to sail until freed by a woman prepared to die for him.

Echoes of Lewin's film recur throughout Jim's work. Pandora is evoked as the embodiment of feminine malice. In *The Drowned World*, Jim describes Beatrice Dahl as a Pandora with a killing mouth and a box of desires and frustrations that she opens unpredictably to release some new affliction. The Vermilion Sands story also employs the film's device of a disinterested narrator who spies on Pandora and her lovers by telescope from his castle. Did Jim, watching the film in a Cambridge art cinema in 1951, intuit what other and more crucial part it would play in his life? In 1964, on holiday in San Juan de Alicante, close to where it was shot, he would push his big Armstrong Siddeley saloon up to 100 mph along the beach, imitating Nigel Patrick in the film, whose attempt on the world speed record ends in flames, doused by driving his into the surf. And it was on that coast that his wife Mary would, like Pandora, sicken and die.

CHAPTER FIFTEEN

CHEMISTRY

Secure behind import restrictions, Carnell had most of the UK market to himself. Old pals such as John Wyndham, E. C. Tubb, Eric Frank Russell, Arthur Clarke and William F. Temple contributed occasional stories, but mostly he relied on part-timers more interested in getting published than making money. New writers of stature were rare. Before Jim, his star had been Brian Aldiss. A lanky, bespectacled Oxford intellectual, Aldiss made his magazine debut in 1954 in *Science Fantasy*, but topped that with an SF story collection, *Space, Time and Nathaniel*, and a novel, *The Brightfount Diaries*, about life as a bookseller, both published in hardcover by Faber & Faber. Carnell was in awe. It took John Wyndham and John Christopher decades to be accepted by such prestigious houses.

Aldiss, more urbane than his five years' seniority over Jim might suggest, had been drafted into the army in 1943 and served in the Far East until 1947, racking up the first exploits of a colourful history that he'd explore in a trilogy of autobiographical novels. Many years later, Jim summed up the difference he perceived between himself and Aldiss. 'He has always made modest claims for science-fiction, while being enormously fond of both SF and its writers. I have made exaggerated claims, and secretly disliked it.' The divide, however, was more fundamental. 'In a consumer society,' wrote sociologist Ivan Illich, 'there are inevitably two kinds of slaves: the prisoners of addiction and the prisoners of envy.' Ballard, the born addict, knew no life but writing, and wanted none. Aldiss, cunning and ambitious, had a relish for intrigue and a wicked tongue. His academic connections and an influential spot as literary editor of the *Oxford Mail* meant he could deal as an equal with London publishers and critics. He cultivated the conservative Kingsley Amis and C. S. Lewis, but at the same time stood his round of proletarian pints at SF conventions for rowdier newcomers. These included extrovert US-born Harry Harrison, gifted but self-important John Brunner and the precocious Moorcock, who had edited *Tarzan Adventures* at sixteen, and the *Sexton Blake Library* shortly after.

In such beery discussions, a gap opened between the old guard, represented by Wyndham, Christopher, Clarke and Carnell, and the newcomers, for whom even the term 'science fiction' had become suspect. ('It's just a label,' one argued. 'So is "leprosy",' snarled another.) Ballard, Aldiss and Moorcock would later be yoked together as 'The New Wave' in British SF, but Moorcock knew little of Ballard until *The Drowned World* was published in *Science Fiction Adventures* at the end of 1961. Ballard and Aldiss shared an impatience with the direction in which SF was heading, but didn't think of themselves as part of any movement. Among other things, they were too busy. 'You could have a short story in every issue of a magazine, for a whole year,' said Jim. 'So there was this great pressure to produce material; and it was a tremendous test of one's talent and imagination.' Carnell's stable of part-timers didn't offer much competition. One of them, Leonard Percy 'Lan' Wright, excited Aldiss's derision by comparing the writing of a story to knitting a sock. Problems with plot, he claimed, were analogous to the challenges of turning the heel. Aldiss wrote, as 'The Knitter of Socks', a gleeful demolition of Wright and others of the second string.

Wright's sock-knitting metaphor appeared in one of the biographical notes printed on the inside front cover of *New Worlds*. A similar profile of Jim, with a postage stamp-sized photograph, accompanied 'Escapement'. Ballard later claimed authorship, but its misstatements and oddities of expression betray Carnell's hand. Among other errors, it names his favourite writers as 'Poe, Wyndham, Lewis and Bernard Wolfe'. No admirer of either John Wyndham or

C. S. Lewis, he meant Percy Wyndham Lewis, modernist author of *The Apes of God*.

Selling to Carnell yielded pocket money, but not enough to live on, so Jim took jobs in the libraries of Richmond Borough and Sheen, besides writing commentaries for a scientific film company. Hearing that he and Mary had a second child on the way, Carnell found him a spot editing *The British Baker*. After six months, Jim moved to the weekly *Chemistry and Industry* as deputy editor. Since Ballard Sr had been a chemist, some discreet string-pulling may have been involved. In many professions, the key question asked of job applicants was 'Don't I know your father?'

Each day, Jim travelled to Belgrave Square in Knightsbridge and the mansion occupied by the Society of Chemical Industry. He soon got to know the business, visiting labs, writing articles and reviewing books. That he had no background in chemistry didn't hinder his interest. Rather, it heightened it, since he was able to enjoy the incidental poetry of technical material and relish juxtapositions never intended by those who put it together. The magazine's editor, William E. Dick, was a professional chemist, and new to the job himself. He left Jim free to shape the design. In the days long before desktop publishing, each page had to be laid out by hand, the text and illustrations pasted on to boards, to be photographed and printed. In the early stages, blocks of meaningless 'body copy', often in Latin, stood in for the text. Such layouts showed Jim that a page could be attractive and informative even when the actual words meant nothing. The work redirected his imagination to the typographical experiments of Bernard Wolfe, and in turn to those of the Dadaists and early surrealists such as Apollinaire.

A second Ballard child, christened Caroline Fay but always known as Fay, arrived in September 1957. Christopher James had been born in an NHS hospital, which forbade husbands from participating in the birth or even observing, so Jim insisted on both Caroline Fay and her sister Beatrice, who followed in the summer of 1959, being delivered at home – in the very bed, he pointed out with some atavistic satisfaction, where they had been conceived. In both cases, he not only observed the delivery but helped the midwife and his sister-in-law deliver the baby by kneeling beside the bed, pressing back Mary's large and bursting haemorrhoids.

With a family to support, Jim experimented with a more slick style in his writing, hoping for US sales. 'Mobile', published in the October 1957 edition of *Science Fantasy*, has a transatlantic feel, beginning with its title; the sculptor Alexander Calder, famous for the invention of the notion of mobiles, had adapted Marcel Duchamp's term for a dangling sculpture, but it wasn't widely known outside the US. Names are based on movies, such as Lubitsch, or Margot Channing (Bette Davis's character in *All About Eve*), and the location is a town called Murchison Falls. For the first time, Jim introduces the concept of allotropism: the capacity of some minerals, because of their crystalline structure, to alter their nature. A sculpture commissioned by Murchison Falls's town council starts to grow like a rabid creeper. Cut up and fed back into the steel works, the metal infects a multitude of buildings, the frames and metal decorations of which begin to sprout. Allotropism, in the form of statues and clothing that respond to movement or even thought, reappears in the later Vermilion Sands stories, while the possibility of an allotropic virus infecting man became the basis of *The Crystal World*.

In the same month as Fay's birth, Jim put in an appearance at the Fifteenth World Science Fiction Convention at the King's Court Hotel in London, the first held outside the US. Two hundred and sixty-eight people attended, including a large American contingent. Carnell, who was chairman, persuaded Jim it would be professionally useful to be there. Events included a talk on the soon-to-be-opened London Planetarium and a demonstration of hypnotism, but the fans expended more energy and invention on the fancy dress competition and subsequent dance. Alan Whicker filmed it for the BBC, with the customary tongue-in-cheek commentary and references to 'little green men'.

The hotel, chosen for cheapness, was run-down, and in the midst of renovation. The staff, unprepared for the unruly fans, were overrun. In later years, Jim, who only went for a single evening, described his visit in apocalyptic terms, claiming the experience so dispirited him that he couldn't write for a year. This appears extreme – all the more so since he never specified what offended him, except to remark, tersely, that 'the Americans were hard to take, and most of the British fans were worse'. Malcolm Edwards, then a fan but later Jim's editor, sees a possible reason. 'There may have been a snobbish element in what happened to him in 1957 – because at that time there were almost no fans who had been to university. They were as far from being an intellectual crowd as you can imagine. Jim was always quite an intellectual person, and he probably went in there, and realised "These people are not on my wave length at all".'

It's possible he also resented the cliquish atmosphere, with old hands such as John Wyndham, Sam Youd, Ted Tubb and even the teetotal Arthur C. Clarke clustering in the bar, discussing everything except science fiction. Nor would he have relished the fans in costume, waving ray gun-like water pistols and sporting beanie caps topped with a propeller, a popular symbol of fandom. SF historian Peter Weston insists that the overall tone of the event was restrained. 'Ted Carnell in particular had been at pains to stress the serious nature of the convention, and the need for the attendees to "put on a good show", as it were, for the press and other outside interests. If Ballard had come for the programme sessions and met some of the many other authors and editors present, he might have been rather more impressed.' Something similar apparently took place, since photographs show Jim in the audience for at least one of the presentations.

'I went to the bar and ordered a drink,' recalled Brian Aldiss. 'Standing next to me was a slim young man who told me that there were some extraordinary types at the convention, and that he was thinking of leaving pretty smartly. He introduced himself as J. G.

Ballard. I had already read his early stories in *New Worlds*; indeed, at that time, his were the only short stories (apart from my own) that I could read there with any pleasure.'

While fans partied, the writers digested some bad news from the US. In June, the largest magazine distributor, American News Company, had collapsed, throwing the business into chaos. Monthlies such as *Galaxy* and *Astounding* lost access to news-stands and thus to their largest readership. The market for short fiction, already shrinking, dwindled as publishers switched to paperback novels that could be sold through bookstores. By 1963, a poll of *New Worlds* readers would show purchases of magazines down to one or two a month, as against seven books. More alarming to British writers, the British government, dismantling wartime tariffs, planned to lift the ban on US magazine publishers distributing in Britain. Carnell's publications, already feeling the pinch, could never survive.

CHAPTER SIXTEEN

CUTTING UP

For the next year, life with a new baby absorbed Jim. He and Mary had few friends. A further awkwardly phrased profile in *New Worlds* explained: 'Outwardly, at any rate, he lives quietly in Chiswick with his wife and baby son Jimmie. He admits that though she doesn't actually write his stories, his wife has as much to do with their final production as he has himself. She hopes to have his novel *You and Me and the Continuum* finished by the end of this year.' In one detail, the profile soon became outdated. With the extra money from his job at *Chemistry and Industry*, Jim and Mary could afford to move from Chiswick to a flat in Heathcote Road, St Margaret's, near Twickenham. The reference to *You and Me and the Continuum* is the first in print to Jim's unfinished experimental novel, and almost the last. When he used the same title for a short story ten years later, he professed not even to remember the earlier project. As for Mary's involvement in his work, this ended at sometimes typing up his manuscripts.

Between November 1957 and November 1959, Jim published only one story, 'Track 12', in *New Worlds* for April 1958. A biochemist and enthusiast for home recording poisons his wife's lover with a drug that drowns him in his own fluids. As his victim suffocates, he plays a thunderous tape of the guilty couple's most intimate moment, exulting that the man is drowning in a high fidelity recording of an illicit kiss. Carnell had reservations about the story, in particular the original title, which used the word 'Atlantis' to resonate with the theme of drowning. Readers of *New Worlds*, Carnell contended, would, seeing

'Atlantis', expect a fantasy. Jim reluctantly altered it, while grumbling that Carnell had been perfectly happy with the title of an earlier story, 'Manhole 69'. 'Track 12' became Jim's most successful early story, and was repeatedly reprinted, beginning with its use by Brian Aldiss in his 1961 anthology *Penguin Science Fiction*, a mark of mainstream acceptance.

Describing his slump later, Jim blamed it entirely on the 1957 Convention. He contrasted the plodding London scene with that in France, where, he claimed, writers and film-makers such as Alain Robbe-Grillet and Alain Resnais were already experimenting with SF. There was no truth in this. Resnais was the obscure director of a few short films. He remained so until 1959 and *Hiroshima Mon Amour*. Robbe-Grillet was equally unknown. He had only just made his name with *La Jalousie*, which Jim didn't read until well after its 1959 English translation, and then disliked. *L'année dernière à Marienbad*, the collaboration between the two Frenchmen that caused Jim to link their names, wasn't filmed until 1961, when he dismissed it as the most boring movie he'd ever seen.

What were the real reasons behind the two-year dry period? The reference to *You and Me and the Continuum* hints that he may have returned to the experimental Cambridge project. David Pringle, a fan who became an authority on his work, speculates:

> My tentative hypothesis is this: Ballard's lost *You and Me and the Continuum* of 1956 was probably a modern-day novel about a botched second coming – or, at any rate, about a 'man who fell to earth' – with a Christ-like central character who is haunted by three personae from his unconscious named Kline, Coma and Xero. Although it didn't closely resemble the condensed novels of later years, it was no doubt unconventional in form, with parts resembling a film script and parts which amounted to prose poetry: a 'hot steaming confection' incorporating a good deal of scientific and psychoanalytical terminology and many surrealistic juxtapositions. Perhaps it was never finished, and it is likely that it would have been considered unpublishable in its day.

But parts of it remain embedded, as literary fossil remains, in *The Atrocity Exhibition.*

Such an attempt, and its failure, would explain some further outbursts by Jim against naturalistic fiction. 'I can't remember who the dominant English writers of the day were,' he said. 'Most of them have vanished into oblivion. Not just the novel, but criticism and the English cinema – I had no interest in that whatsoever. I read on what I'd call the international menu, not the English menu.' This is false naivety. He knew very well which writers held the high ground. Elsewhere, he even named them. 'This was the heyday of the naturalistic novel, dominated by people such as C. P. Snow and Anthony Powell and so on, and I felt that maybe the novel had shot its bolt, that it was stagnating right across the board. The bourgeois novels, the so-called "Hampstead novels", seemed to dominate everything.' He particularly disparaged the aestheticism of Virginia Woolf. 'No one in a novel by Virginia Woolf ever fills up the petrol tank of their car,' he said accusingly.

Why such prejudice against naturalistic fiction? He was at least as accomplished a writer as contemporaries like Stan Barstow and Alan Sillitoe, a fact proved by *Empire of the Sun.* His argument that such fiction wasn't relevant to the technological present is thin. A number of British realistic novelists dealt with technology, ranging from Huxley and Orwell to Nevil Shute, John Pudney and John Lymington. This was a niche Jim could have occupied with ease. Yet he turned his back on this option to embrace science fiction, and then attacked science fiction just as furiously. His truculence could be an aspect of his psychopathology, since it echoes the hostility of someone trying to hide a physical or psychological dysfunction – epilepsy, dyslexia, illiteracy. Perhaps he didn't have the patience to stick with a narrative and a collection of characters long enough to complete a conventional novel. This is borne out by the limp conclusions of his late 'thrillers' *Cocaine Nights* and *Super-Cannes,* which lose momentum a third of the way from the end. Jim wrote in flashes of a delusional, often manic vividness. 'I see him as primarily the creator of powerful, feverishly detailed situations,' wrote the critic Robert Towers, 'situations that give rise not so much to stories as to the nightmarish expansion of images involving, typically, claustrophobia, dismemberment, and apocalypse.' This is not the timber of which the well-constructed novel is made.

Seeking to refine such images drew him to take a minute interest in the mechanics of narrative and the concept of 'story'. He fussed with it, taking it apart like a broken toy, examining each component like a naturally gifted but unschooled handyman who can't understand the manual. Incongruously, he found inspiration at *Chemistry and Industry*. Its opposite number in the USA, *Chemical and Engineering News*, used terms new to Britain – 'coma', 'zero', 'probe', 'zone', 'pack', and names such as 'Kline'. Jim enjoyed their synthetic sound. The character names in his stories began to change. Women are usually identified in full, the men with family names alone – 'Gorrell', 'Stamers', 'Renthall', 'Mangon', 'LeGrande', 'Ryker'. Once he discovered the 'cut-up' technique, they become even more curt. 'Kline' ushered in a snappier transatlantic cast: 'Ricci', 'Laing', 'Payne', 'Steiner', 'Wilder', 'Vaughan' and 'Mallory'. Such names could – and sometimes did – double as brand names, or titles of corporations.

Letraset dry-transfer lettering had just hit the British market, and Jim became proficient at using it to create headings and layouts for the magazine. It reminded him of the adventurous typography of *Limbo 90*, and also of the way in which the Dadaists and surrealists, inspired by the visual games Guillaume Apollinaire called Calligrammes, made collages from cut-up books and newspapers. He would also have read Alfred Bester's *The Stars My Destination*, serialised in *Galaxy* from October 1956 to January 1957. At the climax, its hero, Gully Foyle, experiences synaesthesia, which scrambles his senses. He tastes colours, and perceives movement as sound, effects depicted graphically on the page, in one case in a way that may have planted an idea in Jim's mind.

Foyle opened his mouth and exclaimed.
The sound came out in burning star-bubbles.
Foyle took a step.
'CRASH!' the motion blared.

During 1958, Jim experimented with the possibilities. Clipping headlines from *Chemical and Engineering News*, he combined them with Letraset to create five double-page spreads that initially had no name but which he later called 'Project for a New Novel'. Such a novel, he theorised, would consist entirely of magazine-style headlines and layouts, with a deliberately meaningless text. Typography and design would carry the imaginative content. 'Project' has so much in common with William Burroughs's 'cut-up' texts that it's difficult to believe Jim knew nothing about them. Brion Gysin, Burroughs's friend and collaborator, dated their discovery precisely to 'Room 15 of the Beat Hotel during the cold Paris spring of 1958. While cutting a mount for a drawing, I sliced through a pile of newspapers with my Stanley blade. I picked up the raw words and began to piece together texts.' Even then, it took more than a year for their innovation to appear in a form Jim might have seen. The first cut-up book, compiled by Burroughs, Gysin and Sinclair Beiles, *Minutes to Go*, wasn't published until 1960.

Jim was just one of the many artists in a number of countries who discovered the cut-up technique independently. The subversive idea of turning society's printed matter against itself germinated in a dozen places between the wars. John Heartfield's anti-Nazi collage posters segue into the covers of *Time* magazine cut up and reassembled by Eduardo Paolozzi in 1949. While Burroughs and Gysin sliced and glued in the Beat Hotel, nearby Norman Rubington, as 'Akbar del Piombo', cannibalised antique engravings to create satirical collages in the style of Max Ernst, which Maurice Girodias's Olympia Press published in such books as *Fuzz Against Junk*. Shortly after, in London, future playwright Joe Orton and his partner Kenneth Halliwell made collages of the dust jackets of books in the Islington Public Library and added ribald new texts, offences that earned them six months in prison.

Surrealism had evolved with the same apparent randomness. Throughout the twenties, people drifted to Paris from all over the world to join Breton and Aragon. According to Jean-Claude Carrière, Buñuel's scenarist, 'There is absolutely no reason why Benjamin Peret came from Toulouse to join the group; why Max Ernst comes from Germany, why and how Man Ray comes from the States and Buñuel from Spain, and they get together. There are probably billions of little hazards and coincidences. But something was calling them together. It was something they shared already before belonging to the same group.' Once again, existence preceded essence.

Some time in 1960, Jim taped the five sheets of 'Project' to the fence in the back garden, and Mary photographed him in front of it. (The image appeared on the cover of the January 1963 edition of *New Worlds* that included 'The Subliminal Man'.) Jim sensed the importance of his experiments. They showed that a story need not have narrative. By inserting chapter headings and subheads, varying typography and scattering poetically charged names and proper nouns, one could create an aesthetically pleasing object, independent of any literary meaning. What was narrative anyway but the connective tissue between moments of revelation? Why not dispense with it altogether, or at least minimise it; condense novels into the space of a short story and short stories into a paragraph? Advertisements, comic strips and films did it; why not fiction?

CHAPTER SEVENTEEN

SIDEREAL SHEPPERTON

In 1960, Jim bought the only house he would ever own, a two-storey semi-detached at 36 Charlton Road (later 'Old Charlton Road') in the placid Middlesex community of Shepperton, on the Thames, west of London – and located, Jim later discovered to his surprise, almost exactly on the same forty-ninth parallel as Moose Jaw.

When the Ballards moved in, Charlton Road was, even by local standards, a backwater, with open land opposite. Two ground-floor rooms served as living room and study. Bedrooms and nursery occupied the first floor. The toilet was at the top of the stairs – 'and,' recalls his friend, the editor and writer Charles Platt, 'notoriously difficult to flush. Jimmy once told me that he liked to see how guests would respond to this challenge. How long would they persist in trying to flush it, before they asked for help.' There was no garage and barely enough space off the street to park a car, but the back garden was both large and secluded enough for Jim occasionally to sunbathe nude. Within a few years, neighbours were complaining about this, and by the time he left, fifty years later, the sleepy village had become a dormitory suburb of London.

He scarcely noticed the nearby film studios, except to amuse his children by showing them the spot where, in the comedy *Genevieve*, a vintage car runs off the road into a 'splash' where water flows over the road. Over time, however, he retrospectively cited them as a factor in the decision to move there. As the M3 motorway was built and the sprawl of Heathrow crept closer, both were incorporated into his world view, until 'Ballard's Shepperton', like 'Hemingway's Paris' or 'Warhol's New York', acquired more substance, at least in the imagination of his admirers, than the original. Charles Platt recalls 'one Frenchman made plans to visit him, and became extremely excited as Jimmy gave him directions to find the house. "Ah yes, yes, just like in the book!" the Frenchman exclaimed, referring to *Crash*. Jimmy said if the Frenchman could only see him in his utterly dull suburban home, with Claire [Walsh, his long-time companion] cooking a roast in the oven, and the kids playing in the next room, it might be rather disillusioning.' He came anyway, and later described the journey in terms of Jean-Luc Godard's *Alphaville*, with himself as the traveller voyaging through sidereal space to Shepperton, capital of the universe, with a too-knowing London cab driver as his pilot.

Having his fantasy recoil on him in this way disconcerted Jim, but each attempt to dial down the strangeness merely accentuated it, until he began to wonder if Shepperton wasn't the way his admirers imagined. 'Actually, the suburbs are far more sinister places than most city dwellers imagine,' he said. 'Their very blandness forces the imagination into new areas. I mean, one's got to get up in the morning thinking of a deviant act, merely to make certain of one's freedom. It needn't be much; kicking the dog will do.'

Initially, he rationalised his choice of Shepperton for the reasons important to any young husband and father: the area was cheap, the schools were good, the air clean and the railway provided a quick route into London. It took many years to expose the most convincing motive. In 1991, returning from Shanghai after his first visit since the war, he realised that 'all the people who moved there had come from places just like Shepperton, and so they built and lived in houses exactly like these. I now know I was drawn here because, on an unconscious level, Shepperton reminds me of Shanghai.'

Despite the presence of the film studios, Jim saw few celebrities, except for crooner Dickie Valentine, whose children went to the same school. Parents waiting at the gates were impressed by the white Pontiac in which the star arrived to collect them. Imported from the US, it didn't merely advertise his fame but was roomy enough to ferry the singer, plus his drummer and pianist between gigs. In May 1971, at the height of Jim's preoccupation with car crashes, all three died when, racing at 4 a.m. to a performance in Wales, their car missed a bend at 90 mph. Jim lists Valentine among the celebrity road deaths of *The Atrocity Exhibition*, although, inconveniently for the mythology, at the time the singer was driving his wife's British-made Ford. His newest import from Detroit was stuck in Customs.

How happy was Jim with married life? If his fiction tells us anything, not very. No Ballard story contains a happy marriage nor even a stable relationship. His women are either brisk professionals in lab coats and business suits or languid *femmes fatales* who recline, Martini in hand, in a penthouse or by a pool – characteristics he found difficult to explain. 'I remember my wife reading some of my early short stories, and saying, "Why are there all these tormented marriages, with these strange and rather unappealing women – where do they come from?" Poor husband sort of would hide behind his typewriter and say, "Errrr – well, you've got to understand; I'm not a realistic writer". But it is a point, you know – where do they come from?'

Imprisonment and claustrophobia are recurrent themes in his stories. In 'Manhole 69', experimenters whose brains have been modified not to need sleep feel the walls closing in, until space contracts to a coffin-like capsule. In 'The Overloaded Man', a man's perception of his world shrinks to a single room. The protagonist of 'Build-Up', later retitled 'The Concentration City', seeks open space outside a mammoth future conurbation. Heading west on the transit system, he finds himself, after weeks of travel, back where he started; the city has engulfed the earth. 'Billennium' is particularly nightmarish. Space in the city of the future has become so scarce that each person is allocated four square metres. People sleep seven to a room, or set up house in closets, while neighbours seethe around them, as in a hive. 'The Ballard family's room was a broom cupboard,' Jim recalled of the space assigned to them in internment, 'but I remembered every scratch, every chip of paint. It was Lunghua, not Amherst Avenue, which felt like home.' Though it never entirely disappeared, this claustrophobia dwindled to a persistent psychic ache, externalised in habits such as leaving all the lights on in the house, even on bright days.

Significant international incidents in 1959 included the Cuban revolution, the incorporation of Alaska and Hawaii into the United States, the debut of Motown Records and the unveiling of the microchip and the Barbie doll. It illustrates Jim's single-mindedness that none of these impinged on him. His lack of interest in world affairs was matched by negligible political beliefs. Music, as we have seen, gave him no pleasure, and he never used a computer. However, since the Ballards' third and last child, Beatrice, was born in 1959, it's conceivable he made the acquaintance of Barbie and Ken.

The one event of 1959 that would affect his career took place, appropriately for someone who preferred 'the international menu', in Paris: Maurice Girodias published William Burroughs's novel *Naked Lunch* – adding, in the process, an unwanted '*The*' to his title. It appeared in his Traveller's Companion paperback series that included unapologetic porn such as *Sex for Breakfast* and *Until She Screams.* Later, he issued Burroughs's *The Ticket that Exploded* and *The Soft Machine.* Even in their discreet green card covers, Olympia's titles were too hot for British booksellers, but smuggled copies circulated widely. For years, Moorcock had been sneaking them in by the dozen, mostly the novels of Henry Miller. Occasionally a shipment was seized by Customs. Two Special Branch agents who visited his home, expecting a hardened pornographer, discovered a teenager still living with his mum. They retired in confusion, taking their evidence, which, as Moorcock pointed out, had been read to exhaustion by the lads down at the station.

Burroughs sent a new current into the literary imagination, flooding it with novel and disturbing images. He wrote of drug addicts and aliens sharing the same New York flop houses; of TVs and typewriters not only with lives of their own but sphincters and genitals, too. Jim wouldn't read Burroughs for at least another two years. But just as his 'cut-up' experiments anticipated those of Burroughs, he intuited the implicit lesson of his prose. In a convincing example of Victor Hugo's 'idea whose time had come', the same vision occurred to numerous artists simultaneously all over the world. As *Naked Lunch* appeared in Paris, Jorge Luis Borges in Argentina had just published his essay collection *Other Inquisitions*, and Gabriel García Marquez his first novella, *Leaf Storm.* Meanwhile, Rod Serling in New York was murmuring a Burroughsian introduction to a new TV show:

> You unlock this door with the key of imagination. Beyond it is another dimension – a dimension of sound, a dimension of sight, a dimension of mind. You're moving into a land of both shadow and substance, of things and ideas. You've just crossed over into the Twilight Zone.

All were avatars of the magic realism that had its roots in surrealism. So rapidly did these ideas spread that one could almost believe Burroughs's theory that language was a virus, rushing through the world like wildfire, faster than print, almost faster than thought.

Jim decided Amis was wrong about plot being the hero in science fiction. Narrative was irrelevant. What attracted the reader's interest was *process* – the often minute progress of apparently random activity. The abstract expressionist painters of the New York School experienced a similar revelation after the Second World War. Jackson Pollock, Willem de Kooning and Mark Rothko rejected figuration, believing that painting had outgrown anecdote and illustration: there was only *surface* and *paint.* If Ballard had read anything by Borges (impossible, since none of his books appeared in English until 1962), he would have agreed with the insight in his essay 'The Wall and the Books' that *possibility* was subject enough. 'Music, states of happiness, mythology, faces belaboured by time, certain twilights and certain places try to tell us something, or have said something we should not have missed, or are about to say something; this imminence of a revelation which does not occur is, perhaps, the aesthetic phenomenon.'

CHAPTER EIGHTEEN

TIME

If there was a single science fiction story by which Jim wished to be remembered it was 'The Voices of Time'. The others he published in 1960 are of a piece with his earlier work. In February, 'The Sound Sweep' appeared in *Science Fantasy*, 'Zone of Terror' in the March edition of *New Worlds*, 'Chronopolis' in the June issue, and 'The Lost World of Mr Goddard' in *Science Fantasy* for October. In July, 'Manhole 69' was reprinted in a short-lived US edition of *New Worlds* – Carnell's luckless attempt to counter falling UK sales by entering the equally troubled US market.

'The Voices of Time' ran in *New Worlds* issue No. 99, published in October 1960. In other respects, the issue was banal. Carnell was saving his best for issue No. 100, including new stories by John Wyndham and Brian Aldiss. The cliché cover of issue No. 99 depicted a freighter accelerating into space with a load of containers, while Carnell's editorial fretted over the fate of the US *New Worlds*, mucked about by editors then dumped when it failed to sell. 'The Voices of Time', though the longest story in the issue, didn't lead. That distinction went to James White's whimsical 'The Apprentice', about an alien employed in a terrestrial department store. Nor did Carnell disguise his scepticism about Jim's latest work. His introduction damns him with faint praise, describing him as no more than 'comparable in stature to Brian Aldiss who is undoubtedly the leading British writer of the day'.

'The Voices of Time' begins with what we now recognise as the classic Ballard preamble, down to the premonitory opening

'Later . . .'. The description of an empty swimming pool at the edge of the desert, into the floor of which an obsessed scientist has cut an incomprehensible ideogram, reminded readers instantly of Ray Bradbury, whose Mars-themed collection *The Martian Chronicles* appeared in Britain in 1951 (puzzlingly retitled *The Silver Locusts*). Jim's 1962 essay 'Which Way to Inner Space?' praised Bradbury as someone capable of finding poetry in even so threadbare a setting as Mars. In time, he wearied of him and all American SF writers, dismissing them as

> a collection of truly naive and, if you like, innocent men – people who truly didn't know what they were doing. Ray Bradbury is a prominent example. A few years ago someone sent me a book about him, with many photographs. One of these showed Bradbury in his work room, which is about as large as a tennis court – and every millimetre of this huge workroom is stuffed full of toys: rockets, spaceships, dinosaur models, every kind of monster. A child's room. A wonderful image for the American science-fiction of these times, even for the whole of American culture.

But by then he had absorbed and digested Bradbury's languor, and added his own brand of existential melancholy that turned nostalgia to despair. Entropy drags at the narrative of 'The Voices of Time' as memory tugs at Jim himself, drawing him back to the abandoned swimming pools of Shanghai.

'The Voices of Time' transgressed every rule of science fiction by behaving as if there were none. Fiction traditionally aims to lure readers into a consensual fantasy; to involve them in a story and have them identify with a protagonist. Jim broke with this method. He distances us from identification by fragmenting the narrative into numbered chapters, printing some passages in italics, and interrupting the text with tables of digits and the single out-of-scale word 'YOU' – techniques learned from *Limbo 90* and *The Stars My Destination*, and anticipating *Naked Lunch*.

Scientific concepts jostle for attention, contradicting one another. The text resembles a modern Book of Revelation, both premonitory and poetic in its warning that these are the last days of man on earth. Populations dwindle, harvests fail, and people spend more and more time asleep, while, in an accelerated version of natural selection, frogs concentrate lead in their skins, anticipating increased solar radiation. A scientist theorises that each creature carries a key to the next stage of its evolution in a 'silent' pair of genes that can be activated by radiation. Another suggests DNA is losing its capacity to replicate. Everywhere, machines are running down. Numbers flowing from the constellation Canes Venatici mark a cosmic countdown. The voices of time are saying farewell. Faced with this avalanche of mutually contradictory concepts, sticklers for scientific authenticity echoed the *London Magazine* reviewer of a Burroughs novel who, grappling with the image of 'rectums merging', beseeched plaintively, 'But *how*?'

At a time when most science fiction writers were preoccupied with space, Jim found more food for thought in time. He admired Chris Marker's 1962 film *La Jetée*, made up almost entirely of still images. Its main character vividly remembers an incident in his childhood. Under sedation, he can mentally revisit that moment and, conceivably, change it. Neither Marker nor Ballard was the first to entertain this belief. J. W. Dunne's *An Experiment with Time*, published in 1927, influenced J. B. Priestley, Aldous Huxley, T. S. Eliot and even William Burroughs by rejecting the vision of time as a river, a favourite image of Borges. In his 1946 essay 'A New Refutation of Time', Borges wrote, 'Our destiny is not frightful by being unreal; it is frightful because it is irreversible and iron-clad. Time is the substance I am made of. Time is a river which sweeps me along, but I am the river; it is a tiger which destroys me, but I am the tiger; it is a fire which consumes me, but I am the fire.' Dunne prefigured Marker by suggesting time is more like a book, in which the future has already taken place, and can be accessed in dreams, as memory accesses the past. *An Experiment with Time* inspired Priestley to write the plays *Time and the Conways* and

Dangerous Corner, and T. S. Eliot to include references to variant concepts of time in *Burnt Norton*, one of his *Four Quartets*.

The vision of time as an eternal present, with past and future tantalisingly just out of sight, parallels that of the surrealist painters. Jim echoed Dunne in his credo 'What I Believe' when he affirmed a faith in a non-existent past, a dead future, but an infinitely promising present.

Nobody could ignore the achievement of 'The Voices of Time'. Kingsley Amis chose it for the second *Spectrum* anthology, despite its offending most definitions of SF, as well as the laws of biology and physics. Soon after, he began to doubt whether Jim had ever been a science fiction writer at all, in the sense of someone convinced of technology's capacity to transform society. If Jim was ever such a visionary, this is his last story in the genre. He was no longer listening to its writers, but to other voices in other rooms.

CHAPTER NINETEEN

A VERY ENGLISH ARMAGEDDON

In 1961, Jim felt he was getting old. The strain of the train journey each day into London, and of coming home at 8 p.m. to three children and an exhausted wife, had begun to tell. If he was to break out as a full-time writer, this was the moment. It was Mary who suggested he use two weeks' holiday to write a quickie novel. American paperback houses paid a standard advance of $1,000 – about £300: enough to tide them over the first months of self-employment.

The idea was attractive. Carnell still bought his work, but even though Jim, like Aldiss and a few others, had graduated from £2 2s. per thousand words to his 'secret' rate of £2 10s., that never went far. In February 1961, *Science Fantasy* ran a second Vermilion Sands story, 'Studio 5, the Stars'. 'Deep End' appeared in the May edition of *New Worlds* and in July 'The Overloaded Man'. Jim would have liked to extend his experiments with further short fiction, but magazine sales were declining as readers switched to paperbacks. Carnell, too, urged him to move on to a novel. Somewhat resentfully, he agreed.

He called the story 'To Reap the Whirlwind', and wrote it, he said, straight on to the typewriter. This claim was one of many ways he distanced himself from the book. Another was to insist he never believed in the premise. 'It could have been done on a completely serious level. I nearly did do it that way. I don't know whether it would have been any better, because the wind thing isn't that interesting. So I thought I'd use all the clichés there are, the standard narrative conventions.'

Admittedly the novel was sketchily thought out. A hurricane springs up which, in the course of a few weeks, rips every sign of civilisation from the face of the earth, then abruptly subsides. There's no explanation for the catastrophe, except a reference to 'cosmic radiation'. We're left with the sense of a disaster visited on mankind almost at random. The evocation of arbitrary cataclysm seems driven by an almost Sadeian rage. It recalls the vast canvases and more enormous subject matter of Victorian painter John Martin, whose visions of the end of the world in *The Great Day of His Wrath* or the destruction of Sodom and Gomorrah show nature as it also appeared to Jim: titanic, overwhelming.

Thinking of the US market, he divided his cast between British technocrats and US servicemen. Of his main characters, Maitland is a cliché boffin, while Lanyon captains a US submarine, recalling a similar character is Nevil Shute's bestselling *On the Beach.* Both are technicians, disengaged, prototypes of what critic John Clute calls the 'middle-class professionals, affectless physicians, benumbed apparatchiks [and] deracinated engineers' who carry the narrative through his fictions. We'll meet such Ballardian Men again in *The Drowned World, The Crystal World* and *The Drought.* The most interesting character in 'Storm Wind', as Carnell renamed the novel, is the villain, Hardoon, a construction tycoon with a private army. The name came from Silas (Sileh) Hardoon, a wealthy investor and property owner in pre-war Shanghai – another parallel between the wind and the war. Hardoon responds to the cataclysm by building a concrete pyramid to shelter his enterprises. At the height of the storm, it's the only surviving man-made structure above ground. Once it topples, the wind, inexplicably, dies away.

Ever since 1885, when Richard Jefferies in *After London, or Wild England* returned Britain to a wilderness in the wake of an apocalyptic snowstorm and flood, the novel of ecological disaster had been regarded as a British prerogative. At the 1957 Convention, Jim could have met its two most successful exponents: Sam Youd, who, as 'John Christopher', wrote *The Death of Grass,* and John Wyndham, author of *The Day of the Triffids.* Wyndham describes how flashes in the sky blind most of the world just as it's ravaged by triffids: sentient plants that waddle on tripod legs and kill with poisoned tentacles. In *The Death of Grass*, a virus wipes out all edible grains. Written in a matter of weeks, it made enough money for Youd to leave his day job to write full time – Jim's own ideal.

After Jim had written four novels dwelling on natural catastrophe, a few critics suggested that each was linked to one of the four elements, earth, air, fire and water – something he consistently denied. Rather, 'Storm Wind' attempts to subvert and satirise the disaster novel, and in particular the classics by Wells and Conan Doyle which lay down its foundations. Each of their novels comes with a built-in scientist saviour: the irascible Professor Challenger of *The Poison Belt* and *The Lost World*, and the brotherhood of aviators of *Things to Come*. 'Storm Wind' has a technological wizard, too, but Jim makes him the villain, a megalomaniac. He also questions the assumption that, in responding to a disaster, Britons would act with stoicism and good sense; the Blitz spirit. From what he'd seen in Shanghai, people went to pieces at the same rate as their city. He doubted they would, as in *Triffids*, stockpile canned goods or flee to fortified farms and plant carrots. As someone observes scornfully in 'Storm Wind', most people went down into their basements with one packet of sandwiches and a thermos of cocoa.

An optimistic ending is customary in such stories, as is some explanation of the disaster. But 'Storm Wind' offers neither. For its serialisation in *New Worlds*, Jim added a perfunctory epilogue in which survivors emerge from their cellars and set about rebuilding the world, but he removed it for its paperback publication in the US as *The Wind from Nowhere*. Since Jefferies, such novels had also for the most part been semi-rural, evoking the beauty of the natural world, the better to point up its destruction. 'Storm Wind' overturns this cliché, too. Its action takes place in bunkers, tunnels and bomb shelters, with forays by armoured vehicles on to a surface permanently darkened from the torrent of dust. One would also expect a few likeable characters. But while Lanyon does strike up a romance with the reporter Patricia Olsen, it's perfunctory, and cancelled out by the dysfunctional relationship between Maitland and his spoiled heiress wife, Susan, of whom Jim disposes from the terrace of her high-rise London apartment. One senses his glee as she's snatched by the wind and sent bowling, doll-like, head over heels, across the rooftops.

As anticipated, Berkley bought the novel, for $1,000. After Carnell's 10 per cent, Jim received, as estimated, £300: no fortune, but, since the average British weekly wage was £16, enough to tide him over. Towards the end of 1961, he reduced the hours spent at *Chemistry and Industry*, concentrating mostly on articles and book reviews, which he could write at home. At the same time, he began work on what he thereafter called 'my first novel', *The Drowned World.*

CHAPTER TWENTY

DEATH BY WATER

The Drowned World, *Crash* and *Empire of the Sun* dominate Jim's career, but without the first the others might never have existed. When he started writing it, he was a minor author in a marginal genre. Within a year, he'd been embraced by the literary establishment. *The Drowned World* not only launched him as a serious talent but sparked a new interest in SF among British publishers. Once again, he showed his instinct for the wise career decision. *The Drowned World* was all things to all people: allegory, fantasy, forecast, but also, like John Le Carré's *The Spy Who Came in from the Cold*, a genre novel sufficiently thoughtful to interest the *Times Literary Supplement* yet accessible to the archetypal man on the Clapham omnibus.

The setting is 2145, when the sun has become hotter, melting the ice sheets. Man retreats to the poles, abandoning a flooded Europe. When Richard Jefferies imagined something similar, he visualised familiar trees and bushes running riot until England was one impenetrable forest of oak and ash, bracken and blackberry; the enchanted wood of 'The Sleeping Beauty'. Ballard proposes not rampant natural selection but its reversal. The flora and fauna of this world belong to prehistory. Twenty-metre reeds and python-like tropical vines overwhelm the flooded cities, while alligators, bats and iguanas regress to prehistoric gigantism.

The few humans who linger in London find their mental faculties also receding. In dreams, phantoms of their genetic past carry them back to the Triassic. Their perceptions degrade, returning them to the primitive urges of the id. The hoarse, arrogant bark of the lizards becomes an obbligato to their final days. Jung's theory of a collective unconscious played some part in this conception, but its roots lie in surrealism. As André Masson writes in *Anatomy of My Universe*, 'I let my reason go as far as it can. It reaches finally a wasteland of infinite desolation; it is a truly human place, which creates its own Time.' True to those roots, *The Drowned World* has the stifling vividness of a canvas by Max Ernst.

Global warming as a concept barely existed in 1961. It's ironic that a work so mystical should have been embraced by environmentalists as a forecast. The practicalities of climatology didn't interest Jim at all. Intuiting that the new glamour sciences were biology and biochemistry, he applied his imagination to the concept of memory. Even then, his vision was less clinical than psychoanalytical, embodying concepts so outlandish that even John Campbell might have shied at them. He may have known of experiments done in the 1950s by John Lilly at the National Institute of Mental Health. By immersing volunteers for long periods in lightless tanks filled with warm salt water, a technique he also tried out on himself, Lilly regressed their brains to altered states of consciousness. Once he enhanced the effect with psychotropic drugs such as ketamine and LSD, his subjects imagined they were pre-hominid apes, and fled, gibbering, from non-existent predators. The drug experiments didn't take place until the 1970s, so the novel's biological speculations, like its prediction of global warming, are ahead of their time.

Robert Kerans, the protagonist of *The Drowned World*, is part of an expedition sent back to London to monitor the water level and the heat. (Ballard used the name of the captain of HMS *Amethyst*, the frigate involved in the notorious 1949 Yangtse Incident when the Communist Chinese fired on the ship, then tried to prevent it reaching the sea.) While Kerans's colleagues keep to the research barge and think only of returning to the cooler poles, Kerans surrenders to the lure of the city and moves into a suite on the top floor of the Ritz Hotel. There he becomes the lover of Beatrice Dahl, one of the few survivors to linger in London. Beatrice – the name Jim gave his daughter – inaugurates a parade of anhedonic Ballard heroines, sleek, provocative but untouchable, like the nudes in Delvaux or the models of Helmut Newton, court photographer of Eurotrash, of whose work Ballard was an admirer. She's the sleeping – or at least drowsing – beauty of this flooded city. Surrealist canvases decorate her air-conditioned apartment: an Ernst jungle and a Delvaux showing bare-breasted women dancing with skeletons in formal evening dress.

Women such as Dahl are the human equivalent of Jim's empty swimming pools. To function, they need to be filled, but nobody is equal to the task, so they lounge, bask and shrug off the occasional sexual approach as if it were a troublesome mosquito. Not that either Kerans or Dahl seeks intimacy. For both, the inundated city offers a psychogeographic opiate, with which they lazily self-medicate, unconcerned that, as with most addictions, an early casualty is the sexual urge. Their behaviour reflects an indifference to conventional romance. As Ballard admitted:

> To be honest, the relationships between my characters don't interest me very much. There is only one character I am interested in, by and large. All my fiction is in a sense about isolation and how to cope with isolation. And that's what my novels are about, rather than the relationship that hero X might have with ladies Y and Z: I start with one character in a landscape and then populate.

Kerans accepts incuriously the process that is driving mankind back to its evolutionary roots, even as he intuits that it will lead to his inevitable submersion in the drowned world. All Jim's characters are 'half in love with easeful death' – or, as he put it less poetically, 'my heroes have a bland version of self-immolation'. Kerans's colleague Bodkin is more inquisitive, and decides to experiment on another member of the expedition, Hardman, whose vivid dreams suggest greater sensitivity to the effects of this new environment. Using a radiator, he simulates an even hotter sun, and exposes Hardman to amplified versions of the throbbing that all of them experience in sleep. When the man cracks and flees into the jungle, Kerans intuits that he may have headed south rather than north – towards the heat, not away from it – and goes in search of him. He finds him just where he anticipated, blind, baked almost black, but ready to kill rather than return, and so leaves him there, acquiescing to the inevitability of the process affecting them all.

A gang of African looters, led by an albino named Strangman, invades the city and drains the lagoon in search of treasure. Kerans risks death to restore the water and, with it, forgetfulness. Driven from the city, he sets out southwards, battling heat, rain and predatory animals, searching, Ballard suggests puzzlingly, for a new Garden of Eden in the heart of the disaster, just as Jim stubbornly imagined paradise in the ruins of Shanghai.

Reviewers would repeatedly compare *The Drowned World* and *The Crystal World* to Joseph Conrad, and specifically to *Heart of Darkness*, which Jim insisted he hadn't read at the time of writing these novels, although he obviously did so later. Many of the critics hadn't read it either, or not recently, since the parallels were not as obvious as they remembered. Marlow, the narrator, does travel up the Congo to find Kurtz, but it's the colonial impulse and its corruption by the temptations of Africa that interest him, not the psychogeography of the journey. Jim made the point forcefully in the late 1980s.

> I don't think I'm allowed to forget *Heart of Darkness*. If the phone rings, it'll probably be Joseph Conrad, saying 'Mr Ballard, you stole it all from me'. But to be fair to myself, Conrad in *Heart of Darkness* is not in the least bit interested in the river. The river could be a superhighway. The river is just something that gets Marlow, the narrator, up to Kurtz's station.

Few reviewers mentioned the influences Jim did acknowledge, those of Lawrence Durrell and Graham Greene. Few novels were more respectfully read in the fifties than the four books of Durrell's *Alexandria Quartet*, and traces of their languid, high-coloured style are detectable in Jim's early novels, particularly in the descriptions of interiors and the baroque details of architecture. Greene, however, is the more powerful influence. Both *The Drowned World* and *The Day of Creation* recall *A Burnt-Out Case, Journey Without Maps* – Greene's memoir of his expedition to Liberia – and in particular his two African journals, combined as *In Search of a Character.* Greene and Ballard also had much in common as people, from finding *Ulysses* a bore to liking to drink, and preferring the company of complaisant women to the restrictions of marriage. Both married once, and formed liaisons in middle age with women who remained in the background, aware that their men could be truly faithful only to their work.

Greene rated Jim's *The Disaster Area*, a collection of short stories, among the three best books of 1967, calling it 'one of the best science-fiction books I have read', while Jim admired Greene as 'very much a twentieth-century man [whose] fiction is generated by his experience of the world outside England'. He contrasted him with Kingsley Amis and Anthony Powell 'whose fiction is entirely generated by the closed world not just of England but of a very small part of England. In Greene's fiction one can breathe the smells, see the sights and hear the sounds of the whole world.' He told David Pringle:

> There's something about Greene's handling of solitary characters, externalizing the character's mind in terms of the situation in which he finds himself, the particular landscape. He does this so brilliantly. He can have a solitary figure standing by a jetty in the Far East, looking at some sampans, and he brings in a few things like the local police chief scratching his neck and so on, and within a paragraph one has a marvellous evocation of the psychology of the hero, and of what the hero and of what the book is about. Yes, I probably was influenced by Greene, but I never consciously imitated him.

It's debatable how much of either Durrell or Greene the fiction-averse Jim read. He may just have dipped into a few novels and seen some films; the reference to sampans and a police chief suggests Joseph L. Mankiewicz's 1958 adaptation of Greene's *The Quiet American.* But one doesn't need to read much to see the similarities. Greene, Durrell and Ballard share a sense of tropical lassitude and ennui, and a desire to surrender, first to the flesh, then to the spirit.

CHAPTER TWENTY-ONE

STAYING IN

On 4 October 1957 the Soviets put Sputnik into orbit, sparking a brief world-wide interest in space travel, and inspiring John F. Kennedy to announce in 1961 a national commitment to reach the moon. Neither event excited Jim. With the exception of a few enthusiasts such as Arthur C. Clarke, science fiction writers shared the general indifference to what took place at Cape Canaveral, none more so than Ballard. As he told Chris Evans, 'In the summer of '74 I remember standing out in my garden on a bright, clear night and watching a moving dot of light in the sky which I realised was Skylab.'

> I remember thinking how fantastic it was that there were men up there, and I felt really quite moved as I watched it. Then my neighbour came out into his garden to get something and I said, 'Look, there's Skylab,' and he looked up and said, 'Sky-what?' And I realised that he didn't know about it, and he wasn't interested. No, from that moment there was no doubt in my mind that the space age was over.

Thereafter, his view of interplanetary exploration became progressively more jaded. Stories such as 'The Cage of Sand' and 'The Dead Astronaut' showed Cape Canaveral as he imagined it fifty years on – a decaying monument to vanity and hubris. At a party, Charles Platt tried to introduce him to a NASA engineer. 'No, I have nothing to say to people like that,' Jim snapped. 'To my mind, NASA completely missed the point. They should have put some schizophrenics up there in a space capsule with a tape recorder. Then we might have learned something interesting.' He continued to pour scorn in interviews and stories. In 1990, the critic John Clute wrote:

> He speaks of the psychic and technological out-modedness of the American space programme as anatomised in 'The Man Who Walked on the Moon' and 'Memoirs of the Space Age'; he speaks of the Challenger disaster as 'the blowing of a gasket, the sort of thing that might have destroyed some Pacific locomotive 100 years ago'. The programme was fatally archaic, he says. It is a curious black hole in the continuum of the popular imagination. They'd have had more spin-off if they'd built spaceships out of bamboo and rice-paper, decorated with poems, and they might have got to the Moon sooner that way.

Bamboo and rice-paper whispers of Shanghai. Haunted by his own memories, Jim had no reason to believe that, in travelling to other planets, we would outrun our fears. He urged SF to forget about space flight. Instead, we should look inwards; initially towards our own society, and then into ourselves – the region he described as 'inner space'. He made these comments in 'Which Way to Inner Space?', an essay that became a statement of principles. Periodically, Carnell offered writers and, sometimes, readers the chance to contribute 'Guest Editorials' to *New Worlds*. Early in 1962, with *The Drowned World* completed, Jim used the opportunity to issue a manifesto on behalf of the 'New Wave'.

Some of the ideas for 'Which Way to Inner Space?', including the title, come from J. B. Priestley's 1953 *New Statesman* piece (though W. H. Auden anticipated both in his 'New Year Letter' of 1940). Jim pays tribute, as Priestley did, to Ray Bradbury, and grudgingly acknowledges the achievements of the old school, only to reach back to H. G. Wells to attack his legacy of simple plots, journalistic narrative and stock characters. Having dismissed the writer who was not only the favourite of his own father but of the science fiction world, he allowed himself a moment of pure surrealism. Isidore Ducasse, aka the Comte de Lautréamont, a forerunner of the movement, famously described a boy as 'beautiful as the chance meeting on a dissecting-table of a sewing-machine and an umbrella'. Taking up the idea, Jim proclaimed that he intended to write the equivalent SF story, in which an amnesiac man would lie on a beach, attempting to define the essence of his relationship with a rusty bicycle wheel – an ambition which, fortunately, he never pursued.

As manifestos go, this wasn't incendiary. It reflected the fact that, while he, Moorcock, Brunner and Aldiss shared some ambitions, values and tastes, they disagreed on many others. Aldiss, for instance, admired Wells. Moorcock was indifferent to surrealism but liked art nouveau, which Jim despised. Jim didn't even believe there was a 'New Wave' – or, rather, if there was, it had only one member: himself. 'Which Way to Inner Space?' restated some tenets of surrealism and revisited the argument about tradition versus innovation, but mainly it showed how much closer were Jim's ideas to ideologues in other media, from Freud and Breton to R. D. Laing and Marshall McLuhan. In particular, his belief that we live inside a novel of our own composition echoed McLuhan's claim that 'since Sputnik and the satellites, the planet is enclosed in a man-made environment that ends "Nature" and turns the globe into a repertory theatre to be programmed'. Given his respect for the French and his belief in the primacy of memory, Ballard, even with his dislike of fiction, should also have been an enthusiastic reader of Proust – except that the only memory which interested him enough to explore in depth was his own.

Broke as always, Jim wrote *The Drowned World* for quick sale as a novella. As soon as Carnell bought it for the limping *Science Fiction Adventures*, he got to work increasing it to novel length. 'Jimmy always scaled up, never down,' says Moorcock. By the time the magazine appeared in January 1962, he'd completed the full-length version. In rewriting, he added a new sub-plot and copious description, entwining us even more stiflingly in his psychic jungle. Kerans's suite at the Ritz, perfunctorily described in the magazine version, receives an injection of décor porn worthy of *Vanity Fair*, detailing its furniture and fittings down to the ivory-handled squash rackets and hand-painted dressing gowns. He adds a single new character, Lieutenant Hardman, but he's less an individual than a device; a lab rat on whom Bodkin can experiment.

The most significant addition is the eighteen-page episode called 'The Pool of Thanatos'. Strangman decides to explore the flooded planetarium, and sends Kerans down in a diving suit to search for some notional treasure, but actually in an attempt to kill him. Despite having mocked the claims of Hubbard and Campbell that, under the right conditions, one could remember the moment of birth, even of conception, Jim flirts with the idea that, to Kerans, the spherical, liquid-filled chamber, furred with algae and the waving fronds of marine plants, evokes memories of the womb. His description resonates with a similar passage in *The Kindness of Women* in which a miniature TV camera gives a woman a magnified view of the inside of her vagina, increased to the dimensions of a cathedral, its walls beaded with moisture. It also recalls the 1936 lecture given by Dalí at the New Burlington Galleries in London, which he insisted on delivering in a diving suit. The technician sent to explain the equipment to Dalí asked how far down he intended to go:

'To the subconscious!' Dalí announced.

'We don't go that deep,' said the helper dubiously.

Dalí almost suffocated, just as Kerans nearly dies when his air supply is cut off.

Jim consistently denied that *The Drowned World* was a 'disaster novel', at least in the sense it applied to Wyndham or Wells. In 1983, when the book was chosen by the Book Marketing Council as one of the all-time best British SF novels, he told Charles Shaar Murray: '"Inner space" was the flag which I nailed to my mast, and *The Drowned World* is literally the first Inner Space novel.'

> Up until that point, catastrophe stories were being done on a very literal level, as adventure stories, but the psychological adventure became the subject matter for me. If you look at the Book Marketing Council's list, you'll see that John Wyndham's *Day of the Triffids* is

Downtown Shanghai, 1930s

The Bund, 1930s

1 Amherst Avenue, the Ballard family home (Andy Best)

US marines on guard along the Bund, 1930s.

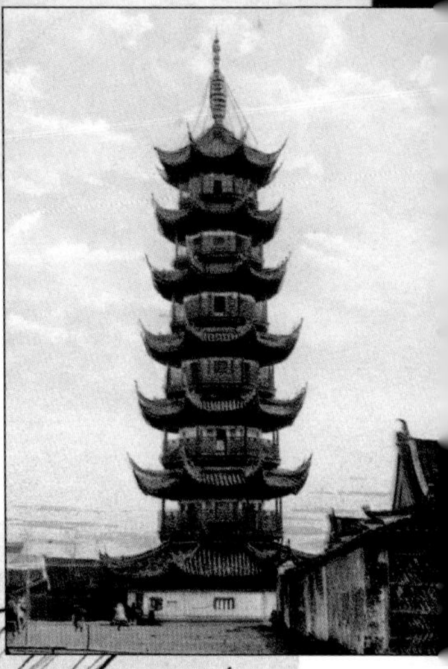

Lunghua Pagoda

Cooking on chatties in Lunghua (Alan Sutton)

Ballard at The Leys School, 1946
(The Leys School)

Dormitory at The Leys (The Leys School)

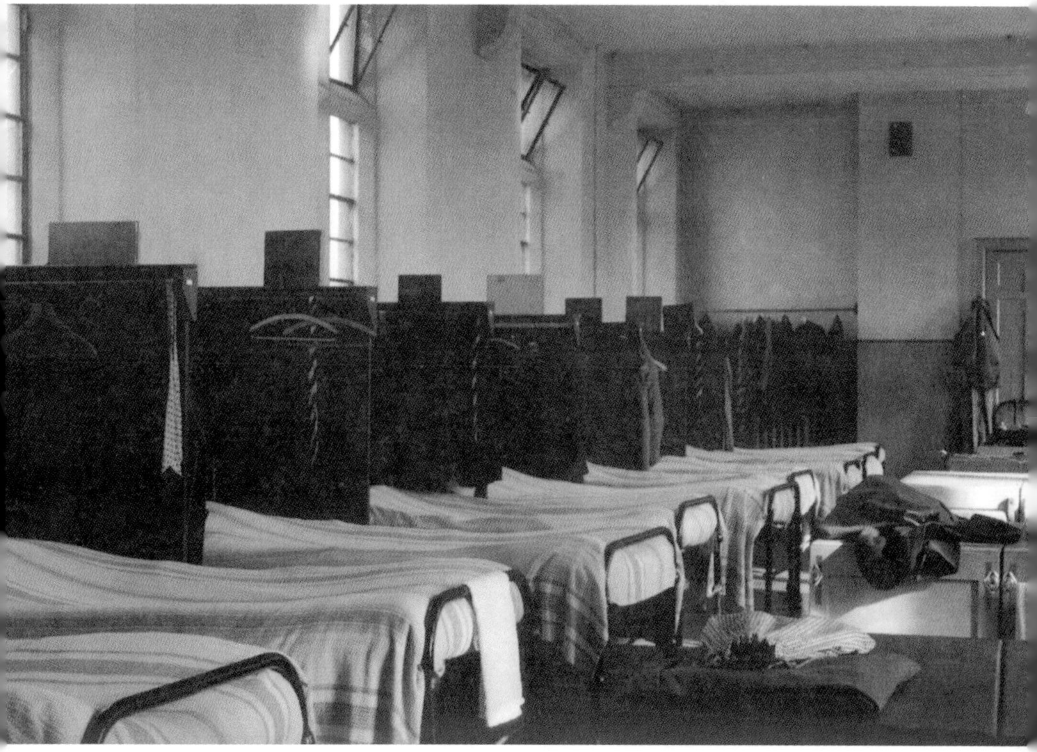

Jim (foreground) at the 1957 World SF Convention

(Estate of Norman Shorrock. Collection of Peter Weston)

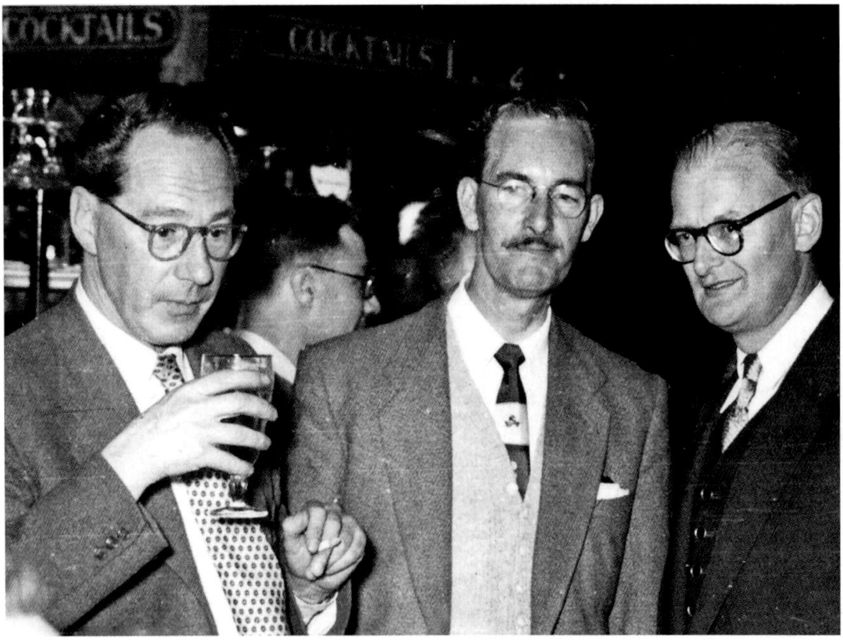

1957 Convention. John Wyndham, Ted Carnell, Arthur Clarke

(Estate of Norman Shorrock. Collection of Peter Weston)

COMPETITION

THE VIOLENT NOON

Revenge: J. G. Ballard

J. GRAHAM BALLARD who shares the first prize of ten pounds with D. S. Birley in the "Varsity" Crime Story Competition is now in his second year at King's and immersed in the less literary process of reading medicine.

He admitted to our reporter yesterday that he had in fact entered the competition more for the prize than anything else, although he had been encouraged to go on writing because of his success.

The idea for his short story which deals with the problem of Malayan terrorism, he informs us, he had been thinking over for some time before hearing of the competition.

He has, in addition to writing short stories, also planned "mammoth novels" which "never get beyond the first page."

First print appearance (*Varsity*)

Ad in *Vogue* for PLJ

(*Advertising Archives*)

LEMON JUICE AT DAYBREAK
Tomorrow, begin a new day freshly with PLJ and water. Nothing's so cleansing and freshening. As all beauty-wise women know, there are sound reasons for making 'lemon juice at daybreak' a daily rule for figure and complexion care; PLJ is the juice of sun-ripened fresh fruit . . . it's full of Vitamin C . . . and it's so low in calories (which is why PLJ plays so vital a part in every slimming diet.) But forget these sound reasons! Just enjoy PLJ's natural tang, the lift that only lemon juice gives, the lift that sends you lilting through the day. Tomorrow, start your day with PLJ.
AND YOU AND THE DAY FEEL SO BEAUTIFUL
PLJ
WEIGHT WATCHERS NEVER ADD SUGAR
24

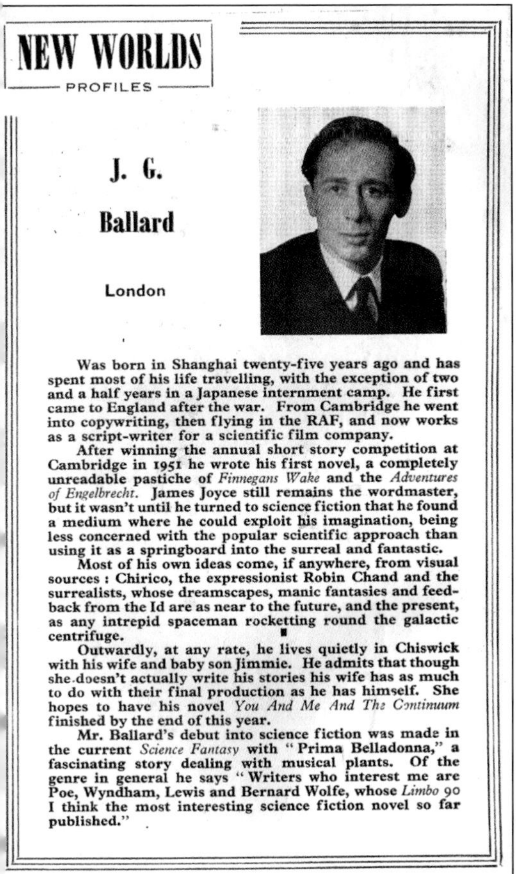

NEW WORLDS

PROFILES

J. G. Ballard

London

Was born in Shanghai twenty-five years ago and has spent most of his life travelling, with the exception of two and a half years in a Japanese internment camp. He first came to England after the war. From Cambridge he went into copywriting, then flying in the RAF, and now works as a script-writer for a scientific film company.

After winning the annual short story competition at Cambridge in 1951 he wrote his first novel, a completely unreadable pastiche of *Finnegans Wake* and the *Adventures of Engelbrecht*. James Joyce still remains the wordmaster, but it wasn't until he turned to science fiction that he found a medium where he could exploit his imagination, being less concerned with the popular scientific approach than using it as a springboard into the surreal and fantastic.

Most of his own ideas come, if anywhere, from visual sources : Chirico, the expressionist Robin Chand and the surrealists, whose dreamscapes, manic fantasies and feed-back from the Id are as near to the future, and the present, as any intrepid spaceman rocketting round the galactic centrifuge.

Outwardly, at any rate, he lives quietly in Chiswick with his wife and baby son Jimmie. He admits that though she doesn't actually write his stories his wife has as much to do with their final production as he has himself. She hopes to have his novel *You And Me And The Continuum* finished by the end of this year.

Mr. Ballard's debut into science fiction was made in the current *Science Fantasy* with "Prima Belladonna," a fascinating story dealing with musical plants. Of the genre in general he says "Writers who interest me are Poe, Wyndham, Lewis and Bernard Wolfe, whose *Limbo 90* I think the most interesting science fiction novel so far published."

Profile in *New Worlds*, 54

The Drowned World

The Old and the New (New Worlds Publishing)

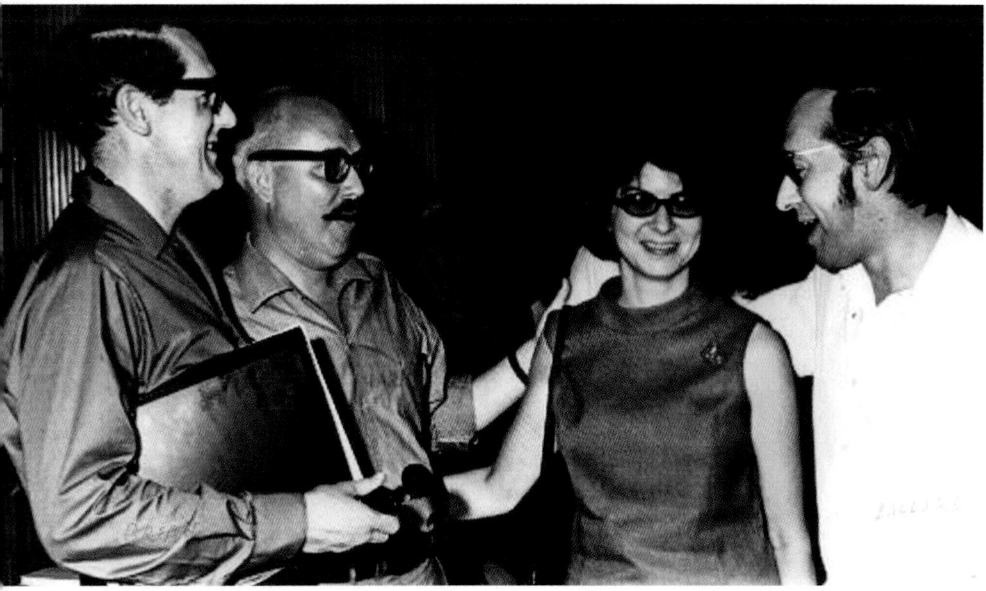

Brian Aldiss, Harry Harrison, unidentified woman and Jim in Rio de Janeiro, 1969
(Philip José Farmer)

LEFT: John and Marjorie Brunner (Estate of Norman Shorrock. Collection of Peter Weston)
RIGHT: The controversial 'Why I Want to Fuck Ronald Reagan' (1968)

Jim (right) with (from left) poet Edward Lucie Smith, Mike Moorcock, Brian Aldiss and ICA director Michael Kustow at the 1968 Brighton Science Fiction Conference (*Sunday Times*)

LEFT: Chris Evans (*Oliver Hatch*) RIGHT: *Ambit* cover, January 1971 featuring Euphoria Bliss, Martin Bax (right), Richard Freeman, Edwin Brock, Michael Foreman, and Ballard. Paolozzi's sculpture *Thunder and Lightning with Flies and Jack Kennedy* in the background. (*Ambit Magazine*)

there. Now it's a fine novel, a classic example of the English kind of Home Counties catastrophe fiction, a very polite society where all kinds of private obsessions are kept firmly buttoned down and people struggle together in the face of an external threat as they did during the Battle of Britain, or as we're led to believe they did during the Battle of Britain. My novel turns all that upside down. The hero embraces the catastrophe as a means by which he can express and fulfil his own nature, pursue his own mythology to the end, whatever that may be. He can accept the logic of his own personality and run that logic right down to the end of the road. That's a different approach. That's what *The Drowned World* is about. That's what nearly all my fiction is about.

CHAPTER TWENTY-TWO

KINGERS

Carnell sold *The Drowned World* to Berkley in the USA. They published it as a paperback original in August 1962 for the standard $1,000 advance, part of which Jim used to purchase his first car, a second-hand Armstrong Siddeley Sapphire.

A sale of the book in Britain posed more problems. It needed a champion and found one in Kingsley Amis, potentially the New Wave's most valuable ally. After six successful novels for Gollancz, Amis had the ear of its owner, Victor Gollancz, and the confidence of Hilary Rubinstein, the publishing director (and Gollancz's nephew) who'd first spotted the promise of *Lucky Jim*. Gollancz published little fantasy, but Amis persuaded them to start an SF list. It included not only his Princeton lectures, as *New Maps of Hell*, but also an annual anthology, *Spectrum*, co-edited with his friend Robert Conquest.

Amis was erratic and sometimes belligerent, particularly when drunk, a frequent state in 1962, since he had become involved with the novelist Elizabeth Jane Howard and was about to leave his wife for her. Since establishing himself as Britain's leading proselytiser for science fiction, his interest had turned proprietary. He believed SF should merge with the mainstream, becoming just another tool in the hands of the professional writer, as it had been for H. G. Wells or Aldous Huxley, who found no inconsistency in switching from *The Time Machine* to *Kipps*, *Brave New World* to *Eyeless in Gaza*. He urged SF writers to abandon their 'cherished gadgets – the rocket-ship, the satellite, the computer, the cybernetics stuff'. This wasn't entirely altruistic, since he didn't understand even the rudiments of technology.

Also, his insistence that SF become intellectually respectable, developing a 'growing concern with contemporary problems; growing self-consciousness and sophistication', matched his own ambition to be seen by the literary community as more than a social satirist.

Those who signed up to Amis's agenda received generous practical support. He persuaded publisher Tom Boardman to back Brian Aldiss and Harry Harrison in *SF Horizons*, a magazine of criticism, inspired by the *Proceedings of the Institute for Twenty-First Century Studies*, the facetiously titled but in other respects sober journal edited in the US by SF writer Theodore Cogswell. He encouraged Penguin to publish a line of SF novels, with Aldiss as editor – a compliment Aldiss repaid by hailing *New Maps of Hell* as a 'pyrotechnic cartographic work'. There was an audible sound of literary logs being rolled and boats pushed out. That Amis would recommend *The Drowned World* to Gollancz was a foregone conclusion, particularly since its synthesis of fantasy and conventional narrative typified the 'crossover' novel he visualised as SF's future. In mid-1962, the fanzine *Skyrack* reported:

> Jim Ballard's long novelette *The Drowned World* in SFA 22 has been written into a novel which is described as 'very powerful' and which will be published about the end of the year by Gollancz, though possibly not as SF. Brian Aldiss and Kingsley Amis have both read it and are tremendously enthusiastic.

Jim's paramount skill was his ad man's ability to remarket himself. Charles Platt called him 'the only person associated with the so-called New Wave who had any clue at all about that most basic requirement for any radical new movement: promotion'. Nobody understood better the importance of strategic alliances. In Lunghua, it had been the Americans. In science fiction, it was Ted Carnell. Now Jim hitched himself to the SF's next generation. His entrée was Moorcock. They had met in Carnell's office in the early 1960s and had a 'nodding acquaintance'. When *The Drowned World* appeared in *Science Fiction Adventures*, Barry Bayley told Moorcock, 'You should read this.'

Moorcock, who had read some of Jim's stories, did so and, realising that Ballard was, in his words, 'the business', called him up.

Through Moorcock, Jim met other writers such as Bayley, Langdon Jones and John Brunner. From early 1962 for a year or more, Moorcock, Bayley and Ballard met regularly at the Swan pub in Knightsbridge, near Ballard's office. The improvement of British science fiction and the widening of its focus were frequent topics of conversation. In the summer of 1962, they decided to convene a meeting of SF writers at a London hotel – 'to just talk about where science-fiction was going,' says Moorcock, 'and what we wanted to do with it. Plenty of people felt things must change, and that we needed to "up the game".'

Immediately, they encountered the personality conflicts that riddled SF. Brian Aldiss declined to attend. 'It may have been because he disliked John Brunner,' says Moorcock, 'or perhaps he thought it would be political, or that we wanted to set up a Communist cell.' Then Brunner withdrew, piqued that Kingsley Amis had also refused. 'When I saw the letter he'd written to him, I wasn't surprised,' says Moorcock. 'It said, more or less, "Dear Kingsley Amis, We are having a conference called 'Whither Science-fiction?' at the Bonnington Hotel, Holborn, on such-and-such a date. It would be very useful if you could come along. By the way, I've just read your most recent book and I have to say it is not up to your usual standard."'

The twenty or so men who did attend were mostly the second string of *New Worlds*, including Ted Tubb, Ken Bulmer, and John Phillifent, aka John Rackham. 'It was obvious from the start that Bayley, Ballard and I were the odd ones out,' says Moorcock. 'We'd hoped to hear some stimulating stuff about, as it were, a new literature for the space age. Instead these guys were only interested in how to break into new markets – TV, comic books, and so on.'

After Moorcock married Hilary Bailey in September 1962 and started his own family, he and the Ballards socialised. 'We saw Jimmy, Mary and their kids pretty regularly,' Moorcock says. 'We all got on very well. Mary would cheerfully contradict him in the middle of one of his rhetorical flights, just as Hilary would remind me of my own exaggerations.' Jim never shared the enthusiasm of Moorcock and his friends for soft drugs, but enjoyed alcohol, particularly whisky. Scotch released his 'intellectual thug'. When the talk became heated, he would overpower objections with the bawled word 'Relax!' – advice he should have heeded himself.

Despite the disappointment of the Bonnington Hotel conference, Ballard, Bayley and Moorcock continued to meet. 'We often discussed founding a magazine,' says Moorcock, 'which was imaginative but ran fiction with, in Ballard's succinct phrase, "the moral authority of a literature won from experience".' Ted Carnell, while cautiously responsive to their ideas, wouldn't change the character of the Nova publications, for fear of losing even more readers. From a peak of about five thousand copies a month, the circulation of *New Worlds* had dwindled to less than 3,500. In May 1963, he folded the runt of the litter, *Science Fiction Adventures.* The magazine's presentation of *The Drowned World* suggests why it failed. Instead of a reeking swamp choking on the jungles of the Triassic, Brian Lewis's cover showed a gleaming condo on a tranquil lagoon, with all the menace of a weekend in Marbella.

The demise of *New Worlds* and *Science Fantasy* was only a matter of time. Until then, the more adventurous writers took turns reassuring Carnell. 'Barry [Bayley] and I persuaded Ted Carnell to run Ballard's "Terminal Beach",' says Moorcock, 'but it's also true that Ballard persuaded Carnell to run my "Deep Fix" [which describes a drug experience in terms of dystopic SF]. Ted was a little uncertain about this "new stuff" and needed encouragement.' Ballard and Moorcock even thought of collaborating on a novel for *New Worlds* – an unlikely idea, since Jim was stubbornly protective of his material, and detested editorial interference. Moorcock says,

> I didn't like his ideas and he didn't like mine. The book I wrote from those ideas was *The Fireclown*, originally commissioned by Carnell,

> but his *New Worlds* went bust before he could run it. I remember discussing the Fireclown idea and seeing Jimmy's face gradually lose its pretended interest, doing his best not to tell me how horrible it sounded.

Gollancz debated whether *The Drowned World* should appear as SF. Rubinstein wanted it published as straight fiction, but Amis insisted a novel by a near-unknown would sell better as a genre piece and persuaded him to put a bold 'Gollancz SF' on the spine, arguing to Rubinstein that it would also be valuable propaganda for SF in general. At the same time, he offered a cover quote that avoided all reference to SF. 'Ballard is one of the brightest new stars in post-war fiction,' he wrote. 'This tale of strange and terrible adventures in a world of steaming jungles has an oppressive power reminiscent of Conrad.' Though dated 1962, the book was deliberately delayed until January 1963, to squeeze the last drop of review coverage before copies reached the shops and it became yesterday's news. Thanks in part to an enthusiastic review by Amis in the *Observer*, it was already reprinting by February, and soon became, as it remains, a steady seller. Later that year, Gollancz published a book of Ballard stories, *The Four-Dimensional Nightmare*, and in 1964 a further collection, *The Terminal Beach*. Before *The Drowned World* appeared, Victor Gollancz bought Jim the traditional lunch. Over the starter, he suggested deleting the references to Delvaux and Ernst, feeling that the novel was diminished by association with the unfashionable and discredited surrealists. He had other problems, too. 'Why does Kerans go south at the end?' he asked. 'Surely he should head north.' When his US editor raised the same point, Jim realised the incomprehension was general.

By allying himself with Amis, finding a publisher in the UK hardcover market and distancing himself from SF, Jim again demonstrated his survival instinct. The wisdom of his decision was confirmed when, late in 1963, Maclaren announced they were folding *New Worlds* and *Science Fantasy* with the April 1964 issues.

Various people, including Kingsley Amis, Brian Aldiss and Moorcock, became involved in negotiations to save one or more of the Nova titles by finding a new publisher. Ralph and David Gold, who, as Roberts and Vinter, published crime paperbacks featuring private eye Hank Janson, showed interest in taking on at least one. Carnell, suffering from arthritis, had no wish to continue as editor of a monthly. Oxford-based art collector and bon vivant Kyril Bonfiglioli was suggested as a replacement, but Carnell designated Moorcock as his successor.

Moorcock opened negotiations with the Golds. 'I told them what I wanted to do,' he said, 'and then they told me what I *could* do.' The Golds agreed to back *New Worlds*, but initially only as a bi-monthly, and providing it adhered to the Hank Janson format of card-covered paperbacks. Unable to handle two titles, Moorcock relinquished *Science Fantasy* to Bonfiglioli. The decision foreshadowed the extinction of Carnell's carefully nurtured enterprise, since 'Bon' was a boozy rapscallion who would lead the magazine into chaos.

As Moorcock scrabbled to create his first issue, Carnell was working on the last issues of his tenure. In March, he featured Jim's landmark story 'The Terminal Beach'. It makes only the most perfunctory nod towards science fiction. The setting is Eniwetok, the atoll in the Marshall Islands that the US seized from the Japanese in the Second World War and turned into a base for nuclear testing. They exploded forty-three devices there between 1948 and 1952, including the first hydrogen bomb. Jim, who confessed to dreaming of Eniwetok and another former base, Wake Island, as stepping stones on a flight back to Shanghai, imagined a pilot making his way back to the island, now abandoned, and wandering among irradiated blockhouses and bunkers. He called him Traven, after B. Traven, shadowy author of *The Treasure of the Sierra Madre.* Traven broods over Claude Eatherly, the USAF pilot whose remorse about the Hiroshima bombing made him a poster boy of the Campaign for Nuclear Disarmament. In reality, Eatherly had nothing to do with dropping the bomb, merely piloting a weather plane, but Traven sees him as a messiah, ennobled by his willingness to assume the blame on our behalf.

Jim acknowledged that 'The Terminal Beach' wasn't a science fiction story so much as a fable about nuclear war and our fears, described in science fictional language. He also called it the first real story of 'inner space', with a direct link to *The Atrocity Exhibition.* Carnell, however, read it as CND propaganda. A Second World War veteran, and apolitical, he had no wish to become involved in the nuclear issue. Added to this, he wasn't comfortable with Jim's subheaded paragraphs or Traven's imaginary conversations with the spirits of dead Japanese soldiers, examples of what Kingsley Amis called 'buggering about with the reader'. It took the combined arguments of Ballard and Moorcock to persuade him it should be published. Though Carnell acquiesced, the April 1964 issue, his last hurrah, defiantly excluded all New Wave material, featuring instead old hands James White, Donald Malcolm and William Spencer. Once Nova folded, he launched a series of hardcover anthologies, *New Writings in SF.* They promised 'new methods and techniques of story-telling', but his Nova regulars supplied most of the stories. At last he was rid of these troublesome newcomers, and he relaxed into the good old-fashioned SF like a tired man settling into a warm bath.

CHAPTER TWENTY-THREE

CRYSTALLINE

In November 1963, John F. Kennedy died in Dallas. The assassination fired Jim's imagination, particularly after he saw Abraham Zapruder's amateur movie of the killing. By slicing the event into instants – Frame 210 recorded the first shot, wounding Kennedy in the neck; Frame 313 the fatal head wound – the film created a species of sentence that could be parsed like any other. Death became susceptible to the rules of grammar, inspiring the fragmentation of books such as *The Atrocity Exhibition.*

Jim also found the killing implicitly erotic. Death in the back seat of a Lincoln Continental; the entire event filmed in colour, the widow, trim and brave in a blood-stained suit – these were the very stuff of his obsessions. He recruited the Kennedys into his fantasies, next to Ronald Reagan, Elizabeth Taylor, Brigitte Bardot, Ralph Nader, Albert Camus and James Dean. In his eyes, no person was exempt from his or her role as a sex object. As he mused to a friend, 'Each of us dies in the unseen erotic corridors of the sexuality of others.' With the assassination of her husband, Jacqueline Kennedy ceased, in his terms, to be the president's widow and became 'Jackie Kennedy', a figure of myth. She entered the shared consciousness of mankind; Jung's racial memory; the public domain. 'I think anyone in the public eye is – horrible phrase – fair game,' Jim told Iain Sinclair. 'If they are that famous, they have already incorporated themselves into our dreams.' To the inconvenient fact that, unlike Oedipus and Jocasta, Mrs Kennedy was still alive, he gave little thought.

This dream-Jackie became the pivot of Jim's provocative short story

'Plan for the Assassination of Jacqueline Kennedy', published in 1967. In quasi-scientific form, it purports to summarise the findings of a team analysing films of Brigitte Bardot, Jacqueline Kennedy, Madame Chiang Kai-shek and Princess Margaret. The researchers measure whether the subjects, at times of stress, kept their legs together or apart. Particular attention was paid to the mouths, a sure indication of aggression and sexual excitement. The Kennedy assassination, the 'report' concludes, was viewed by onlookers in the same way as a multiple car crash, but with sexual overtones.

'Plan for the Assassination of Jacqueline Kennedy' raised a corner of the curtain on Jim's taste for pornography. He seldom spoke about his enthusiasm, and, when he did, it was often in generalities, such as his much-quoted, if enigmatic comments, 'A widespread taste for pornography means that nature is alerting us to some threat of extinction' and 'Pornography is really very chaste – it's the body's unerotic dream of itself'.

About his own tastes in erotica, he was evasive. It's likely that he first encountered print erotica in Lunghua, since the US sailors would have had pin-up magazines along with their copies of *Reader's Digest* and *Saturday Evening Post.* He claimed 'the first pornography I ever read [was] *The Story of O* at the age of 19, which rocked me back on my heels', but *Histoire d'O* wasn't published until 1954, when he was in his mid-twenties, and not generally available in English until the mid-1960s. (It's possible he was confusing *Histoire d'O* with Henry Miller's *Tropic of Cancer*, although the sadism of Pauline Reage appears closer to his personal tastes.)

His earliest experience of film porn also apparently dates from the sixties. In 1968, the new director of the ICA, Michael Kustow, held a private screening of 16mm sex films. 'I was stunned by the novelties of these orgies and other things,' Jim said. 'Some very abstract arty work which was only at second glance pictures of people having sex.' Before the screening, Kustow, aspects of whom went to make up the character of Peter Lykiard in *The Kindness of Women*, asked each of the group of about thirty people to say what they were working on. Jim was amused by the succession of phoney replies, including a plethora of unfinished novels and a biography of Chirico. Of the films, he said only that, after about half an hour, boredom set in – an attitude that typifies his descriptions of sex films in other novels. Although, in his 1991 novel *The Kindness of Women*, his alter ego watches the filming in Rio de Janeiro of a woman having sex with a dog, and in *Cocaine Nights* he describes amateur porn filmed by jaded expat residents of a Spanish resort, in neither instance does he show much enthusiasm.

Appreciating pornography, however, is a case, literally, of 'one man's meat'. A bondage enthusiast watching lesbian sex will be as unmoved as a football fanatic at Lord's. Jim appears to have favoured still photographs, particularly those with a narrative element – a preference shared with Philip Larkin and Kingsley Amis, both of whom were brought up on 'girlie magazines' and pin-ups. The unedited MS of *Crash* includes a detailed and informed description of some bondage magazines collected by Vaughan – based, said Jim, on a collection of such material lent to him by Paolozzi. They show amateur models strapped into halters, gags and masks, and tied to metal fixtures, including the railings of a swimming pool and the rudder and radio aerial of a yacht. This description was deleted from the published version, but one of Ballard's *Announcements*, as he called his simulated advertisements, shows a girl in an old-fashioned bathing suit, wearing primitive snorkelling gear which echoes a bondage mask and ball gag. Once Helmut Newton began creating more polished versions of these tableaux vivants, with models posed in luxury settings that fed a fantasy of decadent sensation seeking, Jim became an enthusiast, describing Newton's images as stills from an erotic movie that had been running in his head for forty years.

Jim incorporated a nude image of Claire Walsh into one of his 'Announcements'. He was intrigued by the Polaroid camera, foreseeing how its technology would encourage amateur porn. This liking for snapshots helps explain the only photograph of Mary Ballard he allowed to be published. Wearing a low-cut blouse or nightgown, she leans forward in a pose that emphasises her breasts, one nipple faintly visible through the thin fabric. The tone is that of a home-made pin-up, and hardly the way most men would wish their wives to be shown in public.

Moorcock's decision to edit *New Worlds* rather than *Science Fantasy* surprised many. 'But *New Worlds* is a much more ambiguous title than *Science Fantasy*,' he argued, 'and fitted the changes I wanted to make.' These were far-reaching. He visualised a quarto-sized monthly combining text and design; *Playboy* without the sex. John Campbell had a similar idea. Bought by the Condé Nast empire, *Astounding*, which he'd already renamed *Analog Science Fiction and Fact* in 1960, re-emerged in March 1963 in the same format as *Time* and *Newsweek*, with sections printed on glossy paper to encourage expensive advertising.

Officially Moorcock took over *New Worlds* on 25 February 1964. To maintain continuity, he needed to produce his first issue, dated May–June, by the end of April. Having achieved, albeit by the skin of his teeth, a means of presenting his agenda, he called in every favour to realise it. His first issues were virtually created 'in house'. He wrote some material himself, both under his own name and as 'James Colvin'. His wife, Hilary Bailey, generated the lead story of the second, and his oldest friend from the days of *Tarzan*, Jim Cawthorn, designed the covers. John Brunner and Langdon Jones also came through with stories, but for the magazine's first serial, Moorcock turned to Ballard.

Jim's contribution to the first issue had been an article on William Burroughs. Copies of *Naked Lunch* had begun to circulate clandestinely in Britain. Moorcock, who had been in Sweden for most of 1961, brought a copy back from Paris. Opinions vary about when Jim first read it, but this could have been as late as 1963. Once Girodias published *The Soft Machine*, *Nova Express* and *The Ticket that Exploded*, Jim asked Paris-born writer Maxim Jakubowski to bring copies from France, and read them at a sitting. They had an electrifying effect – literally, since he says he leaped involuntarily out of his chair in delight as he read the first pages. His enthusiasm is surprising, since, socially and culturally, he and Burroughs had nothing in common. 'There is a huge barrier between us,' Jim said, 'which I have never been able to breach. He is upper-crust, upper-class, mid-western provincial American, and his family strata look down on doctors, politicians, lawyers and feel a sort of off-hand concern for blacks. He's really the equivalent of a Bournemouth colonel and he's also very homosexual and very much into the drugs culture; which leaves me out.'

Jim admired *Naked Lunch* and what Kenneth Tynan called Burroughs's 'precise and wittily sepulchral' prose, but was initially unsure what an 'old-fashioned story-teller' could learn from a novel densely peopled with grotesques, often babbling in private languages. What he eventually took from Burroughs related to style, not subject matter. Every modern novel, even *Ulysses*, was rooted in an existing culture and recognisable characters, including a protagonist who fulfilled the role of Self. Burroughs helped end that. The cracked lens of his drug-skewed vision refracted a present that was also past and future, a world in which fantasy and reality co-existed. Not only were delusion and reality indistinguishable; any distinction was irrelevant, since everyone involved was raving, stoned or insane. Burroughs compared the effect to a cut-up. 'The cut-up is actually closer to the facts of perception than representational painting,' he said. 'Take a walk down a city street and put down what you have just seen on canvas. You have seen a person cut in two by a car, bits and pieces of street signs and advertisements, reflections from shop windows – a montage of fragments. Writing is still confined to the representational straitjacket of the novel . . . consciousness is a cut up.' Jim could only agree.

Always prolific, Jim was particularly so in 1963. Following *The Drowned World* in January, eight of his stories appeared in American and British magazines that year. Gollancz also published a collection,

The Four-Dimensional Nightmare, while a further selection, *Passport to Eternity*, appeared in the US as a Berkley paperback. Before Moorcock's first *New Worlds*, five additional stories would be published, as well as SF Book Club reprints of the two Gollancz titles. He had also mapped out a new novel, *The Drought*. He deserved, needed and, for the first time in his life, could afford a holiday, although he and Mary had to wait for the summer school break. Simple fatigue may have shortened his temper when Moorcock demanded a serial for *New Worlds*. He half-jokingly complained when he delivered the manuscript, called *Equinox*, after only eight weeks, that 'the blood was dripping from my eyes as I wrote this. You made me do it too fast!'

Equinox was the prototype of his 1966 novel *The Crystal World*. He scaled it up from 'The Illuminated Man', a story he'd just sold to *The Magazine of Fantasy and Science Fiction*. Set in Florida, which he'd never visited, it actually takes place in the same imaginary landscape as Vermilion Sands and the vistas of the surrealists. This time, the menace is a virus from outer space. Jim found inspiration in Tobacco mosaic, a disease that creates a not unattractive mottling and discoloration on its leaves. It was the first virus to be discovered, in 1936, when researchers extracted it in the form of crystals. In 'The Illuminated Man', the invading virus coats plants with a crystalline material. Its anonymous narrator, noting that some artificial satellites and even planets have recently changed their character, shining more brightly, speculates that the virus may have been spreading through the universe for aeons, and only just reached our system.

Initially, it sweeps across Florida, affecting mostly trees but also slow-moving animals and humans, whom it embeds while still alive. Only movement arrests the effect. To resist, a man must run and flail his arms. This engenders the novel's central image, of a man, blazing with crystals, racing through a calcified forest. The description appears in all three versions of the story. It begins and ends the shortest, and serves as an epigraph to the longest. Few images are as emblematic of Jim in their loneliness, their beauty and their madness.

For *Equinox*, Jim abandoned the first-person narrative of 'The

Illuminated Man' and moved the location from Florida to French West Africa. The new version begins in the fictitious Port Matarre, supposedly in Cameroon, at the mouth of the Matarre River, the only route to the interior. The main character, the director of a leprosarium, is named Sanders, possibly a reference to the canny colonial administrator of Edgar Wallace's *Sanders of the River* stories. He's come to Cameroon in search of two old friends, one of them a former lover, who together run a clinic in the forest. He finds them but, in the process, realises that other forces draw him and his ex-lover to this place. The crystal world may offer a means to reconcile the conflict in their minds between light and dark – the equinox.

When *Equinox* appeared in book form as *The Crystal World*, reviewers again cited *Heart of Darkness* but missed the more obvious parallels with Graham Greene's *A Burnt-Out Case*, and his diary of the time he spent researching that novel in the Belgian Congo. In October 1961, Greene read extracts of this diary as part of a BBC radio programme, *Life and Letters: Raw Material*. Ballard, a consistent BBC listener, probably heard it. The theme of leprosy; the depiction of a superficially cordial yet restrictive French bureaucracy; the waning colonial presence, represented by abandoned mansions, and empty and decaying arcades of shops: the solemn French and Belgian children, suitcases on their knees, awaiting evacuation; the important character of a priest, Father Balthus, and above all the presence of the forest, repeatedly described as 'sombre' – all these recall Greene rather than Conrad. The writing is significantly more assured than much of his earlier work. For the first time, he dispenses with his reliance on similes. Setting and metaphor seamlessly combine, making it unnecessary to employ those tentative grammatical formulations – 'seemed', 'like', and 'as if' – that were his most persistent stylistic weakness.

In 1956, Gollancz had published *The Lost Steps*, a translation of *Los Pasos Perdidos* by Cuban author Alejo Carpentier, in which a musician travelling up the Amazon, ostensibly to research tribal music, enters a mystical state where religion and music coalesce. When Victor Gollancz bought *The Drowned World*, he told Jim, 'Of course, you stole the whole thing from Carpentier and Conrad.' Jim bridled, claiming that he'd never read Conrad or even heard of *The Lost Steps*. It seems likely, however, that he did consult Carpentier, just as he eventually read *Heart of Darkness*. Moorcock, during editing, removed details such as a mention of balsa trees, which crop up in Carpentier but are found only in South America.

CHAPTER TWENTY-FOUR

DRY

Early in 1964, Jim and Mary began planning their summer holiday in Spain. With charter flights and package holidays still in their infancy, they would have to drive almost 1,000 miles to get there, much of it on indifferent roads. Even so, Jim calculated that their 'tank-like' Armstrong Siddeley was large enough for themselves and the kids, plus luggage for a month. In the meantime, he started work on a new disaster novel, this time involving a worldwide lack of water. Berkley would publish it first in the US later that year as *The Burning World*, a title Jim disliked. In Britain, it was called *The Drought*.

In 1960, Tom Maschler had been appointed editorial director of the staid publishing house Jonathan Cape. Only twenty-six, and formerly of Penguin, Maschler immediately went trawling for talent. 'There was a handful of established writers and no young writers,' he wrote of Cape. 'The youngest "known" young writer was Elizabeth Jane Howard and she was not that young.' His first purchase was Joseph Heller's *Catch-22*, picked up for a mere £250 when another publisher relinquished the rights. He also persuaded Ernest Hemingway's widow to sell him the memoir of Paris in the twenties that became *A Moveable Feast*. Soon Cape was attracting the best young writers from both sides of the Atlantic. Kingsley Amis, encouraged by Howard, went with the flow. In July 1963, Maschler let him use Cape letterhead to write to Robert Graves, C. P. Snow and Somerset Maugham, soliciting original stories for an anthology of 'serious' SF. Interest was tepid, an ill omen for his vision of a synthesis between SF and mainstream literature. Gollancz continued to publish the

Spectrum anthologies until 1966, but when Victor Gollancz died in 1967, Amis would join Howard at Cape. Meanwhile, he recommended his protégés, including Ballard, to Maschler, who agreed to publish *The Drought.*

While Jim never abandoned the novel of ecological disaster, he had higher ambitions for *The Drought.* In its story, pollution has coated the oceans with a polymer that prevents evaporation. Without evaporation there are no clouds, and without clouds there can be no rain, so the earth begins to dry out. A few individuals linger along the banks of the dwindling rivers and lakes but most migrate to the oceans, where desalinisation plants purify a small amount of seawater, producing dunes of salt. Occasionally a tsunami sweeps the beaches, making room for more survivors. But the menace of *The Drought* is more insidious than an absence of water – it is a loss of faith. Despairing and elegiac, the book dwells on a handful of individuals not so much struggling to survive as surrendering to existential despair and ennui.

Once again, a minister of religion figures in the story; not a philosopher priest, as in *Equinox*, but the god-bothering Reverend Johnstone (the name of Jim's maternal grandfather), whose parishioners arrive for his services toting shotguns. A twentieth-century Savonarola, he preaches that man has brought disaster on himself and must face the consequences. One of his more despairing sermons takes its text from the Book of Jonah: 'And it came to pass, when the sun did arise, that God prepared a vehement east wind; and the sun beat upon the head of Jonah, and he fainted, and wished himself to die, and said, it is better for me to die than to live.' After that, local fishermen, resentful of this counsel of despair, torch his church.

Johnstone responds by forming a militia to preserve the little remaining water. Even when travellers offer to pay for a drink, he turns them away at gunpoint. The refugees get help from the central character, Doctor Ransom – a name reused in *Empire of the Sun.* Ransom is another Ballardian male: sensitive, thoughtful, ineffectual.

Habitually suspicious of men of action, Jim assigned that role to a succession of moguls, military bullies and religious fanatics. The effect was often to make his main characters into wimps. Perhaps Maschler pointed this out, since between delivering *The Burning World* to Berkley and selling it to Cape as *The Drought*, Ransom acquires some *cojones*. In the US version, he's a languid visionary on the model of Rimbaud, but *The Drought* visualises him as a tanned Nordic seafarer, a kind of Thor Heyerdahl, clutching a tome by anthropologist Bronisław Malinowski.

Even so, Ransom and his companions, typically for a Ballard book, turn their backs on the fitful promise of salvation – in this case the ocean – and, like Kerans in *The Drowned World*, trek into the heart of the disaster, where abandoned cities are engulfed by dunes of sand. When someone dies, an automobile is excavated and the body laid in this improvised vault – another trope emblematic of Ballard. The end of the story finds Ransom, with equal predictability, beside a drained swimming pool. In the last sentence, it begins, inexplicably, to rain, but like the imposed optimistic ending of *The Wind from Nowhere*, this salvation appears contrived. The *malaise du temps* isn't soluble in rain – only in tears.

Although, in its sparseness and its concentration of a few individuals in a desolate landscape, *The Drought* resembles the Vermilion Sands stories, its desert is less like Bradbury's Mars than the stylised westerns of Sergio Leone or the novels of Cormac McCarthy. Jim explained, 'The few people who survive on the planet are governed by perfectly abstract relations, through an entire geometry of space-time, of emotion and action. It is a completely abstract world, as abstract as the most abstract of painters or sculptors one can imagine.'

In tune with this concept, *The Drought* cites the work of a surrealist painter for whom he had previously shown little enthusiasm, the resolutely non-figurative Yves Tanguy. His table-flat landscapes, interrupted by the occasional blob-like object, had long been looted by US illustrators, notably Richard Powers, who created numerous Tanguyesque SF book covers, including the Berkley Ballards. Penguin also used a detail from Tanguy's 1942 *The Palace of Windowed Rocks* on its 1965 reprint of *The Drowned World.* Though Tanguy lacked the storytelling elements Jim favoured in surrealist art, the emptiness of his work harmonised with the bleakness of *The Drought.* For the chapter describing the edge of the ocean thronged with seekers for water, he borrows the title of a Tanguy canvas, *The Multiplication of the Arts,* in which objects like water-washed stones crowd to a grey, limitless horizon. His text picks up the visual reference, speaking of events from the past being smoothed and rounded by the river of time. The final chapter, describing Ransom alone among sun-baked dunes, is called 'Days of Slowness', from Tanguy's *Jour de Lenteur.* One critic's description of *Jour de Lenteur* captures the quality of existential ennui for which Jim aimed. The painting 'shows a world smoothed, a world of absence and silence; a day of slowness which appears to stretch into the abysses of infinity and space, as in a desert mirage, still as the vision of an unknown planet. As after a disaster, all human presence has disappeared, to give way to strange forms, the shadows of which fall in a supernatural light.'

CHAPTER TWENTY-FIVE

SPAIN

While the Ballards were planning their holiday, Mary became ill with an infected appendix. It was removed at Ashford Hospital but the surgery left her weak and in persistent pain. Jim conceded later that the operation may have lowered her resistance, or that she acquired an infection. The Ballards had dinner with the Moorcocks just before setting off early in August. Seeing her obvious discomfort, they urged a postponement, but Jim insisted the schedule of school holidays made that impossible.

Once into Spain, Jim followed the Mediterranean coast, stopping at Rosas and Barcelona. In *The Kindness of Women*, the narrator speaks of dreaming about the bullring in Barcelona and seeing the famous matador Manuel Benitez Pérez, aka El Cordobés. Since the corrida season ran from April to September, and Pérez was at the height of his fame in 1964, this is probably based on fact.

The solid construction and six-cylinder engine of the Armstrong Siddeley Sapphire suited it to long trips, although at eighteen miles to the gallon it guzzled as much gas as any Cadillac. The specifications also promised a top speed of 100 mph, something Jim was curious to test. Perhaps with memories of *Pandora and the Flying Dutchman*, he headed for the area where the film was shot – the Costa Blanca. They'd rented a flat in El Campello, a beachside town near San Juan, close to Alicante. Jim wrote of the holiday as a carefree romp – 'the kind of holiday,' recorded Bea Ballard, 'in which the biggest excitement was Daddy falling off the pedalo' – but anyone who has been on holiday in a foreign country with three small children will recognise how little this reflects the daily grind of dressing and undressing, bathing, feeding, settling arguments, dealing with minor medical problems while acting as combined babysitter, nanny and entertainer. *The Kindness of Women* describes Jim and Miriam sneaking into the bathroom to have sex – a common stratagem of family holidays. In between picnics and beach visits, Jim also found time to open up the big car on a stretch of empty beach, and was at last able to emulate Nigel Patrick in *Pandora*, coaxing it up to 100 mph.

Mary fell ill during the last days of their holiday. Alicante had only modest medical facilities – and 'modest' by the standards of the day verged on primitive. The British novelist Frederic Raphael, then living in Spain, recalled: 'We went back to England for the birth of our second child. In those days you did not have children born in Spain if you could avoid it, because of the state of Spanish doctors' hands and doubtless other parts.' The infection was virulent, and not immediately identified. By the time a specialist from Alicante diagnosed viral pneumonia, it was already advanced.

Jim, along with the children, moved into the hospital, and remained by Mary's bed. The end came on the morning of Sunday 13 September. In his memoirs, Jim remembers Mary's last words as 'Am I dying?' He believed he shouted an assurance of his love, but by then she was dead. Fay recalls it differently. That morning, she crept into her mother's room for a cuddle and was actually lying beside her when Mary sat up, gave a great sigh and died. This is consistent with a pulmonary embolism, when blood is no longer able to pass through the lungs and the heart stops. In the medical definition, 'A massive pulmonary embolus, common in a patient bed-bound after surgery, especially a female, causes a sudden pain in the chest and stops the right ventricle dead.'

Friends in the UK were shocked to receive a terse telegram – 'Mary died today. Great Heart. Coming Home. Jim.' Too poor to ship the body back to Britain, he buried her in the local Protestant cemetery, at a ceremony attended by only a few neighbours from the apartment building. So sparse was the service that the coffin was trundled to the cemetery on an iron-wheeled handcart. Afterwards the priest took up a shovel and filled the grave himself. Jim then faced the long drive back to London. *The Kindness of Women* includes a number of details that ring true: his daughters helping with the road maps, choosing the hotels where they stayed, young Jimmie's schoolboy French getting them back on the road when they became lost, and the children keeping watch on the whisky bottle Jim held between his thighs. Every half-hour, he was forced to pull over to weep uncontrollably.

Back in Shepperton, Jim faced the reality of life without Mary – not only as wife and companion but as childminder and housekeeper. Initially, the children stayed with his parents, with his sister and with his in-laws. Outside the family, the Moorcocks saw him more than anyone. 'I don't think he really had any other peers,' Moorcock says.

> He talked quite a lot, obviously. We did talk about Mary dying, and him coming back, but there wasn't a great deal to say about it. He would mumble things from time to time. I think he felt guilty about not being with the kids twenty-four hours a day. I think that's understandable. When other friends have lost their wives, they become very protective of their children. They start to worry about them a great deal where they wouldn't have worried before. He was suppressing this but nonetheless feeling that he should be there.

Whether Jim bore any guilt for Mary's death is an open question, but he believed he did. 'Anyone would feel guilty in those circumstances,' says Moorcock:

> whether it was justified or not: you just do. We'd go off to the pub while Hilary cooked the Sunday lunch. There were heart-to-hearts, of a sort. But we were Chaps. We were less interested in relationships than in events. That was how men behaved in those days. What had brought us together in the first place was an interest in the outside world. We were more interested in what was Out There, rather than

reading someone's sensitive account of how the world out there affected them. We weren't interested in how the world affected us so much as how the world worked.

Lunghua had taught Jim the utility of denial. Just as he suppressed memories of the war, so he suppressed those of Mary. 'It unhinged Jimmy for some while,' wrote Brian Aldiss. His self-isolation was exacerbated by the drinking begun on the trip back from Spain. His disconnection from the world continued for years, some might say for the rest of his life. At Shepperton, time, in the best Ballardian tradition, stood still. The children were forbidden to ask about their mother, and any reference to her was discouraged. All photographs of her disappeared. A few were found in Jim's bedside table after his death. Her clothes remained in the wardrobes for years. When he wasn't around, his daughters would sneak into the bedroom to play dressing-up games.

Fay Ballard said loyally, 'Daddy sacrificed everything to bring us up. Our home was a nest – a lovely, warm family nest. We had a lady who came in to change and wash the sheets every Friday, but apart from that he did everything, and he did it brilliantly.' Often, the brilliance was modified by expedience: dresses shortened with the use of Cow Gum and a stapler. According to Moorcock, Jim 'claimed convincingly that the baked bean, the staple gun and a pot of fabric glue were the cornerstones of successful childcare'.

Minimum attention was paid to good manners and politeness. The Ballard kids gained a reputation for wildness. Moorcock's children feared their visits. 'My kids, who weren't exactly repressed, used to be in awe of the Ballards, rather like Romans hearing of Attila approaching.' Charles Platt agreed: 'There was little hint of his genius when he was in family mode. I remember his daughters had a pet rat. One time we all got into his Ford Zephyr to go somewhere, and Jimmy paused for just a second, sensing something not quite right. The daughters were a little too quiet. "There's a rat in this car," he said, playful yet stern. The daughters immediately started pleading, "Daddy, no, let him come with us!" but the rat had to be relocated back in his cage in the house.'

A mythology accreted around the Shepperton house and its supposed neglect, augmented by those who had visited him there, but even more by those who hadn't. A journalist in 1998 observed 'a layer of dust as thick as volcanic ash has settled over the room. Some objects in the house have not been moved for several decades. The house certainly has the feel of a mausoleum: as if he is waiting for someone who will never arrive.' Another spoke of 'a sense of stepping through the looking glass':

> A twenty-year-old Ford Granada of indistinct hue slumps on the narrow driveway, jammed up against the front entrance. Indoors, the curtains, neither open nor closed, are held in limbo by a giant dehydrated plant that has collapsed on to the table, blocking all but the most determined approach. Lost amid the mini-jungle of its dried-up fronds is a dust-covered Collins Dictionary [not by coincidence, presumably, since this was the only dictionary to include the definition 'Ballardian']. Ballard's electrical fixtures would interest the curator of the Design Museum. On a cold day, the rooms are warmed by small heaters positioned in the middle of the floor. The sleek stylist of western consumerism never got round to installing central heating.

Fay Ballard enlarged on the legend in 1987. 'Objects have not moved in twenty years. There is still a revolting rose ornament on the stairs, a blue flipper from an old summer holiday still holds a door open, a peeled orange on the mantelpiece in the nursery has been there for at least fifteen years.' She also explained the presence, noted by visitors, of more than one Ewbank carpet cleaner, the manual variety that one pushed with a long handle. 'Daddy had a routine,' she recalled.

> He would get up quite early in the morning, have breakfast, always do the *Times* crossword, and then settle down to write at his typewriter

> for the morning. And as a way of pausing and thinking of what he was writing, he would come out of his study, take hold of the carpet sweeper, which was just outside his study door, and start sweeping the hallway for . . . I don't know . . . a few minutes. Then go back to his study and do a bit more typing. Then he'd come out again, half an hour later, and do a bit more. Maybe a couple of hours later, he'd come out again, do a bit more. The use of the carpet sweeper was really a device for him to stop and reflect on what he'd been writing.

Favouring writing over housekeeping is usual among authors, and Jim was more diligent than many: as he said, you could do the basics in five minutes if you weren't obsessive about it. While his children were young, he had little time to clean up, and, once they departed, so did the inclination. At the same time, his untidiness had an element of contrivance. A cynic might see it as an exercise in the tradition of Conan Doyle and Sherlock Holmes: a Ewbank in place of the correspondence pinned to the mantelpiece with a jackknife, the desiccated lemon instead of a Persian slipper full of shag, the cigars in the coal scuttle equating to his old manual typewriter, grudgingly replaced by the only slightly less anachronistic electric model. And might not a man so conscious of his image have humoured these journalistic fancies? What was his life, after all, but just another novel?

Above all, the house became a model of the 'eventless present'. The repetition of simple acts over decades caused time to slow, even stand still, an effect emphasised by the two Delvaux paintings he had copied from lost originals. He had reversed time to bring them back to life, and the women in them stood now as guardians.

CHAPTER TWENTY-SIX

WHISKY AND SODA CHAP

What if Jim and not Mary had died on that trip to Spain?

Despite the inspired poetry of *The Drowned World* and the innovations of *The Voices of Time*, he would have been regarded as a rising star doomed never to achieve his potential. Almost everything of substance in his career, anything that attracts the adjective 'Ballardian' – *The Atrocity Exhibition*, *Crash*, *Empire of the Sun* – is a work of his bereavement. The depth of his grief is not in doubt, but neither is its transformative effect. The poet Robert Lowell, no stranger to mental disturbance, believed T. S. Eliot was a paranoiac who wrote best while living alone. Marriage, even one as tormented as Eliot's, assuaged the disturbance that made him great. The same may be true of Ballard. It explains his extremes of feeling, the changes in behaviour and the sense of release that distinguishes almost everything he created after 1964. For good or ill, the violence, the passion and the desire stored up since adolescence and kept in check by his marriage, now gushed out.

William Burroughs went through a similar transformation after the death of his wife Joan, killed in a drunken accident with a handgun for which Burroughs, with some justice, blamed himself entirely. 'I am forced to the appalling conclusion,' he wrote,

> that I would never have become a writer but for Joan's death, and to a realisation of the extent to which this event has motivated and formulated my writing. I live with the constant threat of possession, and a constant need to escape from possession, from Control. So the death of Joan brought me in contact with the invader, the Ugly Spirit, and

manoeuvered me into a lifelong struggle, in which I have had no choice except to write my way out.

John Gray, the social and cultural theorist who rated Ballard Britain's 'most gifted and original living writer', believed that 'the casual cruelty he witnessed in Shanghai, and the tragic early death of his wife Mary in 1964, revealed a world devoid of human meaning. The challenge Ballard faced was to show how fulfilment could be found in such conditions. His writings were the result, a lifelong experiment in imaginative alchemy, the transmutation of senseless dross into visions of beauty.'

Perhaps this is so. Or might the loss of Mary have freed him to indulge in those experiences, from fatherhood to sexual promiscuity, which enriched his best work? If Mary's death induced any transformation, it was one in which rage and guilt transmuted sentiment into the 'Ugly Spirit' of *Crash*.

In *The Kindness of Women*, Ballard's surrogate describes as commonplace the tendency of women to honour the death of a wife by giving themselves sexually to the widower. In *Kindness*, his sister-in-law is the first to offer herself. He frames their brief coupling as a rite of passage; a solace to which the bereaved spouse is entitled by custom, and which is meant as a sort of homage to the dead. In real life, Jim did receive such consolation, but provided by one of the mothers with whom he waited at the school gate to collect his children. For the next three years, until he met his longtime companion Claire Walsh (formerly Churchill), and even after that, during a long hiatus in their relationship, such 'targets of opportunity' distinguished Jim's sex life. He slept with fellow writers and the wives of fellow writers. He sold at least one book after sleeping with a publishing director. He liked and needed women, but left them in no doubt that work mattered more. Though ready enough with a compliment, he lacked the time, patience and, above all, the *savoir-faire* to pay court. Women whom he saw more than once complained that each assignation was a repetition of the first. His behaviour towards his sex partners was not so much gauche as contemptuous, even abusive, which some found to their taste. In *Concrete Island*, his protagonist justifies bullying the old man and the girl with whom he's marooned; they *want* to be mistreated, he writes. They even expect it, since it confirms their low opinion of themselves. The 'intellectual thug' of his schooldays was always just below the surface.

He never considered remarriage, although, as he pointed out in *The Kindness of Women*, a man with three children is an unattractive prospect. That he shouldn't raise his children himself was never an option, even though many in his family strenuously opposed it. 'People were much less tolerant of the idea of fathers being a single parent than they are now,' he said.

> It was very very rare in those days for a man to bring up three children and it was made absolutely clear to me by all kinds of people that I shouldn't really be doing it. People quite seriously told me in no uncertain terms that my children had suffered an immeasurable loss from the death of their mother and no father could ever take her place. It was suggested that I farm my children out to various relatives, which I refused to do. The general assumption was that a man could never take the place of a mother. A man could never be a mother. I never tried to be one. I simply tried to be a father. All you needed to do with the children was love them and let them look after you. I didn't bring up my children. They really brought *me* up.

Seldom reticent in speaking about Mary, he incorporated her into his personal narrative as another tragic victim, like Jackie Kennedy. Any guilt he may have felt at taking her on holiday before she was fully recovered from surgery was subsumed into a scenario that blamed an anonymous but malevolent Other. He called her death 'a crime against this beautiful young woman'. And the criminal? 'Nature committed a terrible crime. I'm very well aware of that.' She became an innocent bystander, collateral damage, the victim of friendly fire – any explanation that laid his remorse at another door.

*

Late in 1964, he started writing again, beginning with the expansion of *Equinox* into *The Crystal World.* 'I was completely drunk while writing that,' he admitted. 'I used to have my first drink at about nine o'clock in the morning, and I would stop drinking at about five.' Alcohol, which helped numb the pain, became the fuel that sustained him. Each morning, after delivering the children to school, he downed a large Scotch. 'It separated me from the domestic world, like a huge dose of novocaine injected into reality, in the same way that a dentist calms a fractious patient so that he can get on with some fancy bridgework.'

His drinking tapered off over the next two decades. 'It was a great sense of achievement,' he recalled, 'when my first drink of the day was not at nine in the morning but at noon and then at eight. Life got much duller as a result.' Profiling him for *The New Yorker* in 1997, Tom Shone noted that

> his body language, like that of many reformed heavy drinkers, still carries within it a distant chemical memory of drunkenness. When he is ascending the conversational foothills toward one of his favourite theories – 'the Normalizing of the Psychopathic', say, or 'the Death of Affect' (he seems to speak in capitals a lot) – his eyes widen a little madly and his laconic drawl rises to an excited declamatory pitch, his white hair shaking loose. The over-all effect is of the Ancient Mariner if he'd been an ex-RAF, whisky-and-soda kind of chap.

David Pringle calculates that Ballard, in expanding *Equinox*, added 23,000 words, including two new chapters, 'Mulatto on the Catwalks' and 'The White Hotel'. He also corrected the few factual errors picked up by Moorcock: details such as the balsa logs, and showing Cameroon as being, like Greene's Congo, under white French administration, whereas the country became independent in 1960.

By May 1965, Maschler had bought *The Crystal World.* The same month, Cape published *The Drought.* Slick presentation minimised the novel's fantastic elements. An abstract cover of a stylised sun and desert reinforced a blurb that began with an Amis quote: 'One of our most individual young novelists takes us further into his strange world. Ballard's landscapes in *The Drought* move and haunt us because they reflect the depths of the human mind.' There was no question of the book being relegated by the press to 'SF Roundup' columns. It was reviewed with other literary novels, and respectfully. *The Drought* and *The Crystal World* made SF, or at least certain sorts of SF, critically respectable. Jim was *sui generis*, his personal style and preoccupations so atypical that, in accepting him, a critic wasn't also committing himself to space opera and Little Green Men, since it was obvious that Jim himself held them in no less contempt.

'The experience Mr Ballard offers is mystical,' wrote the *Sunday Times*. 'It is weird; it is grotesque; it is magnificently Gothic.' The *Daily Telegraph* suggested, 'By arranging a world drought to kill off the majority of people, he brings his characters to a state of timeless, arid obsession with what is left of water and of their own selves. A sensitive, baroque study in decadence.' The *Times Literary Supplement* called it 'a very impressive book by a deeply serious writer, the originality and power of whose vision can be felt', and the *Guardian* 'a strange and rather wonderful book full of haunting landscapes, phantasmagoria and disaster that clangs on the mind. An impressive novel at any level. Its obscurities and surrealist flourishes only heighten the dreamlike atmosphere.'

In May 1965, Kingsley Amis made a last attempt to launch his anthology of 'literary' SF. Inviting Harry Harrison, Bruce Montgomery (aka Edmund Crispin), Brian Aldiss, Ballard and Elizabeth Jane Howard to lunch, he proposed a collaboration. Like C. S. Lewis's Perelandra trilogy, their collective novel would employ futuristic elements but with a contemporary agenda. The provisional title was *Virus from Venus*. Though the meal expired in what Jim called 'a grey miasma of booze', a few ideas emerged. Montgomery outlined a story inspired by the birth control pill, the long-term effects of which were then little understood. It was thought it might possibly delay the menopause. If so, proposed Montgomery, women would age more slowly, living perhaps to 120, resulting in a society of burned-out men dominated by still sexually active women.

Jim suggested a very different plot, hinging on something in which all at the table devoutly believed – alcohol. A virus causes a breakdown in notions of identity. Those infected spontaneously assume other personalities, from dreams, from literature or history, even from TV. Only alcohol neutralises the effect, so people would be truly themselves only when drunk – a tacit acknowledgement by Jim of his lifestyle at the time. He proposed each writer create an episode from the point of view of such a transformed character: Amis an eccentric publisher, Harrison a NASA colonel, himself a Jungian analyst. Nothing came of the project, however.

Jim had become a frequent guest in the Amis household. The informality of having supper on his lap round the fire, then repairing to the pub with Kingsley and his male friends, was a congenial parallel to his own domestic existence. However, this rapport declined after *Virus from Venus* failed. 'The friendship between the two did not survive Ballard's increasing interest in experimentalism,' says Amis's son Martin. At a 1968 Brighton Arts Festival SF Conference, Robert Conquest, in a speech most took to be Kingsley speaking by proxy, inflamed tempers by accusing the New Wave of British SF writers of 'merely repeating the experiments of the twenties and thirties'.

In 1976 and 1980, Amis demonstrated his ideal of respectable speculative fantasy in two novels of 'alternative history', *The Alteration* (the Reformation fails and Britain remains Catholic) and *Russian Hide-and-Seek* (Britain becomes one of the Soviet Socialist Republics). Neither was among his best work. In 1981, he said his last word in an anthology of weary warhorses entitled *The Golden Age of Science Fiction.* The introduction raged against writers ruined by 'restlessness and self-dissatisfaction, by the conscious quest for maturity and novelty, by the marsh light of experimentation'. Jim's work, he wrote, inspired only 'mystification and outrage', even 'physical disgust' and, notwithstanding his earlier championship, his former protégé had, he now believed, 'never been in the genre at all'.

CHAPTER TWENTY-SEVEN

SPOOKY

London in 1965 was coming alive, particularly the former no-go areas of Notting Hill and Ladbroke Grove. The libertarian tradition of SF ensured that sex, drugs and rock and roll were available to any writer or fan who wanted them. 'At the end of February 1965, I threw a party in my tenement,' says Charles Platt.

> Science-fiction fans came from as far away as Liverpool. Former school friends showed up. Moorcock, Langdon Jones, Ballard, John Brunner, Graham Hall, and other New Worlds contributors were there. The lowlifes on the ground floor were smoking hashish (a novelty, in those days). A couple of them were shooting heroin (even more of a novelty, since at that time it could only be obtained by prescription on the National Health Service). On the floor above there was heavy drinking and vigorous dancing, making the floor flex disconcertingly.

Jim was the spectre at this feast. 'He lurked in one corner,' says Platt, 'looking uneasy, clutching a copy of my fanzine which I had thrust into his hands.' He appeared utterly and irretrievably out of his depth.

Firmer ground awaited him in the Hampstead home of John Brunner, who dispensed hospitality just as liberally, but with more discretion. Alcohol and conversation flowed, a powerful strain of marijuana, known as Hampstead Green, flourished at the bottom of the garden, and Brunner and his wife, Marjorie, openly entertained a succession of lovers. Brunner's vainglorious manner, reminiscent of a Jacobean cavalier, could be hard to take. Ostentatiously *engagé*, he'd written songs for the Campaign for Nuclear Disarmament, which is where he met Marjorie. He also endowed a prize for poetry, and answered what he believed was a pressing public interest in his work and personality by printing a glossy autobiographical booklet which he distributed widely.

Sometimes Ballard and Moorcock squabbled over which of them should accept Brunner's invitations. Jim didn't resist too much. Conveniently for him, these soirées took place on Fridays, when he most needed to unwind. They were also an excellent place to meet women. With no time to waste in idle chat, he propositioned them with vigour and had considerable success. One of his earliest partners was the vivacious Marjorie Brunner, but he preferred women he could take home to Shepperton for the weekend, sometimes swinging by Ladbroke Grove to describe the party to Moorcock and show off his conquest.

In the summer of 1965, Jim piled the kids into the car and drove to Greece. Less than twelve months before, he had been in Spain with Mary. But the year since her death had seen fundamental changes in his life, both professional and personal. His work was entering a new phase, and he'd come through bereavement not only intact but more confident. Sitting in a café in Athens, he watched the actor Michael Redgrave cross the street, buy a magazine, chat with the kiosk owner and enjoy a drink in a bar. Though Redgrave had no reason to believe he was known in Athens, he automatically exaggerated his gestures, acting even when there was no audience. It confirmed Jim's conviction, shared by Marshall McLuhan, that we all cast ourselves as characters in a fiction of our own authorship.

In Athens he received an unexpected visit by two emissaries from Stanley Kubrick, then filming *2001: A Space Odyssey* at Shepperton Studios. With the movie almost completed, Kubrick and screenwriter Arthur C. Clarke were wrestling with a conclusion. Before choosing Clarke as a collaborator, Kubrick had set out to read something by every major living SF writer, Jim included. Now he demanded his immediate presence to consult on the film. Jim refused. His holiday and his children took precedence. Such intransigence made Kubrick testy. When Clarke brought other writers to the set, including Moorcock, he ordered them off. Jim saw the completed film at the same preview as Aldiss and Moorcock and, like them, felt it, in Moorcock's phrase, 'a bit cold in the visionary department'. The famously self-confident Clarke was unperturbed. 'He took our poor response with his usual amused forgiveness reserved for lesser mortals,' says Moorcock, 'and told us how many millions the movie had already made in America.'

In 1965, Jim also met William Burroughs for the first time when the writer paid a visit to Britain. The following year Burroughs moved to London and rented a small apartment in the very centre of the city. 'This was in a street called Duke Street, literally about 100 yards from Piccadilly Circus,' recalled Jim. 'That's where all the boys used to congregate, in the lavatory of the big Piccadilly Circus Underground station. It was quite a shock for a heterosexual like myself to accidentally stray into this lavatory and to find oneself in what seemed to be a kind of oriental male brothel.' Burroughs's paranoia also spooked Jim; he warned visitors to keep away from the windows, claiming the CIA and *Time* magazine had him under surveillance from a laundry van.

Kubrick wasn't alone in seeing Jim's work as movie material. Edith Cottrell, a neophyte producer based in Paris, bought the film rights to *The Crystal World* and hired critic Jonathan Rosenbaum to adapt it. Both Jean Seberg and Susan Sontag, already an enthusiast for Ballard, read his script, but it was never filmed. Sensing the new media interest in his work, Jim even wrote, on spec, a screenplay for *The Drought*, hoping to get work as a screenwriter, but he never found a buyer.

In 1964, the BBC had hired US producer Irene Shubik to create a series of fifty-minute SF plays on the model of the US shows *The Outer Limits* and *The Twilight Zone*. She bought stories by Asimov,

Pohl and Bradbury from American agents, then approached Carnell, who sold her stories by Wyndham and Brunner, as well as Ballard's 'Thirteen to Centaurus'. One of his first sales in the US, it appeared in *Amazing* in April 1962, just after the novella publication of *The Drowned World*. The story belonged to the 'claustrophobic' phase that inspired 'Manhole 69'. The characters are again lab rats, twelve people living in what they think is a spaceship en route to Alpha Centauri but which is actually a sealed environment in a subarctic hangar, under constant surveillance. A doctor on board and a team in the hangar monitor the reactions of the crew, gathering data against the day when they make a real journey. Fifty years into the experiment, the doctor discovers that the hereditary captains have long since figured out the deception and even created a peephole into the outside world. They prefer, however, to maintain the fantasy.

The fifty-minute play, in black and white, aired on 13 December 1965, with Donald Houston giving a serviceable performance as the doctor. Allowing for the cardboard sets, the toyshop scientific equipment and the insistence that even the observing technicians dress like Buck Rogers, *Thirteen to Centaurus* did only minimum violence to a story that, in terms of Jim's development, was already an anachronism.

The one fundamental change made by screenwriter Stanley Miller, a veteran of TV adaptations, highlighted the key problem of dramatising Ballard: his stories have no 'third act'. Most end in an irrational action by the protagonist – existentially authentic, but a storyteller's nightmare. Jim's version concludes with the doctor's discovery of the deception, leaving any aftermath to the imagination. Miller rewrote this to show the next candidate for captain overpowering the doctor and brainwashing him into believing the voyage is real. The solution imposes rationality on a writer who never professed to be rational.

In August 1965, another World SF Convention, the twenty-third, took place in London. Jim was still in Greece, but on his return he met one of its guests, Judith Merril, the US editor who'd championed his work. Born Judith Grossman, Merril, seven years older than Ballard and far from beautiful, was as famous for her voracious sexuality as for her militant Zionism and Communism. Ballard called her 'the strongest woman in a genre for the most part created by timid and weak men'. A few weeks after the Convention, she met Ballard and they became lovers.

It was Merril who, exploring the house at Shepperton after having spent the night, discovered Mary's clothes in the wardrobes. 'Spooky!' she confided to friends. Nor was she the first woman to feel offended when Jim packed her off on Sunday night with a clear indication that he had no further use for her until the following Friday. Another woman complained to Jim 'I only see you at night', and Jim admitted that, as he swept down the Thames Valley at sunset each Friday, heading for an assignation, his behaviour did resemble that of a vampire thirsting for fresh blood.

Merril found Ballard's behaviour progressively more disconcerting. During one of her weekends at Shepperton, Langdon Jones, Charles Platt and Moorcock paid a visit. According to Platt, 'Jim had acquired a copy of The Who's single *Anyway, Anyhow, Anywhere.* "I like it much better at 33 rpm," he said. We all started laughing, and he became slightly annoyed. "Well, have you tried it?" he challenged us. Of course none of us had listened to it at 33 rpm, so, we then had to sit patiently while he played it at that speed, and then at 16.'

On her last visit to Shepperton, Merril pocketed as a souvenir Ballard's Parker fountain pen. It had no intrinsic value, only a symbolic one as a relic from life with Mary. Forty years later, he'd still be writing letters with it. Once he discovered the loss, Jim pursued her urgently, eventually arriving at Waterloo station as she boarded the boat train to Southampton. Having wrongly assumed he'd come to see her off, Merril handed over the pen with poor grace. 'Well, *sayonara*,' Jim said, awkwardly, but with an intonation polished in Lunghua. As the train pulled out, Merril, who knew no Japanese but was determined to have the last word, leaned out of the window, fuming, and, aware of how he disliked editorial correction, shouted, 'It's *sayon* *ara*!'

CHAPTER TWENTY-EIGHT

A SCHIZOPHRENIC WORLD

Judy Merril was more than a bedmate for Jim. As an editor, a writer and a former agent with Scott Meredith, she knew the US market intimately. Partly at her instigation, British writers began to desert Ted Carnell to find American agents. Ballard joined Scott Meredith, as did Moorcock, Brunner and Aldiss. Within the next few years, the best authors would all migrate to American agents. At Carnell's funeral in 1972, the air, remarked one mourner, was heavy with guilt.

As Moorcock's *New Worlds* gathered readers, doubling and, in some cases, almost tripling its former circulation, Carnell flinched at the transformation. For the 151st issue in May 1965, he contributed a diplomatic guest editorial that celebrated the magazine's longevity without endorsing its new direction. The New Wave, as long as it consisted only of Ballard, Aldiss, Moorcock and Brunner, had been little more than a pious hope. Now, new American writers like Tom Disch, John Sladek and Norman Spinrad gravitating to London gave it intellectual muscle. Both in how they lived and what they wrote, these newcomers were an affront to those who, like Kingsley Amis, hoped for SF's dignified absorption into the mainstream. But Moorcock was defiant.

> Where mainstream writers still struggle to reproduce the careful, unambitious sentences of Kingsley Amis, the Frenchified retrospective tone of Durrell's *Alexandria Quartet*, the dull authority and over-familiar rhythms of the orthodox American novel of manners, or fall back utterly on pastiche, *New Worlds* writers have kicked all that aside

and are finding and making instruments to do a job, rather than reproduce a riff.

Not everyone in this group shared the same agenda, but it was a house with many mansions. 'The rowdy mob who invaded Mike's *New Worlds* agreed on very little,' wrote Brian Aldiss, 'but they accepted that a version of the future had arrived and they preferred to investigate it rather than look much further ahead.'

> If there was unison, it was in reflecting the schizophrenic world of Vietnam, Oxfam, Twiggy, the invasion of Czechoslovakia, the Beatles, LBJ, Che, the Space Race, and trendy figures like Gagarin, McLuhan, Buckminster Fuller, plus James Bondery, acid, GNP, Swinging London, *That Was The Week That Was*, and the theories of Durkheim, Marcuse, and Laing, with, if you like, Timothy Leary, Wilson-and-Brown, and Marx.

In general, Jim welcomed the new arrivals. Most had read and admired his work, and regarded him with a certain awe. During 1966, Tom Disch even paid him a number of visits.

> These took the invariable form of a trip to the Shepperton train station south of London and then a terrifying ride with Ballard at the wheel of his sports car. At his home, a dilapidated, infinitely cluttered bungalow that he shared with his two children, Ballard, fuelled with whisky, would deliver an oral version of his private gospel. Sad to say, I remember not a single oracle from those occasions, only a sense that the man was, as advertised, a genius hard-wired to the Zeitgeist.

Aside from his confusion about some details – Shepperton west, not south, of London; the house semi-detached, not a bungalow; three children, not two; never owning a sports car – Disch's account does reflect Jim's status; not someone with whom to sink a pint or share a joint, but more a guru and ideologue, to be approached with respect, even trepidation: Merlin to Moorcock's Arthur.

Another newcomer whom Jim got to know well was painter, writer and muse-at-large Pamela Zoline. Daughter of a wealthy Chicago businessman, she'd come to London in 1963 to study art at the Slade School. In the impoverished London art scene, her work attracted awed attention, particularly *$100 Painting*, which was plastered with real dollar bills. She, Disch and Sladek lived in a serpentine-staired flat in the seedy heart of Camden Town. Disch, who had not yet come out as gay, was even engaged to marry Zoline, who relished what she called the 'cohort-based' culture swirling around *New Worlds*. 'The fact,' she wrote, 'that I was lucky enough to run with a bad crowd in London including Tom Disch, John Clute, Mike Moorcock, John Sladek, Jimmy Ballard, etc, certainly gave a certain neighborhood for my stories.'

Zoline's canvases caught the eye of Jim, as did Zoline herself. In 1967, when she and Disch were no longer engaged, they had an affair. He encouraged her to write. Her best-known story, 'The Heat Death of the Universe', was like a Ballard pastiche, but with a supercharged sensorium. A typical passage reads, 'All topographical imperfections sanded away with the sweet-smelling burr of the plastic surgeon's cosmetic polisher, a world populace dieting, leisured, similar in pink and mauve hair and rhinestone shades. A land Cunt-Pink and Avocado-Green, brassiered and girdled by monstrous complexities of Super Highways.' Zoline hoped for publication in the prestigious *Paris Review*, but when they rejected it, Moorcock published the story in *New Worlds*.

Nineteen sixty-seven was the year of the Mary Quant miniskirt, Tom Stoppard's *Rosencrantz and Guildenstern Are Dead* and *Sgt. Pepper*. For a while, London became capital of what Lawrence Ferlinghetti called the Gone World, and *New Worlds* was in the thick of it. In her *Year's Best SF*, Judy Merril printed Moorcock's Ladbroke Grove address and urged visitors to look him up. Shortly after, she returned to London and compiled the anthology *England Swings SF*.

It wasn't the *annus mirabilis* for everyone. By the middle of 1966, *Science Fantasy* was collapsing. The seventeen issues edited by Kyril

Bonfiglioli were marked by falling sales and mediocre material. Assistant editor Keith Roberts effectively ran it, as well as contributing some of the better fiction and designing the covers. Bonfiglioli preferred carousing and dealing in art, activities for which he showed more flair than editing: in 1964, he spotted a Tintoretto at a country auction and bought it for £40.

In a last attempt to revive the magazine, he changed the title to the trendier sounding *Impulse*. The first issue, published in March 1966, included stories by Aldiss and Harrison, but, more importantly, Ballard's 'You and Me and the Continuum', the first of the 'condensed novels' that would make up *The Atrocity Exhibition*. But resuscitation came too late. Leaving *Impulse* in intensive care, 'Bon' took his Tintoretto profits to Jersey, where he became an accomplished writer of tongue-in-cheek crime novels like *Something Nasty in the Woodshed* and *Don't Point That Thing At Me*.

Volatile and paranoid, Keith Roberts was even less suited to be editor. 'He could be a very interesting lunch companion,' said Malcolm Edwards, 'if you got him off the betrayals with which his life was filled. But being with Keith was never relaxing, because you could always sense the volcano of rage, resentment and suspicion just beneath the surface. You were always walking on eggshells. When you were his friend, he would issue praise lavishly and embarrassingly; when he turned on you (always in letters, never in person), it was with an extraordinary mixture of bitterness and relish – his view of his fellow beings had been vindicated yet again.'

Despite his growing reputation, Jim still earned relatively little, and raising three children kept him permanently penurious. In need of a new car, he even tried to sell Moorcock his old Armstrong Siddeley, clapped out after its epic drives to the Mediterranean. He was in no position to turn down work. In 1966, he even wrote a story for the BBC children's programme *Jackanory*. Called 'Gulliver in Space', it was inspired by the same vision as his story 'The Drowned Giant', of a giant found dead by Lilliputians, who demolish the corpse – a memory of his days as an anatomist.

Moorcock proposed that Jim take over as editor of *Impulse*. On paper it seemed a dream deal. Not only would he appreciate the income: with his experience on *Chemistry and Industry*, he could handle both production and content, and relieve pressure on the aggrieved Roberts as well. Moorcock invited both men to Ladbroke Grove for a meeting.

It was not an auspicious time. Jim was still drinking heavily. Already thin-skinned, he could too easily be goaded into losing his temper. A confrontation with mild-mannered poet Peter Redgrove began as a literary disagreement but accelerated out of control – in some versions of the story into a fist fight, in others to a shouting match, but in neither case typical of the usually equable Jim.

All the same, Moorcock had high hopes. 'I thought I could just introduce them, and then they could just go off together and edit the magazine. But it didn't work out that way.'

> Jimmy began by saying, 'We must do something about the covers.' He seemed oblivious to the fact that Roberts was already a fairly accomplished commercial artist who'd greatly improved the look of the magazine. He didn't think the covers were sufficiently 'artistic', by which he meant surrealist.
>
> Keith said defensively, 'Well, I did do a few covers that were more or less surrealist', but they weren't really; just the usual thing you see in science-fiction magazines.
>
> They were both getting more and more angry. As they did, each began to bounce a foot up and down in agitation. With the amount of action they generated, they could have pressed enough grapes to make wine for half of London. Finally Jimmy refused to talk to Keith at all. He'd look at me and say, 'Tell him . . . ', and Keith would say 'Make him understand . . .' I'm trying to pretend we're having a conversation, when really it's Palestine and Israel. And Jimmy was at his worst, raving, really raving, saying, 'If this bloody idiot can't get his act together, there's no point', and Keith saying, 'Well, the best

thing would be for me to resign', and Jimmy replying, 'Just what exactly would you resign from?'

Afterwards, Jimmy rang me and said 'I can't work with these people', but I already knew that. Among other things, he had said during the meeting that, if he did take over the magazine, he would want it to run only stories that were like his. At least it was honest, but I couldn't imagine a magazine lasting long that just had imitation Ballard stories in it.

With the November 1966 issue, Harry Harrison became editor, but he was even less temperamentally suited than Bonfiglioli for the job, and, after four more numbers, *Impulse* expired.

Though *New Worlds* published five of his stories during 1966, Jim disliked many of the writers with whom he shared the pages. He also disapproved of the covers of Langdon Jones and the interior drawings of Jim Cawthorn, two of Moorcock's closest friends. Jones and Cawthorn returned Jim's dislike with interest. For the cover of the January 1967 issue, featuring Jim's 'The Day of Forever', Jones borrowed an ormolu clock and photographed it amidst jungle greenery, in a burlesque of surrealism. The same issue carried a lampoon by Cawthorn, 'Ballard of a Whaler', which captured the more mannered elements of his style. In its entirety, it read:

> Each morning Konrad would go down to the edge of the moraine and gaze across at the skinners stripping the blubber from the whales. Architectural rather than organic, the white bones of the stranded monsters traced the structural relationships of underlying strata with the world above the ice, counterpointing in their curved sequence the prismatic and crystalline complexity of the glaciers, embodying the forms of all sequential aspects of duration. Engrossed by their fundamental geomorphic resonance with the rib-cage of Ulrica Ulsenn, he did not immediately notice the towering figure of Urquart the whale hunter by his side. The harpooner's eyes were sombre and brooding, and when he spun his eighteen-foot lance end-over-end in

a characteristic gesture and drove it splinteringly into the ice, he betrayed by no flicker of a muscle that he had impaled his left foot.

In July 1967, Moorcock achieved his ambition when a new distributor and a grant from the Arts Council, negotiated by Brian Aldiss, helped him take *New Worlds* to the large size he'd always envisaged. A journalist suggested the magazine now belonged in a sisterhood of '*New*'s, alongside the *New Statesman*, *New Scientist* and *New Society*, with a remit to reflect the avant-garde in all its aspects, as *Evergreen Review* did in the US.

Moorcock spoke optimistically of 'that strange cross-fertilisation between the new SF writers, beat and pulp literature, poetry, music, French cinema and pop art painting [that] is becoming identified as some sort of rough and ready movement. Voices of common experience.'

Ballard's belligerence towards *New Worlds* and Moorcock marked the beginning of a new stage in his career, one that would see him, as often in the past, drawing away from a mentor and making new alliances. Increasingly, he saw himself as the heir of Freud and the surrealists, while Moorcock was still, in his eyes, a somewhat naive 'fan'. In 1996, he recalled testily that the Moorcock he knew in the sixties wasn't particularly interested in science fiction, and knew almost nothing about modernism. *New Worlds* art editor Chris Finch recalls 'JGB's idea of modern art seemed to be limited to Dali, Delvaux and Warhol.

He'd begun to spend time in London galleries, acquainting himself with artists like Eduardo Paolozzi, Lucian Freud and Francis Bacon. Jim claimed Paolozzi sought him out, but Moorcock insists he introduced them. References to contemporary art began to appear in Jim's work. In *The Atrocity Exhibition*, he mentions the American sculptors George Segal, creator of life-sized human figures in white plaster, and Ed Kienholz, whose 'environments' often used human dummies arranged in settings redolent of violence and disaster. As these artists were figurative, and preoccupied with the same themes of eroticism and dreams as the surrealists, Jim could see a clear progression.

It led him to make extravagant claims on their behalf, particularly for Paolozzi, of whom he wrote that, were the entire creations of the twentieth century to vanish, its culture could be recreated simply by reference to his work. Jim visualised Paolozzi becoming design editor of the revamped *New Worlds*, and was scornful when, for the first cover in the large format, Moorcock chose *Relativity*, by Dutch artist M. C. Escher. Jim's new friends detested Escher's optical-puzzle pictures of hands drawing themselves and staircases entwined in topologically impossible configurations. 'Jimmy was a bully,' Moorcock told Pedro Marques.

> He had absolutely no input into the magazine (and sulked about it!). We resisted him (much as we were close friends) as well as the 'underground' artists. I came out of commercial publishing and wanted covers that were good and which stood out on the news-stand. In my view he wanted 2nd-rate surrealists. I remember an argument with Jimmy who wanted me to run Dalí and I didn't want to run Dalí etc, because I thought them over-used by that time. I think it was generational. The surrealists meant more to Jimmy but I felt they'd been on the covers of every American magazine since the 1930s. That ten years difference gave us different tastes.

The widening gap between Moorcock and Ballard drew Jim into the circle of Martin Bax and his quarterly magazine *Ambit.* Bax, a physician specialising in child development, but with an interest in art and music, started *Ambit* in 1959, while still at medical school. Intrigued by *The Drowned World*, he tracked down Jim in Shepperton shortly after its publication. They were soon friends.

Bax ran the magazine from his home in Highgate, near Hampstead, a district which Jim, despite his detestation of novels from that suburb, found more congenial than rowdy Ladbroke Grove. The whole enterprise had an air of well-bred dilettantism. There were no editorial conferences. Bax met with each contributor individually, usually in a café. Among them was Paolozzi, who became a consulting editor. The spring 1965 issue included 'The Drained Lake', an extract from *The Drought*, illustrated by Paolozzi.

Jim liked *Ambit*'s photography and art, both modestly avant-garde, reflecting trends in the galleries of Cork Street. He was less enthusiastic about its poetry and prose, and later confessed to the poet Jeremy Reed that all British poetry, from Philip Larkin to Ted Hughes, seemed to him bogged down in the past. Once he agreed to become prose editor, it was with the avowed intention of squeezing out such material. His method, as he'd warned Moorcock when discussing *Impulse*, was to include as much of his own work as possible. Between 1965 and 1988, he was *Ambit*'s most prolific contributor, with a total of forty-one items, including extracts from novels, short stories, concrete poetry, and a continuing series of text fragments and enigmatic graphics called 'The Invisible Years'.

Few other writers satisfied his standards. One who did was eighteen-year-old Michael Butterworth, who'd sold some stories to *New Worlds*. 'I was *Ambit*'s Manchester and Salford distributor for quite a few years,' he said:

> until I got fed up tramping round, and I knew Jim was the Prose Editor, and I sent some pieces to him. I'd met him at least once, at one of the *New Worlds* parties, where he had urged me just to be 'more prolific'. He responded very positively to my work. A correspondence began, and he took the time to edit some of the longer pieces I had sent him. He was generally very kind to me, showing how Burroughs 'subbed down' his work from much longer pieces. He went through my manuscripts with a pen, underlining the sentences he thought 'worked'. No one of his competence had taken this time with me before.

Jim's advice to Butterworth emphasises his growing disillusion with conventional narrative. 'What people read nowadays is advertising,' he told Martin Bax, 'so if you want to have novels that people read, you should publish them as advertisements.' To Jannick Storm, he described advertising as a kind of unknown continent, a conceptual America that the inventive artist could populate with ideas. Some of his stories, he said, could just as well be presented as advertisements, the visual material carrying the burden of narrative, with the text in counterpoint. These could be condensed into single pages, then published in magazines, or even displayed on billboards, bringing his ideas to the widest readership. Not entirely seriously, he applied to the Arts Council for £1,000 to fund such a plan but was turned down. The idea germinated, however. Between 1967 and 1971, he produced five such full-page *Advertiser's Announcements*, which appeared in *Ambit*, *New Worlds*, *Ark* and some continental magazines.

The *Announcements* were 'Homage to Claire Churchill' (*Ambit*, issue No. 32, Summer 1967), 'Does the Angle Between Two Walls Have a Happy Ending?' (*Ambit*, issue No. 33, Autumn 1967), 'A Neural Interval' (*Ambit*, issue No. 36, Summer 1968), 'Placental Insufficiency' (*Ambit*, issue No. 45, Autumn 1970) and 'Venus Smiles' (Ambit, issue No. 46, Winter 1970–71). Most also appeared, gratis, in *New Worlds*. 'Does the Angle Between Two Walls Have a Happy Ending?', the most distinctive of the series, uses a still from *Alone*, a 1964 short film by Steve Dwoskin, showing a nude girl clutching her crotch. Otherwise, Jim employed his own snapshots, or mediocre library photographs. Although, with hindsight, these puzzling pages foreshadowed the next stage of pop art, most readers of the time raised their eyebrows and ignored them. The text just added to their confusion. Only the added credit 'A J. G. BALLARD PRODUCTION' hinted that the pages should be read as literature.

The experiment required that Jim do all the work himself, from finding the illustrations and writing the text to supervising the creation of a block or litho plate, delivering it to the publisher and paying the going commercial rate for the space. At this point, the scheme fell down. Jim had hoped to achieve the quality of the ads he'd helped create for PLJ, and to place them in *Vogue*, *Paris Match* or *Newsweek*. He said that the cost alone prevented him from doing so, but while the copy and concept show promise, his ineptitude in art ensured that no serious magazine would have accepted them.

'Homage to Claire Churchill' celebrated the appearance in Jim's life of a new companion. Churchill was an editor and picture researcher. She'd married at eighteen in 1959, immediately borne a daughter, Jenny, then left her husband, Mike Walsh, and moved into a flat in Goldhawk Road, Shepherd's Bush, which she occupied for the rest of her life, and where Jim was destined to die. She met Moorcock through the Campaign for Nuclear Disarmament, and they had a brief affair, but he sensed that, in temperament but also socially, she was more Jim's type. Not only did she possess the accent and air of good breeding that had distinguished Mary; she was attracted to powerful, even overbearing men. Late in 1966, he brought them together at Ladbroke Grove.

'I knew it was a blind date,' Walsh said, 'but Jimmy didn't.' As always, Jim wasted little time in courtship, but he didn't need to. 'It was a real *coup de foudre*,' says Walsh. 'We were so excited by each other. For a long time in Shepperton, he didn't like it if I left the room even.'

For issue No. 37, Bax handed *Ambit* to Jim, who used it to again celebrate his new girlfriend. He called it 'J. G. Ballard's Court Circular'. (The Court Circular is the notice inserted in daily papers such as *The Times*, announcing what the royal family is doing that day.) The tabloid-format publication rounded up a number of items, including 'A Poem for Claire Churchill', a 'concrete' poem consisting of words such as 'Girl', 'Fuck', 'Suck' and 'Wife' printed repeatedly in vertical columns, and a series of drawings by performance artist and painter Bruce McLean showing a woman, nude except for black stockings, squirming in the passenger seat of an automobile.

Claire became part of Jim's life. He spent at least one night a week in her apartment. They went on holiday together. Jenny became a *de facto* member of his family, to the extent that, in maturity, she described herself as 'the forgotten Ballard daughter'. Though Claire was, in effect, Jim's second wife, Jim kept their relationship tentative. 'Jimmy did occasionally discuss marriage,' says Moorcock, 'getting a new house together, etc., but backed off afterwards.' For forty years, he always referred to Walsh, anachronistically, as his 'girlfriend' and when he died, his will, though munificent to his daughters, left her only a quarter of the sum bequeathed to Bea and Fay.

CHAPTER TWENTY-NINE

FRAGMENTS

Between *The Crystal World* in April 1966 and *Crash* in June 1973, Jim published nothing recognisable as a novel. Rather, he insisted that the realist novel had exhausted itself. Evidence was easily found. The 1966 Nobel Prize for Literature went to the obscure Shmuel Yosef Agnon and Nelly Sachs, and the Pulitzer for fiction to the middle-brow Katherine Anne Porter. Meanwhile, *Star Trek* arrived, Timothy Leary urged the world to 'Tune in, turn on and drop out', The Beatles went to Nepal to meditate with the Maharishi and the Vietnam War continued to escalate. Current events and popular culture were in the ascendant, driven by the forced draught of TV. Reflecting this, the year's bestsellers were not novels but Truman Capote's *In Cold Blood* and Mark Lane's deconstruction of the Warren Report, *Rush to Judgment.*

In 1966, both *New Worlds* and *Ambit* printed 'You: Coma: Marilyn Monroe'. In it, Jim further loosened his ties to conventional narrative. Insofar as it has a story, it concerns a man named Tallis who shares a beachside apartment in a deserted resort with a woman, Karen Novotny, whom he's picked up at a local planetarium. A psychiatrist, Dr Nathan, flies in by helicopter, apparently to see him, but Tallis can't understand what he says over the noise of the engine, so Dr Nathan departs. Shortly after, Tallis kills Novotny. Another woman, Coma, arrives, and she and Tallis leave together.

Ballard fragments the action into a series of brief episodes, each with an enigmatic subtitle. The jolting transitions and arbitrary name changes within these 'condensed novels' make more sense once one knows, as Jim confessed to Charles Platt, that most were 'written with half a bottle of Johnny Walker Red' inside him.

Like the Zapruder film, the sketches preserved the structure of an event but, by cutting it up, rescued it from what Jim saw as the curse of narrative. *La Jetée*, Chris Marker's 1962 short film, or, more correctly *photo-roman* – 'photo novel' – as it's described in the credits, also had its first screening in the UK in 1966. Its structure of sequences made up of groups of still photographs, with only one instant where an image moves, prefigured Zapruder and resonated with Jim's emerging vision of narrative as a succession of discrete fractions of time, each in itself complete. David Hockney, a sometime *Ambit* contributor, would adapt the idea by creating collages of a landscape from hundreds of Polaroids.

If readers of his stories wanted a rationale, Jim suggested, they might think of these pieces as the disturbed fantasies of one man, variously called Tallis, Travers, Talbert and other variations on 'B. Traven', as he undergoes psychiatric treatment for a crime, perhaps the murder of a wife or lover. But he preferred that readers grazed and browsed – proffering the suggestion that they simply turn the pages until a paragraph caught their eye. The method reflected his advertising background, as well as Burroughs's cut-ups and the Dadaist poetry created by picking words from a hat. It also echoed the way a man leafed through *Penthouse* or *Playboy*, selecting a titillating image, then consulting the caption for some detail to bulk out a personal fantasy. As Kingsley Amis explained in one of his sharpest social satires, even as innocent a phrase as 'Girl, 20' could aphrodisiacally ignite the imagination of the middle-aged male – an entire fantasy in a phrase, just as Ballard envisaged.

The fourth 'condensed novel', and the one that would give the collection its title, *The Atrocity Exhibition*, ran in *New Worlds* for September. Doctor Nathan reappears from 'You: Coma: Marilyn Monroe'. The disturbed protagonist is now called Travis and the woman Catherine Austin. Travis is treating – or perhaps only imagines he's treating – a bomber pilot called Webster, whose presence reminds him of the bombing of Hiroshima and Nagasaki, the tests on Eniwetok, and premonitions of nuclear war, elements first explored in 'The Terminal Beach'. As Travis moves around the hospital, of which he may or may not be in charge, we see it through his eyes as through a cracked lens, each segment separated from its neighbour by a line of disjunction that echoes Jim's visual preoccupation – the angle between two walls – as well as his vision of the human mind as an exhibition space hung with private fantasies and horrors.

Celebrities have walk-ons; Lyndon Johnson, Jeanne Moreau, Freud, Garbo, Monroe and, repeatedly, Elizabeth Taylor. Between 1961 and 1964, Taylor was in the news as first Rouben Mamoulian, then Joseph L. Mankiewicz, attempted, initially in London, then in Rome, to complete the film *Cleopatra.* In March 1961, Taylor collapsed from viral pneumonia similar to the type that had killed Mary, but was saved by a tracheotomy. Had Mary become ill in London and not Alicante, she need never have died. In an oblique reference to Taylor's wounded throat and the cut that enabled her to breathe, *The Atrocity Exhibition* imagines the dying actress gasping for breath through gill slits in her throat.

Early in 1964, the report of the Warren Commission concluded that Lee Harvey Oswald alone killed John F. Kennedy. By then, Jim had at least dipped into some examples of the French *nouvelle roman*, and detected a resemblance to the meticulous descriptions of Deeley Plaza and the Texas Book Depository. The Warren Report's analysis of geometric relationships between cardboard boxes in the Depository was, he decided, as lapidary as anything in the novels of Alain Robbe-Grillet and Claude Mauriac. Its compilers even divided the Report into chapters, with titles straight out of a thriller: 'The Subsequent Bullet That Hit', 'The Curtain Rod Story', 'The Long and Bulky Package'.

He pondered how to incorporate this perception into fiction. 'Faction' such as *In Cold Blood* remained, essentially, reportage. Jim wanted something more imaginative, more mythic. He found it in 1965, when new translations appeared of the late nineteenth-century absurdist and precursor of surrealism, Alfred Jarry, author of *Ubu Roi*. Jim's attention was caught by Jarry's 'The Passion Considered as an Uphill Bicycle Race', published in 1907, which describes the crucifixion in the terms of a journalist writing it up for a sports paper. Applying this method to the 'sacred' events and 'sanctified' individuals of our time, Jim wrote 'The Assassination of John Fitzgerald Kennedy Considered as a Downhill Motor Race'. Oswald replaced Pilate as the starter, and Kennedy, not Christ, was first off the grid. Readers who knew the original saw a literary joke with a sting in its tail. To many others, it appeared a monstrous piece of bad taste.

Jim didn't initially write 'The Assassination of John Fitzgerald Kennedy' for a magazine but in response to a call from American writer Harlan Ellison for contributions to *Dangerous Visions*, an anthology of stories too controversial for traditional markets. Ballard asked Scott Meredith to submit the piece, but the agency, fearing for his reputation, failed to do so. By then, he'd sent Ellison another story, 'The Recognition'. Meanwhile, *Ambit* featured 'The Assassination of John Fitzgerald Kennedy' in its Autumn 1966 issue. Moorcock also ran it the following March, the same month in which *Ambit* published another in the same series, the even more provocative 'Plan for the Assassination of Jacqueline Kennedy'. Randolph Churchill, son of Winston and a former MP, protested, claiming these stories might impair the 'special relationship' between Britain and the US, and demanding, unsuccessfully, that the Arts Council withdraw *Ambit*'s grant.

In a letter to an Italian fan, Riccardo Valla, Jim claimed that these five non-linear stories represented a whole new form of narrative, reflecting modern life by showing events out of their normal time sequence. He was less grandiloquent in Britain, though he did try to persuade Cape to produce *The Atrocity Exhibition* in quarto size, illustrated with his own collages, assembled from medical textbooks and car crash records, and reflecting his belief that human anatomy and psychology were intimately entwined. When they refused, Jim grumbled that their idea of illustration ended with a few line drawings by tame figurative artists such as Feliks Topolski or Robin Jacques. Doubleday, slightly more receptive, agreed to commission some illustrations from *Ambit*'s art director Michael Foreman.

In March, as 'The Assassination of John Fitzgerald Kennedy' appeared in *New Worlds*, in its last pocketbook edition before switching to the large format, the left-wing monthly *Encounter* published the title fiction of *The Atrocity Exhibition*: Jim had resold it without mentioning its earlier appearance in *New Worlds*. Disch in particular was angry on Moorcock's behalf, and protested this breach of both ethics and copyright to *Encounter*'s co-editor, Frank Kermode. Those who knew Jim, including Moorcock, shrugged it off. Years of scraping by on Carnell's rates had made him inventively frugal. He often did side deals with foreign publishers, warning, 'No need to tell my agent about this.' He was even more devious at home, as Charles Platt discovered. 'One time I visited Jimmy after having been away in the United States for a while, and I asked him what he had been working on. "The greatest piece of fiction that I will attempt this year," he said, sounding very serious. I asked him what it was. "My tax return," he said. And when I laughed, he followed up, as he so often did, by saying, "I'm serious!"' Moorcock knew the truth of this better than most. During his days as a struggling writer, he had taken work where he could. The magazine *Bible Story Weekly* commissioned him to write a series of well-paid articles about the great cathedrals of Britain, which he researched without leaving his desk. A few months later, Jim told him proudly that, since only three of the articles carried Moorcock's byline, he'd claimed authorship of the others on his tax return, and listed deductions for travel to each location.

As Jim was busy extricating himself from narrative, he received an invitation to wade back in at the shallow end. Producer Aida Young of Hammer, the British film studio specialising in horror and fantasy, asked him to dream up a sequel to its biggest recent hit, *One Million*

Years BC. Don Chaffey's film, a remake of a 1940 Hollywood movie, relied on the sex appeal of Raquel Welch in a suede bikini, and her love affair with husky John Richardson, an interloper from another tribe. Young had read *The Drowned World*, or at least read about it, and decided the giant iguanas and jungle setting conformed to Hammer's hopes for its successor. Essentially, they wanted the same story, only different. Jim wrote a treatment called *When Dinosaurs Ruled the Earth*, from which director Val Guest, a hardened pro, scrubbed anything that didn't replicate the original. In Jim's version, there was no dialogue – 'just a lot of grunts' – but Guest gave the cast a twenty-seven-word 'caveman language', supposedly drawn from Phoenician, Latin and Sanskrit.

The 1968 *Playboy* Playmate of the Year Victoria Vetri replaced Raquel, but the rest of the story, showing prehistoric lovers in leather loincloths evading dinosaurs, changed little. An opening of Busby Berkeley oddity is the film's lone sign of originality. Along the skyline of a towering cliff – exteriors were filmed in the Canary Islands – the Rock Tribe awaits the sunrise. Three pretty but apprehensive blondes are poised on the cliff edge. Men wearing crocodile masks stand behind them, swinging slings filled with stones. A dozen more bang rhythmically with femurs on human skulls. As the sun rises, the blondes will be brained as sacrifices and their bodies flung into the sea. Fortuitously, a portion of the sun tears loose and, in the course of the film, turns into our moon. One would like to think Jim had something to do with this gaudy curtain-raiser, but he always avoided discussing the film. Val Guest received full screenplay credit, 'from a treatment by J. B. [sic] Ballard'. 'They speak high-mindedly about character motivation, psychology, symbolism and so on,' Jim said, 'but, when it comes down to it, it's about one cave man hitting another cave man on the head with a club.'

Publishers aspire to turn writers into product. Their ideal is the author about whom it's unnecessary to say anything, the approach Gollancz adopted when it issued Kingsley Amis's novels with nothing on the dust-wrapper except 'The New Kingsley Amis'. Though *The Atrocity Exhibition* sold poorly, it marked Ballard's emergence as a brand. One could buy his latest book as one could Robbe-Grillet or Burroughs, without knowing or caring what it was about, confident that it embodied an inventive theme and a disregard for form. Reviewing *Rushing to Paradise*, William Boyd said 'Ballard fans know that the conventional ingredients of the conventional realistic novel – story, character, verisimilitude, plausibility – are not of prime importance. These elements function as a kind of mulch upon which the epiphanic Ballardian moments and metaphors may flourish and grow.'

Jim assumed proprietorship not only of his own work but of the influences that inspired it. He alone could decree what belonged in 'inner space'. Subsumed under the umbrella term, the apocalyptic vision of H. G. Wells flowed into the surrealism of Salvador Dalí and Giorgio de Chirico, merging with the eroticism of Georges Bataille and the industrial design of Raymond Loewy to create that vision of the near future that the Collins Dictionary would christen 'Ballardian' – 'resembling or suggestive of the conditions described in Ballard's novels and stories, esp. dystopian modernity, bleak man-made landscapes and the psychological effects of technological, social or environmental developments'.

Such was Jim's gravitas, his obvious intelligence and sincerity, that he could create a children's fantasy for *Jackanory*, invent the plot for a dinosaur movie, contribute to *Playboy*, experiment with LSD and enter the controversy over the banning of Nabokov's *Lolita*, all without impairing his authority. Had he once stepped out of character – succumbed to self-importance like Brunner, or agreed to join those second-string celebrities who endorsed mints, credit cards and wallpaper ('Very J. G. Ballard. Very Sanderson') – his credibility might have been lost. But his seriousness, not to mention his indifference to creature comfort, came to his rescue. He was Teflon. Triviality wouldn't stick.

Like André Breton for the surrealists, Jim defended his franchise from upstart imitators. In 1969, *The Unfortunates*, a novel by young

British writer B. S. Johnson, appeared as a box containing twenty-seven booklets which, aside from the first and last, could be read in any order. Samuel Beckett called Johnson 'most gifted', and Anthony Burgess wrote, 'He's the only living British author with the guts to reassess the novel form, extend its scope, and still work in a recognisable fictional tradition', but Jim dismissed the novel as gimmickry. His judgement was not dispassionate, since he disliked Johnson personally, and condemned him – incongruously, given his own history – for mistreating his wife. He was no less sharp with the *New Worlds* writers, some of whom didn't take dismissal lying down. In 1968, Langdon Jones edited *The New S.F.*, an anthology in which Zoline, Sladek and others demonstrated they could employ numbered paragraphs, typographical oddity and disjunctive narratives just as expertly as he. Jim didn't contribute, except for a transcribed conversation with the poet George MacBeth, but the ease with which younger writers adapted his style would not have been lost on him. Another change in direction was overdue.

CHAPTER THIRTY

BAD TRIP

On 24 April 1967, Soviet astronaut Vladimir Komarov died when the parachute of *Soyuz 1* failed to open. His death, plus the incentive of $1 a word, persuaded Jim to return to the format of the Well-Made Story. 'The Dead Astronaut' appeared in *Playboy* the following May. The magazine had published 'The Drowned Giant' as 'Souvenir' in 1965, and in 1966 accepted, and paid for, 'The Rumour', only to spike it, probably out of belated religious scruples. (It appeared ten years later in *Ambit* as 'The Life and Death of God'.) 'The Dead Astronaut' describes a future Cape Canaveral in almost Gothic terms, as a junkyard of rusting gantries, haunted by souvenir hunters who scavenge for the remains of spacecraft, including the mummified corpses of astronauts, marooned in space and left to die.

The sale inaugurated a disorienting year for Jim. In June, feeling left out in the new culture of mind-altering compounds, he had his first and last experience of drugs when he ingested some LSD. It was by no means the drug of choice with most people. Burroughs, for instance, smoked hashish, and scorned acid, writing, 'Listen: Their Garden of Delights is a terminal sewer . . . Their Immortality Cosmic Consciousness and Love is second-run grade-B shit . . . flush their drug kicks down the drain – They are poisoning and monopolizing the hallucinogenic drugs – learn to make it without any chemical con.' Some people, including Tom Disch, contracted infections from polluted acid, or experienced bad trips. Above all, it was unwise to drop acid on top of alcohol, or, if a newcomer, without an experienced and unstoned guide. Nevertheless, Jim was insistent, so Moorcock gave in.

> I got him a sugar cube and I said to him 'Don't take it now' because he was as drunk as a skunk. And of course, being Jimmy, he took it immediately. [The effects were] appalling, psychotic – snakes all over the bed; everything bad about Shanghai, on top of everything bad about everything else.

Though *The Kindness of Women* fictionalised his LSD experience as transcendental, it was a nightmare, convincing Jim that drugs didn't alter states of mind but, rather, released memories properly kept locked in the Pandora's Box of the imagination. Under their influence, fears that crept out manageably in his dreams or in story form were briefly permitted to escape, uncontrolled, into daily experience, invading and overpowering his sensibility. It was a terrifying episode, and one he had no wish to repeat. Thereafter, he became cautious of any medication, even aspirin.

The ordeal did motivate him to offer a prize of £40 and publication in *Ambit* to the best piece of fiction or poetry written under the influence of drugs. On hearing this, Lord Goodman, chairman of the Arts Council, and a crony of Prime Minister Harold Wilson, threatened prosecution. This played right into the hands of Ballard and Bax, who explained that they were equally interested in the effects of legal drugs – tranquillisers, antihistamines, even baby aspirin. Novelist Ann Quin, who attracted some attention in 1965 by admitting to an illegal abortion, won with a story about the transformative effects of the oral contraceptive. This time, however, the Arts Council caved in to the controversy and withdrew the magazine's grant.

A willingness to oblige his admirers led Jim into some poor decisions, nowhere more than when he allowed Bill Butler, an American-born but Brighton-based poet, bookseller and amateur publisher, to produce a limited edition of the piece he called 'Why I Want to Fuck Ronald Reagan'. Why, most people asked, would anyone wish to have intercourse with the Republican governor of California? Physically, emotionally and intellectually, the one-time minor movie star was unappetising. He lacked even the aphrodisiac of power, since he hadn't yet entered national politics, and wouldn't do so until 1976, losing the presidential race to Gerald Ford. He didn't become President until 1981. Even then, people were incredulous that an actor, and a second-rate one at that, could be elected. Remembering the supporting roles in which he'd specialised, they joked, 'No, *John Wayne* for President. Ronald Reagan for Best Friend'.

In the sixties, however, movie personalities were sufficiently rare in politics for Reagan to intrigue Jim. Seeing beyond surface impressions, he sensed what insiders already knew; that Reagan was a turncoat. Originally the left-wing president of the Screen Actors' Guild, he'd reversed his position in the late forties to become a proselytising Republican. Watching him on TV, Jim noted how he used his skill as an actor to divert attention from his political message. Assuming a folksy, off-hand and smiling persona, he pushed his conservative agenda in a way that suggested he was saying the exact opposite. Given the later revelation that Reagan sometimes confused his own life with his movie roles, the observation was prescient.

Jim wrote 'Why I Want to Fuck Ronald Reagan' as a quasi-scientific report, another experiment, following the unsuccessful *Announcements*, in presenting a concept without recourse to narrative. Its portrait of Reagan is unsparingly grotesque, equivalent to a scatological eighteenth-century broadside. Taking his dishonest presentation to its logical conclusion, the 'report' suggests that psychopaths, asked to fantasise about Reagan, imagined him involved in acts of an anal-sadistic nature, while his lopsided grin betrayed homosexual tendencies.

Butler, who was gay, and regarded publishing Jim's text in part as a gesture of homosexual activism, assumed the small printing of only 250 copies would attract no attention. Ballard didn't offer the piece to either *Ambit* or *New Worlds*. It appeared only in *International Times* and *Ronald Reagan, The Magazine of Poetry*, a short-lived (two issues) magazine edited by Tom Disch, John Sladek and Pamela Zoline. That might have been the end of it had not police, visiting Butler's shop in search of drug-related material, found three copies of 'Reagan' in a sealed envelope addressed to Anne Graham-Bell, head of public relations for Penguin Books. These were seized, and in August 1968 Butler appeared before the Brighton Assizes, charged with offences under the Obscene Publications Act.

From the start, the case went badly. The three magistrates refused Butler's request for legal aid. Jim declined to testify. Mostly he was frightened, though he later claimed he withdrew at the suggestion of Butler's solicitor. Asked to explain how he would argue that 'Reagan' wasn't obscene, Jim replied that, in his opinion, it *was* obscene, and he'd written it in that spirit. 'Mr Ballard, you will make a very good witness for the prosecution,' snapped the lawyer. 'We will not be calling you.' In his place, George MacBeth argued, plausibly, that Ballard was 'concerned with American politics and society and the ways in which, as he sees it, the feelings of sexual desire and love can only be aroused by violence and violent stimuli. [It] shows the connection between the different kinds of violence, for example car crashes, Vietnam and racial violence.' Anne Graham-Bell testified that she'd offered, as a favour to Butler, to show copies of 'Reagan' to possible reviewers. Since review copies are traditionally free, she'd paid nothing for those in the envelope, so no sale had taken place.

Neither she nor MacBeth moved the magistrates, who agreed with Michael Worsley, prosecuting, that 'Reagan' was 'just the meanderings of a diseased and dirty mind'. The chairman announced how 'appalled my colleagues and I have been at the filth that has been produced at this Court, and at the fact that responsible people including members of the university faculty have come here to defend it. We hope that these remarks will be conveyed to the university authorities.' They fined Butler £419, plus his own costs – in total, about £3,000, mostly owed to his lawyers. Impugning the defence witnesses earned the magistrate a rap on the knuckles from the professional journal of the judiciary, but the fines stood. In an ironic footnote, in 1980, as Ronald

Reagan finally ran for President, some ingenious joker printed 'Why I Want to Fuck Ronald Reagan' on the stationery of the National Republican Congressional Committee, and distributed copies at the Republican Party Convention under the title 'Official Republican 1980 Presidential Survey'. Nobody took the slightest notice.

For a while after 'Reagan', Jim kept clear of topical material involving living celebrities. Part of this was caution following Butler's conviction, but he also lacked a theme. Late in 1969, Charles Platt took over editorship of *New Worlds* and asked Jim for a story. 'Apparently he spent a lot of time walking around Foyle's bookshop, looking for inspiration. He stumbled upon a plastic surgery handbook which gave him the memorable phrase, "In the experience of this surgeon, skin is never in short supply", which he transposed directly into his own text.'

That line isn't in this piece (though it appears in 'Coitus 80: A Description of the Sexual Act in 1980', published in *New Worlds* issue of January 1970), but in other respects 'Princess Margaret's Face Lift' uses the same flat medical terminology. Party-going, heavy-drinking Margaret was one of the sights of Swinging London, and Jim relished the chance to skewer her as he had Reagan. 'Face Lift' appeared in the March 1970 *New Worlds* and caused no particular furore. Moorcock, speaking at the Milford Writers Workshop in Milford, Pennsylvania, praised Ballard for 'drawing on his own medical education, his work as a scientific journalist, his relish for the rhythms and resonances of techno-prose'. Some years later, Jim repeated the exercise with 'Queen Elizabeth's Rhinoplasty', 'Mae West's Reduction Mammoplasty' and 'Jane Fonda's Augmentation Mammoplasty', all faux-scientific 'reports' about cosmetic surgery inflicted on women of power. These fictions merged with his *Advertiser's Announcements*, all of which show women, usually naked, in situations of weakness or submission.

A nude Claire Churchill features again in the last of them, 'Venus Smiles', also the title of a Vermilion Sands story. In July 1970, she and Ballard had gone to Phun City, a chaotic two-day rock concert taking place outside the seaside town of Worthing. Jim didn't attend for the music but because William Burroughs had been invited. When Jim arrived at the gate, the Hell's Angels retained as security told him 'Dad, you're in the wrong place'. According to Maxim Jakubowski, 'all the writers present were utterly bewildered as to why they should be there, and never made it to the stage, although the dj kept on saying through the sound system that all these fab groovy people were there'. (Some took this amiss. Paul Ableman, reviewing *Hello America* a few years later, recalled how 'an amplified voice kept bawling aggressively that we would shortly be addressed by "the greatest writer in the whole world, Jimmy Ballard"'.) Fleeing the music, Ballard and Churchill retreated to the beach, where she impulsively waded into the surf wearing only a light dress and Wellington boots. When these became waterlogged. Jim dragged her out. As she shivered, naked, in the passenger seat, her body blotched with pieces of seaweed, Jim snapped her picture, and used the photograph in 'Venus Smiles', crediting the source as 'Claire Zephyr V8 J. G. Ballard'.

The minor furore in Britain over 'Why I Want to Fuck Ronald Reagan' mirrored changing attitudes inside the publishing establishment. Editors had begun to bristle at the unconventional material arriving on their desks, some of it remote from the outlines that led them to commission it. Agents were equally resistant. Jim, trying to find a publisher for the *Atrocity Exhibition* pieces, complained to Jannick Storm in October 1968 that Scott Meredith had refused to handle them. Shortly after, he left to join the tiny London agency of John Wolfers.

Wolfers had been brought up in China, but any shared history mattered less to Jim than the fact that he paid special attention to foreign rights, and employed a junior agent, Maggie Hanbury, to deal with them. His style didn't suit every writer. When he died in 1998, his obituarist wrote: 'His passion was to help bring about the publication of books he thought important. If an author passed his exacting standards, there was nothing he would not do to help – he was insanely generous with his time, his home, his advice, his friendship – but if his sympathies (and it must be said his prejudices) were not engaged, he was as likely to tell a budding writer "to take your stinking fish elsewhere".'

According to Hanbury, Wolfers and Ballard met occasionally for lunch and attended a few publishers' cocktail parties, but neither wished for a more personal relationship. Wolfers had an immediate success when he sold the US rights to *The Atrocity Exhibition* to Doubleday. Its publishing director, Larry Ashmead, was a law unto himself within the company, and the controversial text would not have fazed him. Jonathan Cape remained dubious, however, and Doubleday scheduled publication for June 1970 without any British publisher in sight.

The difficulty in getting *The Atrocity Exhibition* published dramatises the fragility of Ballard's career before *Empire of the Sun*. Though well known within the counter-culture, he was regarded elsewhere as marginal. Except for a few *Playboy* sales, he never cracked the major US magazines. From mid-1968 to mid-1970, his output diminished to the occasional story in *New Worlds*. The sole book to appear in that period was Storm's Danish translation of *The Atrocity Exhibition* in October 1969. Talking to the press, Jim didn't hide his irritation at the obtuseness of publishers. Of *The Atrocity Exhibition*, he told the *Times Educational Supplement*,

> It's not a book that you would sit down and read as you would, say, a book by Kafka or Raymond Chandler. It needs a more fragmentary approach. With the narrative technique I use, I'm able to move rapidly from public events to the most intimate private events in the space of a few lines, almost a cinematic technique of rapid cutting. I can annex an enormous amount of material into it that I wouldn't be able to in a conventional narrative. Some people seem to be complaining that it isn't a nineteenth-century novel. Why the hell don't they go and live in the nineteenth century? I'm living in 1971.

Illustrating Robert Lowell's contention about Eliot's marriage, the presence of Claire arguably deprived his writing of urgency. He made no secret of his delight at having a willing sexual partner, particularly one with a 'posh' veneer. Just as he'd boasted of Mary's connection to Cecil Rhodes, so he encouraged Claire to retain her single name, with its distinguished associations. (After her break-up with Ballard, she reverted to her married name.)

Like Graham Greene, who boasted of having sex with his mistress behind the altars of numerous Italian churches, Jim enjoyed sex in unconventional locations. Less playful automobile impulses emerged when Jim was drunk.

Claire appeared at parties with facial bruises, usually hidden behind sunglasses, and it was no secret that they had terrible fights. Most people took it for a sign less of sadism than of his obsessive devotion and a concomitant jealousy directed at anyone who seemed to rival him for Claire's affections, or in whom she evinced an interest. Such conflicts between partners were not unusual, and people generally let them settle them privately. As Jim and Claire weren't married, they could always split up, which eventually they did.

Even within the counter-culture, however, Jim's preoccupation with Claire was regarded as disproportionate and sometimes irrational. Towards the conclusion of a well-lubricated London party, he confided to Charles Platt that he planned to stage a car crash, with Churchill as the 'star'. It would be an act of love, he explained, or, at least, of passion.

Placing his palms on her cheeks, he said, 'Look at this beautiful face. Can't you just imagine the shape of a radiator grille superimposed?'

As Platt was digesting this, Jim continued, 'I want you to be the driver. What kind of car should it be?'

Platt, whose father had been an automobile executive, named the most overtly erotic of Detroit's creations, the luxury convertible whose front bumper boasted the protuberant bosses known as 'Dagmars', after the breasts of a classic dumb blonde actress of 1950s TV.

'Cadillac Eldorado?'

'Yes, exactly!'

It was a flash of headlights from what would become *Crash*.

CHAPTER THIRTY-ONE

CHRIS

Anyone in the 1960s with the urge to paint, play or perform but lacking the talent didn't want for opportunities. Once the composer John Cage had defined music as 'anything I listen to when I choose to think of myself as a music listener', the last barriers fell. In 1952, his *4' 33"* demonstrated that even sitting silent and immobile at a piano could, when viewed in this spirit, be art. As warehouses and factories became galleries and the upstairs rooms of pubs turned into theatres, thwarted creators pressed forward, eager to express themselves in performance, installations and 'happenings'.

Ballard was among them. The new possibilities revived his schoolboy ambitions to be an artist. He experimented with collages, juxtaposing images of Churchill and illustrations from gun magazines. According to Fay Ballard, who became a professional painter, 'I remember when I was very tiny, Daddy making a couple of sculptures in the garden out of old milk bottles, cement, chicken wire. One was red and white. When I was very small, he had a go at using oil paint. He was fascinated by the technique of oil paint and always said he wished he could have been a painter, but he had no talent.' The backyard sculptures, stunted and abstract, with orifices that might have been gaping mouths or vaginas, confirmed this judgement.

With Churchill's help, Jim made new friends in the world of graphic art. One was Steve Dwoskin, who arrived from New York in the mid-1960s and, though disabled by polio, became a successful designer, lecturer and, eventually, film-maker. Claire commissioned artwork from Dwoskin for books she edited.

She was also instrumental in him meeting psychologist Christopher Evans, Chief Scientific Officer at the National Physical Laboratory at Teddington. Technically, the NPL established measurements and carried out tests for the government; Barnes Wallis had refined the Dambusters' bouncing bomb in the water tanks it used for tidal studies. Telegenic, ebullient and imaginative, Evans stretched the remit of the job almost to breaking point. He was frequently on TV and radio, explaining scientific advances or anticipating them. He conducted experiments in extra-sensory perception: his wife Nancy had worked with Joseph Rhine on his research into telepathy and other psi talents at Duke University. He investigated dreams, suggesting, controversially, that they performed the same function in our brains as the clearing of extraneous data from the memory of a computer. He helped programme a computer to write a science fiction novel. His book and associated TV series about computers, *The Mighty Micro*, appeared in 1979, poignantly coinciding with his death the same year, at forty-eight, of cancer.

Around 1967, Evans was trawling art schools for innovatively designed alphabets to use in a series of experiments in stroboscopic perception. According to David Pringle, 'Chris Evans visited Moorcock in Notting Hill. Charles Platt, Moorcock, and a couple of others went for a drink with Evans in one of the local pubs. After the meeting, when Evans had departed, they all chorused as one, "We must introduce him to Jimmy!" A meeting was engineered and, sure enough, Jimmy was smitten.'

Jim enjoyed the company of alpha males. Moorcock, Paolozzi and Evans were all physically large and powerful. He and Evans also complemented one another. Evans provided the scientific expertise he lacked, while Jim encouraged Evans to widen his horizons. At Jim's request, Evans began to send him each month what he called 'the contents of his waste basket': brochures, abstracts of scientific papers, announcements of new products – any technical literature that passed over his desk and that he didn't wish to keep. Though Jim understood only a fraction of it, he enjoyed sensing the texture of current technology, testing the precise temper of the cutting edge.

Jim came to regard Evans with affection and admiration. As 'Dick Sutherland', he's a character in *The Kindness of Women.* He also inspired aspects of car fetishist Robert Vaughan in *Crash.* Vaughan and the fictional Ballard indulge in some sweaty sodomy. There's no suggestion this ever took place. Nevertheless, long after his death, Jim still spoke of Evans with visible emotion.

Not everyone shared his enthusiasm. To some, Evans appeared just one more exponent of what TV critic Clive James labelled 'sci-bull': pop technology, closer to stage magic than science. Moorcock dismissed him as 'a false scientist: a pseudo-scientist, a charlatan' – judgements that infuriated Jim. While not blind to the showbiz aspect of Evans's character, he excused it as part of the job. In *The Kindness of Women*, Dick Sutherland is a victim of his popularity, forced into becoming a spokesman for popular psychology but itching to return to research. Like Evans, Sutherland transforms his image once he discovers the power of TV, trading in his leather jackets and gold medallions for tweed jackets and knitted ties. Again like Evans, Sutherland writes a bestseller; not about computers but sex. An American publisher funds him to compile a new version of Masters and Johnson's *Human Sexual Response*, using the latest miniaturised cameras to show arousal and orgasm from inside the body.

Jim was tolerant of his friend's success, but occasional references in the novels suggest that it rankled. Long after Evans's death, shady media personalities crop up, such as the Bracewells in *Rushing to Paradise*, who film the environmental activists in their battle with the French, or Sanger in *The Day of Creation*, who travels the hinterland of Africa, trying to foist tons of charitably contributed rice on people who have previously never eaten it, always making sure his efforts are recorded by his personal cinematographer.

The willing collaboration of Claire Churchill nourished Jim's fantasies about the sexuality of the car accident. Under their impetus, he wrote a short prose satire, called simply *Crash.* It appeared in the ICA's

'Eventsheet' in February 1969, and only later as a chapter of *The Atrocity Exhibition.* Jim called it the progenitor of the novel, but the connection is tenuous. Once again, it uses the 'report' formula. Subjects are asked to view films of automobile accidents and assess their degree of sexual arousal. Appearances are made by Jayne Mansfield, James Dean, Albert Camus and the Kennedys – all by now looking a little tired. Jim felt the same, since this fiction shows him modifying his style, returning to more conventional narrative. In the earliest condensed novels, the 'chapter headings' that broke up the text appeared random and unrelated. Beginning with 'Plan for the Assassination of Jacqueline Kennedy', he substituted phrases which, once connected, became coherent sentences. The return signals his impatience with the fragmented form. The later condensed novels have the blurred quality of a poem or piece of classical music transposed into pop – a whiter shade of alienation.

Already intrigued by Steve Dwoskin's disability, Jim was doubly impressed to find that they shared similar erotic inclinations. In a profile of Dwoskin, he commented on the chrome tubing of the film-maker's wheelchair, and announced that the director proposed to use Claire Churchill, nude, in his next film, but that she really deserved a movie all to herself. Dwoskin never made such a film, and probably never intended to, but Jim used a still from his *Alone* in the *Advertiser's Announcement* called 'Does the Angle Between Two Walls Have a Happy Ending?'. In the film, a girl, clearly bored, lounges on a bed, then masturbates, though 1963 restrictions forced Dwoskin to keep this ambiguous.

In 1968, Dwoskin made the short film *Me, Myself and I.* Like Andy Warhol's *Blue Movie,* aka *Fuck,* produced the following year, it set out to record the interaction of a man and woman forced into close proximity for a long period – in Dwoskin's case, confined for twenty-four hours in a bathroom. He recruited actor Neil Hornick and American dancer Barbara Gladstone, in whose Notting Hill flat the film was shot, and ordered them to improvise. They chatted, shared a bath and flirted, but, unlike Viva and Louis Waldron in the Warhol movie, refrained from having sex. In those pre-video days, Dwoskin used a clockwork Bolex 16mm camera that needed rewinding every twenty-seven seconds. After eight hours, running out of film and with nothing much taking place, he terminated the experiment.

Dwoskin screened his first compilation for Churchill. 'She must have told Ballard about it,' says Hornick, 'because he asked to see this unedited footage too. Having done so, he requested some stills.' Seventeen of these photographs became the basis of 'The Bathroom: A Film In Pictures by Steve Dwoskin. Text by J. G. Ballard'. It appeared in the July/August 1968 issue of *The Running Man*, the short-lived (three issues) magazine of theatre producer/director Charles Marowitz. In Jim's facetious captions, Hornick became 'Roger, a young British actor' and Gladstone 'Louise, an American medical student'. Jim joked about Hornick's restraint in the face of Gladstone's heavy breasted sexuality – a fine example, he suggested, of the Dunkirk spirit that moved the British to endure but never surrender.

In 1968, the Institute of Contemporary Arts moved to new premises on The Mall. Jim had become friendly with its director, Michael Kustow, who invited him to its events, including a private show of pornographic short films. As part of the same liberalism, singer and surrealist George Melly was invited to lecture at the Institute on 'Sexual Imagery in the Blues'. As he began, a fellow musician in the audience asked politely if it was permissible to wank during the presentation.

Seizing the opportunity provided by this new openness, not to mention the ICA's extra space and his enhanced access to Kustow, Ballard, Paolozzi and Evans proposed a performance piece called *Crash*. It would trace the significance of the automobile in a young man's life, from buying his first car to his death in a crash, and his subsequent elevation to the status of a secular saint, a mythic sacrifice to the freeway. The set would include a real wrecked car. Paolozzi offered to create his version of the dummies used in simulated crashes, and Jim to write a commentary, which Evans would narrate.

Again showing his flair for promotion, Jim leaked details to the sensation-seeking *Sunday Mirror.* The resulting report by June Rose, headlined 'If Christ Came Again, He Would Be Killed in a Car Crash', appeared on 19 May 1968. It promised that 'all the horror and realism of an actual road smash will be played out in front of the audience':

> The young driver, in blood-covered track suit, will lie beside the mangled car. His girl friend will kneel beside him, caressing him. Dummies will mouth words about the beautiful and desirable features of the motor car. Behind them, film of cars crashing will make up the stark and terrible accompaniment.

She quotes Ballard as saying:

> Crash victims like Jayne Mansfield, James Dean, Aly Khan, Jim Clark and President Kennedy (the first man to be murdered in a motorcade) act out the Crucifixion for us. Their deaths heighten our vitality in a blinding flash. The death of Kennedy was a sacrificial murder, connived at by the millions of people who watched it endlessly recapitulated on television. If Christ came again, he would be killed in a car crash.

Crash, the play, never happened. Before it developed beyond a concept, another group offered the ICA a different Ballard-based event, an adaptation of his 1966 story 'The Assassination Weapon', subtitled 'A Transmedia Search for Reality'. It had already previewed at the Arts Laboratory, the venue in Drury Lane run by maverick promoter Jim Haynes. The creator, Stewart McKenzie, assembled the piece with The Human Family, a collective of acting and design students for whom the Arts Laboratory had become a showcase. The show took Jim's text from 'The Assassination Weapon', says McKenzie:

> with early analog electronic distortion and music, and played this back in surround stereo around a vertical circular screen, about ten feet in diameter, which revolved slowly at the centre of circles of concentric

> seats separated by access corridors at the four cardinal points. Once the audience was seated, the recording of 'The Assassination Weapon' was played back and four projection tables shooting down the access corridors combined images on the revolving screen which could take front and back projection. The projection tables had a variety of image and light emitting paraphernalia, still and movie projectors, boiling liquids, rotating colour filters, strobes, smoke machines, etc.

Punch theatre writer Jeremy Kingston evoked the experience. 'In the centre of the room a large white disc slowly rotates,' he wrote:

> Projectors in the four corners flash images on to this double screen while a voice sonorously reads passages by the ex-science-fiction writer J. G. Ballard. The superimposed photographs, surrealist paintings, charts and mandalas, coupled with Ballard's dense distressed sentences, have the texture of an unhappy dream. A Max Ernst worldscape of mighty fragments – flyovers, deserts, dark reservoirs, radio-telescopes – following the private logic of an hallucinating mind. Puzzling, frequently powerful, devised and invented with ingenuity and skill.

'We put on a demo at the ICA,' says McKenzie, 'and Ballard came to see it. He loved it and invited me to join him in a video about the sexuality of car crashes which, I confess, sounded unappealing.' The ICA dropped the project, which Jim would revive, controversially, in the *Crashed Cars* exhibition of 1970. In any event, he had plenty to occupy himself, since David Frost and Hazel Adair had bought the film rights to *The Drought*. Ballard showed them the script he'd written in 1965, but Adair, a veteran of TV soaps such as *Crossroads* and *Compact*, wanted something more down to earth. Frost retained the property but never made the film. Ballard complained that later potential producers were scared off by the high price demanded by Frost for the rights.

CHAPTER THIRTY-TWO

FLYING DOWN TO RIO

In Britain, the literary establishment continued to scorn SF. Newspapers reviewed SF books in bunches, with each title lucky to get a paragraph. In all his years at Jonathan Cape, grumbled Jim, he invariably received a congratulatory call from his editor when a book was published, but no communication of any kind from the publicity department.

Thus handicapped, writers relied on their fan base. Attending conventions and conferences, appearing at signings, supporting limited print-run 'collectors' editions' and simply replying to fan letters were tools of survival. Few writers used these skills more actively than Jim, particularly in forging connections with admirers in other countries. Since he never sold well in the US, he needed readers in continental Europe and Scandinavia. Robert Louit in France and Jannick Storm in Denmark not only translated his books but interviewed him for magazines and sometimes agented his work.

He spoke more frankly to these men than he ever did to British fans. In 1969, Storm mentioned a plan to raise money for Damon Knight's Science Fiction Writers of America by publishing a collection of autobiographical profiles. Jim scorned the idea. The great majority of British and American SF writers were totally uninteresting, he told him, and had no original ideas. He would refuse to contribute to such an anthology, and had nothing but contempt for the SFWA, which he found backward and unimaginative.

He was equally direct with Riccardo Valla. In 1967, Valla sent a list of his stories that had been translated into Italian. Jim, with his customary attention to the black ink, noted he hadn't been paid for some of them, then complained that only one example of his experimental work of the previous two years had appeared in Italy, and that this, 'The Assassination Weapon', was greeted with complete indifference. After dismissing the work of writers such as Isaac Asimov and A. E. Van Vogt, who were popular in Italy, he revealed he was working on a book about the conceptual auto-disaster – something which Italians, in his opinion Europe's most dangerous drivers, would, he suggested, appreciate.

In March 1969, Jim made a rare trip outside Europe when he visited Rio de Janeiro for an International Symposium on Science-fiction in Literature and the Cinema, part of the Second Rio de Janeiro Film Festival. The organisers, supported by a generous government grant, flew in dozens of writers and film-makers, including Brunner, Ballard, Harrison and Aldiss from the UK and a larger contingent from the US, led by Robert Heinlein, but also including Harlan Ellison. When Jim took Ellison to task for refusing to use 'The Assassination of John Fitzgerald Kennedy' in *Dangerous Visions*, he denied having received it. The duplicity of Scott Meredith confirmed to Jim the rightness of his decision to join John Wolfers.

The Rio trip features in *The Kindness of Women*, but Jim doesn't distinguish invented details from the real. Some of the latter were stranger than fantasy; for example, the mercurial but diminutive Ellison using a few moments in a lift to show Jim how to kill a man in three seconds with his bare hands. In the novel, Jim goes to Rio in the company of Dick Sutherland, who's there to report on a retrospective of science documentaries. They meet a decrepit Fritz Lang and the cast of *Star Trek*, whom Jim compares to a group of greying morticians. In real life, Evans didn't attend, and, while Lang was there, the actors of *Star Trek* were not. Moreover, the series debuted only in 1966, meaning its stars would still have been spry in 1969.

Ballard and Sutherland pick up two whores, who take them to the apartment where they pursue their day job, performing in porn movies. Women and children are working there, cobbling together festival souvenirs. The prostitutes are ready to service both men with the workers looking on, but Jim bribes them to step into the corridor. He then has sex with one woman on the semen-stained bed, the floor around it scattered with wadded Kleenex from previous encounters. Sutherland retreats to another room where, to Jim's surprise, he only fools around with his girl, and never removes his clothes. Once again, Jim feels that Sutherland has set out to humiliate him, not so much out of malice as to emphasise the disparity in their statuses.

David Pringle speculates 'Just possibly, the character of Dick Sutherland is here based – in part – on JGB's recollections of his friend and fellow writer Brian Aldiss'. Whether or not Aldiss inspired these incidents, the Rio visit did mark a watershed in relations between the two men. After Rio, Jim's comments on Aldiss became increasingly dismissive. In 1980, he was still friendly, if a little sarcastic, in introducing him at a Birmingham convention. 'I'm delighted to learn that Brian is the Guest of Honour at your convention,' he joked, 'though I was under the impression that Brian was the Guest of Honour at *every* convention!' He went on to praise him as a 'wise, witty and good companion, the best man in the world to spend an evening with in a bar on Copacabana Beach'. Jim and Claire appeared in 1986 at the launch of Aldiss's history of SF, *Trillion Year Spree*, and again at his surprise sixty-fifth birthday party in 1990. At the latter, Jim recalled, how, on Copacabana, they had planned a further convention, to be held somewhere equally exotic – perhaps Venice, Palm Springs or Casablanca. No publishers, agents or fans would be invited. At this, Aldiss had said, 'What a wonderfully dotty idea. But are you sure you want me along?' The anecdote suggested subliminally how competitive the relationship became – confirmed by Aldiss. 'We were once, as I imagined, close friends,' he says. 'Ah, the tropics! Then suddenly he decided that he would be a great writer, and associate no more with riff-raff. I wrote to him several times, the last time being an admiring postcard from Florida, where I read a collection of his articles [*A User's Guide to the Millennium*, published in 1996]. Brilliant, I thought. No response. Finito.'

Back in London, Jim delivered *The Atrocity Exhibition* to Doubleday. Like a literary equivalent of Paolozzi's scrapbooks, many of its episodes show their origin as cut-ups and collages from his earlier work, his life, and from surrealism: Chirico's esplanades by an empty beach, afternoon sex in four-star hotel rooms, the iconography of nuclear war – airfields, blockhouses, black helicopters, concrete bunkers – and of the freeway: the yin and yang of Dallas's black Lincoln Continental and London's white Pontiac. In an introduction to Storm's Danish translation, Jim spelled this out, evoking the nuclear explosion at Nagasaki, which he called a symbol of potency. He suggested that Freud's pessimism in *Civilization and Its Discontents* about our ability to control and direct our instinct for violence has been replaced by a relish for it, and for those who wreak havoc.

The illustrations commissioned by Doubleday from Michael Foreman for *The Atrocity Exhibition* bore little relation to Jim's vision for the book, which wouldn't be realised until the magazine *Re/Search* issued a revised, illustrated large-format edition, with his annotations, in 1990. The Doubleday cover, calculatedly cool, showed three sets of closed lips floating against a blue sky, a reference to Man Ray's painting *Les Amoureux: A l'Heure de l'Observatoire*, in which the lips of his mistress Lee Miller, blown up to the size of a dirigible, float above the Paris Observatory. The US sale stimulated British interest. On 11 June, Jim wrote to Storm to announce that one of the stories, 'Tolerances of the Human Face', which he completed before Rio and which he regarded as the best in the book, had been taken by *Encounter*, and that Cape, encouraged by the Doubleday sale, would do a British edition of *The Atrocity Exhibition.* He expected it to come out at the same time as the American. In this, he was mistaken.

CHAPTER THIRTY-THREE

DEAD SAD DODGEMS IN A BLACK GHOST'S FAIRGROUND

The *Crashed Cars* exhibition of April 1970 transformed Ballard's career and his mythology. It inaugurated a new phase in his work that culminated in the publication of his most innovative novel, *Crash*. Confusion shrouds the event, mostly generated by Jim himself. Yet it's this imprecision that confers on the show its glamour. What appeared to be a work of conceptual art was in part an inspired exercise in self-promotion.

Jim's experiments with advertisements fizzled out after the Arts Council refused a grant to place the images on billboards. The mass-market magazines he approached all demanded unaffordable sums for space. The three *Announcements* following 'Homage to Claire Churchill' appeared in *Ambit* or *New Worlds*, either for a token payment or gratis. With a sense that his project had become a sermon to the choir, Jim looked for other means of expression that didn't involve formal narrative.

Of London's many new exhibition spaces, the Arts Lab in Drury Lane attracted the most attention, thanks to its flamboyant director Jim Haynes. By the end of 1969, however, after only fifteen months in operation, it was foundering. In particular, film, video and art groups resented Haynes's preoccupation with performance which had installed The Human Family as a more or less resident company. The dissenters broke away and, as the Institute for Research in Art and Technology (IRAT), set up in north London. Without their support, the Arts Lab collapsed. Haynes moved to Amsterdam, where he applied his energies to sexual liberation, directing the Wet Dream Festivals and editing the magazine *Suck*.

The group located a former pharmaceutical warehouse in Robert Street, just across Euston Road, in the liberal borough of Camden. 'IRAT was founded by about twenty-five artists, of which I was one,' says photographer and videographer John 'Hoppy' Hopkins:

> [The building] belonged to the council, which planned to demolish it and put up a block of flats in its place, but that required a lead time of several years. Some bright spark realised that it could be used, providing the people using it got out when they were asked. We made a joint application and got this building, three storeys plus ground floor, for no rent.

If one didn't mind the cold or the dirt, there was room for everyone, according to film scholar David Curtis.

> IRAT ran a cinema (me), theatre (John Lifton), TV lab (Hoppy), print studio (John Collins), and housed the London Filmmaker's Co-op's first workshop (Malcolm LeGrice). Pam Zoline, with my partner, Biddy Peppin, ran the Gallery (as they had done at Drury Lane).

The Institute registered itself as a private club. This relieved it of many regulations, including censorship, although anyone attending an event had to become a member. Sally Potter, later to direct the films *Orlando* and *The Tango Lesson*, but then a nineteen-year-old student, remembers IRAT with affection. 'The people were a ragbag; intellectuals, artists, starters out; there was something of a drug and alcohol haze; lots of idealism; political idealism. Very few women, and none of them taken very seriously. But I loved it.'

Jim learned of IRAT through Pamela Zoline. She persuaded him to join Chris Evans and architectural historian Reyner Banham as trustees, though their role was honorary, and they played no part in running the place. Initially, Jim regarded this new outpost of the counter-culture with bemused disbelief. Noting large holes in the ceilings and floors, he fantasised that these were ventilation shafts designed to funnel off the omnipresent pot smoke. They were actually the remains of the shaft for a demolished lift. When these were boarded up, parts of the building became quite cosy. 'We promised not to,' says Hopkins, 'but after a while some of us thought it would be interesting to live there, so we moved in.'

There was no 'Eureka!' moment for *Crashed Cars*. Jim had long been disturbed and excited by car wrecks. A woman in a smashed car, nude for preference, and under duress, had featured in his work since *The Violent Noon*. In 'The University of Death', one of the fictions in *The Atrocity Exhibition*, his protagonist organises an exhibition of crashed cars in an automobile showroom. Catherine Austin, the story's embodiment of sensuality, leans against a Pontiac, the curves of her thighs mirroring those of the car, while another, Karen Novotny, prowls among the exhibits. The *pièce de résistance* of the exhibition is the same model, a Lincoln Continental, as that in which John Kennedy died. Dummies of JFK and Jackie are arranged in the back seat, complete with a smear of brain matter reproduced in acrylic on the trunk.

He took a further step towards the show when he proposed incorporating a real wreck into the planned *Crash* performance at the ICA. Its house-proud administration would never have risked their new décor, but IRAT were less finicky. In fact, Robert Street might have been made for such a show. At the formal opening of the centre on 4 October 1969, which he attended as a trustee, Jim noted the fire-station-red double doors at street level which would permit a tow-truck to drive right into the building. Also, unlike the ICA's pristine flooring, IRAT's was only dirty concrete. In one of his few preparations for the event, Jim paid to have it painted black.

The idea of a show of real wrecked cars developed in conversations with Pamela Zoline, who, with Biddy Peppin, was in charge of exhibitions. Though the real inspiration was pure fetishism, Jim offered an intellectual rationalisation. 'All this was designed to provoke the audience,' he told Iain Sinclair. 'The whole thing was a psychological experiment – to see if my basic hunch about the latent, hidden psychology, the depth-psychology of the car crash, was on the right track. Whether my hypothesis was accurate. It was a test. I was lab-testing *Crash*.'

Zoline and Peppin didn't need much convincing. The show had legitimate artistic precedents. Jim Dine had presented a 'happening' called *The Car Crash* at New York's Reuben Gallery in 1960. In 1963, French sculptor Arman dynamited a white MG in a quarry near Düsseldorf and exhibited the remains as *White Orchid*. Car wrecks appeared in Andy Warhol's *Death and Disaster* screen-prints of the early sixties, and *Dodge 38*, by American sculptor Ed Kienholz – a wrecked white car with the plastic dummies of a Third World War pilot and a girl with facial burns making love among a refuse of bubble gum war cards and oral contraceptive wallets – features in *The Atrocity Exhibition*. In 1968, Jean-Luc Godard filmed part of *Sympathy For the Devil* in a London car junkyard. The front cover of the first issue of *International Times* for 1970 showed a heap of smashed cars with the caption 'Beautify Junkyards! Throw something lovely away today'.

If anything, Peppin felt the space was not good enough for the show. 'It was a dark, industrial building,' she says, 'lit with a few strip lights. The show should have been in a proper art gallery, where the contrast [between the wrecks and the setting] would be more obvious, but at IRAT they were all of a piece. I was worried that, because of the nature of the site, people might think the crashed cars were just the sort of junk that happened to accumulate in arts labs.' However, Ballard was more than pleased, and offered to pay all the show's expenses, even the wine for the opening. For the penurious IRAT, this was a considerable incentive.

Zoline and Peppin suggested Ballard create a catalogue, or at the very least some explanatory text, but he insisted that the show consist of nothing but the cars; anything more would pollute public reactions. Once the exhibition had closed, he remained adamant that there had been no supporting graphic material of any kind.

Zoline and Peppin had no problem with this. Shows they'd sponsored at Drury Lane included an event conceived by John Lennon and Yoko Ono, to which Lennon's contribution was an empty drawer from a broken bureau, laid on the floor, and, like the rest of the objects on display, unlabelled.

Cruising London's scrapyards, Jim found few big American cars, but Motor Crash Repairs on Finchley Road had a 1950s white Pontiac of the type Dickie Valentine drove. Proprietor Charlie Symmonds agreed to rent the Pontiac, a Mini and an Austin Cambridge A60 for the show. Art historian Simon Ford thought the choices revealing. 'The Pontiac represented a particularly baroque phase in American car styling, while the Mini symbolised the fun-loving mobility of the swinging sixties. The sober and conservative saloon, the A60, stood for the Mini's exact antithesis. All however, through the catastrophe of the car crash, were now in a sense equivalent; smashed and levelled to the raw material of their crushed metal, broken glass, and stained upholstery.' Symmonds took a less aesthetic view. 'I detest cars,' he said. 'But maybe it's a good idea to show crashed cars. It's frightening.'

Since cars were routinely ferried about, Jim had no trouble installing his choices at Robert Street. Word of the show got around, and people dropped by. Steve Dwoskin watched the delivery of the Austin. The building had no wheelchair access, so he had to walk with crutches, supporting his legs with steel callipers. Jim examined these appliances closely and asked many questions. They inspired the braces worn by accident victim Gabrielle in *Crash*.

The presence of Hoppy Hopkins and his video lab as part of IRAT excited Jim's imagination. He suggested Hopkins video the show's private view, and run the images on closed-circuit monitors. Hopkins went one better. 'We had one of the three portable TV outfits in London. The camera weighed two or three pounds, and there was a back pack. You could walk around with one of those for about half an hour.' He proposed that, if Jim or someone else would circulate among the guests and interview them, he would follow with his camera. As for the show's intellectual pretensions, Hopkins dismissed them: 'The whole thing was thought of as being a "happening",' he says. And the keynote of a happening was spontaneity.

'I suggested we hire a young woman to interview the guests about their reactions,' Jim said. It was implicit in his suggestion that the woman be nude. The girl who accepted the job, Jo Stanley, wasn't part of the IRAT collective. 'I believe Jo was a model,' says Hopkins. 'She had big breasts, so that was quite an eye-catcher, and exciting for the blokes anyway. She was quite natural and spontaneous. She became a personal friend very quickly. She was a lovely person.'

On the telephone with Jim, Stanley agreed to appear naked, but once she met him and saw the cars, she changed her mind. 'It was so delicious,' Jim recalled to Iain Sinclair, still excited three decades on. 'She walked into the gallery. She said, "I won't appear naked. I'll only appear topless." I thought, "That's interesting." She saw the sexual connection.' It inflamed him that she understood this wasn't simply an art show, but the realisation of his sexual fantasy.

Crashed Cars commenced with a preview on 3 April 1970 and ran to 28 April. The day of the preview, a photojournalist asked for someone to sit in the Pontiac while he took pictures. Sally Potter obliged. The journalist asked why, if this was 'new sculpture', no price was shown. Rather than explain that Jim didn't own the wrecks and had no intention of selling them, someone came up with the figure of £3,000. This was hurriedly lettered on a piece of cardboard which Potter held in the empty windscreen space.

At the preview, Jo Stanley, bare-breasted, circulated with a microphone, followed by Hopkins with his camera. Jim's description of the result was breathlessly sensational:

> I'd never seen 100 people get drunk so quickly. The show went on for a month. In that time they came up against massive hostility of every kind. The cars were attacked, windows ripped off. Those windows that weren't broken already were smashed. One of the cars was upended, another splashed with white paint. Now the whole thing was a speculative illustration of a scene in *The Atrocity Exhibition.* I had speculated in my book about how the people might behave. And

in the real show the guests at the party and the visitors later behaved in pretty much the way I had anticipated. It was not so much an exhibition of sculpture as almost of experimental psychology, using the medium of the fine art show. People were unnerved, you see. There was enormous hostility. The topless girl was almost raped in the back seat of the Pontiac (or so she claimed). A woman journalist from *New Society* began to interview me among the mayhem, but became so overwrought with indignation, of which the journal had an unlimited supply, that she had to be restrained from attacking me.

The paint-daubing was blamed on a Hare Krishna group. In some versions of the story, wine and urine were also poured over the cars, windows smashed and side mirrors torn off. Supposedly, Charles Symmonds, when the wrecks were returned, was shocked by their condition. Despite the improbability of a junkyard proprietor being surprised by damage to cars already wrecked, nobody questioned this or any other details of the event as recounted by Jim. Hearing that authoritative voice, how could one doubt him?

Contemporary videotapes ran for only twenty minutes. Hopkins managed to capture eighteen minutes of the event, filmed at various times through the evening. Video technology was so primitive that the tape was neither edited nor copied, and subsequently disappeared. As press coverage was perfunctory, the photograph of Sally Potter in the Pontiac became the sole evidence of the event. Jim's account filled the vacuum and was accepted as reliable evidence of what took place. In 2010, however, Hopkins unearthed the original videotape, which has been restored. Jo Stanley's article for *Frendz*, long forgotten, also came to light. Augmented by reminiscences from those involved in the show, these give a different account of that night.

The tape, despite some deterioration, shows none of the violence Jim described. Jo Stanley, mockingly aware of the effect of her semi-nudity on the predominantly male guests, elicits coherent opinions from people obviously knowledgeable about contemporary art. A woman with a German accent suggests the show might receive more sympathetic attention in Cologne. Someone else thinks the effect would be improved if the cars included dummies, as in the work of Ed Kienholz, or even real corpses, but Jim, he tells her, insisted that emptiness made them seem more 'glacial'. At the end of the tape, Jim is glimpsed being interviewed by a woman. 'What is this for exactly?' he demands, glass in hand and sounding belligerent. 'You're not Karen Novotny, are you? Or Coma?'

From time to time, Stanley does squeeze into the Pontiac with both men and women, but space is so tight that they remain there only a few moments, and without any signs of violence. The claim of 'near-rape' is made more doubtful by her behaviour in the days following. 'As a result of that exhibition night,' says Hoppy Hopkins, 'she stayed around for a few days, on and off, and more or less lived with us video people on the top floor.' Nor is any attack, either on the cars or her, mentioned in her review of the show. Headed 'Ballard Crashes', its tone is banteringly contemptuous, and amused at the show's pretension.

> I wonder just who was being taken for a ride at J G Ballard's exhibition of crashed cars? This in fact consists of 3 cars in several states of smashed-ness, left in the gallery of the arts lab – dead sad dodgems in a black ghost's fairground. On 3rd April he held a private view at the lab. in Robert Street – flashing promises and wine and a semi-naked chick (me) in the faces of the establishment media unfreaks – who remained completely undazzled – and inviting specially suitable friends along for the trip. Amazingly the Arts Lab countenanced this bourgeois binge, but maybe this is related to the fact that he is one of their trustees.
>
> Ego-tripping around with the mike for the Arts Lab video team, I found that most of the people thought that the price [of £3,000] was a big joke, but were totally uninterested in being interested, or even in being uninterested. The stock of wine was decreasing though and smiles were getting wider – maybe it was quite a funny joke after all.

> Bored speculation from heavies and heads as to whether or not it was a gib-con [gyp-con?]. What is it intended to be and what are Jim Ballard's real motives? Is this Art? What is art? *The Times* Art critic (no less) thought that it wasn't anyway. General reaction was that the whole thing was rather pointless.

About rampant Hare Krishnas with paint pots, those involved with the show, including David Curtis, Biddy Peppin, Hoppy Hopkins and Sally Potter, are sceptical. Nobody recalls such vandalism – to achieve which, they point out, the perpetrators would have had to become members of IRAT, making their identities known. 'I was there every day,' says David Curtis. 'The place stank of petrol and oil dripping from the cars – I remember that. And the cars were an ominous presence for the month they were there.' But as for the alleged violence and attempted rape, 'I would have been aware of anything like that. I was there on the preview night. After that, the place was mostly empty.'

Despite Jim's claim that 'there was no supporting material whatsoever' for the show, the manifesto he distributed, essentially a reprise of the *Sunday Mirror* article, attracted little attention. The few who attended can recall only a sense of dark and lowering threat, characterised by John Clute as 'Gigeresque'. Since such a response counted, in terms of Jim's experiment, as a failure, he should have abandoned the novel. Instead, in a well-established tradition of scientific research, he faked his findings, inventing the desired violence, or at least exaggerating the little that did take place.

Perhaps he intended to do so all along. His more passionate supporters, particularly in continental Europe, would claim that, had he made this choice in advance, he would once again have shown himself ahead of his time. In 1994, Jean Baudrillard proposed a new model of artistic discourse that accommodated this elastic concept of truth.

> It is no longer possible to fabricate the unreal from the real, the imaginary from the givens of the real. The process will, rather, be the opposite: it will be to put decentred situations, models of simulation

in place and to contrive to give them the feeling of the real, of the banal, of lived experience; to reinvent the real as fiction, precisely because it has disappeared from our life.

CHAPTER THIRTY-FOUR

THE NASTY

In April 1970, as Jim presented *Crashed Cars*, *New Worlds* expired. It would briefly revive as a quarterly, but Moorcock's dream of a multicultural monthly was wrecked by the most common of all hazards, distribution, which was monopolised in the UK by the conservative W. H. Smith chain. Battles with its management, particularly over the serialisation of Norman Spinrad's novel *Bug Jack Barron*, ended with the magazine effectively denied a place on the racks.

Charles Platt, who edited the last issues, contrasted the marketing skills of Moorcock and Ballard, as demonstrated by *Crashed Cars* and *New Worlds*:

> It was Jimmy who got publicity by staging the crashed-car show, Jimmy who was written up in the newspaper because he bought an ad in *Ambit* and used it as literary form, promoting Claire. Jimmy would have liked to promote *New Worlds* in a similar way, I think. Mike Moorcock had no instincts for promotion at all, and Brian Aldiss wasn't much better. Brian obtained the Arts Council grant, but getting patronage from a government agency is a long way from getting press in a national newspaper. If Jimmy had had a more active involvement in *New Worlds* as a collaborator rather than as a contributor, the magazine might have been much more successful. Mike has complained subsequently that Jimmy was always telling him what to do. Maybe he should have listened.

Jim was about to achieve additional publicity, this time unsought.

On the day in June when the US edition of *The Atrocity Exhibition* was due to appear, he received two telegrams from Doubleday. One congratulated him on publication; the other announced the book had been withdrawn and the entire printing pulped. No reason was given for this decision, but an introduction to a later edition of the book confidently asserted that 'idly flicking through an advance copy, the firm's head, Nelson Doubleday, had hit upon "Why I Want to Fuck Ronald Reagan". Doubleday, a close friend of Reagan's, immediately moved to kill the book.' Jim included this version in *Miracles of Life*, even though a glance at *Who's Who* would have shown it to be false. Nelson Doubleday Sr died in 1949, and Nelson Jr, aged thirty-seven in 1970, was not yet president of the company. Moreover, Nelson Jr seldom read anything, devoting his energies to baseball as owner of the New York Mets. The true culprit in the pulping was John Turner Sargent, who had married into the family, and was CEO from 1961 to 1978. An active Democrat and friend of the Kennedys, he objected not to the Reagan piece but to 'Plan for the Assassination of Jacqueline Kennedy'. After Aristotle Onassis died, Jackie joined Doubleday as an editor, under Sargent.

Reviews of the Cape edition of *The Atrocity Exhibition* published the following month ranged from baffled through respectful to contemptuous. Jim particularly resented a piece by crime writer Julian Symons, which referred to his 'evident relish for the nasty'. Symons had also compiled *Crime and Detection. An Illustrated History*, about which Jim (while admitting to owning a copy) was scathing.

> Great fat book, with hundreds of photographs; an encyclopedia of crime with descriptions of every conceivable criminal act from rape to mass murder. It's quite well done because it's got all the gory details: how many little girls the Cannibal Killer of Cologne ate between 1927 and 1933. This is a man who says I've got an evident relish for the nasty! That's one of the paradoxes: everything becomes so conventionalised that you can write about 'crime'. Very genteel and refined people make a living writing about crime for fifty years. Polite society

> allows this, no one raises an eyebrow. Someone comes along with a slightly fresh or original approach: 'Oh, my god. Relish for the nasty'. It's absurd.

By late 1970, Jim was deep into researching the novel of *Crash*. Pressed later for its inspiration, he would nominate various 'moments of truth'. Sometimes he said the idea came to him when, driving past a fatal traffic accident, he saw the body of a beautiful woman, half naked, spread over the back seat. Conversely, he assured film-maker Harley Cokeliss that working with him on a BBC film about *The Atrocity Exhibition* had been his inspiration. While none of these was entirely untrue, *Crash* had too many fathers for all to be given credit.

Eduardo Paolozzi played a more important role than most. He'd begun to collect, photograph and create his own versions of the dummies used in crash tests. A show of these at a London gallery towards the end of 1970 also attracted the attention of the BBC. Making the connection with *The Atrocity Exhibition*, the producers of the current affairs programme *Panorama* commissioned American director Cokeliss, who lived in London and had interviewed Jim for an earlier BBC film about science fiction, to film one specifically about his preoccupation with car accidents.

In October, Cokeliss taped a long interview with Jim and used this to compile a four-page treatment. Jim was supposed to write a script, but still hadn't finished it in December. As a stop-gap, he sent Cokeliss a list of ten locations, with notes on their possible use. The list included, as Ballard wrote in his synopsis, highways and freeways, cloverleafs, and multilevel interchanges, which he suggested should be shown as sculpture, and cinematically melded into images of a woman's body. He also wanted to shoot in multi-storey car parks, nominating one at Sunbury, near Shepperton. Car showrooms were important, particularly if they could incorporate a woman in some sort of erotic dream sequence. The breakers' yard, with wrecks, of course. And a carwash.

He was very keen that Cokeliss should film this from inside the car, like the sequence from *Psycho*, with Janet Leigh. Ideally, he wanted a girl in the car, and she should be nude. Including an attractive woman at every point of the film was very important to him – if only in the background, he said, like the artist's model in the paintings of Delvaux or Ernst. She would also feature in a dramatised sequence from *The Atrocity Exhibition*, showing a woman getting out of the automobile after a crash.

To play the nameless woman, Cokeliss hired Gabrielle Drake, familiar from the SF series *UFO*, in which she showed off her figure in high boots, tight sweaters and miniskirts. He filmed her and Ballard roaming junkyards and a Watford lockup, and cruising motorways together, occasionally exchanging enigmatic stares. Drake also acted out the slow-motion episode of a bleeding victim, in the moments after a crash, opening a car door and toppling out. There are shots of her stockinged legs in high heels as she scissors them into the front seat of a car, and a closely observed moment as her breast lingeringly subtends a corner of upholstery. Refused a nude shot of Drake in a car, Cokeliss compromised with a shower sequence that explores a nude body of a woman whose face we never see.

Panorama broadcast Cokeliss's film in February 1971. Presenter James Mossman captured Ballard's tone by introducing the item while sitting opposite a dummy borrowed from Paolozzi.

Shortly after, inspired by the film, the Automobile Association's magazine *Drive* invited Jim to join a veteran car event celebrating the seventieth anniversary of Mercedes-Benz and marking the launch of a new car, the 320SL. He became a passenger on a seven-day drive by a caravan of eighteen vintage cars, terminating at the Mercedes factory in Stuttgart. His vehicle was a 1904 Renault. Since the cars were too slow for the autobahn, they had to use B-roads, which took them through the outskirts of some large towns. Cruising these neatly tended avenues, Jim realised he was seeing the future of Europe: not the stainless-steel towers and glass motorways of the SF magazine covers, but miles of identical villas, each with a BMW and a boat in the driveway, and not a crumpled hamburger wrapper or empty cigarette pack in sight. In short, the future was a suburb of Düsseldorf. He also intuited why Germany had become an exporter of urban terrorism. This was the breeding ground of Andreas Baader and Ulrike Meinhof, a world where the only freedom was to be found in madness. This insight would return to motivate the dystopic fantasies of the last phase of his career, *Millennium People* and *Kingdom Come*.

Ballard featured in two other events involving an *Ambit* regular, a Trinidadian woman – avant-garde performance artist by day, Latin Quarter stripper by night – who called herself 'Euphoria Bliss'. To commemorate *Ambit*'s fiftieth issue in January 1971, Bax assembled its principals – Richard Freeman, Edwin Brock, Martin Bax, Michael Foreman, Paolozzi and Ballard – at the Royal Academy to be photographed for the *Sunday Times*. With Paolozzi's sculpture 'Thunder and Lightning with Flies and Jack Kennedy' in the background, Ms Bliss, watched by this bemused group, posed in what looked like a G-string and a shrimping net.

Also for *Ambit*, Jim compiled 'The Side Effects of Orthonovin G', made up of edited testimonies from American women of the sometimes alarming psychological damage of taking this birth-control drug. One became obsessed with football, moved to Britain in an attempt to meet the English World Cup team, then went on to Brazil, where she became friendly with the world-famous Pelé. Bax, asked to stage a 'happening' at Kingston Polytechnic, suggested reciting Jim's texts with jazz backing, and hired Bliss to read them. 'There were two pieces,' says Bax. 'One about soccer. For that one, she said, she'd dress in soccer boots and shorts. The other was about a woman – it just describes an American life – and she looked at it and said "I'll read that naked".' Bliss sat demurely on stage in a long green coat and hat while Bax introduced her. Then he moved behind her chair and, as she rose, pulled off her coat. 'The students just sort of fell off their seats while she read,' he recalled with satisfaction. English literature had never had it so good.

CHAPTER THIRTY-FIVE

CRASH

The gap between the publication of *The Atrocity Exhibition* in July 1970 and the delivery of *Crash* to Jonathan Cape early in 1972 attests to the effort of creation. The most condensed of Jim's novels, *Crash* is also the one on which he lavished greatest effort. Martin Amis rightly called it 'his most mannered and literary book, its sprung rhythms and creamily varied vowel-sounds a conscious salute to Baudelaire, Rimbaud and Mallarmé'. Jim usually burned his manuscripts, but in this case both the first draft and a corrected typescript survive. The former is a barely decipherable maze of over-scrawled second, third and fourth thoughts. Even the clean copy he delivered to Cape early in 1972 is littered with his handwritten corrections. The intensity of his effort is palpable.

Describing the novel as a 'psychopathic hymn', Jim claimed to have created it in a state of what he called 'willed madness' – self-induced erotic hysteria. He gave the narrator his own name – to show, he said, that he identified with all the characters, no matter how extreme their actions or fantasies.

That said, he doesn't much resemble his fictional persona. The novel's James is a prosperous producer of TV commercials. He's married to Catherine, an attractive bisexual. Latently bisexual himself, James appears not yet to have had a homosexual experience. Injured in a motorway collision that kills the other driver, Ballard is treated in the same hospital as the man's widow, Helen Remington. While recuperating, both are visited by Robert Vaughan, whom James takes for a staff doctor. He is actually a car-crash fetishist who stages reenactments of the accidents in which celebrities such as James Dean and Jayne Mansfield died.

Later, James and Helen re-encounter one another in the pound where wrecked cars are stored. Their sexual attraction is reinforced by the presence of the vehicles in which people, including her husband, have died. They start to meet for sex, which takes place only in cars. James, Catherine and Helen gravitate to the group orbiting Vaughan, with whose members they begin to have sex, culminating in James sodomising Vaughan. When Vaughan is killed in an accident, James and Catherine plan a similar death.

With *Crash*, Jim returned unreservedly to the well-made novel. There are no interpolated excerpts from scientific reports, no typographical experiments. As firmly as he had rejected the tyranny of story, he re-embraces it with a prodigal's fervour. The straightforward first-person narrative is entirely appropriate to what he called 'the first pornographic novel based on technology'. As he intuits, pornography is conservative. It functions as a delivery system for sexual satisfaction. Narrative and characterisation exist only as spacing between erotic 'arias'. The reader's fantasy gives faces to the characters who are, in every other way, ciphers; the same practice, as it happens, that he employed in *The Atrocity Exhibition.*

Detroit designers of the fifties exploited the sexual fetishism of the automobile by adding breast-like 'Dagmars' to front bumpers, and creating the vaginal grille of the Edsel. *Crash* lifts this concept to new levels, making lascivious suggestions for the refinement and distillation of the sensual pleasures of flesh juxtaposed with leather, chrome and steel, and the vertiginous lurch of collision.

Having found the courage to reveal his imaginings, Jim is determined to shock, and knows exactly how to do it: set up a situation that elicits pity, sympathy and concern and then deride the sentiments. Thus the most provocative passages in *Crash* involve Gabrielle, whose body, dreadfully scarred, is enclosed in a steel and leather harness. Edmund Wilson caused a scandal with 'The Princess with the Golden Hair', an episode of his 1946 novel *Memories of Hecate Country*, which described the erotic appeal of a leather and metal spine brace. *Crash* explores this fetish in even more intimate detail. Most of Chapter 19 is devoted to a description of James and Gabrielle having sex after an aphrodisiac visit to the Earls Court Motor Show. Sensing that the conventionally erogenous junction points stimulated in the sexual act – anus, vulva, nipple and clitoris – no longer function in a body so damaged, and so reliant on machinery, he follows her urging and penetrates her wounds, ejaculating into a fissure in her thigh, a cavity in her armpit and another under one breast.

For all the importance accorded the female characters, it's Vaughan on whom *Crash* concentrates. A glamorous villain/hero on the model of Count Dracula, Svengali or the Phantom of the Opera, he looms over the story, guiding its action with demonic omnipotence. Scarred, unwashed, priapic, innocent of both fear and shame, he's a Pan figure from ancient myth, a satyr, celebrating sex and death, not least in his own life. Jim gives him the reckless commitment of the enthusiast who's not afraid to pursue his obsessions to their logical conclusion, in self-immolation.

Christopher Evans wasn't gay, nor, however much Jim admired him, did they ever, as far as one can discover, have a sexual relationship. Nevertheless, there are plenty of correspondences between Evans and Vaughan. James describes Vaughan as a 'fugleman' for the new sexuality, an antique term Jim applied elsewhere to Evans. His Road Research Laboratory recalls Evans's National Physical Laboratory. Charles Platt doesn't doubt the similarities. 'I once asked Jimmy if he had talked to Evans about this. Jimmy said he had given a copy of the book to Evans, but they had never talked about it at all, even though they were fairly good friends. This suggests another attribute of Jimmy. He was very old-school British and quite repressed in his everyday life. The ruthless ripping away of conventional mores only occurred in his fiction.'

Publisher and author David Britton was in no doubt that Evans inspired Vaughan. 'Shortly after first reading *Crash* in the early 1970s,' he wrote, 'I'd seen [Evans] give a talk at an SF convention.'

> It was quite a revelation: here in the flesh was Vaughan in all his feral erotic intensity. Evans prowled the stage just oozing sexuality. He wore a black biker's jacket and a blue denim shirt open to the midriff. You might have got into a car with the doctor, but you wouldn't have accompanied him up a dark alley. Of his talk, I can't remember anything, just his physicality remains in my mind. No doubt this subjective observation made by a stranger isn't a full picture of Evans's personality, but I'm sure it was this aspect of his friend that Ballard homed in on. Evans had been one of the catalysts for the book, lifted from life and conjured into a deviant Minotaur by Ballard's imagination. A sweet image to me: Evans and Ballard haunting the motorways of England for auto-sensation.

Jim also incorporated Gabrielle Drake into the novel. In the first draft, she appears under her own name as one of the celebrities pursued along the motorways by Vaughan and James. The published version removes the direct reference, but retains her Christian name for the paraplegic star of Vaughan's coven of car-crash ghouls.

Jim liked to introduce Claire as 'the woman in *Crash*', and originally wanted to use her name for one of the characters, though for many years he avoided identifying which one. He finally admitted he imagined her as the promiscuous, bisexual Catherine Ballard. Yet Helen Remington seems a better fit, given the way Walsh often figured in Jim's automobile sex fantasies. James and Helen have sex only in automobiles. In her bedroom, he can't get an erection, but in traffic on a crowded freeway he's instantly excited by the propinquity of an unseen audience of fellow drivers.

In *Crash*, Jim flirts with the remark in the *Crashed Cars* manifesto that, in twentieth-century terms, the crash bore a similar relationship to the cult of the automobile as the crucifixion to Christianity. Conflating the personae of the sacrificed messiah and his crusty avatar, John the Baptist, Jim draws Vaughan as a shaggy crypto Christ whose fascination with automobiles is as mystical as it is fetishistic. Taking James to the long-stay car park at Heathrow, Vaughan forces him to wait as he walks among the expensive American and European cars, caressing their exotic fixtures and alien bodywork.

Exasperated, James shouts 'Vaughan! For god's sake!' The published version ends there, but in the typescript Vaughan chooses to treat the protest as a pious outburst. These metal fittings, he lectures Ballard, deserve comparison with the chalice of the mass. If anything, their holiness is even greater, since, during an accident, they partake of a ritual where, instead of wine, the Eucharist is celebrated with actual blood. By linking automobile fetishism to the Catholic mass, *Crash* audaciously opens a door on an entirely new vision. It harks back to Jarry's 'The Passion Considered as an Uphill Bicycle Race' and anticipates young Jim's sanctification of the Japanese Zeros and their pilots in *Empire of the Sun.* But in *Crash* Jim recoils from its implications. He not only dropped the passage from the published text but heavily crossed it out in manuscript.

Jim never complained that Cape censored him, and length rather than content appears to have dictated most deletions. The most provocative episodes remained intact and, if anything, more flagrant for the removal of the literary undergrowth. Only occasionally was an image so outrageous that the editors intervened. They retained James's fantasy about the body of his own mother, which he imagines, after a succession of accidents, being fitted with new artificial orifices of ever-greater abstraction and ingenuity. Nor did they cut a Burroughs-like evocation of elderly pederasts tonguing the simulated anuses of colostomised boys. They insisted, however, on removing a passage where, after sex with Catherine, James scrapes shit from her rectum with a finger and smears the words 'LOVE' and 'CRASH' on her thigh.

Crash caught the *zeitgeist.* Jim agreed with Paolozzi that 'violence is probably going to play the same role in the seventies and eighties that sex played in the fifties and sixties', and in 1971 the whole of Britain appeared equally convinced. That year saw a series of memorably bloody films, all produced in the UK: Stanley Kubrick's exercise in 'ultra-violence' *A Clockwork Orange*, Sam Peckinpah's rape-and-revenge drama *Straw Dogs*, Mike Hodges's retributory gangster film *Get Carter*, Richard Fleischer's *Ten Rillington Place*, telling the story of John Christie, whose murders had interested Jim two decades before, and, most flagrant of all, Ken Russell's *The Devils*, in which a handicapped Mother Superior channels her lust for a charismatic priest into accusations of demonic possession, leading to his torture and burning at the stake. Testing as always the limits of public taste, Russell filmed a sequence, known as 'The Rape of Christ', in which the nuns, their libidos liberated by the pretext of 'possession', fling themselves naked on a giant crucifix and fornicate with its sorrowing larger-than-life-size Jesus. Horrified, distributors demanded its removal.

As in all these films, and Ken Russell *passim*, sex in *Crash* is inseparable from violence, and also from collectivity. The fetishists of *Crash* accept group sex as a given. Jim even suggests that, in the future, copulation will take on a new complexity, requiring not only the participation of additional human partners but also of machines, or at least the products of technology. His proposition that 'Sex x technology = the future', provocative at the time, appears commonplace in the era of the Multi-Speed Waterproof G-Spot Vibrator and computerised sex manikins, complete with body heat and heartbeat.

In an image recalling Jim's fantasy of a radiator grille superimposed on the face of Claire Walsh, James becomes excited watching Vaughan sketching on the photograph of a film actress, transforming the planes of her face into something closer to the front view of an automobile. The subsequent passage, surprisingly deleted from the published version, is an inspired exercise in theme-and-variations that shows Ballard at the peak of his powers.

What if, he speculates, sex in the future could only take place with the participation of some artefact of technology, or an element of consumerism? The scenarios he proposes are redolent of the car pornography he asked Jannick Storm to search out on his account: a bank manager having sex with his teenage typist against a metal counter grille; a garage attendant and a suburban housewife coupling against a petrol pump; an oil executive on a transatlantic flight pleasuring the bored widow in an adjacent seat, fingers exploring her vagina with the skill of a watchmaker probing a complex escapement, and his *bonne bouche*, a three-way coupling in a travel agency during the planning of a honeymoon trip, where, as the new bride sprawls across a laminated map of the world, husband and agent penetrate her anally and vaginally in a triple orgasm that joyfully salutes the package holiday.

For more than two years, *Crash* monopolised Jim's attention. He finished the first draft just before Christmas 1970 and began work again in the New Year. During the whole of 1971, he published nothing new. Not only an intense effort of imagination, the writing also demanded extensive research in the motoring press and books on car-crash injuries. Never social, he became even less so. 'When I visited England every six to twelve months,' said Charles Platt, 'I would usually telephone him',

> and he would go through the 'come and visit' ritual.
>
> 'We'll go to the local pub and hoist a few pints,' he said.
>
> I suspected that drinking at the local pub was not high on his list of pleasurable pursuits. The one time we did it, he had difficulty finding the pub, and was eager to leave. I think he was just simulating what he believed other people did socially; trying to do what he thought they would want to do. Of course I may see it that way because I have similar problems myself. But he was truly reclusive.

While certainly reclusive, Jim was more impatient with casual socialising; 'hanging out'. Interacting with others meant more if he could learn from it. During 1971, he and Paolozzi, possibly for an article in the magazine *Studio International*, visited some of London's museums of science, technology and war. They were photographed looking at an Apollo space suit in the Science Museum in South

Kensington and sitting together in a jeep at the Imperial War Museum – an incident referred to in *Crash.* Also in 1971, Jim met Jorge Luis Borges at a party at the home of John Wolfers. Critics like to assign some of Jim's more visionary prose to a Borges influence, but there's no evidence that either took much interest in the other. 'Burroughs wasn't a disappointment, when we finally met him,' says Moorcock, 'but Borges was. Burroughs pretty much lived as he wrote, while Borges was a rather conservative man with a keen interest in G. K. Chesterton.' Jim was unfortunate not to have met some of the more radical writers of the day, such as Yukio Mishima, whose militaristic homophilia and suicidal tendencies would have interested him more. However, if anyone did send him Mishima's *Confessions of a Mask* or *The Temple of the Golden Pavilion,* they ended up on the bonfire in the back garden, like Rushdie's *Midnight's Children.*

Otherwise, his little free time was spent with Claire. In the summer, they went on holiday together along the Mediterranean, usually to Spain, but sometimes to Antibes, where Graham Greene had also retired, or to Greece. Most weeks, he visited her flat in Shepherd's Bush on Friday evenings and remained there for the weekend. 'He would drive up on a Friday,' Walsh said, 'and even after all these years I couldn't help waiting at the window, and going out to meet his car in the street. And whenever he went back to Shepperton, we would always part as if we were leaving each other for a very long time.'

Night-time drives on relatively empty dual carriageways fed Jim's fetishist enjoyment of the automobile experience. In particular, he found iconographic importance in the elevated Westway, or Western Avenue, as he sometimes mistakenly called it. Charles Platt observed his fascination at first hand:

> One time when I visited him at his home in Shepperton, he suddenly pulled out a stack of 4x6 black-and-white photographic prints.
>
> 'I took these myself,' he said, sounding a bit uncomfortable about it. 'You might want to take a look. They're . . . they're not very good.'
>
> He passed them to me in the embarrassed, furtive, yet prurient style

of someone sharing some home-grown pornography. Feeling as if I were being invited to share something of special and perhaps disturbing significance, I looked at the pictures. I was somewhat disappointed, yet not entirely surprised, when I found that all of them depicted the underside of the elevated section of the M4 motorway at Hammersmith.

Opened in July 1970, the Westway stood out as a lone piece of modern construction in a nation where roads still meandered, and traffic could tail back for miles, halted by some narrow High Street or at road works left unattended while workers enjoyed their tea break. Just as he relished pile-ups more than progress, Jim, like Federico Fellini in *Fellini's Roma*, saw that traffic jams, far from being static, were avalanches of frustration, momentarily stilled, yet poised to sweep on, crushing all in their path. But the real reservoirs of suppressed violence existed within Ballard himself. *Crash* released them. Angela Carter, herself gripped by a dark and violent imagination, wrote approvingly of how he confronted 'that hard-edged aesthetic of the horrid, all open wounds and black humour, the baleful sexuality of the car crash. A particular obsession peaking in *Crash*, a mutilatory and inconsolable novel that could have sprung from the pen of some Maldoror of the motorways.'

CHAPTER THIRTY-SIX

DRUNK AT THE WHEEL

Jim delivered the manuscript of *Crash* early in 1972, and, conscious of a huge task completed, relaxed for the first time in two years. Inevitably, he drank. And, while drinking, he drove, refusing to believe it impaired his reactions; Vaughan spoke for him in the novel when he observed that a few drinks always made a car go better. The result was foreseeable. In February, possibly earlier, Jim was driving back from, he thinks, a West End movie preview – conceivably that of Stanley Kubrick's *A Clockwork Orange*, on 12 January – when, around midnight, his car left the road at the bottom of Chiswick Bridge, demolished a road sign, turned over and slid to a halt on the opposite carriageway.

The accident became part of the Ballard mythology, accumulating detail with each telling. At the time, his account was curt: simply 'I rolled a Zephyr across a dual carriageway and ended up on my head in the oncoming lane, tucked under the wall of Mortlake Cemetery'. By 1983, he'd added more detail:

> I was driving along a dual carriageway at the bottom of Chiswick Bridge at about midnight. I think one of the tyres blew out. The car swerved to the right, crossed a traffic island demolishing a sign, rolled over onto its roof and carried on along the oncoming lane. Cars were coming towards me but luckily nobody hit me. I was wearing a seatbelt, and I remember as the car moved along upside down my face was only about eighteen inches from the road which was rushing past, lit by the headlamps. I remember this sudden explosion of glass as the windshield

> collapsed. Then, suddenly, I could hear people shouting 'Petrol, petrol', and discovered I could not open the doors because the roof had been crushed. But finally I managed to climb out. About twenty people gathered and we rolled the car over and I attempted to drive off but was stopped by the police. I spent three days with a splitting headache, then went out, hired a car, drove to where the wrecked Zephyr was stored and photographed it. I'd developed exactly the obsession I'd described in *The Atrocity Exhibition.*

The blowout, a later addition, is suspect. A car with a blown tyre is virtually undriveable. The photos he took of the car while it sat in the police pound don't include a shot of the blown tyre – an obvious subject – and from what one can see of the front tyres, both appear intact. Charles Platt insists: 'He said nothing about a blowout. I pressed him on the cause of the accident, and he threw up his hands and said, "It just went out of control!" Of course I have no doubt he had been drinking.'

That Jim was charged with driving under the influence remained a secret for more than thirty years. He made the first public reference in an interview given in 1986 but not published until 2005. Even then, he simply said, 'Alcohol is a big problem here. There's a mandatory year's ban, which I've been through.' A fuller description appears, by inference, in his 2003 novel *Millennium People.* The protagonist, David Markham, is arrested after a brawl, and appears at Hammersmith Grove magistrates' court, as Jim would have done. The book describes convincingly the miasma of guilt and despair, and the ceaseless coming and going of lawyers, prisoners, policemen and witnesses, whom Markham compares to characters out of Lewis Carroll. He is fined £100 and bound over to keep the peace. Jim, too, was fined, his licence was suspended for a year, and he had to pay a further £100 to replace the demolished sign. The replacement, he noticed wryly next time he passed, was of a more sophisticated design.

Without a car, Jim felt marooned. 'After a while, I found that I never went anywhere. I would take walks to the horizon, which for a man of my height is roughly about half to three-quarters of a mile away. That was as far as I would be able to walk. So in effect I was living on this planet about a mile wide, and never going anywhere. My whole universe just shrank.'

He wasn't, however, entirely morose. To have survived an accident induced a perverse excitement. Like a neophyte member of the hunt, he had been in at the kill, and been 'blooded'. Once the police released the car, he insisted on having it repaired, even though it had been sitting in the open for weeks. Mike Moorcock went with him to drive it back. 'He's arguing with the blokes and he gets the car back. It's not running, it's rumbling along. It stinks of death. It reeks of damp and mould. We're doing about ten miles an hour. Everything steaming and banging. And he's insisting it's all right.'

It never took to the road again. In July 1973, more than a year later, a French journalist remarked on 'an old American car, with numerous dents' still parked in front of the house. It became his private *Crashed Cars* exhibition, both a *memento mori* and his 'red badge of courage'. Charles Platt says, 'After the total, almost maniacal immersion which the book entailed, maintaining an obsession with car crashes for more than a year, I think he really needed a crash, in the same way that his protagonists often needed to follow a path to oblivion, which Jimmy justified because they were achieving "psychological fulfilment".'

Despite the accident, Jim didn't forgo his usual month in Spain with Walsh. In 1972, he chose Rosas, on the Costa Blanca, not far from Salvador Dalí's home at Port Lligat, and rented an apartment in one of the blocks along the Mediterranean. He returned there after the grandiose Dalí Museum opened in 1974 in the rebuilt Municipal Theatre of nearby Figueras. The proliferation of tower blocks along this coast disturbed and stimulated him, becoming the setting for 'Low-Flying Aircraft', the title story of his next collection. It imagined a future in which mankind, hoping to reverse a falling birth rate, builds 'Venus Hotels' along the Mediterranean coast, where erotic décor, sex shops and porn films hopefully encourage procreation.

With a censorship-free Denmark now acting as a conduit to channel every imaginable form of erotica into the rest of the world, the story restated his belief that the proliferation of pornography, far from being a corrupt diversion for a bored populace, was society's way of stimulating a flagging birth rate.

Jim's excursions on foot around Shepperton reintroduced him to the landscape. When he moved there in 1960, these fields had been rural and bucolic – the background to the charmingly naive landscapes of Stanley Spencer in not too distant Cookham. Since then, they'd been overrun by dual carriageways, shopping centres and housing developments, not to mention the spread of Heathrow Airport. But signs of the original streets, culverts and canals remained, and Jim rediscovered them as a pedestrian. This knowledge informed the book he was gestating. Called *Concrete Island*, it became the most self-searching of all his novels, an attempt to realise his adolescent ambition to conduct his own psychoanalysis.

Jim always wrote a synopsis before starting work: a single page for stories, but more for novels. 'I don't mean a rough draft,' he said, 'but a running narrative in the perfect tense with the dialogue in reported speech, and with an absence of reflective passages and editorializing.' His outline for *Concrete Island* is twenty-four double-spaced pages long, and differs in only a few details from the book. His main character, called, once again, Robert Maitland, like the protagonist of *The Wind from Nowhere*, is a successful architect. Driving home mid-afternoon along the Westway, he experiences the same accident as Jim, although the car, rather than overturning, plunges below road level into a steep-sided miniature valley, an 'island' between roads where he can no longer be seen, and from which, having hurt his leg, he finds it impossible to escape. Sustained by a case of wine in the boot of his car, he explores the archaeology of former occupancy: the remains of the suburban street demolished to make way for the road, the subterranean ruins of a cinema, and an air raid shelter from the Second World War.

In one of many parallels with *The Tempest*, the concrete island is full of voices. Its Miranda is a young prostitute, unnamed in the outline but called Jane Sheppard in the book. She lives in the air raid shelter and climbs back to ground level to work. It also has its Caliban, a simple-minded but powerful tramp named Proctor. Maitland, their Prospero, subdues both with relative ease, using his superior intellect, lubricated with wine. The girl heals his leg and has sex with him, at a price. Proctor shows him where to find food dumped by local restaurants. Freed of concern about his job, wife and mistress, Maitland surrenders to his enforced isolation. He realises that the girl and Proctor were not his captors; rather he had become theirs. In his outline, Jim acknowledges that the Maitland character is in no hurry to escape. His very presence there is an escape – from his past, from his childhood, his wife and friends, with all the affectations and demands. This reflection culminates in his ultimate revelation – he *is* the island.

Concrete Island is littered with correspondences to Jim's life, aside from the topical one of his virtual confinement in Shepperton for a year while under the drink-driving ban. His pleasure in casual sex is reflected in his attitude to the greedy Jane. An episode in which she berates Maitland is taken from real life with Claire. 'That is a transcript of a secret tape recording I made of my then-girlfriend in a rage,' he admitted. 'Well, "secret" is the wrong word; she was simply too angry to notice that I had switched the machine on.' Some of his more Freudian first thoughts didn't survive into the book. Proctor has created a shrine to an old mentor, decorating it with scraps of shiny car trim. Initially the shrine's centrepiece was the man's mummified body, but Jim removed this detail, as well as the fact that Jane's stillborn child is buried on the island.

At 42,000 words, *Concrete Island* is among Jim's shortest books. The premise is too flimsy to bear the weight of a novel, and could have been fully explored in a novella. After the muscularity of *Crash*, the writing is flaccid. It also exposes the sameness of his settings. Once again, a man imprisoned within concrete walls grapples with questions of ontology, finding relief in sex and violence. But Iain Sinclair sees virtuosity in Jim's narrowness of focus:

> The material of *The Atrocity Exhibition* is revised for the middle-brow audience with *Crash*, *Concrete Island*, and *High-Rise*, but doesn't work as well. Then there's *Empire of the Sun* – a break with the past; acclaim; the film, Spielberg. After that, he uses the material yet again, in a series of ecological fantasies – *The Day of Creation*, *Rushing to Paradise* – and yet again in the form of some almost Agatha Christie novels – *Cocaine Nights* and *Super-Cannes*: tourist fiction. A wonderfully controlled career; exemplary.

Though few novels are more preoccupied with the Self than *Concrete Island*, nobody challenged Jim on his former antipathy to introspective fiction. And perhaps not unfairly, because the events that transpire on the island lack the precise social observation of the 'Hampstead novel'. They hardly seem real at all. It would be no surprise to have the book end, like Lawrence Durrell's *Cefalu*, published in 1947 (which it in some ways resembles) in the revelation that all the characters are dead, a device Jim uses in his novella *The Dead Time* and with which he flirts in *The Unlimited Dream Company*. The imprecision of *Concrete Island* and its aims was dramatised in its packaging. For its cover, Cape chose a characterless steel-grey triangular column. Farrar, Straus & Giroux, no more appropriately but closer to Jim's ad-man spirit, showed Maitland contemplating a crevice between flyovers, slyly drawn to suggest a woman's spread thighs, complete with pubic thicket.

In July 1970, Cape had published *The Atrocity Exhibition* in Britain to general, if muted, acclaim, though its reputation would grow until it became one of the most respected of Jim's works, if not the most commercial. Following the Doubleday pulping, Dutton bought the US rights, but when their lawyers demanded numerous changes, including the removal of all references to Reagan and Jackie Kennedy, Jim terminated the deal. In 1972, the more adventurous Grove Press, which had already used extracts in *Evergreen Review*, published a US edition, with an introduction by William Burroughs, but, despite Jim's objections, under a title taken from one of its episodes, *Love and Napalm: Export USA*. The cover design of a grinning skull, painted with flowers, was redolent of hippiedom, and the use of 'napalm' implied the subject was Vietnam. Jim protested that, despite an occasional reference, the book had nothing to do with war. Grove went ahead anyway.

Reviews boxed the compass. 'Enviable, admirable Ballard!' wrote Susan Sontag, calling the book 'subtle, brutal, cerebral, intoxicating'. In *The New York Times Book Review*, however, Paul Theroux labelled it 'a stylish anatomy of outrage, full of specious arguments, phony statistics, a disgusted fascination with movie stars and the sexual conceits of American brand names and paraphernalia'. He continued, 'Man is more than warm meat, but Mr Ballard's attitude is calculated. He says love when he means sex, and sex when he means torture, and there is nothing so fragile as sorrow or joy in the book. It is not his choice of subject, but his celebration of it that is monstrous.' Such reviews, coupled with the Doubleday experience, warned major US publishers off Jim. He didn't hide his resentment. For his last few novels, he told his agent not to seek US publication at all.

These reverses pushed Jim into further drinking, which in turn affected his relationship with Claire, who turned up at the Moorcock's door one night, claiming he had pushed her out of the car following an argument. After she appeared at some social events in tears, or with dark glasses to disguise a black eye, Moorcock confronted him about his abuse. 'Jimmy was knocking Claire about,' he said, 'and I had to speak to him about it.' Ballard's reaction was expectable. 'I pretty much knew how it would run. What do you call a clam with both parts of its shell duct-taped together? This being Jimmy, he withdrew completely – bingo, I wasn't there any more.' The two old friends didn't speak for years.

CHAPTER THIRTY-SEVEN

UP!

At 476 pages – more than 100,000 words – the typescript of *Crash!*, both in size and content, shook Jonathan Cape. As they debated their options, copies were sent to readers – outsiders with the expertise to assess a book's commercial potential. According to Jim, one was the wife of a 'well-known TV psychiatrist', who concluded: 'This author is beyond psychiatric help. Do not publish!' Leaving aside the improbability of any psychiatrically competent person describing someone as 'beyond help', and of making such a judgement on the basis of a book alone, there were no psychiatrists on British TV in 1972. Moreover, in practice, such a verdict wasn't particularly damning. Cape saw hostility as an indication of potential controversy and, thus, sales. As for Ballard, who was the only source of the anecdote, the frequency with which he retold it suggests he took the judgement as a compliment. Nor did he particularly disagree, acknowledging that his motives for writing *Crash* were confused. Reading the proofs nine months later, his first reaction had been 'the guy who wrote this must be nuts'.

As *Crash!*, Cape put the book into its summer catalogue to retail at what was then a hefty £2.75, as against £1.05 for his previous books. But during editing, second thoughts prevailed, at least about length. Jim conceded only that, at Cape's request, he made it 'slightly shorter'. In fact, when the book hit shops on 28 June 1973, a third of the text had been deleted, as well as the title's exclamation mark. The published version sold at £2.25 but was just 70,000 words long.

Unsure of how to package or promote it, Cape assigned the task of designing a cover to Bill Botten. 'I knew that by using the content I would probably end up with something rather savage,' he said, 'so plumped for a design that I hoped would indicate that this was a monumental book and that *Crash* involved cars.' It owes much to Nick Castle's pop art logo for Kubrick's *A Clockwork Orange.* That featured a massive letter 'A', from within which a smiling Malcolm McDowell brandished a sadophallic dagger. Botten rendered Ballard's title as a monolith in marble, looming behind a thrusting purple-pink gearstick, bulbous knob decorated with a semen-white comma of gleam. Jim disliked the design, but preferred it to the one created by Lawrence Ratzkin for Farrar, Straus & Giroux, who published simultaneously in the US. Ratzkin catered to Ballard's SF readership with a futuristic car whose contours approximated a female body, tapering at the rear to red-varnished toenails.

The jacket copy of both editions soft-pedalled the novel's erotic relish. Cape called it 'a cautionary tale, a warning against the brutal, erotic and overlit future that beckons us, ever more powerfully, from the margins of the technological landscape'. Farrar, Straus preferred 'visionary portrait', and stressed the *Clockwork Orange* parallel – a risky strategy, since Kubrick's film was attracting a storm of controversy and baseless accusations of copycat crimes.

Critical reaction ranged from revulsion in the conservative press through embarrassment among Ballard's SF fans to an awed respect in the counter-culture. *The Times* rubbished it. 'Ballard has a brilliant reputation but this novel's obsession with sado-masochism via deliberate car-crashing is repellent. The fact that he writes well makes it creepier.' Martin Amis in the *Observer* was almost as unsparing, calling it 'heavily flawed: loose construction, a perfunctory way with minor characters, and a lot of risible overwriting make it hard not to see the book as an exercise in vicious whimsy'. The *New York Times* conceded it was well written but dismissed it as 'a crazed morbid roundelay of dismemberment and sexual perversion'. Jim claimed he never read any of the notices. He was cheered, however, by a new interest in his work from film producers. *Concrete Island* had been optioned almost immediately after publication, and it remained under option to various producers, but the film was never made. A number of interested parties would also option *Crash*, though none found a way to film it until David Cronenberg's 1996 version.

Back in Shepperton, Jim contemplated a new novel. It owed part of its inspiration to an incident observed on holiday in Rosas. One of the ground-floor tenants in the building where they rented an apartment was infuriated by cigarette butts tossed from upper floors on to his patio. Lurking on the beach, he snapped the offenders with a long lens and posted their pictures in the foyer. This memory fused with the appearance in west London of new blocks of flats, replacing the Victorian bedsits of his student days. Large-panel construction, in which prefabricated concrete units were bolted together at the site, made cheap high-rise housing affordable. At the same time, luxury office and apartment buildings were appearing in former Thames dockland, abandoned when the use of container ships forced freight docking and handling downstream.

'I did research before sitting down to write,' Jim said. 'For example, in cities, the degree of criminality is affected by liberty of movement; it's higher in culs-de-sac. And high-rises are culs-de-sac: two thousand people jammed together in the air.' His primary source was architect and city planner Oscar Newman, whose book *Defensible Space* appeared in 1972. Citing statistics on crime prevention and neighbourhood safety in New York, Newman suggested that densely populated buildings suffered more crime because residents felt no responsibility for an area occupied by so many people. In *Cocaine Nights*, published in 1996, Jim cites 'Goldfinger's theory of Defensible Space' – a reference to Ernő Goldfinger, the British architect whose Trellick Tower, a thirty-one-storey block of flats in north Kensington, also opened in 1972. Bearing out Newman's theory (and Jim's), Trellick Tower and similar low-rent housing became notorious for vandalism. Lifts were wrecked and walls defaced with graffiti. The spaces between buildings became no-go areas, prowled by street gangs.

What if, Jim speculated, the same hooliganism took place in a luxury block? He imagined a tower of forty floors, containing a thousand apartments, dwarfing Trellick's 217. His nameless tower has two thousand tenants, all prosperous professionals. Lower floors are occupied by a 'proletariat' of film technicians and air hostesses, the middle levels by doctors and lawyers, accountants and tax specialists, and the top ten floors by minor tycoons and entrepreneurs, television actresses and academics. It stands with five others in what was still, at the time of writing, a wilderness of abandoned warehouses near the Isle of Dogs. The novel describes how it might look when these were demolished: a table-flat landscape, Tanguyesque in its emptiness, dotted with towers lonely as monoliths. A sea of parking lots laps the buildings. Once tenants lock their cars, there's little reason to leave, since each tower, a vertical suburb, offers a supermarket, an off-licence, a school, a crèche, a restaurant, doctors' surgeries and a sports and swimming complex. Informally, a few tenants supply other services, including massage and sex. After a number of title changes, from *The Towers* and *The High Life* to *Up!*, Jim decided on *High-Rise*.

Work commenced with his usual outline. 'It was about twenty-five thousand words, written in the form of a social worker's report on the strange events that had taken place in this apartment block, an extended case history. I wish I'd kept it; I think it was better than the novel.' The premise was straightforward. As the last tenants move in, the quality of life starts to deteriorate. Rivalries develop and fester. From an argument about the use of lifts, the tension, exacerbated by technical breakdowns, explodes into warfare between the three strata.

Many reviewers read the novel as a parable of the British class system, but Jim denied any such intention. He visualised the story taking place in the near future when social standing depended on professional accomplishment rather than a 'good family', and a high salary counted for more than 'old money'.

> There's a new class emerging which I guess didn't really exist until the thirties, or the twenties in the US, a sort of professional class which

includes everyone from cost accountants to dentists to air-traffic controllers. These people, regardless of their background, have more in common with each other than with the children they played with at home. High technology has given these people a very strong sense of identity. I was interested in studying this new class and wondering what would happen if it came under extreme internal stresses.

We watch the escalating chaos through the eyes of three men – Laing, a doctor-turned-lecturer, Wilder, a documentary film-maker, and an architect, Royal, who helped design the building. The first warning of impending anarchy is a wine bottle from an upper floor smashing on Laing's balcony. Visiting the roof, he's menaced by the guests at a cocktail party, despite the presence of Royal, who appears content to stand back and observe. Within weeks, Royal and Wilder are dead, and the building ruined, its walls covered with graffiti, barricades of furniture blocking corridors and stairwells, its swimming pool clogged with corpses. Laing, the primary narrator, survives only by reverting to the law of the jungle. As calm returns, Jim describes him sitting on his balcony, contentedly dining off the roasted hindquarters of Royal's pet Alsatian.

Beginning with this surrealistically incongruous image, the book flashes back to the events of the conflict, which Laing catalogues with relish. For all its superficial social satire, *High-Rise* is a celebration of Sadeian violence. In the way the privileged lock themselves in with their victims, the book echoes *The 120 Days of Sodom*, in which four wealthy sensualists congregate in a château with four equally corrupt brothel-keepers, and resolve to inflict on forty-six innocents every depravity they can imagine. Jim called *Sodom* 'a masterpiece, a black cathedral of a book, forcing us to realise that imagination transcends morality'. The high-rise war unfolds as a similar monstrous conspiracy. The staff shut their offices and flee, while the residents keep silent about the carnage, even lying to the police when the first victim falls to his death. *High-Rise* also recalls *Lord of the Flies* in acknowledging that, relieved of social restraints, a group of civilised humans will revert swiftly to savagery, but Jim makes the violence more calculated – as if some boys in Golding's book had engineered the plane crash in order to experiment on the weakest.

Nowhere does Jim deplore the mayhem. Rather, his protagonists either revel in it or observe it dispassionately – literally so with Wilder, who films it for a documentary. Laing eating the dog is a satisfied man, for whom anarchy has brought not disquiet but contentment. His experience demonstrates the benefits that accrue to those strong enough to seize them. As the society of the building breaks down, unattached women and the wives of weaker men gravitate to the more powerful males, just as the American sailors in Lunghua became a magnet for the sexually frustrated females of the camp. As Laing gets drunk in preparation for seducing one of them, he acknowledges that he and his neighbours see trouble as a means of enlarging their sex lives. He ends up sharing his apartment with two complaisant female companions. Meanwhile, Royal has sex with a woman while his wife watches. This isn't presented as an incident of erotic complaisance in a so-called 'open marriage' but, rather, as a demonstration of tribal solidarity, the wife ceding total deference to the leader of the clan.

The building in *High-Rise* is itself a model of aspiration, but the things to which the tenants aspire – sex, violence, the domination of others – are, as Freud pointed out in *Civilization and Its Discontents*, the very elements that undermine society. In embracing them, people release their tensions, restoring normality, for a time at least. In *Cocaine Nights* and *Super-Cannes*, Jim would argue the point in more detail, and show how the philosophy functions in practice. *High-Rise* stands as a crude sketch of the Freudian interpretation – the building a forty-storey penis and the novel its orgasmic emission.

The lawlessness of *High-Rise* reflected a period in British politics typified by a loss of influence overseas and, at home, a debilitating war with the unions as they fought a rearguard action against the advance of technology. The novel articulated a common frustration with Britain's decline, to which Margaret Thatcher would give a voice, speaking of 'a feeling of helplessness, that a once great nation has somehow fallen behind'. Many passages foreshadow the manic cry of Peter Finch as the deranged newsreader in the film *Network* who urges listeners to open their windows and shout, 'I'm mad as hell and I'm not going to take it any more!' By the time Thatcher became prime minister in 1979, Jim was her supporter, although, as in his preaching of anarchy, admiration was mixed with desire. He happily confessed that, given half a chance, he would gladly have sex with the Iron Lady, if possible on the back seat of the prime ministerial Daimler V8. It was an ambition that, fictionally, he would achieve in the novel published in 1994, *Rushing to Paradise.*

Once Canary Wharf and its associated developments began to transform the Isle of Dogs, opponents of this invasion, assuming Jim meant *High-Rise* as a Dreadful Warning, tried to recruit him to their cause. In 1991, BBC TV's *The Late Show* brought him back to inspect the complex then colonising both banks of the Thames. Other contributors to the programme excoriated the violence done to the traditional architecture of the area by the building of Canary Wharf, Iain Sinclair labelling it a 'swampland Manhattan', but Jim was more benign. 'I think it would be an exciting place to move the entire British people into,' he said. 'Perhaps people should be forced to come here for a fortnight every year. It might radically change the national character. We might become more like the North Americans.' He paused to smile at the remoteness of this possibility. 'I may move in tomorrow.'

CHAPTER THIRTY-EIGHT

LOW FLYING

Writing of Ballard in his early forties, his friend John Clute remarked, 'Jimmy Ballard had developed into a remarkably attractive figure':

> He was of medium stature, with swept-back receding hair, and a gaze that seemed both bland and impatient. He was bonhomous in a fashion that somehow suggested to his companions that he might not, in truth, be that easy to please. Without seeming to notice his effect on others, without ever claiming to do much other than work hard in Shepperton, he gave an impression of almost dangerous worldliness, as though he understood too much. Perhaps because he seemed physically denser than other people, they orbited him. He was charismatic. He gave audience. He loved in particular women, and for years after 1965, he was intensely involved with more than one partner.

One such partner was the writer and editor Emma Tennant. In the mid-seventies, independent literary fiction almost disappeared from British news-stands. No magazine specifically served the counter-culture as *Village Voice*, *Evergreen Review* and Andy Warhol's *Inter/View* did in the US. Tennant, seeing a niche and admiring the tabloid format of *Inter/View*, launched *Bananas*, a lookalike quarterly that, unaccountably, took its name from Woody Allen's eponymous 1971 film about a nebbish who bumbles into the leadership of a South American revolution.

Bananas was as unconventional as its editor. A novelist manquée and journalist for magazines such as *Vogue* and *Queen*, Tennant was also the independently wealthy daughter of the 2nd Baron

Glenconner, though much of her fortune was lost bankrolling the magazine *New Left Review.* She edited *Bananas* from her house at 2 Blenheim Crescent, off Ladbroke Grove. Former *New Worlds* contributors John Sladek, Tom Disch and Mike Moorcock were all regular visitors. She took both Sladek and Moorcock as lovers, inspiring the six-foot-six-inch flame-haired bisexual empress Gloriana I in Moorcock's *Gloriana, or the Unfulfill'd Queen*, while his ex-wife, Hilary Bailey, became a close friend and *Bananas* contributor.

The first issue of *Bananas* appeared in January 1975. Tennant's aggression and seductiveness, combined with her imposing height, good looks and unapologetic snobbery – she dismissed Anthony Powell as 'a parvenu' – made her an effectively iconoclastic editor and publisher. 'The magazine began to be attacked in critical quarterlies – always a good sign,' she wrote with satisfaction, 'and Auberon Waugh called it "pretentious rubbish".' Ballard and Moorcock had each encouraged Tennant as a writer. Her novel *The Last of the Country House Murders*, published in 1974, is dedicated to Jim. He also agreed to become associate editor of *Bananas*, and contributed a story to almost every issue, beginning with 'The Air Disaster' in issue No. 1.

About the time *Bananas* was launched, Claire Walsh had been surprised and pleased to be asked to tea by Tennant. Her suspicions weren't even aroused by the way conversation kept returning to Ballard, and she left with the sense that she'd made a new friend. There was no second invitation. Instead, she discovered Jim was now sharing Tennant's bed. That year's Spanish holiday would be their last for a long time. After what Walsh called 'a blazing row', they parted, apparently for good.

Tennant and Ballard were not a good fit, and the relationship didn't last. She'd been charmed when, on their second meeting, he arrived with the gift of a potted plant, but disconcerted when, on every subsequent occasion, he gave her an identical plant, until they cluttered up the flat. Tongue in cheek, she reciprocated with the gift of a large aluminium palm tree. Jim installed it in his living room, another eccentricity to puzzle visiting journalists. His replacement in Tennant's affections was Ted Hughes, who inspired her to write a *roman-à-clef* about their relationship, and a sensational memoir.

In 1974, Penguin reprinted *The Drowned World*, *The Terminal Beach*, *The Drought* and *The Wind from Nowhere* as a boxed set with new artwork. For the first time, Jim had some say about how his books appeared. Penguin's new head of design, David Pelham, was a friend of Paolozzi, who took him to Shepperton.

> I admired the bleak style of his catastrophe novels, and their heartless depiction of technological and human breakdown and decay. Grim perhaps, but wonderfully written. Drawn to the romance of his apocalyptic imagery, I wanted to illustrate his covers myself. I quickly airbrushed a postcard-sized image to show him the idea, and talked to him about his other titles in the list.

The covers depict what Pelham called 'the debris of our society' – a Centurion tank, a Detroit-made automobile, the first atomic bomb, the art deco summit of the Chrysler Building, a Second World War bomber – but in each case in eccentric juxtaposition with the material world: the Chrysler Building almost completely underwater, the bomber and the car nosed into sand, the tank doing a somersault. Drawn with pop art precision and in vivid colours against black backgrounds, the images strike the balance between surrealism and technology that Jim strove to attain. As illustrations to his work, they remain unsurpassed.

In 1975, the magazine *Science Fiction Monthly* ran a competition for fantasy paintings. The American artist Brigid Marlin won with a canvas titled *The Rod*. It showed a woman holding a rod in one hand and in the other a burning newspaper with the headline 'WAR'. Behind her stretches a desert, littered with cars half buried in the sand, and invaded on one side by a city of high-rises, on the other by an oil refinery. Jim wrote an enthusiastic letter of appreciation, the only fan letter he ever sent to a painter. *The Rod* could, he told her, have made a perfect cover illustration for one of his novels, particularly since it included the buried cars of *The Drought.* Marlin mislaid the letter for ten years, so never had a chance to tell him that the landscape was a more or less accurate depiction of the Kuwaiti desert, where she'd spent some time. The locals really did buy cars, drive them off into the desert, crash or overturn them and just walk away.

The British publication in November 1975 of *High-Rise* was an unexpected success. 'Ballard's finest novel! A triumph,' trumpeted *The Times.* The *Daily Express* praised it as 'another eerie glimpse into the future. A fast-moving, spine-tingling fable of the concrete jungle.' *Time Out* found it 'a gripping read, particularly if you like your thrills chilly, bloody and with claims to social relevance', while Martin Amis in the *New Statesman* called it 'an intense and vivid bestiary, which lingers unsettlingly in the mind'. Nobody reviewed it as science fiction. Rather, it belonged to the expanding genre of 'Condition of England' novels. These took a national tendency and exaggerated it for the purposes of satire – a form of speculative fantasy that approximated to Kingsley Amis's ideal for a low-tech, essentially British SF.

On paper, Jim sounded increasingly like a convert to Amis's ideas. 'I believe that SF will become more and more an aspect of daily reality,' he told a German interviewer. 'It has migrated from the bookshelf to daily life.' If he was a convert, however, he was a heretical one. Where Amis argued that SF should adapt to literature, Ballard proposed that literature and the arts adapt to SF – that they were, in fact, in the process of doing so. He even reversed his former rejection of Moorcock and the counter-culture.

> One sees the landscapes and imagery of SF, one sees their contents playing a part in the world of pop music, of film, even that of psychedelic experiences. The reason being, that SF was always concerned with psychological perceptions, and the world of pop music, film and psychedelic experience is now greatly concerned with the senses, with perspectives of our own psychological space-time, and has not so much to do with questions of individual histories, the past and

> so forth, as were the prejudices of the literature and cinema of the past. I believe that in the last ten years the entire basis of SF has changed rapidly.

The film rights to *High-Rise* were optioned by Euston Films, the features-producing division of Thames Television, known almost entirely for low-budget crime films spun off from series such as *The Sweeney*. Bruce Robinson, later writer/director of the hit comedy *Withnail and I*, wrote a screenplay. 'Bruce put a lot of work into it,' noted an acquaintance. 'He researched the architectural side of the story, as well as some particularly gruesome torture devices available to "ordinary" people.' The script would have cost an estimated $35 million to film. 'It was dumped,' says the same source, 'because Bruce believed it would never be made.' Paul Mayersberg, who wrote *The Man Who Fell to Earth* and *Eureka* for Nicholas Roeg, did another adaptation – though not, he insists, for Roeg.

> I made it into a story about a man breaking into the building. He was a computer man. I placed it quite differently. In my version, the building existed in the middle of a desert in Arizona. It was like a totem. When he looked at it, he saw two buildings, but when he arrived there, he found only one. It was just a site. People would come along, look at it, then go away again. Inside it there was just decay, and the man came in to try and find out what was going on. I delved into character vignettes, overlapping lives and relationships. It wasn't a project for Nic, though. Some producer came to me and asked me to write a script. He didn't like it. The rights reverted.

Film-maker Chris Petit pointed out the irony of Ballard living within walking distance of a major studio, yet none of his repeatedly optioned novels and stories ever being filmed. In truth, this was not so remarkable. The 'writing in pictures' praised by David Lean was negated by his self-absorbed, uncommunicative characters and a lack of interest in the relationships between them. These drawbacks defeated screenwriters until David Cronenberg 'licked' *Crash*, at the cost of turning its crazed polemic into melodrama. Film-makers closer to Jim's sensibility, such as Alain Resnais, Chris Marker and Michelangelo Antonioni, never tried to adapt his work, although it's impossible to speak of any of them without invoking Ballard, so tangled are their shared obsessions. Resnais's time-travel story *Je t'aime, Je t'aime* scales up Chris Marker's film *La Jetée*, while Antonioni's cityscapes at nightfall, and his lingering stares at fizzing street lamps invigilating streets void of all life, look forward to Ballard's empty cities, and concrete bunkers seared by nuclear light.

As if to counterbalance the indifference of film-makers, the tin-eared Ballard increasingly, and ironically, acquired iconic status among musicians. *High-Rise* inspired a song of the same name by Robert Calvert of Hawkwind, the rock group with which Mike Moorcock performed. Joy Division's Ian Curtis, in search of inspiration, would lock himself in his study with his favourite books, including titles by Ballard. His 1980 album *Closer* includes the track 'Atrocity Exhibition'. In 2001, Madonna recorded a song called 'The Drowned World'. The Clash, Joy Division, Throbbing Gristle, Cabaret Voltaire, The Sisters of Mercy, Radiohead, Ultravox and The Human League all paid tribute in song. Best of all for Jim, Grace Jones, for whom he confessed a *béguin*, covered The Normal's 'Warm Leatherette', the *Crash* anthem *sans pareil*.

Meanwhile, loonier fans door-stepped Jim in Shepperton or lurked under the Westway, seeking the exact location of his concrete island. It would never have entered their minds to follow Kerans by checking into the penthouse at the Ritz. Socially or architecturally, 'Up' was not a Ballardian direction. He was the People's Guru, the patron saint of grunge, a psychopathic Peter the Hermit, leading his followers away from the music, towards the hum of the motorway and the sallow wash of light from the mercury vapour lamps.

After 'Low-Flying Aircraft' appeared in the second issue of *Bananas*, dated 'Early summer' and published in June 1975, Jim didn't publish anything for six months. He occupied his time writing his own screenplay of *Concrete Island*. This attempt to jump-start his career in a new medium reflected his disquiet about his relative lack of commercial success and stubbornly modest income. The fiction market was separating into high brow and low brow, and nowhere more than in fantasy and SF. C. S. Lewis, J. R. R. Tolkien, Alan Garner and T. H. White all enjoyed enthusiastic readership and critical support, but 'mid-list' writers such as Ballard lacked the numbers to compete. Cape encouraged some to try fiction for young adults. Thriller writer Lionel Davidson made a new career in the genre, but Kingsley Amis's 1973 *The Riverside Villas Murder*, an attempt at a detective story with a schoolboy investigator, fell between stools.

As well as the screenplay, Jim worked on a novella called 'The Ultimate City' which, David Pringle suggests, he meant for the juvenile market. Such a change of direction would be characteristic of Jim's need to rebrand himself with every third or fourth book. He had already flirted with writing for children with his 1966 *Jackanory*. In 1973, grounded by his drunk-driving conviction, he developed a book called 'Last Rocket to the Moon' with *Ambit* art director Michael Foreman. 'It was about an old astronaut living in an overgrown and neglected Cape Canaveral,' said Foreman. 'It was to be a picture book so Jim's text was short. I did a cover and a dummy and several pictures, plus a complete layout.' Collins expressed interest, but the book was never published. Possibly, after *Crash*, nobody wanted Jim within barge-pole proximity to young minds.

Halloway, the main character of 'The Ultimate City', is a young and frustrated technophile in a future that has rejected machines. His home, Garden City, is a Green Party poster community, plant-filled and solar-powered. Frustrated by its inertia, Halloway explores the workshop of his late inventor father, builds a sailplane from his designs and flies it to the ruined metropolis on the other side of the bay, now a graveyard of abandoned technology. Wandering its streets, he finds pyramids created from TV sets, washing machines, cars. They turn out to be the work of a sole surviving industrialist, Buckmaster, who detests the world of waterwheels and solar panels. His monuments are cenotaphs, celebrating the unappreciated contributions of rampant high technology. Inspired, Halloway recruits other renegades and criminals who've taken refuge in the city. They round up the last reserves of oil and briefly restore power to one small district. Halloway savours the return of electricity to the streets and supermarkets. When the tanks run dry, he sets out across the continent, aiming to outdo Buckmaster in erecting ever more imposing monuments – of airliners, freight trains and missile launchers.

Halloway has his Holden Caulfield aspect, and the elements of hobbyism, youthful rebellion and father worship are straight off the juvenile fiction playlist. Unfortunately the story is obscure where it should be clear, and chill where it demands intimacy. Mostly, it betrays Jim's ambivalence towards his own parents. Halloway admires his father and acknowledges his influence, but there's no denying that, like fathers in most Ballard fiction, he's dead. In building the sailplane, he's in effect reincarnating him. Crashing the craft into his own reflection in the mirrored façade of a skyscraper, he's reborn in the back seat of an abandoned car, the softly upholstered interior of which he compares to the womb. Before going on, he takes a last look at the wreckage of the sailplane, which reminds him of the body of his father.

CHAPTER THIRTY-NINE

WILLIAM BLAKE'S LEFT FOOT

That Ballard's mid-life crisis came late, in his forties, didn't make it any less debilitating. His autobiographical novel *The Kindness of Women* describes a fictional Jim moping around his deserted home, mourning the departure of his children, and comparing the house to the set of a long-running family sitcom that's just been axed. He took refuge in repetition – evoked by Iain Sinclair.

> Fixed routines served him well. So many hours, so many words. Breakfast. *Times* crossword. Stroll to the shops to observe the erotic rhythms of consumerism. Lunch standing up with *The World at One* on the radio. Back to the study. Forty-minute constitutional down to the river. TV chill-out meditation – *Hawaii Five-O* and *The Rockford Files* rather than Kenneth Clark.

Not mentioned was alcohol, though when describing the same working day to a journalist, Jim concluded his summary with 'then, at six, Scotch and soda, and oblivion'. His casual reference disguised the major drinking problem he'd gradually brought under control. When Lynn Barber asked how difficult it had been, Jim said, 'It was like the Battle of Stalingrad.' Writing had become systematic; second nature. 'Every day, five days a week,' he said:

> Longhand now, it's less tiring than a typewriter. When I'm writing a novel or story I set myself a target of about seven hundred words a day, sometimes a little more. I do a first draft in longhand, then do a very careful longhand revision of the text, then type out the final

manuscript. I used to type first and revise in longhand, but I find that modern fibre-tip pens are less effort than a typewriter. Perhaps I ought to try a seventeenth-century quill. I rewrite a great deal, so the word processor sounds like my dream. My neighbour is a BBC videotape editor and he offered to lend me his, but apart from the eye-aching glimmer, I found that the editing functions are terribly laborious. I'm told that already one can see the difference between fiction composed on the word processor and that on the typewriter. The word processor lends itself to a text that has great polish and clarity on a sentence-by-sentence and paragraph level, but has haywire overall chapter-by-chapter construction, because it's almost impossible to rifle through and do a quick scan of, say, twenty pages. Or so they say.

He didn't mention his practice of dictating the final version into a tape recorder for transcription by an audio typist. In the context of his monastic existence, this small concession to technology was an apostasy.

SF was changing as the focus of interest shifted to film and TV. In the US, writers such as Richard Matheson, Harlan Ellison and Ray Bradbury regularly wrote for Hollywood, or had their work adapted. Frank Robinson and Thomas Scortia collaborated on a novel that explored what might happen if fire broke out in a high-rise. 'The Glass Inferno' became a successful film, retitled *The Towering Inferno*.

In Britain, the hopes of Amis and Ballard that SF writers would move into the mainstream were being realised, but not as expected. Many did turn to literary fiction, but abandoned the fantastic entirely. Tom Disch's novels *Clara Reeve* and *Neighbouring Lives* explored nineteenth-century literary London, John Sladek wrote crime stories such as *Black Aura*, while Mike Moorcock varied his output of fantasy with modernist fiction like *Mother London*.

In 1970, Brian Aldiss began a trilogy of autobiographical novels with *The Hand-Reared Boy*. Thirteen publishers rejected his bawdy celebration of adolescent masturbation and rowdy behaviour in the army abroad, but, once it appeared, the response was enthusiastic.

This success nudged Jim into experimenting with memoir. The failure of 'The Ultimate City' added weight to the argument. Cape published it with eight other stories in December 1976 as *Low-Flying Aircraft*. It made little impression, and as Wolfers couldn't interest a US buyer, the book would never appear there.

True to his surrealist roots, and taking a cue from his parents, Jim despised religion. Though never descending to the snarling anarchy of Buñuel's 'I shit on God' or Benjamin Peret attacking nuns and priests in the street, he scorned the deity as no more than a clever wheeze of mankind. 'They really came up with a good idea there.' At the same time, to someone with his mystical inclination, the phenomenon of faith was as tantalising as alcohol. During the seventies, his interest increased, powered by a declining libido and intimations of mortality. One of the first products of this introspection, the novella 'The Dead Time', was written during the last half of 1976 and appeared in *Bananas* for March 1977. For the first time, he evoked his Shanghai childhood. The story's anonymous twenty-year-old narrator has been interned by the Japanese. As the guards flee, he sets out to find his parents, imprisoned in a camp nearby, and is offered use of a truck if he agrees to haul the bodies of some Western casualties, including a nun, to a Protestant cemetery.

The landscape of paddy fields and flooded ditches, many choked with corpses, would become familiar with *Empire of the Sun*. Driving across it, the narrator imagines the dead rising from the fields and moving towards him, as to a saviour. He rescues a starving child and feeds her bits of flesh from a wound on his own body. As he approaches the camp, he experiences an epiphany. Seeing his parents standing at the gate, awaiting him, he realises all of them are dead, and his war with life at an end.

'The Dead Time', so different from Ballard's usual work, confused the few people who read it. Even in the 1982 collection *Myths of the Near Future*, it attracted little interest, and after *Empire of the Sun* everyone pigeonholed it as a rough sketch for that book, whereas its real concerns are very different. The story's 'dead time' is the afterlife. The narrator symbolically transits a wilderness with a cargo of dead souls, bound for a place of rest. Christ-like, he offers his own flesh to feed the starving child ('This is my body, this is my blood ... ').

As he had done by evoking the Eucharistic elements of the automobile collision in *Crash*, 'The Dead Time' imports the secular mysticism of surrealism, Eliot and Burroughs into the Christ legend. The story dramatises Jim's special brand of atheism. God is not so much Our Father as *a* father, keeping an eye on things while his son carries on the family business, feeding the living and ushering the dead into his calming presence. His Reaper isn't Grim, just uninvolved. Jim imagined him as one of the enigmatic, faceless presences in the canvases of Francis Bacon, a man in a herringbone jacket, sitting in a garden with a machine gun by his side.

Jim didn't feel he'd exhausted this vein, since he immediately returned to it in the novel he began afterwards, at the end of 1976. The theme was, again, death and resurrection, but taking place close to home – much closer, since the locale is Shepperton, or at least a transmogrified version of the community. Pressed to summarise the plot, he did so in undramatic terms that hardly do justice to its eccentricity. 'It's about a young pilot who steals a light aircraft and crashes it into the Thames and, in a sense, dies; drowns in his aircraft but frees himself by an enormous effort of the imagination, and through his imagination transforms Shepperton into a kind of Edenic paradise full of exotic plants and animals.'

Alcohol probably played a role in his decision to write such a wildly visionary work. It had the reeling narrative invention that characterises some Beat literature, the sense of 'don't get it right, get it written'. Jim said he had read both Kerouac's *On the Road* and Allen Ginsberg's *Howl*, and kept up with Burroughs, on whose concepts the book to some extent draws. Additionally, there are resonances with the 'magic realism' of Carlos Castenada and other writers of the drug experience. Variously called *Fury* and *The Stunt Pilot*, the novel emerged as *The*

Unlimited Dream Company, a title he came to dislike. It sounded, he said, like the name of a jeans emporium.

Aside from calling his protagonist Blake, Jim said nothing about the sources of his ideas, sensing, rightly, that only a scholar would spot the parallels with William Blake's epic poem *Milton*. Written between 1804 and 1810, *Milton* is mainly remembered for the passage that provided Hubert Parry with the words for the hymn 'Jerusalem'. Around the time Jim wrote the novel, Blake scholars such as Northrop Frye and John Howard were reviving interest in the poet. They reminded people that there was more to *Milton* than 'arrows of desire' and 'dark Satanic mills'. Frye made a programme about it for the Open University, and it's likely Jim heard it, since his use of the text mirrors their interpretation.

Blake admired John Milton and in particular *Paradise Lost* but felt that the poet's puritanism limited his humanity. *Milton* begins with Blake theorising that mankind is divided into three categories – the Elect, the Redeemed and the Reprobate. It was the Reprobates who achieved true divinity, because they had sinned but were forgiven. Blake believes that Milton, as one of the Elect, will never be truly great unless he embraces the feminine side of his character. Hearing this lament in heaven, Milton descends in the form of a comet and, finding Blake in his cottage in Lambeth, enters his left foot.

From that moment, Blake perceives the world in new and mystical terms. He visualises the five senses as a sandal with which he can walk into the City of Art.

> And all this Vegetable World appeard on my left Foot,
> As a bright sandal formd immortal of precious stones & gold:
> I stooped down & bound it on to walk forward thro' Eternity.

A skylark metamorphoses into a twelve-year-old girl named Ololon. Blake assumes she's one of his muses, and invites her into his cottage, only to find she's Milton's long-lost feminine aspect, hoping to be united with him. With her help, and the intervention of other spirits, the two poets explore a London transformed by their combined vision.

With the help of Ololon, Milton achieves self-awareness. At the end of the poem, he returns to heaven, leaving Blake as his anointed heir. With his new powers, Blake is able to confront and defeat Lucifer, and see London transformed into the New Jerusalem.

There are obvious correspondences between the poem and *The Unlimited Dream Company*. A man named Blake, who has failed at being a pornographic writer, a medical student and a Jesuit novice (Reprobate, Redeemed and Elect) steals a small Cessna and, even though he's never flown before, gets it into the air long enough to reach nearby Shepperton, where, like Milton, he plunges to earth in flames, dousing them in the Thames.

Jim never decides whether Blake survives the crash to become the town's messiah, or drowns, and, dying, imagines all that follows, like the protagonists of William Golding's *Pincher Martin*, Lawrence Durrell's *Cefalu* and Ambrose Bierce's short story 'An Occurrence at Owl Creek Bridge'. Blake may even be deranged, and hallucinate everything. Since we see events only through his eyes, we are committed to his solipsistic view. In that vision, he's unable to cross the motorway into the world at large, but can work magic within Shepperton itself, where he assumes increasingly celestial and benevolent powers. From healing the sick, he progresses to absorbing the inhabitants into his body. Able to ejaculate semen like a hose, he fertilises the plants and flowers, and attracts all sorts of exotic birds to flock and wheel over the town. They inspire him to take to the air himself, in preparation for the apocalyptic conclusion of the story, where he leads the entire population, living and dead, as they dissolve in a sea of light.

Weaving through this vision are the customary autobiographical threads. Like the Blake of his story, Jim was a pilot. During the time he couldn't drive, he was also, like the fictional Blake, confined to Shepperton. Blake shares Jim's hostility to 'father figures' – literally so, in this case, since the man, Wingate, is a priest. After the crash, Blake is nursed by Miriam St Cloud, an earthy, complaisant woman with whom he falls in love. As in *The Kindness of Women*, Miriam

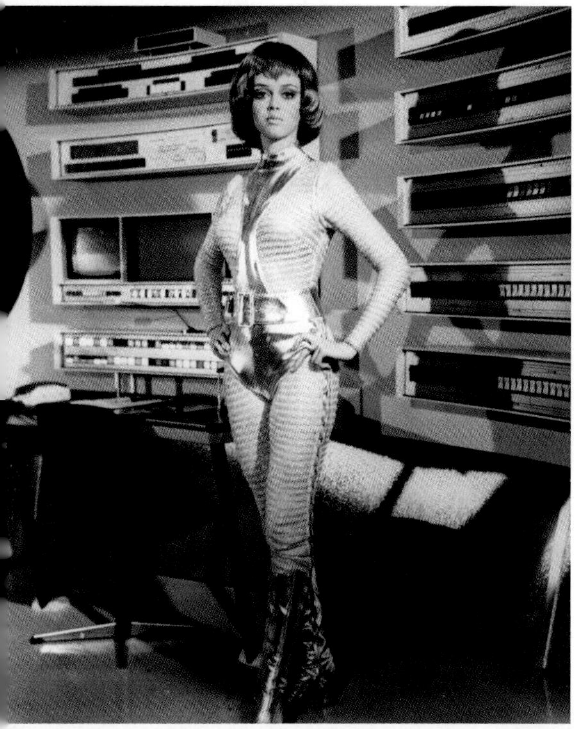

LEFT: Gabrielle Drake in *UFO*
ABOVE: Jim during BBC *Atrocity* filming, 1971
BELOW: The Crashed Cars Show, 1971. Jo Stanley, from the video at the private view.
(John 'Hoppy' Hopkins)

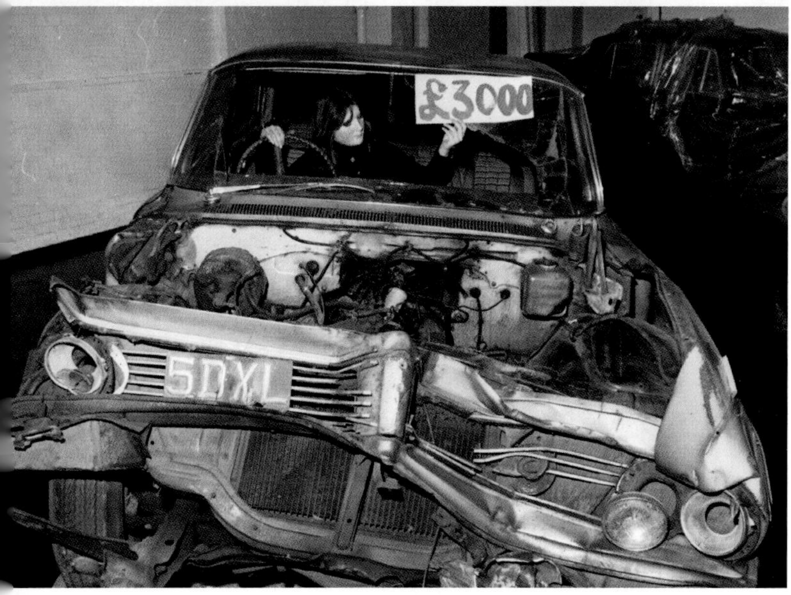

Sally Potter poses in the crashed Pontiac.
(Getty Images)

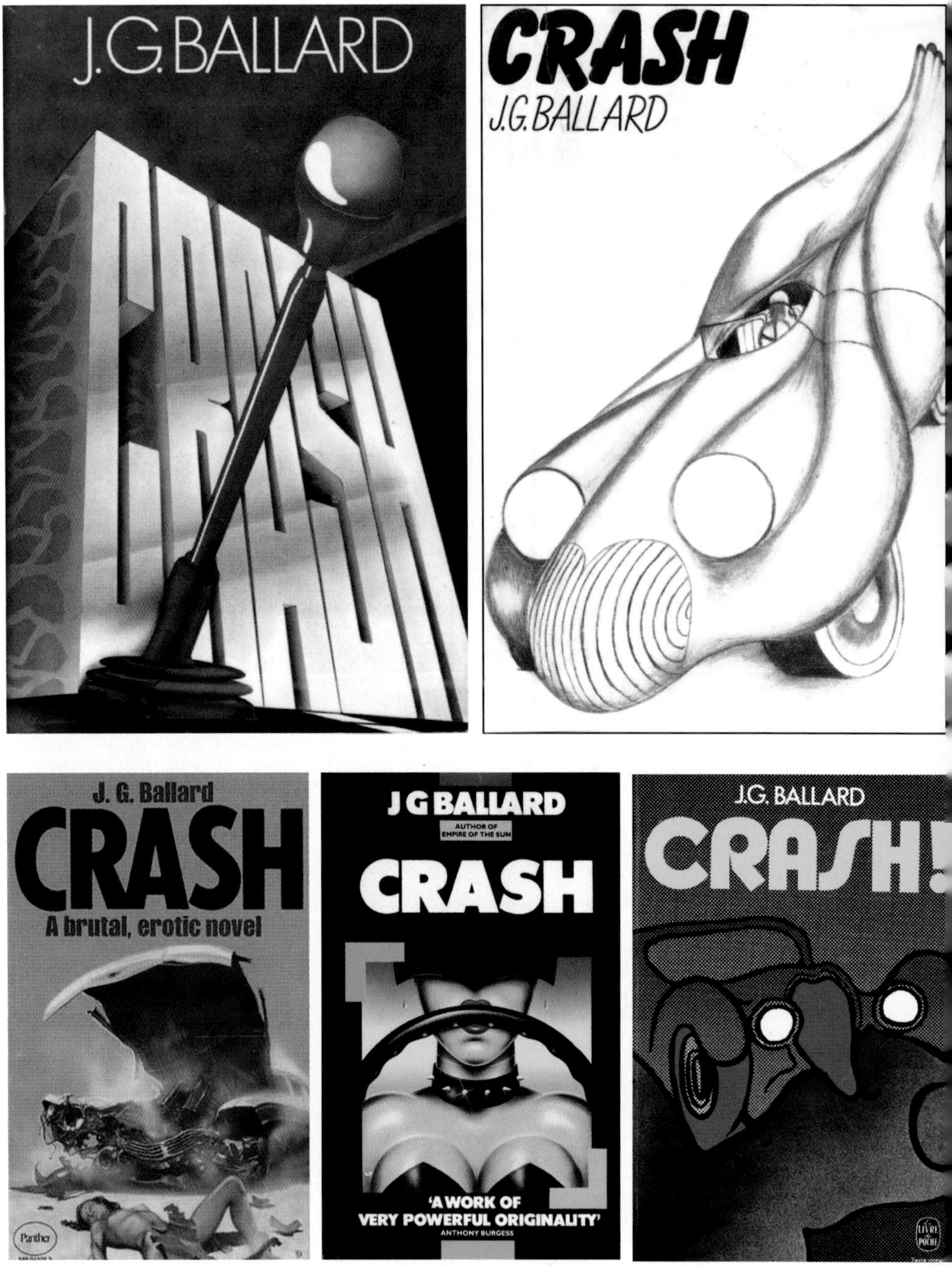

The crash heard round the world. The UK and US first printings.
CLOCKWISE FROM TOP LEFT: Bill Botton (Jonathan Cape, 1973) and Lawrence Ratzkin (Farrar, Straus & Giroux, 1973); Atelier Pascal Vercken (Livre de Poche, 1973); James Marsh (Triad, 1985); Chris Foss (Panther, 1975).

Judy Merril at the 1965 Worldcon, 'Telling It How It Is' to British science-fiction writers, including William F. Temple (Peter Mabey)

Pamela Zoline by Roger Robinson (Roger Beccon)

Unusually dapper, Jim sports a flower in his button hole for Jorge Luis Borges, about 1975

Jim with his children

Portrait of Jim by Brigid Marlin, 1986 (Brigid Marlin)

Jim and Claire Walsh after the revival of their relationship in the mid-1980s.

With Mike Moorcock at a signing of *Empire of the Sun* at Forbidden Planet. bookshop in London in 1984.

Signing session for *The Day of Creation* at Forbidden Planet.

Brigid Marlin
(Brigid Marlin)

Jim at home
in front of *The*
lirror, one of the
wo Delvauxs she
opied (Rex Features)

Brian Aldiss

Mike Moorcock, Jim and Claire Walsh, 2007 (Linda Steele)

corresponds to Mary, his dead wife. In *Dream Company*, she possesses some of Mary's qualities; her sensuality, a willingness to mother him and also to act as his pupil.

As his powers increase, Blake teaches Miriam to fly. They marry in mid-air, then cruise over Shepperton. On an amusement pier that juts into the river, a handsome blond man named Stark has created a sad zoo with a handful of animals. Supposedly sympathetic, Stark is actually a sinister figure, the equivalent of Lucifer in Blake's poem *Milton*, and with the same ambivalent character: a fallen angel, but an angel all the same. Just as Blake is about to fuel his surge into the infinite by absorbing every living thing in the town, Stark shoots him, and Blake is reborn as newly compassionate and healing. At the end of the story, Stark dredges up the wrecked aircraft to reveal Blake's corpse in the cockpit. Blake wrestles with his own skeletal body and defeats it, helped by shoals of fish that miraculously replace his torn flesh.

Some of these scenes suggest a further inspiration for Jim's story – the painter Stanley Spencer, who lived and worked in Cookham in the early part of the twentieth century. His homely canvases recast biblical incidents in terms of village life, with local tradesmen standing in for patriarchs and farmers' daughters for saints. A painting such as his *Saint Francis and the Birds* (executed in 1935 but rejected for that year's Royal Academy Summer Exhibition) captures some of the same strangeness. The ducks, chickens and pigeons crowding around the odd-looking, spade-bearded saint in his flapping bathrobe could have inspired the flocks that circle over Jim's Shepperton.

The Unlimited Dream Company was as long in the writing as *Crash*. 'It was imaginatively exhausting,' Jim said, 'a real set of balancing acts.' The first year was spent compiling a synopsis which, at about 70,000 words, was longer than the published novel. Since he refused to discuss the impulse that motivated him, we'll never know why he chose such obscure material. He may have hoped to create a fantasy to rival those of C. S. Lewis and Alan Garner, thereby winning new younger readers, though the image of Blake, naked, erect penis in hand, spouting gouts of semen as he raced through Shepperton, might have raised some librarians' eyebrows.

It's more likely that he took a leaf from the Beats, or from Marquez, Borges, Castaneda and the other magic realist writers of Central and South America then in vogue. He never read any of their books, but magazines such as *Time* published long profiles of Carlos Castaneda in particular, which would be enough to ignite his imagination. When Blake goes on his inseminating rampage, the plants that flower in his wake are all tropical – bamboo, coconut, mango, Spanish moss, orchid, lily. They strangle Britain's tepid flora. Lianas twine around dying elms, and the postman struggles to deliver letters as tiger lilies envelop them. In particular, the presence of a condor among the birds circling Shepperton hints at an acquaintance with Carlos Castaneda, for whom the condor had both symbolic and magical significance. The Peruvian anthropologist claimed to have been apprenticed to a Yaqui shaman named Don Juan Matus who fed him peyote cactus, 'magic mushrooms' and datura, or 'loco weed'. Under their influence, Castaneda saw desert spirits, including 100-foot tall insects. Matus also showed him how, by rubbing himself with datura, he could fly.

Above all, *The Unlimited Dream Company* returns to the sunlit surrealist landscape of Vermilion Sands. In their stiff, archetypal nature, the figures of the novel – reducible to the Father, the Mother, the Woman, the Magician – recall Magritte or Delvaux, but the arrangement, as often in such canvases, is awkward, and the treatment clichéd. An American reviewer commented, 'Some readers will find this book a brilliant flight; others will be troubled by the unanswered questions left in the dust.'

CHAPTER FORTY

GOODBYE AMERICA

In 1977, Holt, Rinehart & Winston published, without much success, *High-Rise*, and, in 1978, *The Best Short Stories of J. G. Ballard.* The care with which they avoided mentioning science fiction in either title or flap copy recalled British publishing in the 1950s. Invited to choose a representative selection of his work, Jim began with *New Worlds* stories such as 'Manhole 69', but concluded defiantly with 'Plan for the Assassination of Jacqueline Kennedy' and 'Why I Want to Fuck Ronald Reagan'.

In an introduction, Anthony Burgess scrabbled to find consistencies between 'The Drowned Giant', a surrealist-inspired take on *Gulliver's Travels*, with a community first admiring, then harvesting the corpse of a giant cast up on its shore, and 'The Garden of Time', a sustained dying fall in the style of Ray Bradbury, peopled by wafting sages whose most extreme expression of emotion is a drawn-out sigh. Cover artist Carlos Ochagavia, no less stumped, tossed together a ragbag of Ballard images – sailplanes, stone roses, rearing stallions and thunderheads over a Monument Valley landscape straight out of a John Ford western. It was an irony of Jim's background in advertising that, though he could rebrand himself repeatedly for Europe, he was as helpless before the monolithic US market as a man trying to sell cricket bats or crumpets.

As Jim delivered *The Unlimited Dream Company* to Cape in the middle of 1978, an interview he gave to Chris Evans appeared in *Penthouse.* Shortly after, Evans discovered he had cancer. He died on

10 October 1979. In *The Kindness of Women*, his character, Dick Sutherland, a media man to the end, suggests filming his last weeks for a TV programme. Jim, when he learned of his own terminal illness, proposed a book titled *Conversations With My Doctor*, which would have covered similar ground. Jim felt the loss of Evans profoundly. When Moorcock commiserated, he responded morosely, 'I'm now down to 1 friend – you.'

In October 1979, Jonathan Cape and Holt, Rinehart & Winston simultaneously published *The Unlimited Dream Company*. In a 1976 article, critic Martin Hayman had noted 'a coarsening and degrading of the quality of Ballard's imagination and the stultification of his lucid prose style'. *Dream Company* helped correct that impression. Anthony Burgess, solicited for an advance opinion, called it 'blindingly original. Moving, thrilling, exquisitely written. Surely the best thing this fine writer has ever done.' He included it in his list of the ninety-nine best modern novels. Feeling, rightly, that drawing attention to his inspiration would open him both to attack from Blake scholars and baffled questions from his admirers, Jim had said nothing about *Milton*. He needn't have worried, since no reviewer noted the similarity, beyond picking up the hint that William Blake was involved somewhere. Malcolm Bradbury in the *New York Times* referred to *The Marriage of Heaven and Hell*. John Mole in the *New Statesman* suggested that it might relate to the poet's *Songs of Innocence and Experience*. The jacket copy doesn't mention Blake at all, but gives a clue to Jim's intention when it calls the book 'a brilliant fable'.

In an even more surprising accolade, *Dream Company* caught the attention of the actor Richard Gere, who wanted to play Blake in a film version. 'I met him in London,' said Jim, 'and was very impressed by him – highly articulate, thoughtful, serious-minded':

> He's very interested in Buddhism, does work on behalf of various Buddhist missions. Reincarnation through one species to another is very much a part of Buddhist thought, and obviously that is what

> intrigued him about the novel. What would have been the insuperable obstacle of filming the flying sequences is no problem these days – they can do that extremely convincingly. But one must assume, to be sensible, that nothing will come of it.

Nothing did.

Asked about the best director to film his work, Jim usually nominated David Lynch, with George Miller, creator of *Mad Max 2: The Road Warrior*, a close second. (At the foot of a 1982 letter to Moorcock, he scribbled 'See *Mad Max II* – a stunner'.) It was Lynch's fable of small-town sadism, *Blue Velvet*, that he called not only the best film of 1980 but of the decade; a conflation of *The Wizard of Oz* and Kafka, as visualised by Francis Bacon. He was less impressed by Ridley Scott's *Alien*, and declined to write a novelisation: 'I knew nothing about the film, which I was never shown, and when I read the script I liked it even less. It struck me as an unoriginal horror movie with almost no connection with SF. They offered me $20,000 but it was surprisingly easy to turn down – the film is very glossy, but empty at its centre.' The job went to Alan Dean Foster, who had ghosted the novelisation of the first *Star Wars* film.

Jim looked more kindly on *Star Wars* than *Alien*, finding Lucas's creation likeable, though juvenile. He praised the quirky attention to detail; its sense of the 'used universe', with Han Solo's spaceship as rusted and dented as an old tramp steamer. He was almost envious of Moorcock, who, facing tax debts in the UK and with family problems besides, was living in the US. With Claire out of his life and his drinking much reduced, Jim had become reconciled with his old friend, who had been lured to Los Angeles in 1979 by Irvin Kershner, director of the *Star Wars* sequel *The Empire Strikes Back*, to write the screenplay for an heroic fantasy set in Arthurian Britain. Moorcock's letters to Jim mocked the oddities of the film colony and of Kershner, whom he described as having 'the imagination of a tub of coleslaw, the creative gift of a cockroach, the emotional age of a nine-year-old schoolboy, but the power to summon up millions and millions of dollars'. Jim published the first letter in *Ambit*, and requested more, inaugurating a series collected in the 1986 *Letters from Hollywood*.

In an industry where bad years far outnumber good, 1981 was worse for British publishing than usual, particularly in the independent and fringe sectors. After *Bananas* expired in 1979, Emma Tennant launched a quarterly series of original paperbacks, each devoted to an original novella. Unconventionally produced with wire spiral binding, Next Editions sold initially on subscription, but never looked like making money, even with contributions from Harold Pinter and Angela Carter. Jim agreed to supply two titles, including 'The Neurosurgeon's Tale', but the series folded before it could be published. Retitled 'Myths of the Near Future', it was published in 1981. *Ambit* ran a second story, 'News from the Sun', which also appeared as a limited-edition booklet with the debut issue of *Interzone*, a new quarterly SF magazine edited by a consortium including David Pringle and Malcolm Edwards. A third story, 'Memories of the Space Age', featured in the second issue of *Interzone* and became the title story of the collection Cape issued in September 1982.

Another victim of the slump was Philip Dunn's Pierrot Publications. Aiming for something between trade paperback and coffee-table book, Pierrot published outsize paperback editions of science fiction and fantasy-related titles with lavish colour illustrations. Brian Aldiss, Harry Harrison, Malcolm Edwards, Robert Holdstock, Moorcock and Ballard all wrote for Pierrot, and some of what they wrote actually got published. Among titles still in preparation when the company failed in 1981 with rumoured debts of £500,000 were Moorcock's 'The Entropy Tango', and a Ballard fantasy called, provisionally, 'Hello America'. Once Pierrot failed, Jim sold it to Cape.

Hello America, set in a future where Europe has lost touch with a North American continent which disastrous attempts at climate control have turned to desert, conflated the self-absorbed mythology of the modern USA, as depicted wittily by Moorcock in his Hollywood letters, with the boys' adventure novels Ballard read in

Shanghai. In a plot that echoes *Captains Courageous, Treasure Island* and *The Gorilla Hunters*, the story is told through the eyes of young Wayne, who stows away on the *Apollo*, the ship carrying the first expedition from Europe in generations.

They land near New York, where sand has silted up the canyons of Manhattan, to find that the few surviving Americans are camel-riding nomads. Since Jim had barely been to the US except for a few excursions across the border during his time in Canada, his vision was drawn from advertising and in particular movies, and shares with the Vermilion Sands stories the sense of a manufactured, artificial world where improbable characters perform against painted backdrops.

The expedition heads for California, lured by indications that some technological genius is at work there; a Wizard of Oz with the instincts of a showman, who can summon enormous laser-generated mirages of western movie heroes such as John Wayne, Gary Cooper and Henry Fonda to loom over Dodge City's Boot Hill cemetery. Arriving in Nevada, they find Death Valley has become rainforest and Las Vegas is half-submerged in a lake, its quenched lights a symbol of America's lost glory. Vegas is the new capital of the USA, or what remains of it, administered by President Charles Manson, who rules it from the suite at the Desert Inn formerly occupied by Howard Hughes. The only humans are a few henchmen kept by Manson as guards. The remaining inhabitants are robots. In the nightclub, a mechanised Rat Pack performs the old routines of Sinatra and Dean Martin, aided by a Judy Garland still the pig-tailed, gingham-clad teenager of *The Wizard of Oz*. Elsewhere, a group of robot former Presidents – inspired by similar electronic puppets at Disneyland – harangue one another. When Manson decides to leave earth in the last functioning space vehicle, Wayne, unwilling and unequipped, becomes the new President of the USA.

Hello America might have worked as a novella for the juvenile market, with slightly tongue-in-cheek illustrations, but at novel length the satire caved in for lack of structure. Extracts from a diary kept by

Wayne and chapters of heavy-handed irony betrayed their source in tourist brochures and the US TV series such as *Dallas* that Jim watched so enthusiastically. David Pringle points out the parallels between *Hello America* and Bernard Wolfe's *Limbo 90* – 'up to and including the near-nuclear-holocaust climax. JGB's character Wayne keeps a diary, as does Wolfe's Dr Martine. Ballard's depictions of Durango, Las Vegas, etc., are highly reminiscent of Wolfe's description of a ruined Miami. In short, *Hello America* is a deliberate homage to Wolfe's *Limbo.* Even the stylistic tics are sometimes the same – notably the substitution of a mere comma for "and" in many sentences.'

The book shows signs of second thoughts and hurried adjustments. Jim meant not Manson but Howard Hughes to be President. In 1977, he reviewed *The Hughes Papers,* which delved into the mogul's final years. He confessed to admiring Hughes for the way, not unlike himself, that he shut out the world. The novel betrays *passim* a hostility towards the consumer society that sits oddly on a man who showed a natural flair for advertising. America is represented as a decayed hell of selling. Wall Street is dominated by the two-hundred-storey OPEC tower, its neon sign pointing towards Mecca. Brand names have largely replaced language. The expedition's obligatory *femme fatale,* Anne Summers, shares her name with a chain of sex shops. The nomads who wander the central desert are called Heinz, Pepsodent, GM, Big Mac, Texaco, and 7-Up. All women are called Xerox – because they make good copies. Their tribes include the Astronauts, the Gays, the Gangsters, the Gamblers, and an all-women group called the Divorcees – who promise to marry you, explains one of the nomads, then steal your camel and cut your throat. This information is imparted in a scene that is almost a self-parody. These new arabs have taken shelter in an abandoned swimming pool, where they grill a rattlesnake.

That Jim had never visited Disneyland or Las Vegas is evident from the second-hand nature of his inspiration. Many readers who had not been offended by his co-opting of John and Jackie Kennedy into his personal mythology regarded his recruitment of Manson as conspicuously bad taste. From the US, Charles Platt reported the negative reaction to 'the unfortunately titled *Hello America* (to which editors here have replied "Goodbye, J. G. Ballard")':

> I spoke to Don Hutter, editor in chief at Holt, Rinehart and Winston, a year or so ago about this book, and again this last summer. Don is not the sort of editor to shy away from 'controversial' material. Rather, he seemed to feel simply that the book is lightweight and lacks a first-hand understanding of what America is all about. I agree to the extent that I think it would have been better, ideally, if JGB could have visited the USA. It's not that the book is factually incorrect; simply that it lacks a sense of authenticity which matters to an American audience. Americans are actually very tolerant of outsiders satirizing their culture – in fact they have invited it, over the years. But only if the outsider meets them on their own terms; which is fair enough. Personally I like the book, and tried to get a piece of it excerpted in *Omni* (without success). But I doubt it will sell here.

He was right. Nobody wanted *Hello America.* It wasn't published in the US until 1988, when *Empire of the Sun* had made Ballard briefly 'hot'.

In a letter to Platt, Jim joked about his unpopularity in the USA. To cheer him up, Platt announced that a poll of customers at SF bookshops across the country had voted 'Myths of the Near Future' the year's Best Short Story. 'On my next visit to England,' Platt wrote, 'I visited Jimmy and presented him with the award (made of Lucite, depicting the planet Saturn, as I recall). He was surprisingly agitated about it. "I don't think I have ever received an award before," he said. This must have been around 1980, and is an interesting indicator of his continuing relative obscurity prior to the success of *Empire of the Sun.* He seemed to be quite emotionally touched by it.'

Later, Platt learned the award was faked. 'There were only a handful of votes for the category which Jimmy won, so it was a trivial matter to rig the outcome. I certainly wasn't going to tell him that it was the result of a few Ballard fans fixing the vote.' Jim, as it happens, was already sceptical. In a letter to Platt, he joked that his two biggest fans, whom he visualised as a twelve-year-old computer freak and a retired linotype operator, must have toured the SF bookstores from NYC to LA, stuffing ballot boxes. Jim's also-ran status in the US market was summarised by the 1983 poll run by the trade magazine *Locus*. It voted his latest collection, *Myths of the Near Future*, thirteenth in a field of eighteen. Moorcock consoled him that he remained as potent a symbol as ever in certain parts of society. The girlfriend of Crazy Charlie, president of the Notting Hill Hell's Angels, had just changed her name to Vermilion Sands.

CHAPTER FORTY-ONE

DECLARING WAR

Asked why he waited until his fifties to write about his wartime experiences, Jim wasn't very convincing. 'I was so bound up with the present,' he said vaguely. 'I was very interested in the 1960s: in this whole new world we lived in.' By some convoluted logic, he shifted part of the responsibility to his children. 'While they were the same age as I was in [*Empire of the Sun*], I couldn't really begin to write about my younger self, whom I protectively saw as one of my own children. Once my children were adults, I felt free. I could face anything that happened to my younger self.'

The real pressures were more practical. In 1982, he felt threatened and beleaguered. Britain was at war with Argentina over the Falklands, while at home the IRA continued to bomb almost with impunity. The sense of a threat on the doorstep was palpable. He hesitated even to leave the house. Crossing the street, he told Moorcock in Los Angeles, had become a feat, on the level of Marco Polo's voyages. He feared he was starting to resemble some of his own characters, so morbidly attached to their home that they rejoiced in their isolation and were happy nowhere else. Reflecting this, the house gradually shrank in Ballard's perception. In 1986, he confided to Brigid Marlin that he felt like his characters in the story 'Manhole 69' who sense space diminishing around them. 'He was worried,' says Marlin, 'because he began by only being able to write in one part of the house, then only in one room, and finally only in one corner of that room. He didn't know how this was going to progress.'

To add to Jim's troubles, John Wolfers announced he was giving up his agency and moving to France. At the same time, Jim's relationship with Jonathan Cape had reached an impasse. At its Christmas party, one of the sales force angered him by joking of *Low-Flying Aircraft*, '"Low-flying" was the right term for that one all right.' He was even nostalgic for SF. In Belfast, Paul Campbell, with Dave Langford as non-fiction editor, had launched a new magazine called *Extro*. Aldiss, Sladek and other old hands contributed stories, but nobody asked Jim, and he assumed his experiments had made him *persona non grata* in conventional SF circles. In June, he wrote to Moorcock with a startling suggestion: 'He wanted to know when I was going to re-start *New Worlds*,' says Moorcock. 'He said it was the right time – "not unlike the early 60s in many ways".' However, *Extro* only ran to three issues, folding in August 1982. Nor was Moorcock interested in getting back into the magazine business, which had cost him dear in both time and money.

In October 1982, David Pringle's Ballard newsletter *News from the Sun* reported Jim was deep into the new project, the nature of which he wouldn't reveal. In June 1983, he wrote 'J. G. Ballard's latest novel (title not yet announced) is a semi-autobiographical work set in the China of his childhood. It is not SF, nor even a fantasy, though he says the events have been "heightened" somewhat. A first draft has been completed, and Ballard is currently revising and polishing with a view to a possible 1984 publication date.'

Until then, Jim had doubted that his life was interesting enough for a book. But the success of Aldiss's *The Hand-Reared Boy* and its sequels suggested he was wrong, as did *Hell's Cartographers*, the collection, edited by Aldiss and Harry Harrison in 1975, of memoirs by SF writers, first floated by Damon Knight some years earlier. His always effective instincts also told him it was time for a change.

Once he began the book that became *Empire of the Sun*, he realised he'd been writing about Shanghai all along – just calling it other things. The visions of cities on the horizon in 'The Ultimate City' and *Hello America* echoed Shanghai's towers as seen across the paddy fields, while his years in the cramped surroundings of Lunghua induced the claustrophobia implicit in early stories such as 'Manhole 69' and 'Billennium'. Family names such as Ransom, Maitland and Osborn that turned up repeatedly in his stories had all been those of corridor neighbours at Lunghua. Above all, the psychic damage inflicted by the violence with which he'd been surrounded is explicit in 'The Dead Time' and implied in *The Atrocity Exhibition* and *Crash*. The wounds were old and deep, and they went to the bone. John Sutherland in a review described *Empire of the Sun* as having risen from Jim's childhood 'like a slow bruise'.

The question of who would agent and publish the new book remained unresolved, until, fortuitously, the Book Marketing Council chose *The Drowned World* as one of the twenty best British SF novels to be included in a promotion of science fiction. At a dinner in October 1983 to mark the event, Ballard met Victoria Petrie-Hay, the attractive publishing director of his former publisher, Gollancz. The company had revived under new management, with Malcolm Edwards among its editors. It boasted a list of innovative writers, including friends such as Angela Carter, but also former *New Worlds* writers Tom Disch and M. John Harrison, not to mention American authors Philip K. Dick and Ursula Le Guin.

Jim and Petrie-Hay left the dinner together. Shortly after, Petrie-Hay advised John Wolfers that Gollancz was interested in the book Jim provisionally called *The Empire of the Sun*. Wolfers didn't much care. His house was up for sale and he proposed to close the agency in February 1984. He offered Maggie Hanbury the opportunity to buy him out, but she havered. Shrinking from the aggravation of seeking new representation, Jim urged her to take his offer, promising his backing. As one of the few remaining clients of any significance, his support was crucial. At last, she closed the deal and took over the Wolfers operation, with *The Empire of the Sun* her first property.

Hanbury couldn't discuss the book with Gollancz, since Cape had an option on it, even though the editor, Liz Calder, had read nothing. Petrie-Hay told her that, should Cape fail to exercise its option,

Gollancz would pay a £25,000 advance. Much depended on Cape assuming sales of the new book would be as mediocre as for other recent Ballard titles, and making its customary modest offer. As expected, Calder proposed a similar advance to his previous books: about £10,000. 'At that point,' says Malcolm Edwards, 'Maggie rejected Cape's offer, and accepted ours.' When Hanbury took the book to the Frankfurt Book Fair in October 1983, word was already out.

On 17 December 1983 *The Bookseller* announced the sale of UK and Commonwealth rights to Gollancz. In February 1984, John Wolfers formally relinquished the agency to Hanbury. At almost the same time, she announced that Simon & Schuster had bought the US rights for $75,000. Jim's editor there would be Don Hutter, who had published some of his earlier books at Holt, Rinehart & Winston (and also turned down *Hello America*). Victoria Petrie-Hay left for Weidenfeld & Nicolson shortly after, so Edwards became Jim's editor. It didn't lead to a lasting bond. 'With some writers, the editor becomes their best friend,' says Edwards. 'That was never on his agenda. Writing was his job. When he finished a book, he brought into play the cast he needed – his agent, his publisher. But for the rest of the time, he didn't want much to do with us.' At Edwards's suggestion, Jim removed the first definite article from the title. Copies of the typescript were sent to prominent writers, inviting advance quotes. Graham Greene obliged with 'An admirable novel' and Angela Carter speculated that the book 'may well be that great British novel about the last war for which we've had to wait forty-odd years'.

CHAPTER FORTY-TWO

VISIONS OF EMPIRE

Most people assumed the 'empire' of *Empire of the Sun* was Japanese. In fact, the book takes the superiority of the Japanese empire for granted but offers a wan vision in microcosm of Britain's colonial power in decline and America's in the ascendant. Of the three, Jim prefers the Japanese. It's superior in all the values he came to respect: effectiveness, discipline, honour. A century before, he could have found these qualities in British life, but his father's generation, as lamented by Hargreaves, the rubber planter in 'The Violent Noon', had surrendered the colonies that gave weight and dignity to national pride. If the Battle of Waterloo was won on the playing fields of Eton, the British Empire was surrendered in the overcrowded classes of a dumbed-down suburban grammar school.

But even as Jim complained about Britain and its institutions, he clung to his Englishness. Britain gave him standing, relevance, a role, all of which he would forfeit if he moved abroad. Following the success of *Empire of the Sun*, his pose as an unwilling Briton who preferred 'the international menu' wore thin. In 1995, he told an interviewer: 'I go to the Côte d'Azur every summer and, if I could afford it, would happily live there for the rest of my life.' His personal fortune at the time exceeded £4 million.

Though Jim insisted he'd never read Charles Dickens, *Empire of the Sun*, in its detail, its pathos, its larger-than-life characters and its emphasis on the things one will do to survive, is intensely Dickensian. (The first person to option the film rights was David Lean, who had directed both *Oliver Twist* and *Great Expectations.*) Basie, the American sailor at the centre of the story, is an archetypal Victorian villain/hero, a conflation of Fagin in *Oliver Twist* and Magwitch in *Great Expectations,* with echoes of Long John Silver in Stevenson's *Treasure Island* and the gentleman smuggler Jeremy Fox in J. Meade Falkner's *Moonfleet.* Models of adult corruption, these men both seduce and inspire, challenging the young hero to decide between virtue and sin. For Jim, the choice is automatic. Oliver Twist is treated cruelly by the people charged with protecting him, but finds a refuge with Fagin and his gang of pickpockets, becoming their willing confederate. In the same way, Jim betrays everything his parents stand for, guiding Basie and Frank back to his old home in Amherst Avenue and fingering houses worth burgling.

Reviewing *Empire of the Sun* in the *Los Angeles Times,* Richard Eder recognised the book's nineteenth-century roots, praising its insight into the contradictions of imperial morality. 'Kipling's *Kim* did it for the panorama of empire in British India. Dickens' *David Copperfield* and *Oliver Twist* did it for Victorian England, and the cold, unsparing children of [Richard Hughes's] *A High Wind in Jamaica* did it for our modern rediscovery of original sin.' He might have added *Lord of the Flies* to the list, since both Golding and Ballard use the formulae of Edwardian and Victorian juvenile fiction to suggest that even the most disciplined sons of empire cave in under pressure. Cruelty, cowardice and self-interest are inborn, and will flourish in the youngest, given half a chance, while compassion is a luxury of adulthood that has to be learned, and paid for.

Once the book became a bestseller, Jim was badgered about what was real and what was invention. One Lunghua survivor protested that, contrary to Jim's version of the camp, 'it was very well run – like a small town, with a school, hospital, churches, clubs for entertainment, study, sport and games and we turned the rough ground into productive and beautiful gardens'. It troubled some readers that the book showed Jim surviving alone when he was actually interned with his parents and sister, and shared a room with them for more than two years. Jim joked that, as he'd spent forty years forgetting the war, some detail was bound to be lost. In truth, he'd suppressed so much that *Empire of the Sun* became almost as much a work of pure invention as *The Drowned World.* When his French teacher from the camp, Peggy Abkhazi, formerly Pemberton-Carter, wrote her memoirs, *Enemy Subject: Life in a Japanese Internment Camp 1943–45*, and the British publisher asked Jim for an introduction, he acquiesced, but remarked, with mild embarrassment, 'I wish I could remember her in person.'

Empire of the Sun, thanks to Jim's imagination, parades a rich cast, starting with himself, observant, winning and resourceful, part Oliver Twist, part Artful Dodger. Other figures in the story were constructed on the armature of less interesting originals. The long-suffering Mr and Mrs Victor, on whom he's inflicted in the story, are usefully distant, without the emotional baggage associated with his parents. The inspiration for the fictional Doctor Ransom was a Methodist missionary. Also in Lunghua was another Methodist missionary, Reverend George Osborn, who was headmaster of the camp school. The son of a rich Sheffield steel family, he became friendly with Jim's father after the war, and urged him to send him to his old school, The Leys, in Cambridge. Osborn served as a better metaphor for naive but well-meaning colonial values than the real-life Pemberton-Carter, just as Latin, a dead, imperial tongue, was more appropriate as the language Jim learns from Ransom than the French Pemberton-Carter tried and failed to teach him.

Once Steven Spielberg filmed the book, people remembered the story in terms of the movie. Jim didn't discourage them. In interviews, he repeatedly reminisced about the pleasures of pre-war Shanghai, and the bike rides that took him to every corner of it. These excursions occupy only twenty of the book's 270 pages. Once the Japanese invade, Jim spends forty pages scavenging around the occupied city, until he meets Basie, its most fully realised character, and the one who is to change his life. The remaining two hundred pages chart the contest for Jim's soul, competed for by the devious but indolent Basie, the principled Ransom and the Japanese, who, for all their cruelty, embody honour and self-respect. This, finally, is why Ballard excluded his parents from the book. Morally null, they play no part in Jim's choice of corruption or redemption. It's when they disappear that he's forced to make choices, and to reveal his true character, or lack of it. As Jim observes with precocious insight, his entire upbringing had been aimed at preventing him from meeting people like Basie, but the war, with its new ethos of survival, changed everything.

In contrast to Ransom, who teaches Jim a dead European language, Basie coaches him in living American reality. He passes on the skills learned as a steward on cruise liners: how to befriend the women of the camp by helping fan their cooking fires and to curry favour with authority by kowtowing to the Japanese officers. The need to survive trumps all other motives. Jim lurks by the dying, ready to grab their uneaten food. In a significant episode, recounted in the later *Miracles of Life*, he and another boy steal coal from the communal stock. Jim takes his share back to his family, but later sees his confederate, troubled by ethics that Jim has long since discarded, toss his away. Expediency and cynicism abrade the thin layer of morality imposed at school and by his parents. Before the war, an infringement against some parental rule would put him in disgrace for days, whereas Basie shrugs off any error and moves on to the next scam. The capacity to act without morality or fear of consequences exhilarates him. For the first time in his life he is free.

Instead of quizzing him about his parents, commentators on the book should have asked if Basie and his toadying sidekick, Frank, were based on real people. On the balance of probabilities, they, too, were probably pure invention. The Americans in the camp were merchant seamen from a freighter unlucky enough to have been moored in Shanghai at the outbreak of war. They spent their time loafing in E Block, occasionally rousing themselves to play a game of softball. As food became more scarce, they set traps for the pheasants that foraged on waste ground around the camp. Jim helped them, while suspecting that the traps were just a ruse to scout an escape route.

Jim liked their indifference to class and their casual manner, but above all their possessions: everything from copies of *Reader's Digest* and *Popular Mechanics* to novelty fountain pens, cowboy tie clips and transparent celluloid belts. In *Empire of the Sun*, he re-imagines E Block as a kind of court, an embassy of the rich, sensual America he admires. For the women of the camp, it's a magnet. A succession of adolescent girls, single British women and even a few wives make their way there, responding to needs which Jim recognises as much like his own.

He also admires the Japanese kamikaze pilots, and feels some comradeship with them, based on the fact that he is almost their age, and that he was part of the work gang repairing the runway from which they take off. They represent the brighter face of the imperial coin. He notes their vitality and commitment in cheering the emperor as they go to their deaths, and contrasts this with the unpatriotic self-interest of the Americans, although both are superior to the lethargy of the British, many of whom descend into a torpor, staring at the walls, or endlessly examining their own hands.

Both *The Kindness of Women* and *Miracles of Life* add new details and characters to the Lunghua story, sometimes contradicting the first book. Many relate to Jim's evolving sexuality and the ambiguous relationship with Basie, whom one assumes to be homosexual. The eleven-year-old Jim of *Empire of the Sun* was a sexual naif, imaginative but emotionally immature, more concerned with games and fantasies than people. He noted the Chinese prostitutes in the streets of Shanghai, but showed no interest in them, any more than he does the girls in the camp, aside from a little flirting.

Miracles of Life tells a different story. It introduces another internee, the older, more knowing Cyril Goldbert, who will eventually change his name to become the actor Peter Wyngarde, star of the TV action/adventure series of the seventies *Jason King*. Jim also invents a friend from the expatriate British community, David Hunter, who, before the war, entertains Chinese girlfriends in his parents' home. In the camp, Jim has a playfully sexual relationship with a girl named Peggy Gardner, who becomes his lover once both return to England. In *Kindness*, the adult Jim, visiting Los Angeles for the premiere of *Empire of the Sun* in 1987, has sex with the White Russian woman who was formerly his nanny.

Jim never volunteered any more information about his adolescent sexuality, though it's evoked in marginal details such as a comment made when, revisiting the camp fifty years later for a BBC TV documentary, he stood in the tiny room he'd shared for four years with his parents and sister, and remarked, 'I came to puberty here.' Steven Spielberg sensed the deficiency, since he inserted a scene in his film where Jim spies on the Victors, the couple who shelter him, while they have sex – something which, given the lack of privacy, he must have done frequently.

Of all the day-to-day details of life in Lunghua which Jim recalled in his various semi-autobiographical books, it's the gratuitous violence inflicted on the Chinese by the Japanese that exhibits an almost Proustian verisimilitude of recall. He is unflinching in the detail with which he describes the instant life slips away from a body. There's no pathos in these episodes – just the chill, uninvolved stare of the psychopath ('Cast a cold eye/On life, on death'). In his depiction of death and destruction, there is no pity; merely lust and awe. Whether in the slow strangling of the young Chinese or the snarling low-level runs of the US Mustangs as they bomb the airfield, the naked exercise of power arouses and exhilarates him. Its apotheosis is the flash of the Nagasaki bomb, seen only in his mind's eye, but no less real to him for being imagined. In that instant, Jim shows his affinity with the ideas that inspired surrealism. 'To attack the sun,' wrote Sade, 'to deprive the universe of it, or to use it to set the world ablaze – these would be crimes indeed.'

CHAPTER FORTY-THREE

SALMON

Before the text of *Empire* was either copy-edited or typeset, thirty facsimiles of Ballard's typescript, bound in the plain blue covers of uncorrected proof copies, were circulated to potential buyers of the UK paperback rights. By April 1984, Granada had offered £55,000, beating off bids from Dent, Fontana, Futura, Pan and Penguin. Granada hadn't paid this much for a book since John Fowles's *The French Lieutenant's Woman*, but publishing director Nick Austin believed that *Empire of the Sun* ranked with *Nineteen Eighty-Four* and *Catch-22* among the great novels of the century.

Gollancz published in September 1984, and Simon & Schuster in the US the following month. Success in the UK was immediate. It was serialised in *The Times*, and Martin Amis profiled Ballard for the *Observer*. It was called 'one of the most enthralling novels of the year' by the *Daily Mail* and 'a book of quite astonishing authority and power' by Paul Bailey in the *Evening Standard*. In the *Observer*, Anthony Thwaite wrote: 'I think I have never read a novel which gave me a stronger sense of the blind helplessness of war.' Anthony Burgess, more sceptical of its factual basis, called it 'a brilliant fusion of history, autobiography and the kind of imaginative speculation of which Ballard is an acknowledged master'. It went straight to No. 4 on the *Sunday Times* bestseller list. The first printing of 15,000 copies soon sold out and Gollancz printed an additional 6,000. It eventually sold 55,000 copies in hardcover.

The *Guardian* concluded its review, 'it should go straight on the short list for the Booker Prize'. The Booker panel of Professor Richard

Cobb, Anthony Curtis, Polly Devlin, John Fuller and Ted Rowlands, MP, agreed. It joined Angela Carter's *Nights at the Circus*, *Flaubert's Parrot* by Julian Barnes, *Hotel du Lac* by Anita Brookner, *In Custody* by Anita Desai, *According to Mark* by Penelope Lively and *Small World* by David Lodge. Even before 18 October, when the winner was announced at a ceremony in the Guildhall, London, the *Guardian*, *Observer*, *Sunday Times* and the trade magazine *The Bookseller* all tipped it to win.

Maggie Hanbury was seated at one of the large round tables, opposite Jim, as the chairman rose to announce the winner. As he did so, an insider journalist leaned over to her and whispered, 'I'm sorry.' Too far from Jim to convey the bad news, she had to sit immobile while the prize went to Anita Brookner for her sentimental *Hotel du Lac*. Many guests didn't hide their astonishment, but Ballard showed no emotion, just raising his arms and letting them drop limply back to his chair. *Empire* went on to win other awards, including the James Tait Black Memorial Prize, shared with Angela Carter, and the *Guardian* Award for fiction, but its failure to take that year's Booker is regarded as a major injustice. To Angela Carter, the choice betrayed the snobbery endemic in British literature. 'Ballard is rarely, if ever, mentioned in the same breath, or even the same paragraph, as such peers as Anthony Powell or Iris Murdoch. Fans like Kingsley Amis and Anthony Burgess praise Ballard to the skies but they themselves are classified differently, as, God help us, "serious writers" in comparison.'

Even before *Empire* was published, Jim started a new novel that was really an old novel in disguise. Once again, it was the story of a loser in a desert. Provisionally called *The Day of Creation*, it harked back to *The Drought* and *The Crystal World*. He'd told one interviewer, 'I hope *Empire of the Sun* will be the locomotive that pulls the rest of my work out of the tunnel', but since there could be no true sequel and he had no further ideas about the Second World War as a subject, this was a train with only one carriage. To add to the sense of anticlimax, *Empire* maintained Jim's disappointing record in the US. With gallows humour, he sent friends copies of the standard letter from Simon & Schuster, inviting him to purchase the thousands of unsold copies at a generous discount. Journalist Nicholas Fraser sensed Jim's pessimistic state of mind, which seemed reflected in the new novel:

> *The Day of Creation* follows a doctor who attempts to tame the flow of the underground river he has accidentally uncovered in Africa. He's successful, creating wealth from the desert; but so much damming and distorting of the river causes it to dry up, destroying everything that has been momentarily created. It is the fate of humans, Jim believes, to struggle violently and purposelessly, to be crazed with ambition or stuffed with delusions. There can be no guarantee of success, even if the goal is a worthy one.

This attitude was reflected in the uncategorisable text 'What I Believe' that appeared in the January 1984 issue of the French magazine *Science Fiction* and in the summer number of *Interzone*. It read like a formal resignation from the role of guru and seer which he found increasingly burdensome. Readers and the press continued to demand, as Aldiss had complained, that SF writers be 'a cross between Old Moore and the Air Ministry roof'. By offering a credo that endorsed irrationality, prejudice and psychosis, 'What I Believe' suggested they look elsewhere.

Fortunately, before Jim could enfold himself once again in the comfortable complacencies of despair, *Empire of the Sun* attracted the attention of the movies: *Chariots of Fire* producer David Puttnam paid £10,000 to option the project for director Roland Joffé (*The Mission, The Killing Fields*). Once the book began to sell, it came to the attention, possibly at the suggestion of Canadian novelist Mordecai Richler, of Robert Shapiro, head of Warner Brothers' European operations. Jack Clayton, on the script of whose *Room at the Top* Richler had worked, was briefly mooted to direct, but Shapiro preferred London-based, US-born Harold Becker (*The Black Marble, The Onion Field*) and agreed to invest $25 million in a production.

He commissioned a screenplay from Tom Stoppard and in October

1985 Shapiro, Becker and Stoppard made a reconnaissance trip to Shanghai. From there, Shapiro rang Ballard to say how impressed they were with the almost perfectly preserved Bund and downtown areas. However, they were refused entry to the remains of Lunghua camp, and were having problems finding the old Amherst Avenue house. In any event, explained Shapiro, they would shoot the camp scenes in England, not China. Ballard was amused to think that his own neighbours might be recruited to play detainees – more or less what happened when the film was made.

By the time the three men did find the house, now occupied by a number of families, and Lunghua camp, back in use as a school, it was clear that the costs of shooting anything in China were prohibitive. Back in London, Becker started scouting locations in Spain. On hearing this, Jim protested. Even if they recreated the camp elsewhere, he insisted some of the film be shot in China.

> The architecture of Shanghai, these great western banks, Midland Bank Classical, rolling down the Bund for two miles, absolutely expressed the peculiar nature of this city, the greatest city in China, created not by Chinese but by the British, the Americans and the French, a city created by my father and people of his generation. Shanghai is an important presence in the novel. Jim is forever hovering between his dreams of East and West; he's infatuated with the Japanese, but at the same time he can see the great apartment towers of the French Concession. He's obsessed with American cars which fill the streets of Shanghai and with the American style of life. The Chinese form a sort of ghostly background, as they did in my youth. I think it had to be established that the Shanghai created by the Americans and Europeans was a Western city, not a Chinese city with pagodas and so forth.

Chance helped resolve the impasse. At the 1985 Bafta Awards in London, Steven Spielberg arranged to be seated at the same table as his hero David Lean, who was looking for someone to fund the restoration of *Lawrence of Arabia.* Spielberg offered to do so, and to put the film back into circulation. And, he added, if Lean had a film project, he was ready to produce it. Lean mentioned *Empire of the Sun*. Spielberg immediately told Warners of his interest, which bumped Becker from the picture.

For the moment, the project remained on the shelf, since Spielberg was preoccupied with his TV series *Amazing Stories*. He even invited Lean to direct an episode, but Lean pleaded his commitment to a film of Conrad's *Nostromo*, for which he was working on a script with Christopher Hampton. Lean did take time off to visit Shanghai, and decided, like Becker, that the logistics, not to mention the bureaucracy, made filming there impossible. He inclined towards making *Empire of the Sun* in Singapore. He also planned to involve Jim in the screenplay. 'Ballard would be almost the best script advisor we could have,' he observed in his notes. 'He writes in pictures, knows the China end of things, and might come up with some very bright ideas for all sorts of things.'

Both *Amazing Stories* and *Nostromo* faltered through 1985. Spielberg sent production manager Norman Reynolds on a world tour that took in Buenos Aires, Liverpool, Stockholm, Lisbon and Vienna, none of which sufficiently resembled pre-war Shanghai to shoot there. Having fought Hampton to a standstill over *Nostromo*, Lean asked Spielberg to adjudicate. 'Lean had a meeting with Spielberg in the US,' said Hampton, 'but came back very annoyed, with a load of notes handed to him by Spielberg. He couldn't believe it. David thought Spielberg's offer to produce the film was a courtesy, and didn't think he would actually offer opinions about the script.' Ignoring Spielberg's suggestions that he add more action and adventure, Lean persevered with his version, leaving Spielberg in sole charge of *Empire of the Sun*.

At another time, Spielberg might have made a different film – perhaps embodying the unflinching view of war that he brought to *Saving Private Ryan*. In 1985, however, he aspired to be taken seriously by Hollywood, and believed that, for all his popular success with science fiction and fantasy, it would never do so unless he worked with respectable literary material. He'd just filmed Alice Walker's *The*

Color Purple, and was contemplating Thomas Keneally's *Schindler's Ark*. *Empire of the Sun* promised to be the kind of film he needed to make.

He hadn't yet met Jim, but his executive producer, Frank Marshall, was based semi-permanently in London, sitting out the scandal over the death of actor Vic Morrow and two Vietnamese children in a helicopter accident during the making of *The Twilight Zone: The Movie*. Marshall assured Jim that Spielberg would shoot in Shanghai, but wanted some changes in emphasis. 'In the book,' explained Stoppard, 'Jim is really the centre of a wheel with a number of spokes, principally towards the English doctor. But Steven was really fascinated with the relationship between Jim and Basie. In Steven's mind, it connected with other stories of boys coming under the formative influence of experienced men. *Captains Courageous*, for instance, which he often mentioned.'

Jim agreed, mostly because of the money. His down payment on the film rights came to $250,000 – more than the combined earnings of his entire writing life. Prosperity changed nothing, however, except the quality of the whisky he drank, and the occasional meal he shared with friends such as Moorcock. 'Have you noticed, Mike,' he asked on one such occasion, 'how rude customers in restaurants have become?' Moorcock responded, 'I'm not sure it's that, Jimmy. I think we can now afford to eat in the rude people's restaurants.' Jim never owned a credit card but, as he'd done for years, withdrew £100 each Monday for pocket money. In 1990, on the way to lunch with a journalist, he stopped at an ATM. Looking over his shoulder, the journalist saw his balance – more than £1 million.

'But why have all this money sitting in your current account?' he asked.

Genuinely puzzled, Jim replied 'Where else would I put it?'

Wealth embarrassed him. While Brigid Marlin was painting his portrait, he told her that he'd been talking with some builders – 'men with a big build, looking cocky, with money in their pockets to burn'. As he turned to leave, he caught his reflection in a mirror and, for a moment, took himself for one of them. Such surprises made him even less inclined to change his lifestyle. After depositing his film advance, he stopped at a supermarket in Shepperton, reviewed its cornucopia of products, but left with what, given his modest scale of living, he still considered a luxury – a tin of salmon.

CHAPTER FORTY-FOUR

DELVAUX RISING

An unexpected by-product of *Empire of the Sun* was the revival of his relationship with Claire Walsh. 'Out of the blue, I rang him,' she said, 'because I had seen a car going down the road that reminded me of his. He just said, "I was waiting for you to ring" and from then on we got back together.' In her recollection, the relationship resumed more or less where it had broken off almost a decade before. Once again they met for dinner every Wednesday, and spent weekends together at Walsh's flat. 'We had moved from the normal kind of volatile relationship people have,' she said contentedly, 'to becoming a sort of Darby and Joan.'

Jim didn't share this vision of domestic tranquillity. His alienation from British life, numbed for so many years while he watched his family growing, had begun to return as they left for university. The fictional Jim in *The Kindness of Women* speaks for the real Ballard in complaining that, after having spent his whole adult life with children, he finds himself at fifty facing an emotional vacuum for which nature offers no solution. In Jim's case, he feared that the space would be invaded by an old sense of loss and despair. 'I felt a sense of strangeness coming on again,' he fretted.

Nor did he regard the reconciliation as a commitment to fidelity. In 1986, while still writing *The Day of Creation* and negotiating the film of *Empire of the Sun*, he'd met the artist Brigid Marlin. In June, she had a show of her work in London. In compiling a guest list for the private view, she found Ballard's letter of a decade earlier, complimenting her on her prize-winning painting *The Rod*. His name meant nothing to her, but when a friend explained his importance, she invited him to the show. After they met in person, Jim wrote her a letter which, though still addressing her as 'Mrs Marlin', was playfully flirtatious. Her paintings made him nostalgic for surrealism, he said. They also suggested a way in which he could have some fun with his movie windfall. 'He asked whether I would accept a commission to produce an exact copy of another painter's work,' says Marlin, 'specifically two early paintings by Paul Delvaux, both of which were supposed to have been destroyed in the war, and survived only as black and white photographs.'

The Rape and *The Mirror*, both painted in 1936, disappeared during the Blitz. *The Rape* shows three women posed formally in front of a classical landscape. Two are bare-breasted, one of them facing out of the picture, hands held out, palms upraised in welcome. In the middle distance, another woman sprawls on the ground, naked. In *The Mirror*, a fully-clothed woman sits in front of a mirror that reflects her body nude. 'Jim asked what I would charge to produce a 5 ft x 4 ft easel painting in oils that was an exact copy of a Delvaux. He seemed to think I might be offended at being asked to replicate the work of another artist, because he said he'd heard that Dalí did copies of Vermeer. He also said, rather surprisingly, that he would have no problems if someone asked him to do something similar – for instance, to re-write *Moby-Dick* from memory.' (The offer was cheeky, given that he had never read it.)

Marlin disliked Delvaux, who mixed black into his colours, unlike the luminous Mische method in which she'd been trained. However, she agreed to copy *The Rape* for £500. As Jim only had black and white reproductions, she discreetly improved on the original, brightening its colours. Initially, she also gave more realistic skin tones to the women, who, to her, resembled plastic sex dolls. 'They have no expression. They're like vacant cows.' But Jim resisted this, and she realised that their pallor and passivity conformed to his standard of beauty. The final version delighted him. He laid out £164 on a gilded frame, and in August 1986 wrote enthusiastically of the way the painting had become part of his life, to the extent that he felt he could almost take up residence within it, a companion to the woman on the left of the picture, who held out her arms in mute acceptance.

Jim made several trips to Marlin's home in rural Berkhamsted. They enjoyed flirtatious conversations in which, as usual, he did most of the talking. Marlin was struck by his resemblance to Stanley Kubrick, whom she knew well, as a friend of Kubrick's wife, Christiane, also a painter. 'They were not dissimilar,' she said, 'except Kubrick only needed one woman. Ballard seemed to need quite a few.' It was obvious to Marlin that he had decided to make her one of them.

When he suggested she continue with a copy of *The Mirror*, Marlin made a counter-offer. She would do it for nothing if he agreed to sit for his portrait. The suggestion took him aback. He temporised. In October, as they tried to fix a time to meet and discuss it, he pleaded work on *The Day of Creation*, which was almost ready to go to the audio typist. When she didn't respond, he wrote again, querying if she'd thought better of the portrait and offering to pay more for the second Delvaux if that would encourage her. Among the things that worried him, it emerged, was whether he was expected to buy the portrait.

> He made it very clear that he wasn't in the market for it, and that he couldn't see why anyone else would be, unless he won the Nobel Prize. Once I explained that I'd do it just for the pleasure, and because he was an intriguing subject, he showed more interest. He even started proposing ideas for how he might be posed. Some were bizarre. For instance, he suggested I should dress him in the uniform of a Japanese Air Force officer!

In the end, Jim agreed to sit for her – partly, it appears, in the hope that, while spending more time in her company, he would coax her into bed. She resisted both his overtures and the surrealist options for the portrait. In it, he wears a sweater and shirt, and sits at a plain deal table, pencil in hand, correcting pages of typescript. Marlin found him an exhausting subject.

> When I tried to make an appointment for a sitting, he would groan. I'd say, 'You act like you're going to the dentist!' and he'd say, 'It's worse than the dentist!' Other sitters would give themselves to you. They would admit you into their world. But Ballard wouldn't do that. He was always asking questions. I was trying to paint him into my fantasy world and he was trying to write me into his. He hated sitting – even physically. He would get up and roam around the room, in spite of my cries of annoyance. He would also peer at the picture and give advice, and when I said, 'Do I advise you not to write like Enid Blyton?' he said, 'I know I'm a Mr Buttinski. My children are always complaining about that.'

He asked Marlin to give him drawing lessons, but proved as inept as ever, unable even to sketch something as simple as an apple. Following one half-hearted attempt, he shoved the paper across the table and requested she finish it. 'He hated to fail,' said Marlin, 'and to be seen to fail. Later, he asked if I could give him lessons over the phone!'

In December 1986, with *The Day of Creation* completed and serious work on the film of *Empire of the Sun* about to start, Jim made an all-out attempt to seduce Marlin, who refused him firmly. In two cards sent later in the month, he took her rejection in good part, swallowing his disappointment and urging her to start on the second Delvaux, even specifying the dimensions – 4 feet x 4 feet 10 inches. Marlin did so, but without enthusiasm, preferring to work on refining the portrait. Her first attempt at *The Mirror* displeased him. 'He said it lacked an element of the mysterious,' she says. She repainted it until it conformed to his vision, if not that of either Delvaux or herself. Once he was satisfied, the copy joined *The Rape* at Shepperton.

Thereafter the canvases appeared prominently in most photographs of him taken in his home, and few journalists failed to comment on them. Of *The Rape*, he said, 'I never stop looking at this painting and its mysterious and beautiful women. Sometimes I think I have gone to live inside it and each morning I emerge refreshed. It's a male dream.' When the Centre de Cultura Contemporània de Barcelona held a Ballard exhibition in 2008, the curator asked to borrow *The Mirror*. Jim refused. 'It's the most precious thing I have,' he told them. They then asked Marlin to paint another copy. More aware now of the work involved, she charged £2,500. (The original of 1936 hadn't in fact been destroyed. It was sold at auction by Christie's in 1999 for £3.2 million.)

Though he was right to call the paintings 'precious', Jim may have been speaking in terms other than those of art appreciation. Commissioning them was a coup of rebranding as effective as his embrace of 'inner space'. Once the paintings were in place, he seldom moved more than a few metres away from them. Over the next decade, as his personal space contracted within the house, the paintings moved with him, *The Rape* sitting on the floor next to his desk – almost, as he said, as if he could step into it. With such lovely chatelaines at his elbow, he no longer risked being pigeonholed as a sad old man, tapping away in a tumbledown suburban house. They made him a glamorous eccentric, a star in his own fantasy, and a fixed point in the cultural cosmology of his time. Did he even notice them any longer? Who knows? They served their purpose; that was enough. Seldom has £500 been so shrewdly spent.

Jim saw Marlin's completed portrait but, as he'd warned, didn't offer to buy it, asking only for some postcard-sized photographs. 'He said it made him look "mysterious",' she says. 'He didn't seem comfortable with that. He thought that, while women were flattered to be called mysterious, men took it as an accusation of secretiveness.' The National Portrait Gallery acquired the painting in 1987. When they included it in a show of twentieth-century writers, he went along like any punter, and sent Marlin a congratulatory card. He also wrote an introduction to a book of her paintings. Given this apparent cordiality, Marlin was all the more shocked by *The Kindness of Women*. In an episode of drunken sex in Moose Jaw's Iroquois Hotel, Jim and

David Hunter share two part-time whores named Yvette and Brigid. Jim senses a bond with Yvette, who is, like Marlin, a robustly built blonde, and boozily offers to take her back to England. She fobs him off. Even though his account transposed the names, Marlin doesn't doubt that she inspired the unsavoury portrayal of Yvette.

CHAPTER FORTY-FIVE

CREATIONISM

Gollancz scheduled *The Day of Creation* for publication in September 1987. Meanwhile, Warner Brothers negotiated a deal to shoot part of *Empire* for twenty-one days in Shanghai during the spring. They were promised 10,000 extras and enough police to keep them under control. Everything else would have to be imported, pushing the budget from $25 million to $35 million. Except for John Malkovich as Basie and Joe Pantoliano as Frank, Spielberg cast all the roles in London, including that of the young Ballard, played by twelve-year-old Christian Bale, chosen from four thousand candidates after Spielberg's then wife, Amy Irving, had worked with him on the TV film *Anastasia: The Mystery of Anna*. 'He was like the character of Jim,' Ballard said. 'A not-very-nice little boy.'

The Shanghai shooting concentrated on the Bund, the one element without which, Jim was convinced, the film would lack authenticity. The scenes of a Japanese ship bombarding the city, and of Jim lost in the mobs fleeing the invading army, were achieved with the expertise for which Spielberg had become famous. As some of the first Westerners to film in the 'new' China, cast and crew were dazzled by the richness of its culture and the buying power of the pound and the dollar. When their 747 was preparing to take off at the end of shooting, it was found that there was too much baggage in the hold. A second aircraft therefore had to be chartered to carry 'souvenirs', which included silk carpets, antique urns, statuary and entire dinner services.

Shooting continued in Spain, where Spielberg recreated Lunghua. The landscape resembled that around Shanghai. Moreover, the

Spanish Air Force had the largest number of airworthy Second World War planes. In lieu of Japanese Zeros, the production retrofitted Harvard trainers of the kind on which Jim took lessons. In *Super-Cannes*, his main character, an amateur pilot, flies a restored Harvard on which Japanese markings from its film use are still visible.

After that, the production moved to London, and Jim at last met the director.

> He was nothing like the Spielberg I'd been led to believe. He was being presented as a sort of suburban sentimentalist, and the man I met was nothing like that. The man I met was adult, had a hard, mature mind, was very thoughtful. As far as *Empire of the Sun* was concerned, he cut no corners. He certainly wasn't trying to sentimentalise the book: quite the opposite.

For the scenes on Amherst Avenue, scouts scoured London's upper-middle-class suburbs for the houses Shanghai architects had used as models, and found them in Sunningdale, Berkshire, not far from Jim's home. It underlined Jim's realisation that he'd chosen Shepperton in the first place because of its resemblance to Shanghai. Spielberg suggested he speak a line of dialogue in the film, or even the opening commentary, but Jim begged off. Instead, he was given a cameo in the Christmas party scene that opens the film. When the costumier tried to fit him out in Roman armour, Jim balked on finding it was resin, not metal, so he appears instead, fleetingly, as John Bull, complete with Union Jack waistcoat – and, of course, glass in hand.

The Day of Creation was launched with the fanfare due an author whose last book had spent six months on the bestseller list and was 'Soon To Be A Major Motion Picture'. Grafton bought the paperback rights for more than had been paid for *Empire of the Sun*, and Farrar, Straus & Giroux outbid Simon & Schuster for the US rights – which, reading between the lines, they were not sorry to lose, given the poor sales of *Empire of the Sun*. William Boyd, Doris Lessing, Angela Carter, Michael Moorcock and Graham Greene contributed advance quotes.

Greene alone struck a less than ecstatic note, volunteering only that Ballard was 'a writer I always read with pleasure and interest'.

The setting of the book, as with *The Crystal World*, was once again France's former colonies of West Africa, in this case the Central African Republic, the former French Congo. A doctor with the World Health Organisation, Mallory is supervising drilling work at the fictional Port-la-Nouvelle in hopes of tapping the aquifer under the dried-out Lake Kotto, which gives the town its name. He's thwarted by warlords and guerrillas, who, in the name of one political creed or another, but often just out of malice, destroy his equipment, and harass the few remaining aid workers and expats.

By chance, a tractor driver tears out a tree by its roots. In the hollow, a spring wells up, becoming a Nile-like river that promises to turn the arid wastes into a garden. Mallory names it for himself, but after seeing the uses to which greedy locals and rapacious foreigners put the water, decides to sail to its source and kill it rather than let its power pass into the hands of the warlords. Refloating an old car ferry, the *Salammbo*, he loads it with the surviving Europeans, and heads upriver.

His ragbag of passengers turn the steamer into a 'ship of fools'. They include the African policeman Kagwa, from whom Mallory 'bought' the river, and Sanger, the phoney frontman for the useless and corrupt aid movement, Africa Green. They're joined by Mrs Warrender, a former zookeeper who has gone into the brothel business. Her floating bordello, staffed by teenage whores, is proudly named the *Diana*, complete with a figurehead of the 'Queen of Hearts'. Also on board is Noon, a twelve-year-old African girl with an ulcerated mouth for whom Mallory conceives, rarely for a Ballard character, a sexual passion. This is consummated, when Mallory, suffering from malaria, has sex with someone he thinks is one of the whores, hallucinating that she and he are performing in a porn film. Only when he sees traces of pus and blood on the pillow from Noon's mouth does he realise the identity of his partner.

After the reticence of many of Jim's previous novels, the erotic vigour of this passage, with its images of gushing water and ripping cloth, suggests a Ballard enjoying a revival of sexual energy, even if only in imagination. The character of Mallory shares other elements of autobiography. Raised in Hong Kong and trained as a doctor, he edited a medical journal in London, became a lobbyist for the pharmaceutical industry, and finally joined the WHO in the hope of redeeming his so far unproductive life by doing some good in Africa. Inevitably, his dream of a river to irrigate its wastes comes to a nightmarish end. Polluted by everything from condoms to corpses, the water ceases to flow. Most of the characters are killed or flee, even Noon, who melts away into the dwindling forest, leaving Mallory scrabbling in the sand for the last trickles of his creation. An epilogue finds him back by Lake Kotto, now completely dried up. He's become a classic Greeneian figure, part burned-out case, part whisky priest, watching the Sahara inexorably invade, and dreaming of the lost Noon and the even more regretted river – as Jim, one might think, dreamed of a lost Shanghai.

Many readers felt the book should have ended with Mallory dying when his river ceased to flow, but Jim argued vehemently against this. In identifying his protagonist with the river, even to its name, he linked its waters, as his title implies, to the concept of creativity, and to his own fear of waning inspiration. 'I think it is important that he survived his own dream so he can reflect upon it,' Jim said of Mallory. 'At the end, the dream disposes of him. The river is rejecting him and dismisses him. I think it is important that he is able to reflect upon his dream, which remains ambiguous to the end. The whole thing is a vision of his own deepest possibilities and it touches his own imagination.' His attachment to the image is understandable. Nothing was so central to Jim's nature as his ability and desire to write. He had seen his wife die and his children move away. He had nothing but his work. Once that died, he would die with it.

After a *succès fou* like *Empire of the Sun*, only a modern-day *Moby-Dick* could have excited anything like the same interest, and *The Day of Creation* was hardly that. Had it appeared immediately after *The*

Crystal World, it would have been hailed as a major refinement in his work. The language is richer, the characterisation less formulaic, any science fiction influence almost completely absent. His protagonist, Mallory, isn't one of his over-intellectual observers but a blighted visionary with at least as much emotional baggage as any character from Greene. In the wake of *Empire of the Sun*, however, it read as a relic of simpler times.

In the *New York Times*, SF writer Samuel R. Delany gave an even-handed account.

> Certainly from close-up, in paragraph after paragraph, Mr Ballard constructs a moody and well-modelled landscape with as fine a writerly intelligence as we might hope for. But almost as frequently, when the actions of his characters come under his writerly eye, his account becomes thin, his dialogue wooden. The long view gives his book a rich allegorical air, a sense of quest and a steady rise in action – helicopter raids, blown-up dams, mysterious sexual trysts and clashes with Captain Kagwa – to suggest a near-classic adventure. But when we move in to look at the people, the relations between them, or the simple succession of events, things get very cloudy.

Martin Amis, doomed by family associations and personal acquaintance to be assigned to review each new Ballard work, had some good-natured fun at its expense:

> I don't know what post-Empire converts will make of this new novel, but I know what old Ballarders will make of it. Dialogues like the following are easy to imagine (indeed, I have shared in one or two myself).
>
> 'I've read the new Ballard.'
>
> 'And?'
>
> 'It's like the early stuff.'
>
> 'Really? What's the element?'
>
> 'Water.'
>
> 'Lagoons?'

'Some. Mainly a river.'

'What's the hero's name. Maitland? Melville?'

'Mallory.'

'Does Mallory go down the river?'

'No. Up.'

'Yes, of course. Natch. Does he hate the river or love it?'

'Both.'

'Is he the river?'

'Yes.'

'And does the novel begin "Later . . . " ?'

'Not quite . . .'

It actually begins, evocatively, with images of Mallory lulled by the sound of water heard through the wooden walls of a boat. Reading these sentences, loyal Ballardians, alienated by *Empire of the Sun*, bought *The Day of Creation* gratefully, reassured that it was the kind of visionary fiction they associated with him – unconcerned that it was a type he found increasingly uninteresting to write.

In October 1987, Jim was the guest of Toronto's Harbourfront Centre International Festival of Authors. To promote *The Day of Creation*, he did his first ever public reading from a novel, a trying experience. He was in Los Angeles for the December opening of Spielberg's *Empire of the Sun* – necessary to qualify for the Academy Awards. It was nominated for six, but all in lesser categories – sound, editing and music. Warners threw a lavish opening party, closing off a downtown street so that guests could walk from the cinema to the marquee that housed a giant Chinese buffet and Asian dancers jiving in forties costumes. He returned to the US in March for the Oscars, preceded and followed by a two-week book tour that took in New York, Miami, Chicago, Seattle, San Francisco and ended in Los Angeles. As he joked in a card to Moorcock, he could only judge where he was by reading the names on the hotel towels.

At the Oscars, he found himself seated behind a nervous Stoppard.

'Perhaps I should find another seat,' Stoppard suggested diplomatically, but Jim reassured him he was entirely happy with his adaptation. This was more than could be said for many people Jim met on his tour. 'What surprised me,' he said, 'was the degree of hostility of the American press towards Spielberg. Most of them seemed to have an almost knee-jerk negative reaction towards him. I remember someone saying, "Why did you allow him to film your book?"' Many critics agreed that Spielberg sentimentalised and glamorised *Empire of the Sun* as he had *The Color Purple*, imposing a Hallmark Cards prettiness, with misty vistas of Shanghai, reminiscent of David Lean. The opening is certainly over-calculated, with an angelic-looking Jim in choirboy robes soloing in a dubbed treble on the Welsh hymn *Suo Gân*. Reflecting this criticism, the film didn't live up to Warner Brothers' hopes or those of Spielberg. Its first release returned only $22 million domestically on a $38 million investment, and though the film limped into profit with overseas sales, it was regarded as a failure. It won just one Oscar, for Michael Kahn's editing. Ironically, that year's big winner – Bernardo Bertolucci's *The Last Emperor* – had also been shot in China.

For its UK release, *Empire of the Sun* was accorded a Royal Command Performance. Despite his anti-royalist sentiments, Jim dressed up, allowed his hand to be shaken, but felt a smug satisfaction that the Queen, poorly briefed, had no idea of the identity of his neighbour in the presentation line, legendary power broker Steve Ross, CEO of Warner Brothers, without whom the film would never have been made.

Jim remained on good terms with Spielberg, who was as prone as Kubrick to ringing out of the blue with news of a fresh scheme. A couple of years after *Empire of the Sun*, he proposed that Ballard script a remake of William Castle's cheesy 1959 ghost story *The House on Haunted Hill*. Starring Vincent Price, it had been rendered memorable by one of Castle's notorious gimmicks, 'Emergo', which, at a key moment, sent a luminous plastic skeleton skittering on a wire over the heads of the audience. Who would not be tempted? But Jim declined.

CHAPTER FORTY-SIX

PROFESSOR PLODD

In 1978, the Cambridge University magazine *Granta* was relaunched as a quarterly devoted to 'new writing'. Many major authors had stories that didn't lend themselves to novel length, and some of the best ended up there. Hoping to tap the same market, Hutchinson launched Hutchinson Novellas in 1987. Buying world rights, and guaranteeing US publication through Farrar, Straus & Giroux, they gambled that these illustrated hardcovers would succeed where Emma Tennant's funkier Next Edition paperbacks had not. But despite writers as eminent and/or popular as Paul Theroux, Colleen McCullough, Malcolm Bradbury, Anthony Burgess and Ballard, the series failed on both sides of the Atlantic and in 1990 was discontinued after sixteen titles.

Jim's contribution was the 25,000-word *Running Wild.* Following his practice of scaling up from shorter fiction, he based it on 'The Object of the Attack', written for *Interzone* in 1984, and reprinted in 'War Fever', Jim's 1990 short-story collection. In 'Attack', Dr Richard Greville, deputy psychiatric adviser to the Met, is called to Daventry prison to examine Matthew Young, a boy who's attempted to bomb Windsor Castle from a home-made ultra-light aircraft. At the time, those present included the royal family, the Reagans and Apollo astronaut Colonel Tom Stamford – who, unconventionally, proves to have been Young's primary target, having founded a cult devoted to expunging all non-Christians by zapping them with lasers from space.

Jim didn't read much crime fiction – or, indeed, much fiction at all – but British TV in the eighties reverberated to the tread of flat feet and he was an enthusiastic viewer. *Running Wild* resembles an episode of the television series based on Colin Dexter's Inspector Morse books, which made its debut in 1987. The *Morse* formula, a protracted conversation between John Thaw's opera-loving, ale-bibbing, emotionally impoverished Oxford detective and his loyal but often baffled assistant, dated back to Sherlock Holmes. The same year *Inspector Morse* first appeared on screen, a man ran amok with an automatic rifle in Hungerford, Berkshire, killing seventeen people, wounding sixteen more, before killing himself. In *Running Wild*, Greville is sent to Pangbourne, in Berkshire, some thirty miles west of London, to investigate why thirty-two adults have been murdered in a single night, and to find out what became of their thirteen children. Readers would not have missed the parallel with the Hungerford killings, nor Jim's point: that such random violence was hopelessly at odds with the systematic rationality of TV detective work.

The real Pangbourne does exist, but the murder scene is a cynical Ballard invention, a mating of English rustic village with US gated community, where CCTV cameras track every movement along its leafy lanes, and armed guards lurk behind the variegated privet. With Scotland Yard thoroughness, Greville considers every conceivable explanation for the killings. Discarding the notion of it being the work of a single assassin, he contemplates the possibility of a Manson-like cult, an SAS unit sent to the wrong address, a renegade Spetsnaz or Stasi hit team from the old Soviet bloc, a London mob gang, and even the maids and chauffeurs conspiring to eliminate their employers *à la* Jean Genet's *The Maids*. He briefly entertains a cuckoo suggestion from the BBC's *Panorama* that the perpetrators were unemployed workers from the north, roused to violence by Pangbourne's display of privilege. After rejecting a theory that it might be the work of extraterrestrials, or that the parents were themselves their own killers, in a mass suicide, he arrives, well after the reader, at the obvious truth that the kids did it.

A minute-by-minute reconstruction follows, explaining how the adults were variously shot, stabbed, electrocuted, and, in one case, torn limb from limb by an exercise cycle in overdrive. Greville proposes no motive, except to theorise that an apparently perfect community such as Pangbourne, where every action is observed, may frustrate those urges Freud isolated as the basis of the pleasure principle – sex and violence. His discovery in a boy's room, under the expected copies of *Playboy* and *Penthouse*, of 'real pornography' – gun magazines, extensively annotated – is as close as he gets to confirmation.

Having committed the crime, the children, he discovers, resourcefully put on tracksuits and, unsuspected, jogged away from the scene, as if taking their morning exercise. An epilogue suggests that the group may have metamorphosed into urban terrorists on the pattern of the German Red Army Faction or Baader-Meinhof group, and are plotting to assassinate Margaret Thatcher. Transiting the silent, clean, characterless suburbs of Düsseldorf in his 1971 tour by vintage car, Jim had intuited that he was seeing the future of Europe. Pangbourne is the British equivalent of those suburbs, and the murderous reaction of its children parallels those German and French urban terrorists who rebelled against a similar pampered upbringing by attacking the paragons of their own culture.

The open conclusion of both 'The Object of the Attack' and *Running Wild* suggests Jim may have hoped to link them with others into a novel. If so, he didn't persist, although their similarity points to the next stage in his career. *Running Wild* in particular reads like a sketch for his four final novels, *Cocaine Nights*, *Super-Cannes*, *Millennium People* and *Kingdom Come*. All begin as investigations of murders that prove to be symptoms of social malaise. In each case, the inquiry goes nowhere, and little is either solved or explained. This is existential fiction in a classic mould, harking back to the novels of Robbe-Grillet and Mauriac, and the films of Antonioni and Resnais. *Running Wild* evokes an even earlier model – one that inspired Jim to become a writer: case histories were the preferred narrative form of Sigmund Freud.

CHAPTER FORTY-SEVEN

UNKINDNESS

Hoping the film of *Empire of the Sun*, plus the novel's British success, would stir new US interest in Ballard, New York publishers Carroll & Graf reissued some titles that were out of print or which, like *Hello America*, had never appeared there. Anticipating enthusiasm from their author, publisher Kent Carroll found Ballard 'remarkably disinterested', a reaction echoed by the American reading public. Jim had helped define what was meant by the word 'modern' and had anticipated post-modernism, but now even his brand of post-modernism was out of date.

For his sixtieth birthday in 1990, Claire gave him something he'd always claimed to want: a unicycle. It gathered dust in the living room, along with everything else, including Emma Tennant's palm tree. For the gift giver, Jim was that nightmare, the man who truly had everything he needed – since all he needed was to write. The gift he would have valued most was a readership. 'Many people tell me I should write more short stories,' he said,

> and I reply that I don't know where I'd publish them. When I began writing, nearly every paper and magazine published short stories, some of them even every day. And then there were of course the science-fiction magazines, which had an almost insatiable appetite for short stories. The SF magazines in those days were an entirely wonderful training space for budding authors. One could pursue one's obsessions, one's fantasies; one could discover what kind of writer one wanted to be. It's a little like the way that, in one's youth, one has a lot of affairs:

one learns how to make love. It's different now: most young authors don't know how to make love, and they don't know how to write.

His 1990 short story collection *War Fever* illustrates the shrinking market. *The Magazine of Fantasy & Science Fiction* published the title story, but the rest come from *Ambit*, *Interzone*, *Bananas*, the *Observer*, the *Guardian* and the listings magazine *City Limits*. All to some extent are fragments: postscripts, footnotes or obituaries. They reflect a preoccupation with marginalia. Jim said he wanted to write about 'the next five minutes', but much of what he wrote in this period was a look back over his shoulder at the last five minutes. In the title story, war has been eradicated except in Beirut, where it's permitted, indeed encouraged, for study purposes, in the way virologists retain samples of a virulent disease. In other stories, Cape Canaveral is derelict, and a united Europe has become 'The Largest Theme Park in the World'. 'The Index' is a list of topics in a non-existent book and 'Answers to a Questionnaire' a set of responses to imaginary queries.

The book should have concluded with an announcement that the Atrocity Exhibition had closed indefinitely for lack of support – except that *The Atrocity Exhibition* had, paradoxically, become the emblem of Jim's achievement. Though never a commercial success, it earned widespread critical respect. In 1990, the San Francisco magazine *Re/Search* issued the collection in the illustrated large format he'd planned originally, though now with his comments, footnotes and updates. These, while interesting to the scholar and fan, smoothed the jagged edge of the original.

The appearance of this respectful edition showed once again how Revolt – whether surrealism, *les événements* of 1968, Dean, Elvis, Che or punk – degrades into Style. The term 'Ballardian' no longer defined a stance in relation to the future but a look and a sound. Already embraced by pop music, it had entered the common currency of advertising, graphic novels, movies. Irvin Kershner's film *The Eyes of Laura Mars*, released in 1978, begins with a fashion shoot in which three half-naked models brawl around a burning car wreck *à la* Ballard.

A cologne called Diesel, marketed as 'Fuel for Life', is already on the market. Can *Crash: The Musical* be long coming?

The jacket copy of *War Fever* mentioned *Empire of the Sun*, and announced that Ballard was 'currently at work on its successor'. This book, *The Kindness of Women*, appeared from HarperCollins in September 1991, publicised as 'the sequel to *Empire of the Sun*', but the description is misleading. While it does continue the story of *Empire*'s fictional Jim, it also revises, augments, corrects and, at some points, contradicts the original. Before everything else, however, it is a sexual memoir, albeit an existential one, though bold enough for *Private Eye* to label Ballard 'a fruity old perv'.

The opening chapters serve as an epilogue to the first book, covering the Japanese surrender and concluding with Jim sailing for England. His father waves to him from the dock, but he doesn't respond, a mean-spirited act he will regret all his life. Or will he? Can we trust *The Kindness of Women*? It may be a *roman-à-clef*, but the text, like Ballard's life and career, has many doors, some of which open on to imaginary worlds.

Unlike *Empire of the Sun*, *Kindness* is told in the first person, which confers a superficial authenticity. The cover blurb insists that Ballard 'plunges into the maelstrom of the 1960s, using himself both as instigator and subject of every aspect of cultural, social and sexual experimentation'. The 'I' of the book does study medicine, fall in love, enlist in the air force, train in Canada, return and marry the girl, who dies while on holiday with him. But unlike 'I', Jim never flew solo, nor set out to find a lost aircraft in the Canadian tundra, nor did his wife, as in the book, die from a fall. A lone drug experience is described in glamorised form, but a long affair with whisky is barely mentioned. We meet two new characters from his Shanghai days – Peggy Gardner, who becomes his mistress, and David Hunter, who persuades him to join the RAF – and the media personality Dick Sutherland, based on Chris Evans. He lingers on the unhappy life of the imaginary Hunter, who ends up in a mental hospital, and on his friendly rivalry with Sutherland, but omits any reference, even fictional, to Moorcock, Brunner, Bax, Paolozzi, Tennant, Zoline, or anyone else in the counter-culture or SF.

Women may have been kind to Jim, but he doesn't return their kindness. His sexual descriptions have the quality of autopsy reports. They evoke with lubricious relish a mucus-lubricated anus, a wrinkled pink vulva, yawning amid dark hair, a nipple flicked erect with the same motion as a nurse swelling a vein to draw blood. Even sex with his wife is forensic. To enjoy some time alone on holiday, they retreat to the bathroom, a common stratagem for couples with kids. Once the door's locked, the maternal Miriam turns lustful exhibitionist. Gymnastically contorted, watching herself in the mirror, she regards their coupling without expression, as Jim, inspired by the sterile surroundings, imagines them as astronauts having sex in an orbiting space capsule. Taking its cue from *Crash* and the theory that sex in the future will involve more than two people, the sex in *Kindness* is frequently communal and voyeuristic. It invites comment like Rupert Birkin's tirade against Ursula Brangwen in D. H. Lawrence's *Women in Love*: 'What you want is pornography – looking at yourself in mirrors, watching your naked animal actions in mirrors, so that you can have it all in your consciousness, make it all mental.'

It's not kindness the fictional Jim requires from women but acquiescence. Like the consoling (and fictional) sex offered by his sister-in-law following the death of Miriam, he accepts satisfaction as his right. Walking in on Sally Mumford fucking a stranger, he rationalises that she has engineered the interruption as a way of teaching him not to be jealous. Once shed of that encumbrance, he will be free to enjoy her promiscuity as much as she does. Such solipsistic scenes show Jim becoming the Abraham Zapruder of his own sex life, isolating, parsing, analysing. Though he calls his sexual activities 'making love', there are no expressions of joy, let alone passion. They would be as much out of place here as in his description of Princess Margaret's nasal surgery. Only violence engages his feelings. He calls the *Crashed Cars* exhibition 'a repository of the most powerful and engaged emotions, a potent symbol in the new logic of violence and sensation that ruled our lives'. Compared to carnage, having sex is weak stuff – women's work.

The promotional blitz for *Kindness* included numerous magazine and newspaper profiles, TV and radio interviews, almost none of which commented on the fact that, in coming clean about his life, the genial Jim Ballard had elected to talk dirty. For *Shanghai Jim*, a documentary film for the BBC series *Bookmark*, he returned to Shanghai for the first time since the war. He also appeared on the BBC's *Desert Island Discs*, an emblem of cultural acceptance as significant to the public as an OBE, though an ironic one for someone who disliked music. Never lost for words, he gave a plausible imitation of a man who loved the stuff. Of being marooned, he claimed, 'I'd thoroughly enjoy it. To some extent it's an extended version of the situation in which I find myself now. I'm sort of marooned on the British Isles. Many people would say, looking at my ramshackle home, that I've lived like a castaway all these years.'

As the one book allowed on the island, apart from the Bible and the complete works of Shakespeare, he nominated *Moby-Dick*, which he would never finish, and as his one luxury the unicycle given to him by Claire, which he would never ride. The songs likewise were chosen not for musical appeal but as cues to stories. 'The Teddy Bears' Picnic' recalled a wind-up gramophone he owned as a boy and the one record he played on it; 'The Girl From Ipanema' his visit to Rio; and in Bing Crosby singing 'Don't Fence Me In' he even found a joke in the experience of Lunghua. His most eccentric selection, 'Put the Blame On Mame' from the film *Gilda*, starring Rita Hayworth, sparked a fantasy about another movie entirely. In Orson Welles's *The Lady from Shanghai*, Hayworth plays a woman who has lived in China, a fact that inspired a Ballard improvisation. Had such a woman as her character actually existed, he speculated that he could, as a boy, have met her. 'That [film] was made in 1948 and she must have been in Shanghai about the time that I was – she was probably a bar girl, or something even worse – and I've always liked the idea that she might, like a lot of bar girls in Shanghai, have worked as a nanny, and she might conceivably have been *my* nanny.'

'Next record?' croaked the nonplussed presenter.

For *Shanghai Jim*, he gave as plausible a performance of The Stranger's Return as he had of a music lover. The scene in the film where he sits, silent, in the fetid hutch in which he lived for two years with his family, and muses 'I came to puberty here', played poignantly onscreen. Few viewers realised they were watching an improvisation. That night, he sent Moorcock a postcard, admitting that, as he waited to be flooded with memories, nothing came. All the effort to expunge those years, combined with the fantasising of *Empire of the Sun*, had worked too well. He scrabbled together enough reminiscences to satisfy the film-makers, who hired a local boy to duplicate young Jim's bike rides, which some people – even himself – were beginning to regard as at least partly imaginary. Jim became far from the first person to follow the advice enshrined in the work of film-maker John Ford – 'When the legend becomes fact, print the legend.'

CHAPTER FORTY-EIGHT

DEMI-PARADISE

For most of his life, Jim expressed no political beliefs, beyond the reflex *noli me tangere* libertarianism of most sixties artists. This modified with age into a law and order conservatism in which he and Kingsley Amis were not so different. Both conceded that if leaving them alone to work required an ICBM silo at the bottom of their garden targeted on Libya, so be it. Jim did, however, take a medically inclined interest in politicians as physical beings. The realisation that the people who controlled the population's lives and deaths also ate and crapped and, in particular, had sex like everyone else, aroused the same mingled envy, curiosity and lust that he felt in considering the Kennedy assassination.

Of all post-Cold War political figures, none was more attractive to him than Margaret Thatcher. Like Ronald Reagan, the Kennedys, the Queen and the other celebrities whom he sometimes literally dissected in his fiction, she intrigued him as much with her body as her beliefs. 'I've had sexual fantasies about her,' he admitted. His litany 'What I Believe' included a panegyric to Thatcher that added an additional appeal: her association with the violence of the war in the Falklands. It imagined her, in a variation on one of Helmut Newton's tableaux, having sex in a motel room with a young Argentine soldier while a tubercular gas station attendant looked on. Not surprisingly, the Conservative Party omitted to invite Ballard to campaign on its behalf.

Jim liked to speculate on the appeal of political figures, in particular the role played by sexuality in the decision to vote. Convinced, like Nixon's lawyer Charles Colson, that 'if you've got them by the balls, their hearts and minds will follow', he proposed that selectors should look for candidates in show business. 'You can imagine somebody like Madonna,' he said, 'with the will and brains and the ideological drive of Margaret Thatcher.' Above all, they must be women. 'When one looks at the bumbling male leaders of the day – Major, Clinton, Yeltsin – they hardly have a grip on anything. The charismatic dictators of the future will have to be women in the Margaret Thatcher mould. Only women will be able to tap the deep need of the male half of the population to be led, to be drilled, to be frightened. It won't be Big Brother in the future, Big Brother has had his day, it'll be Big Sister.'

To put a powerful and mediatique woman at the heart of a novel made good sense in the early nineties. Even after Thatcher was eased out of office in 1990, public life didn't lack women with her quality of schoolmarmish aggression. The ability of animal trainer Barbara Woodhouse to boss dogs about as well as their owners made her a TV celebrity. Mary Whitehouse campaigned aggressively and publicly against sex in the media. Esther Rantzen protested tirelessly for worthy causes. *The Female Eunuch* author Germaine Greer addressed feminist issues with the snarl of an attack dog. Even TV cooks such as Delia Smith laid down the culinary law with a smiling steeliness.

Aspects of Whitehouse, Woodhouse, Greer, Rantzen and Smith converged with that of Thatcher in the character of Barbara Rafferty, the driving force of the novel *Rushing to Paradise*, published in 1994. 'Dr Barbara', as she's known to her acolytes, is a feminist environmentalist, devoted in the first instance to saving the supposedly threatened albatross by occupying a tiny Pacific atoll where it nests. However, as Jim makes clear, her political agenda is subordinate to the act of revolt. She's already been struck off for euthanasia, and will, by the end of the book, have moved beyond animal survival to planning the creation of a master race. Rafferty embraces Abbie Hoffman's Revolution for the Hell of It, with echoes of Brando's Black Rebels' Motor Cycle Club in *The Wild One*. Asked 'What are you rebelling against, Johnny?' he answers languidly, 'Whaddya got?'

Rafferty is always ready with a view on any topic, pro or con, as media and money dictate. When Neil Dempsey, the hapless teenage surfer she's recruited to her cause, expresses doubts about invading the Pacific island of Saint-Esprit, shortly to be used by the French for nuclear tests, and cites the sinking of Greenpeace's *Rainbow Warrior* in Auckland harbour as an example of the risks, she goes into what Jim calls 'full interview mode' – something he knew intimately, since he was a master of it. Their opponents won't dare, she explains. With a satellite dish and a film crew on hand, any action will immediately be transmitted to CNN and the BBC. The Ultimate Deterrent is no longer a nuclear strike but a damaging sound bite.

Both Neil's fears and Rafferty's expectations are realised. On landing, he's shot in the foot by a French soldier, whereupon Dr Barbara uses her TV link to make him a martyr. A millionaire offers money, and Saint-Esprit becomes a haven for cranks, hippies and the media. Club Med surveys it for a possible resort. A Polynesian helper wants to make it the capital of a new Pacific empire, free of European colonialists. An elderly Japanese arrives with the ashes of Hiroshima's H-Bomb survivors. People send every kind of endangered animal but, as canned food gives out, the colonists eat them. Thwarted, Dr Rafferty turns Neil out to stud in a doomed eugenics scheme to make him the father of a super race.

Given its topicality, the resonances with Jim Jones and David Koresh, the resumption of French nuclear tests on Mururoa, and the Falklands War, *Rushing to Paradise* might have been a bestseller to rival the work of an infinitely less gifted Michael Crichton. But Ballard lacked Crichton's slickness, his ease in crafting congenial characters and narratives that transfer effortlessly to the screen. *Rushing to Paradise* reads less like a novel than a report, and its dialogue like transcribed testimony. Though nobody drew the parallel, Paul Theroux's 1981 novel *The Mosquito Coast* dealt more effectively with similar material – ironically by adopting Jim's technique from *Empire of the Sun*, of telling the story through the eyes of a boy.

In defending the book, Jim argued that his concerns went beyond popular fiction.

> To some extent, *Rushing to Paradise* is a satire. I make clear that I thoroughly approve of Dr Barbara Rafferty. She represents what for me is a very appealing strain of archetypal womanhood, often cruel, incredibly strong-willed, messianic, ruthless, far stronger than most men, and capable of inspiring fanatical devotion, which the archetype of woman through the ages has done. My feelings toward her are very ambivalent.

In Dr Barbara, Jim comes closest to acknowledging the mixture of desire and dislike he felt towards his own mother. An incestuous attraction on Neil's part is more than implied, notably in a scene where he discovers a crude mural that a disaffected colonist has smeared on the wall of a concrete bunker. It shows a rampant goat about to mount a woman resembling Rafferty. It's been painted with her blood, using one of her wadded-up blouses as a brush. As Neil contemplates the image, he squeezes blood from the fabric, imagining he is wringing sex from her vagina. A spark leaps from this scene to the 'psychic surrenders' of observing Edna's body in her Shanghai bedroom and the dissection of 'Dr Elizabeth Grant' in Cambridge, to illuminate the darkest corners of Ballard's troubled imagination.

Rushing to Paradise was published in September 1994 in Britain, but not until the following May in the US. British reviewers received it respectfully, but hardly with enthusiasm. Almost nobody in either country spotted the Thatcher/Rafferty parallel. Many British reviewers opted for an easy but imprecise comparison with *Lord of the Flies*, and praised Ballard for past triumphs rather than accusing him of present mediocrity. One reviewer, citing Golding's book, went on to call *Rushing to Paradise* 'Ballard's most powerful novel in years, a terrifying, all-too-real "what if". Which is exactly what Ballard does best, what-iffing Armageddon-like possibilities in this paradise we call Earth.' Another asserted that:

> nobody can fault either the intensity or the conviction of J G Ballard's obsessions: nuclear test sites, dead albatrosses, empty swimming pools and abandoned cities. Submerged enemy aircraft filled with skeletons, dead astronauts orbiting the earth in beeping satellites, and motorists stranded on collapsed freeway off-ramps. For more than 30 years Ballard has mined and re-mined his subconscious with a sort of clinical exactitude. He has created original and perplexing new landscapes with such skill and consistency that even his strangest imaginings have come to seem familiar.

The valedictory tone gave these reviews the quality of obituaries. Ballard, it seems, had had his day.

CHAPTER FORTY-NINE

TESTICULES FLAMBÉS

In 1995, Beatrice Ballard married fellow BBC producer Nick Rossiter at the Jesuit Church of the Immaculate Conception in Farm Street, Mayfair, London's most fashionable Catholic venue. Among Rossiter's discoveries was Sister Wendy Beckett, an art historian who was also a Carmelite nun. She featured in a number of series, always in full habit, lecturing in a style many found charming but a few disliked. According to a colleague,

> Nick Rossiter was not a Jesuit but a Benedictine. His refugee parents had converted to that branch of Catholicism. He used to fret about whether there was something 'deceitful' in being a Catholic born to parents who were themselves born Jewish. What JGB thought of his daughter's choice of partner is hard to determine. He was pretty pained that Bea was getting married in church. But he agreed to attend, on condition that Sister Wendy wasn't there. Ballard loathed her. There were very few people in the church, perhaps thirty or so, in a great barn of a place. JGB was sitting somewhere towards the back. The service was about to begin when a door opened and Sister Wendy scurried through it. JGB turned to look and then announced, very loudly indeed: 'They've smuggled in the nun!' It was a sheerly wonderful moment.

Anyone meeting Jim in his mid-sixties might have assumed he saw himself as being in the twilight of his career. With a prominent pot, a straggle of untrimmed grey hair trailing over his collar, and usually dressed in open-necked shirts and unfashionable jackets, often in mismatched fabrics, such as tweed and flannel, he resembled a retired butcher of eccentric habits.

He knew few of his immediate neighbours in Shepperton, none of whom ever entered the house. Even his admirers were kept at arm's length, fended off with notes and postcards. After writing an unsolicited letter of praise to the poet Jeremy Reed, he agreed to contribute introductions to two of Reed's collections, but though the two men exchanged occasional letters and postcards, they almost never met, except when Jim surfaced in the West End for a signing. Novelist Will Self visited him once, but when he suggested a further meeting, Jim, friendly but firm, decreed their relationship should continue 'on a textual level'. Years later, when they met once again in person, Jim asked puckishly, 'Why don't you ever come to see me?'

Jim embodied at its most extreme the dictum 'The unconsidered life is not worth living'. Any expedition away from Shepperton was endurable only if it became a performance or a ritual. 'Jim himself is a creature of habit,' said a friend. 'He eats out twice a week, at least once every three weeks in the Esarn Kheaw Thai restaurant in Shepherd's Bush, with Claire. To get there, he never varies his trajectory. Overground train to Richmond, District line to Turnham Green. Then walk.' Once having decided to assume the part of Jolly Jim, he played up to the role. Iain Sinclair remembered 'his wonderful paternalistic presence when he went into his favourite Chinese restaurants, his arms around the Thai waitresses, that booming voice; he ordered for everyone else'. If the party was large enough to fill two tables, the women sat at one, the men at the other, allowing Jim to hold court. It was made clear that men were for talk, women for fun. Female attempts to enter the conversation were laughed off or ignored.

In calmer moments, Jim was content to drift on the surface of popular culture, letting the current carry him. His taste for TV was voracious but discriminating. He was one of the first people to recognise the appeal of the *CSI* forensic series, and foresee their astonishing popularity. He also became fascinated by *Big Brother*. 'Most television is low-grade pap, it's so homogenised it's like mental toothpaste. But *Big Brother* is a slice of reality – or what passes for reality. It was like Tracey Emin's *My Bed*.' He speculated that the show's hypnotic appeal stemmed not from its content but from the brain's capacity to fixate. 'If you focus on anything, however blank, in the right way, then you become obsessed by it. It's like those Andy Warhol films of eight hours of the Empire State Building or of somebody sleeping. Ordinary life viewed obsessively enough becomes interesting in its own right by some sort of neurological process that I don't hope to understand.' He would have preferred the concept's ultimate extension – a film in which people didn't realise they were being filmed, such as the *Candid Camera* television series of the sixties, and Peter Weir's *The Truman Show*, where a young man finds he's the unwitting star of a TV reality programme.

Some Sundays, he and Walsh took tea at the Heathrow Hilton, watching 747s take off for destinations where he wasn't tempted to follow them. Airports and air terminals share with the freeway and high-rise a timeless functionality. The events that take place there resemble one another to such a degree, and pass in such quantity and rapidity, that we can no longer differentiate between them, any more than we can isolate a single water molecule in a river. They remain as untouched by time as the eventless present of the surrealists, a quality Jim found reassuring.

The Hilton, designed in 1992 by Michael Manser, became his favourite building in London, a reminder of Chris Marker's *La Jetée*. He called it a white cathedral, the closest to a religious building that one can find in an airport, and used his own snapshot of the façade as a postcard. Revealingly, he celebrated the fact that the building neutralised all emotion. In his eyes, it was unlike other public buildings, such as the National Gallery or the Louvre, in that one could never fall in love there, or need to. He appeared to find the fact consoling.

Though he no longer burned all his manuscripts, Jim kept no archive, nor, since he refused to use a word processor, were the texts of his many reviews and essays readily accessible. Fortunately, David Pringle, also now his bibliographer, had collected everything. At Pringle's suggestion, he compiled *A User's Guide to the Millennium: Essays and Reviews*. 'The book was pitched to various publishers before HarperCollins,' says Pringle. 'Eventually he and Maggie [Hanbury] decided that it had to be from his main publisher – and of course by 1994, when it went to him, Malcolm [Edwards] was quite happy to publish it.' When it appeared in 1996, reviewers were agreeably surprised to be reminded of the range of Ballard's interests; not only Dalí and the surrealists but Andy Warhol and David Hockney; Sigmund Freud but also Hitler, Disney, Darwin and Winnie-The-Pooh. However, the influential trade magazine *The Bookseller* remarked, 'The real problem with this collection, apart from its lack of focus, is that Ballard the essayist is not nearly as compelling as Ballard the creative writer', and the book enjoyed only modest sales.

Jim was still the person to whom any literary editor sent the uncategorisable book, and whom a journalist called on a slow news day. In September 1995, the *Observer*, for a piece about odd bequests, invited him to answer the question, 'What would you leave to whom, and why?' Jim said, 'I would leave Andrea Dworkin my testicles. She could have *testicules flambés*.' Anti-pornography campaigner Dworkin was a close friend of Mike and Linda Moorcock but a *bête noire* of Ballard's.

A project to film *Crash* had kicked about for years. At one time, Sandy Lieberson, producer of *Performance*, envisaged it for Nicholas Roeg. Playwright Heathcote Williams wrote a screenplay which set the story in Los Angeles, and imagined Jack Nicholson as the star. (Jim disliked its Disneyfied style.) Chris Petit admired the book, but did his own takes on it in his novel *Robinson* and the movie *Radio On*. Jeremy Thomas, producer of *The Last Emperor*, which had beaten *Empire of the Sun* for an Academy Award, also optioned it, but gave up when the production threatened to be too expensive. Jim took no part in these projects, just banking the option cheques and, if asked for a comment, saying he thought the book was unfilmable, at least as he had written it.

Early in the nineties, during an interview with Canadian director David Cronenberg, New York journalist Toby Goldstein recommended the novel and sent him a copy. He read about a third of it, and was initially repelled. Later, however, he saw its cinematic potential, particularly if he could transfer the action to his native Toronto. He raised the possibility with Ballard, and was encouraged by his response. Earlier producers assumed he would demand any film be shot in England, but Jim surprised Cronenberg with his indifference to location. To him, a freeway outside Liverpool was interchangeable with one near Bucharest, and the cars on both, wherever manufactured, were identical. As for sex and death, they, too, were global.

Cronenberg seemed an odd choice to direct such a film. The world still knew him mainly for his exercises in 'venereal horror'. In *Rabid*, former porn star Marilyn Chambers played a cosmetic surgery patient turned vampire, with a penile barb in her armpit that infects her victims. The slugs in *Shivers* slither into the intestines of unsuspecting toilet users, transforming them into sex maniacs. His greatest success was *Dead Ringers*, a surrealist love triangle starring Jeremy Irons in a double role as twin-brother doctors, experts on the reproductive system, who fall out over Geneviève Bujold – their ideal woman, since she has three vaginas. For Ballard, however, an admirer of David Lynch and Italian dramatised 'shockumentaries' such as *Mondo Cane*, Cronenberg was an entirely appropriate choice.

Cronenberg had problems interesting producers in the project. In May 1993, Ballard wrote to an Italian fan, Luca del Baldo, that the project was stalled, perhaps indefinitely. It remained so until, in 1994, while filming William Burroughs's *Naked Lunch*, Cronenberg suggested *Crash* to his producer, Jeremy Thomas, unaware of his prior interest. When Thomas first contemplated a film, he'd wondered how to find a credible double for Elizabeth Taylor, and to get the original's permission to be shown in the film, but from the start Cronenberg excluded Jim's fetish stars. With this hurdle out of the way, an adaptation presented fewer problems. As David Lean had noted when he considered filming *Empire of the Sun*, Ballard wrote in pictures.

Crash was never going to be a blockbuster, a fact that, paradoxically, helped persuade Jim to support it. No concessions needed to be made to temperamental stars. Thomas clinched the deal by taking Jim out for a spin in his Ferrari. At the time, Jim drove a 2.9-litre Ford Granada, which he described as being 'about the nearest you can get to the size, the space and the Detroit glamour of an American car'. But Thomas's car was another order of experience entirely. The way Jim caressed the leather upholstery and dashboard as the car raced up the motorway revealed to Thomas that he was a fellow 'petrolhead'.

With Ballard behind the project, Thomas raised the modest $9 million budget from independent production company New Line, owned by TV entrepreneur Ted Turner. Hearing of the project, Will Self wrote to Ballard, diffidently suggesting he might write the screenplay, but Cronenberg insisted on doing so himself, an exclusion that rankled slightly with Jim, who would have liked, at least, to be consulted. Thomas and Cronenberg announced the project at the 1995 Cannes Film Festival, with a cast already attached. Holly Hunter had long wanted to work with Cronenberg, and would have accepted almost any role he offered. James Spader played Ballard, Canadian actress Deborah Unger his wife Catherine and Rosanna Arquette the crippled Gabrielle. Another Canadian, Elias Koteas, would portray Vaughan. To capture the right frame of mind, he drove the three thousand miles from Los Angeles to Toronto.

Once Ted Turner, who financed the film, learned of its sexual content, he did his best to distance himself, and even to have the production shelved. Jim had frankly labelled the novel as pornographic, but Cronenberg felt he had to defend his film against the charge. He told a journalist, 'Pornography is created to arouse you sexually and has no other purpose. It's obvious *Crash* is not pornographic. People say it's sexual but not erotic, as though that was a criticism.' He praised Arquette's performance as the crippled Gabrielle. 'I'm not saying the movie is striking a blow for the disabled, but there is a sense in which that's true. She's saying, "My disfigurement is not disfigurement, it's a transformation and a mutation and it can be sexual." Scars have been sexy for years.'

Most people agreed Holly Hunter was too meek and dowdy for Helen Remington, who, in the novel, is another of Jim's omni-competent professionals in a white medical coat, strong, young and commanding. The slack is taken up by Deborah Unger as Catherine Ballard, a sleek blonde with the impassivity of a car bonnet emblem, and a body that lends itself to being placed in conjunction with curved enamelled metal. Her first appearance in the film, bent over the wing of a small aircraft, skirt hiked up to reveal naked buttocks and thighs, ready to receive the penis of an anonymous lover, sets the tone, reinforced in the next sequence, where she stands, similarly exposed, at the balcony of the Ballards' apartment, overlooking a motorway, the shot a specific reference to similar photographs by Helmut Newton of women, sleek as Brancusis, posing high above the city. In the first draft of Cronenberg's screenplay, this sequence was followed by another in which Catherine and her secretary, Karen, try on lingerie together in a department store changing room, the camera dwelling on the marks made on Catherine's body by the straps and clips, but the sequence slowed down the development, and was cut, even though it would have been useful in setting up Ballard's later interest in similar but deeper impressions made on Gabrielle's flesh by her orthopaedic harness.

Unger is more skilful than the other women of the film in capturing the hieratic nature of Jim's writing, the sense of ritual. As for Catherine Deneuve in Buñuel's *Belle de Jour*, lust makes her dreamy. She disappears into an erotic haze, sleepwalking through acts of depravity with the slowness and deliberation of someone underwater. By contrast, Arquette plays Gabrielle, as she plays almost everything, with impish humour, effectively so when she and Ballard visit the auto show and persuade a perversely excited assistant to let them sit in the front seat of an expensive new car. Gabrielle asks for his help, handing him her cane, then letting him kneel to move her legs inside the car. One of her callipers rips the leather upholstery. 'Oh, this is bad,' murmurs the assistant. 'This is really bad.' But we're never sure whether he's lamenting the damage or relishing the erotic effect of chromed metal against net-stockinged thighs, and the way Gabrielle's hand is fondling James's penis through his trousers.

All the car crashes were filmed in real time, without slow motion or other special effects, and many of them from inside the cars, the camera experiencing the same disorienting jolt as the victims. The crashes matter less in the film than in the book, since Cronenberg concentrated on the unconventional love story of the Ballards and the tensions within the group around Vaughan. Jim reserved his particular enthusiasm for the scene where James drives through a car wash, the brushes whoosh-whooshing, water gushing, as Catherine and Vaughan have sex in the back seat. He watches in the rear-view mirror while they grapple, Vaughan clawing at Catherine's face and neck. She extends one hand towards James, sticky with juices, but falls back helplessly into the pit of gratification. This was automobile sex as he had always fantasised it. 'One of the greatest scenes in cinema,' he enthused to Iain Sinclair, 'marvellously erotic too. Brilliantly done. The sound is so wonderful.'

Cannes accepted *Crash* in competition at the 1996 festival, which Jim attended. Helmut Newton photographed the cast, giving Ballard a chance to praise Newton in person. The commitment of the actors impressed him, particularly when a film journalist sat down next to Hunter and, not recognising Jim, asked, 'Holly, what are you doing in this shit?' Jim recalled, 'Holly sprang into life and delivered a passionate defence, castigating him for his small-mindedness and provincialism. It was the festival's greatest performance, which I cheered vigorously.' The jury awarded the film a Special Prize, but reaction was polarised, with accusations of 'pornography' that promised not to disappear.

CHAPTER FIFTY

BURNING DOWN THE HOUSE

Since publicity for *The User's Guide to the Millennium* made no reference to a new novel, the arrival of *Cocaine Nights* the same year surprised many. In April 1995 Jim had let slip to an interviewer that his next book was 'a psychological study. Oh God, it sounds crazy. It's about the necessity of crime.' After that, however, he spoke of the unnamed novel as a return to his more radical and experimental style of *The Atrocity Exhibition*. When he recommended to Will Self that he read *The Black Box*, a compilation of recordings salvaged from crashed planes, he added that his next novel might be inspired by it – something Self intuited was a lie. 'He was always suggesting story ideas to me. I knew it was because he had already thought about it and had abandoned the concept.'

Throughout 1995, Jim was writing, in effect, his first thriller, the publication of which HarperCollins timed to coincide with the British release of *Crash*. This was frustrated by the *Evening Standard*'s habitually shrill right-wing film reviewer Alexander Walker, who, in Jim's words, 'halfway through *Crash*'s press conference at Cannes [...] suddenly got up with a flourish and walked straight out. And when he got back to London, he wrote a piece calling *Crash* the most depraved film ever made. To me, this represents Total Artistic Success!' Such grandstanding was a Walker trademark. His report described *Crash* as 'beyond the bounds of depravity'. Because of the campaign he helped orchestrate, the film, while opening promptly in France and other countries, didn't appear on British screens for another year.

*

Cocaine Nights, despite resonances with *High-Rise*, *Running Wild* and some of the short stories, was a major departure for someone never comfortable with the restrictions of genre. Reflecting this, its plot only occasionally respects the rules. It's a whodunnit in the same way that *The Drowned World* is a science fiction novel; the shoe fits, but it's a Manolo Blahnik in black kidskin, with its three-inch heel buried in someone's flesh. As Nicholas Wroe wrote admiringly of the author in the *Independent*, 'his continued ability to keep coming up with new J. G. Ballard-isms is extraordinary. It is now 40 years since the publication of his first short stories, yet he is still conjuring up the most dazzlingly original and unsettling images, coupled to unfailingly depressing and plausible visions of the future.'

Yet in one sense *Cocaine Nights* also returned Jim to Shanghai. As he told Kevin Jackson,

> What I'm saying is that over the last 20 or 30 years in Europe – longer in the US (and it was evident in the Shanghai I lived in before the war) – a minority of middle-class professionals – any term you like – retain the greatest energising and creative input into life. And they've decided for reasons of security to remove themselves from the hurly-burly of city life. American cities were the first to show this; it's now happening here, Nairobi, Singapore. They're subtracting themselves from the whole of these civic interactions that depend on them, virtually conducting an internal immigration – and that's dangerous.

Writing again in the first person, Jim tells his story through the eyes of travel writer Charles Prentice, beginning as he passes through Gibraltar, heading for the retirement community of Club Nautico, near Estrella de Mar on the Costa del Sol. Until recently, his brother Frank, for whom he's always felt responsible, managed the resort, but a house has burned down, killing five people, and Frank, having confessed to setting the house on fire, is in prison.

Cocaine Nights is calculatedly old-fashioned. It depicts the Costa del Sol with a stylised emptiness that recalls art house films of the sixties, in particular those of Michelangelo Antonioni. It even employs the plot device that made Antonioni's *L'Avventura* a *succès fou.* In the film, a girl disappears from a yacht during an Adriatic cruise. Her lover and her best friend stay behind on a deserted volcanic island to search for her, drift into their own liaison – and forget the missing woman entirely, as do we. Her disappearance is never explained. It wasn't the point.

In the same way, the explanation of how and why the house in *Cocaine Nights* went up in flames is cursory, even silly. As in *Running Wild,* Jim dispenses with suspense halfway through, the better to deal with his real subject, the *cafard* of modern life in Europe and his recipe for livening it up. He puts his suggestions into the mouth of the club's tennis pro, Bobby Crawford, a taskmaster who chivvies the residents into activity as a serving machine barrages him with deliveries of greater speed and intricacy. Nicholas Wroe's review evokes this mechanism's star appearance: 'a single magnificent image which perfectly encapsulates the book's main thesis'.

> An unmanned tennis machine sends down a fizzing supply of kicking, swerving and biting services onto a baking Spanish court, empty but for a broken wooden racket and a bloody corpse. It's all you really need to know. The future is leisure plus technology and it's not for the squeamish.

Once he and Charles become friendly, Crawford owns up to the thefts, fires and accidents, but argues in justification that they have energised the once moribund resort. To be burgled or mugged jolts people out of their complacency. No longer content to drowse on the couch watching a DVD, they join the tennis club or amateur theatre group. From there, it's a step to performing in porn films or experimenting with drugs. (Crawford, a full-service Pandarus, imports hashish by speedboat from Morocco.) The community psychiatrist, Dr Irwin Sanger, reinforces the lesson. Only violence can lure people from their TV sets or swimming pools. Burning down the house was a joint project by a few residents. The victims were sacrificed to instil a communal guilt that would maintain the momentum developed by

Crawford. Even Frank contributed, by confessing to the arson he didn't commit. Charles, too, becomes complicit when Crawford moves to a new and larger community and starts his work again. After he's murdered on his tennis court, Charles, though innocent, confesses to the killing.

Over this bare, even perfunctory mystery, Jim drapes a cloak of cultural references. A few are surrealist: Chirico in the colonnades and white walls of the club's white architecture; Hans Bellmer in the opening sequence, a traffic jam at the Gibraltar border with Spain, during which a customs officer fumbles through a truck loaded with naked blue-eyed dolls. The tone, however, is post-surrealist, more Edward Hopper than Salvador Dalí, with echoes of Helmut Newton. The tall, well-tended professional women of *Cocaine Nights* and *Super-Cannes* could have stepped out of Newton's 1976 collection *White Women.* Some of Jim's descriptions read like scenarios of photographs Newton hadn't yet got around to shooting. As in his images, Jim's characters often appear to have paused momentarily in a game of complex sexual charades from which we voyeurs are frustratingly excluded, since, like everything at Club Nautico, this is Members Only.

Jim originally submitted the novel with the title *The Dark Side of the Sun.* 'I thought (a) it sounded too generic,' says Malcolm Edwards, 'and (b) it was the title of a Terry Pratchett novel. I looked down the contents page (all the chapters had titles) and *Cocaine Nights* just leapt out as a potentially commercial title.' That said, cocaine doesn't play a large part in the story. One of the residents, burned-out jazz singer Laurie Fox, is a user. Charles never tries it. We're told that, as a young man, he dabbled in opium and brothels, an admission that establishes him ineluctably as Old School, and easy meat for Crawford and Sanger. Unable to see beyond the surface of anything, Charles is always a step behind. He wants to play tennis with Crawford, but never gets the chance. He wants to drive his Porsche, too, but the one time he's allowed, Crawford overrides him, pushing his own foot on to the accelerator and swerving the car in front of a truck. Glumly,

Charles notes the imprint of the sole of Crawford's sneaker on the upper of his shoe. Did Ballard see the 1973 film *The Wicker Man*, in which an innocent policeman is lured to a remote island, supposedly to investigate the disappearance of a girl during ancient fertility rites, and realises too late that he's there to be sacrificed? As in poker, if you can't spot the patsy, it's you.

The London Film Festival screened *Crash* in November 1996, inciting the *Daily Mail* to demand on its front page 'Ban This Car Crash Sex Film'. While admitting she hadn't seen it, Virginia Bottomley, then Heritage Secretary, urged Westminster Council to exercise its prerogative and bar the film from the cinemas under its control, including the prestigious first-run theatres of the West End. The British Board of Film Classification had begun to consider it the month before, but at arm's length and a snail's pace. They consulted a psychologist, who reassured them it wouldn't encourage people to indulge in car-crash sex. A QC concluded it didn't contravene the Obscene Publications Act. They held a screening for eleven paraplegics. Not all enjoyed it, but most approved of Rosanna Arquette's characterisation as a disabled woman who was not only sexually active but hot with it.

In March, the Board rated *Crash* suitable for audiences over eighteen, and released it uncut. That only hardened resistance and ramped up the level of abuse. Until the day it opened in May, the conservative press relentlessly attacked the BBFC and its members, even publishing photographs and personal details of these 'liberals' who were ready to unleash this dangerous work. Westminster Council demanded the film be cut and, when the distributors declined, banned it from all West End venues. But neighbouring Camden, traditionally more liberal, allowed the film to play intact. Controversy settled down until August 1997, when Princess Diana was killed in a Paris car crash, replenishing the sexual mythology of the automobile, and proving Jim, once again, to have been prescient. Since 1984, he'd extemporised freely in interviews and described in prose the special power and mystery of collective hysteria, and the capacity, even eagerness, of the public to surrender to frenzies such as that evoked by Diana's death and interment. If there is a Ballardian era, it dates from August 1997. After that, nobody challenged his right be considered Max Ernst's successor as, in André Breton's phrase, 'the most magnificently haunted mind in Europe'.

CHAPTER FIFTY-ONE

DU CÔTÉ DE CHEZ JIM

In 1998, Edna Ballard died in Claygate, Surrey. Jim hadn't seen his mother for years, and resisted visiting her on her deathbed until his sister persuaded him.

Once *Crash* went on release, he participated vigorously in its defence, including giving interviews to Iain Sinclair for a British Film Institute book on the film. An unabashed admirer, Sinclair confessed to accepting the commission in part for the chance to meet Jim in the flesh, and they remained friendly until Jim's own death. Sinclair possessed the breadth of vision to see both novel and film in the context of the post-modern cultural landscape.

For a perspective on the *New Worlds* days, Sinclair interviewed Moorcock, resident in Texas with his third wife, Linda. Of much that Jim held sacred, Moorcock was dismissive. He called Chris Evans 'a pseudo-scientist' and the *Crashed Cars* exhibition 'pretty dull'. He stigmatised Paolozzi as a phoney, and Jim as his dupe.

> Paolozzi went to Germany and came back speaking this ersatz jargon. He and Jimmy were so banal. Everything they thought about. It was like an Emma Tennant dinner party. I wonder if this is just public school barbarism? You can hear echoes of Jimmy in Martin Amis. Boy-techno stuff, presented in an aggressive way. Amis extended his narrowness through Jimmy. It gave him a channel.

On the record, Jim shrugged off these attacks. 'Mike's a mythologist,' he told Sinclair. In private, he was furious, complaining to David Pringle in a July 1999 letter of the 'provincial' Moorcock denigrating Paolozzi and Chris Evans, who were both, he claimed, his superiors in intelligence. While praising Sinclair's book, he urged Pringle to take all Moorcock's comments with a huge pinch of salt, insisting that almost everything he said was out-and-out invention.

A sense of grievance also permeated his relationship with another former supporter, the radical publishing enterprise of Savoy Books, managed by David Britton and Jim's former protégé from *Ambit*, Michael Butterworth. Britton proposed to reissue a series of de luxe limited editions of fantasy classics, including Maurice Richardson's *The Exploits of Engelbrecht*, which had interested Jim at Cambridge, and David Lindsay's *A Voyage to Arcturus*. Each would be accompanied by a CD of extracts from the book, read by actress Fenella Fielding in her trademark insinuating, near-baritone purr. Fielding agreed to record some extracts from *Crash*, with a view to a similar reissue. According to Butterworth,

> Fielding has the allure of Hollywood about her, while having an eccentric English demeanour, and has what we think is the perfect voice for reading *Crash*. It took us a great deal of effort to get her to do it. At first, she was cautious, because she didn't want to do anything that she thought might demean women. After protracted discussion, which went on for about a year, she finally took the advice of an ex-BBC director friend, who assured her that it would be OK. She did the reading, but would not read some of the more violent heterosexual sex scenes involving women.

Butterworth sent the CD to Ballard, along with the proposal, but he refused to cooperate. 'He claimed that he had always disliked "book worship" in any form, and did not subscribe to the "industry of limited editions"; he thought books should be mass-produced and disposable. When I asked whether he would mind us releasing just the Fielding reading on its own, he said not, preferring that "a book should just be a book".' This hardly squares with his readiness to inscribe books for collectors, nor the signed and slip-cased editions of *Empire of the Sun* and *Miracles of Life*, and a number of occasional limited editions. He may have felt that involvement with Savoy and Britton – who had already served two prison terms under the Obscene Publications Act – risked once again placing him in hazard, as had been the case with 'Why I Want to Fuck Ronald Reagan'.

Jim's visit to Cannes for the film festival reminded him of how the Côte d'Azur had changed. Ferried by limo between Antibes and Cannes, he'd seen at close quarters the disappearance of the casinos and *belle époque* hotels of the old Riviera. Gobbling up estates, techno parks such as Sophia Antipolis metastasised through what had been the summer refuge and retirement region of the Parisian bourgeoisie. The pine woods, private beaches and secluded villas of *Tender Is the Night*, in which Gerald and Sara Murphy entertained Scott and Zelda Fitzgerald, had become France's Silicon Valley. A sprawl of white office complexes and laboratories, spas, gymnasiums, fountains and hectares of car parks, apartment blocks, offices and business hotels squinted into the sun, *brises-soleils* like RayBans. Only an occasional patch of grass or grove of trees, as domesticated as a flock of sheep, interrupted the man-made monotony.

The transformation didn't repel Jim, quite the reverse. He found it so soothing that he started a new novel set in one of these complexes. Inspired by Sophia Antipolis, he called his techno park Eden-Olympia. As a title, *More Cocaine Nights* would not have been inappropriate, since the book replicated both the plot and argument of the first, though with more polish and confidence. However, he decided instead on *Super-Cannes.*

Its main character, Paul Sinclair, is another hangdog Ballard hero, limping after a flying accident that left both knees shattered, along with his confidence. Abandoning the aviation publishing company he helped found, he accompanies his new wife, Jane, a doctor, to her new job at Eden-Olympia. She's replacing her former lover, David Greenwood, who supposedly went on a killing spree, murdering seven people before himself dying. Nobody quite knows why, but an unhappy love affair is suspected – an explanation almost as outlandish in this haven of complaisant infidelity as death by meteorite.

Having created a plot almost identical to that of *Cocaine Nights*, Jim barely deviates from it. The alpha male of Eden-Olympia isn't a tennis pro but the psychiatrist Dr Wilder Penrose. Though no less a lord of misrule, he exhibits an athleticism that is intellectual rather than physical: less Wimbledon Centre Court, more *Brain of Britain*. He can swap aviation lore with Sinclair and appreciate the finer points of his vintage Jaguar. The two men bandy quotes from Cyril Connolly's *The Unquiet Grave*, in particular the description of driving south to the Côte d'Azur in the good old days, his girlfriend with the Michelin guide open in her lap and the plane trees going sha sha sha past the window. It's implicit in the exchange that Connolly's Riviera has gone for ever.

Super-Cannes also ramps up the scale of psychopathic violence. Where Bobby Crawford used house invasions and porno pics to ginger up Estrella de Mar, Penrose stages vigilante raids on the nearby dormitory towns inhabited by immigrant workers. 'Undesirables' are beaten up and occasionally killed. Like Anderson, Penrose is convinced that violence stimulates creativity. A few *sans papiers* with broken heads are, he insists, a small price to pay for the possible emergence of another Bill Gates or Akio Morita. When Sinclair responds drily that the victims might not agree, Penrose suggests it's no more than they expect. In fact, in satisfying their expectations, the raiders might be doing them a good turn.

Believing Greenwood was murdered, Sinclair allies himself with the dead man's ex-lover, Frances, who soon becomes his lover also. But before they can unravel the mystery, she's killed in an attempt to fake a suicide pact that should have ended with both of them dead. With his marriage in meltdown and his wife surrendering to the sensual pleasures of sex and drugs, Sinclair decides to complete Greenwood's task and purge the evil that is taking over Eden-Olympia. He will kill Penrose and his confederates, then, before the killings are discovered, fly to London and give himself up, preventing the crime from being concealed, like Greenwood's death, by the corrupt French police. He takes some satisfaction from the fact that Jane will be the first witness for the defence. They'll be brought together again, even if only at the Old Bailey.

Jim may never have read the shopping and fucking novels then in vogue, but he understood their tricks. Historical factoids, tourist tips, restaurant recommendations and descriptions of clothing are scattered through *Super-Cannes*. His early experiments with Letraset and cut-up headlines demonstrated how capitalised proper names caught the eye. Clothing, cars and aircraft are invariably identified by brand; not just a car but a BMW or a Range Rover; not merely a hotel but the Noga Hilton; not an anonymous office but the headquarters of American Express. Reading paragraphs riddled with such names resembles a game of minigolf, the ball of one's attention ricocheting randomly from irrelevant specifics as from a jutting cornice or rockery.

During the writing of *Super-Cannes*, Jim burned the accumulation of scientific documents Chris Evans had sent him. 'It was wonderful stuff,' he said wistfully. 'I kept it in the coal shed for years. When I finally cleaned it out, I could hardly bear to throw any of it away. I can't have enough information coming into my life – I want to read everything. I want to eavesdrop on the shop talk of specialists in any field.' He could incinerate the material with indifference, since he now had a new source of technological gossip: the internet. Jim never owned a computer, and had barely been persuaded to upgrade his old manual typewriter to an electric. Claire, however, was an energetic web surfer and acted as his researcher, dredging up what Alan Bennett in *The History Boys* calls 'gobbets' – lumps of raw fact which, judiciously dropped into otherwise pedestrian material, engage our attention and provide the illusion of omniscience.

Jim doesn't apologise for the plethora of product placements in *Super-Cannes*. If anything, it was the point of the book. 'The main theme,' he explained,

> is that in order to keep us happy and spending more as consumers, capitalism is going to have to tap rather more darker strains in our

> characters, which is of course what's been happening for a while. If you look at the way in which the more violent contact sports are marketed – American football, wrestling, boxing – and of course the most violent entertainment culture of all, the Hollywood film, all these have tapped into the darker side of human nature in order to keep the juices of appetites flowing. That is the risk.

The clearest impression left by *Super-Cannes* and Jim's defence of it, as well as by the numerous enthusiastic reviews, is of Britishness. Possibly he did spend time at one of these parks, and even spoke to employees, though nothing in the acknowledgements suggests this. Claire undertook much of the research, working online. Moreover, to probe Sophia Antipolis in depth, he would have needed to know some foreign languages, particularly French. His characters are overwhelmingly Anglo-Saxon, or, if putatively French, speak impeccable English and act like Britons – as, for instance, when one of them, Delage, discourses to Sinclair on Bonnard, Picasso, Matisse, and the possible influence of Provençal light and the quartz in the Permian rock on their work. Delage is supposed to be a senior executive, but this lecturette has the tone of a twenty-two-year-old, fresh from the École Normale Supérieure, who's been designated to take an American visitor on a guided tour.

The rants of Wilder Penrose (perhaps named for British surrealist Roland Penrose?) are similarly Anglocentric, though riddled with Germanic rhetoric. He cites an understanding of man's latent psychopathy as a key to the success of Hitler, who didn't impose anti-Semitism but tapped into the deep-seated and entirely natural fear of strangers. He argues that those resentments remain in our psyche, ready to be evoked by a sufficiently skilful ideologue. Advertising already did so, by playing on some of the more benign elements of this shared consciousness. The next step, he suggested, would be more sinister.

Though the sociopolitical element is new, this wasn't the first time Ballard had voiced such sentiments. His identification of psychopathy as the engine of creativity went back to his days at Cambridge. But this was dangerous ground. Political correctness had made even so detached a historical perspective on Hitler and his policies at best an act of bad taste, and at worst a sort of moral heresy. For the first time, one sensed Jim moving not so much five minutes into the future as five minutes sideways.

CHAPTER FIFTY-TWO

OLD-SCHOOL REVOLUTION

The reflections inspired by *Super-Cannes* would find their voice in another novel, *Kingdom Come*, but for the moment Jim elected to deal with more topical themes in a novel suggested by the beginning of the third millennium.

As a word to sell products, 'millennium', like 'bicentennial', never lived up to its promise. Moreover, nobody was entirely sure whether 2000 marked the beginning of the millennium or the end. No surprise, then, that *Millennium People*, Jim's 2003 novel of middle-class revolt in trendy London, arriving as it did two (or three?) years after the event, was no celebration, but a sour literary reflection on white elephants like the Millennium Dome and the wreck of a balance sheet of achievement of the Blair government.

As with Margaret Thatcher, Jim responded almost entirely to New Labour through its leader rather than its policies. Tony Blair irritated him. He resembled, he said, a restaurant 'greeter' who comes towards you with an obsequious smile, hand outstretched. 'Blair has this evangelical commitment to what he believes is right,' he said, 'and he invents the truth when he can't find it out in front of him. I think we're living in dangerous times and most people aren't really aware of it. They're worrying about asylum seekers or abortion or paedophilia.' For a former member of the plague-on-both-your-houses party, this interest in politics was not typical of Jim, and may have had more to do with Claire's militant leftism. One of the most active terrorists in *Millennium People* (and the lover of the protagonist) is named Kay Churchill.

Millennium People, like the millennium celebrations, treads a fine line between the predictable and the ridiculous. The ex-wife of psychologist David Markham is killed by a bomb on a luggage carousel at Heathrow on the day that Markham, quite separately, is due to fly out of the same terminal with his new wife. Co-opted into a search for the bomber, Markham joins the movement that appears to be responsible, winning its confidence by participating in a demonstration and being arrested. He becomes friendly with its ideologue, a discredited paediatrician and political activist named Richard Gould, who confesses that the real target was Markham himself. Having heard him speak on TV about the increasing meaninglessness of existence, Gould resolved to jolt people out of their complacency by blowing up the very man who warns of this anomie. The death of his ex-wife was an error – collateral damage – but just as effective in igniting greater and more effective violence.

The unacknowledged heroine of the revolt, and the book, is Jill Dando, the TV personality shot in broad daylight on her doorstep in 1999. The man convicted of the killing was acquitted on appeal, and her death remains a mystery. Jim co-opts it to his story, suggesting that the randomness of her shooting points to a fanatic such as Gould. 'What all these murders – Hungerford, Dunblane, Jill Dando – have in common,' he said, 'is that they appear to be meaningless. There are no motives. Dando wasn't even a celebrity. It may be that this is their great appeal.' The rationale is worthy of Josef Goebbels, recalling how the Nazis blamed a nonentity, Marinus van der Lubbe, for burning down the Reichstag, and the equally innocent Herschel Grynszpan for assassinating Ernst vom Rath, the act that triggered *Kristallnacht*.

Millennium People takes place mostly in Chelsea Marina, an imaginary Thames-side development built on the site of an old gasworks but inspired by Chelsea Harbour. The residents, furious at the soaring cost of living well – with higher parking fees, maintenance charges and taxes – rise in well-bred wrath. They begin by smashing parking meters and defying the police by putting up barricades, but by the end of the book, they've been decamped en masse, leaving some of their homes in flames.

While the British middle class make improbable revolutionaries, Jim points out that the most dangerous radicals in Italy, France and Germany came from privileged backgrounds. These people have studied political science at university and know the relevant authorities – Marcuse, Fanon, Hoffman. Their class also places them above suspicion. Initially, nobody can believe they would stoop to physical violence. Jim enjoys describing their choice of targets: points of cultural interest, such as Tate Modern and the V&A, and the National Cat Club show at Olympia. Kay Churchill, a film scholar, plants smoke bombs in video stores, a campaign that culminates in incinerating the National Film Theatre.

Though more than ready to play to the crowd at readings, and to emphasise the book's parodic elements, Jim denied he meant *Millennium People* as a social satire. 'What I try not to do when writing is to poke fun at the middle classes,' he told a journalist. 'They're such an easy target. I don't want to become a dime-store satirist. There's no satire in this book at all.' But Adam Mars-Jones, in one of the more thoughtful reviews, found no shortage of cheap shots at the expense of the insurrectionists.

> *Crash* succeeded in part because of a rigorous avoidance of humour, while in *Millennium People*, Ballard seems content some of the time to play things for laughs, or at least smiles. The bourgeois revolutionaries of Chelsea Marina remain bourgeois even as they take on the system that has both spoiled and exploited them. They order a dozen skips before they riot, and tidy up afterwards. A Volvo may have been burnt out in the mayhem, but it has been properly left in a parking bay. When making Molotov cocktails, the revolutionaries use burgundy bottles, with regimental ties for wicks.

He might have added that, as the police arrive to quell an incipient riot, they are pelted not with paving stones, as in *les événements* of

Paris in 1968, but holiday souvenirs – colourful stones picked up on holiday in the Seychelles, Mauritius or the Yucatán. His credit card terrorists block the entrances to Peter Jones and the London Library, Legoland and the British Museum, travel agencies and the V&A, a Hendon shopping mall and a minor public school. Smoke bombs explode in Selfridge's Food Hall and the Dinosaur Wing of the Natural History Museum – a reminder of the war cry of the Futurist Marinetti, 'Destroy the Museums'.

Quoting Marinetti, a cultural hero of the sixties, puts the stamp of *vieux jeux* on the *Millennium People* revolt. The book's twenty-first-century setting is misleading. Its references to cinema and urban terrorism are redolent of forty years earlier. Some of Jim's comments to the press while promoting the book have the ring of 1968. 'When you're a young writer,' he said, 'you want to change the world in some small way, but when you get to my age you realise that it doesn't make any difference whatsoever, but you still go on. It's a strange way to view the world. If I had my time again, I'd be a journalist. Writing is too solitary. I think journalists have more fun!'

The burning of the National Film Theatre induces a special glee. Killing time until they torch the place, Markham and Churchill watch the *film noir Out of the Past*, a Ballard (and *Cahiers du cinéma*) favourite. For a few years, the NFT had an annexe called the Museum of the Moving Image, an imaginative but not very popular installation that closed in 1999. Churchill, with Markham's reluctant assistance, starts the fire there, among the posters for Hollywood films. He protests at the immolation of benign cultural heroes such as Burt Lancaster, Humphrey Bogart and Lauren Bacall, but Churchill is adamant; such people rotted the brains of their audiences, she says, drowning them in dreams.

More intense press interest in his work since *Empire of the Sun* had made Jim media savvy. Journalists wishing to discuss *Millennium People* were seldom invited home to gawp at the Delvauxs and snigger at his poor housekeeping. A reporter from the *Sunday Telegraph* who did so saw a flash of the bully. 'Please! Don't ask me about the dust! Everyone is fascinated by my dust – there must be more interesting things to talk about.'

He met another journalist at the Hilton International Hotel in Holland Park, a real-life equivalent of Chelsea Marina, but enthused about the perspective offered by Shepperton – 'a close-up view of the real England – the M25, the world of business parks, industrial estates and executive housing, sports clubs and marinas, cineplexes, CCTV, car-rental forecourts. That's where boredom comes in – a paralysing conformity and boredom that can only be relieved by some sort of violent act; by taking your mail-order Kalashnikov into the nearest supermarket and letting rip.'

While *Millennium People* resembles *Cocaine Nights* and *Super-Cannes*, the similarity is only plot-deep. In those books, the man instigating the violence had a clear aim. Gould's aim is aimlessness. It makes *Millennium People* both surrealist and existentialist, in a form even purer than *L'Étranger*. Nobody commented, and Jim didn't stress the point, that such random killing was a scaled-up version of the archetypal surrealist *acte gratuit* – to fire a gun at random into a crowd. By putting the rhetoric of the novel into the mouths of film critics and media psychologists, Jim disguises his point with jargon. It's only when we swallow the bait that we feel the barb.

While he was in the news, the government proposed Jim for a CBE. He refused, calling the honours system 'a Ruritanian charade that helps to prop up our top-heavy monarchy'. His indignation didn't neutralise an enjoyment of the absurdity, however. Not entirely seriously, he asked if the Commander of the Order of the British Empire entitled him to style himself 'Commander'. 'When they said no, I told them I couldn't see the point.' He became one of that distinguished group of more than three hundred people who, over the years, had also declined, among them performers Albert Finney, David Bowie, Dawn French and Jennifer Saunders, and sculptor Anish Kapoor. What if Margaret Thatcher and not Tony Blair had offered? Another of those unanswered Ballard questions.

*

Still every journalist's first call on a dull day, Jim answered more than his fair share of dumb questions from the press. Asked to comment on the 2004 death of structuralist philosopher Jacques Derrida, he fed the *Guardian* some skilfully improvised waffle. 'Do I even partly understand him? If I'm honest, not really. For 20 years, I've been floating around Derrida like a space capsule whose landing instructions have got lost, and I have never really made contact. Only professional philosophers and Eng. Lit. deconstructionists can really explain him.'

He was on firmer ground when the *Observer* queried 'What do you eat?'

'I'm bored,' he told them. 'I've eaten everything' – if not literally true, then at least defensible: who else had ingested both greyhound and weevils?

> I wake at 8 a.m and have a couple of cups of tea. Midmorning I make a coffee to get my brain in gear. Alcohol used to provide a large proportion of my calorie intake and my life enhancement, but I'm too old for that now. For lunch I eat odd things: Parma ham with a few drops of truffle oil. Dinner is usually an omelette. If I'm out I like some lobster, and I order a lot of crab dishes. I still enjoy a nice juicy steak. I'm also very fond of game. I love quails but I like grouse best of all.

Food also motivated *Home*, a twenty-three-minute adaptation, broadcast on BBC 4 in October 2004, of 'The Enormous Space', a 1989 story that first appeared in *Interzone.* Richard Curson-Smith wrote the script, and directed Antony Sher as Gerald Ballantyne, a middle-aged technologist who, after a spell in hospital following a car accident, and the subsequent defection of his wife, goes quietly insane. He decides never again to leave his middle-class two-storey suburban house, but, rather, to survive on whatever it contains.

The original story is chilly and interiorised, more interested in Ballantyne's increasing sense of transcendence than the practicality of his acts. Sher and Curson-Smith round him out. In the story, he heads a vaguely defined 'research department' in a merchant bank, but in the film he's a food scientist. This gives at least a superficial motive to his attempt to 'live off the land', which Gerald describes as an experiment, and documents in a video diary.

An admirer of Roman Polanski, Curson-Smith was attracted by the similarities between Ballard's story and Polanski's *Repulsion.* We sympathise so much with shy, pretty Catherine Deneuve, alone in an alien London, that it hardly seems strange when she starts carrying the rotting carcass of a rabbit around in her handbag. Short, soft-spoken, unblinking, Sher gives a disturbing, credible picture of a mind disappearing into itself. He and Curson-Smith interviewed polar explorers, dieticians and agoraphobes to build the character of Gerald, who never raises his voice, least of all when he's describing how to make earthworms edible. Cats and dogs are easier meat, and TV repairmen simplest of all. Everything he says in his video diary makes perfect sense, even when he comes to believe the upstairs rooms are expanding into infinite Blakeian spaces of mystical revelation, while downstairs a black garbage bag sags in the corner of the living room, a human leg-bone protruding.

CHAPTER FIFTY-THREE

EFFIGY

In October 2002, Iain Sinclair and Chris Petit staged an event at the Barbican to mark the launch of Sinclair's book *London Orbital* and Petit's associated TV film, both of which celebrated in Ballardian terms the roads around London. 'The whole point,' says Sinclair, 'was to walk the motorway spaces, and thereby suck out information slowly and gradually from the ground.' For the Barbican performance, some of the people mentioned in the book, including Jim, had agreed to appear in person while Petit's road footage was projected on three screens behind them. At the last minute, he begged off because of ill health, so Sinclair and Petit enlarged a photograph of him to life size. At the point where he was supposed to appear, they placed it on stage and recited alternate strophes of his 1984 essay 'What I Believe', which had come to be regarded as Ballard's credo. The Barbican expected to sell 400 or 500 seats, but in the end they had a full house of 2,000. Jim had entered the Pantheon, complete with his own effigy.

At the conclusion of the *London Orbital* film, Jim urges Sinclair, 'Iain, I want you to go out and blow up the Bentall Centre, I want you to destroy Bluewater.' Both were US-style multi-storey shopping malls on the outskirts of London, with cathedral-like atriums and piled galleries of shops. Few of the shops sold essentials. Rather, they served a market increasingly ready to make credit card purchases of clothing, shoes, electrical appliances, CDs and DVDs: 'adult toys', as a character calls them in Ballard's next and last novel, *Kingdom Come*. In it, he imagines a mall the size and form of the Millennium Dome dominating Brooklands, the satellite community once home to Britain's motor racing and aviation pioneers. The Metro-Centre is a consumer's cathedral, with more worshippers than any Christian church. It serves the inhabitants of Sinclair's 'orbital London', of which Shepperton was a part, but from which Jim felt increasingly alienated. The ring of motorways on which were strung many such temples of excess seemed to him less like a necklace than a noose.

It was a new and unsettling experience to see Ballard – the ideologue of rampant expansion and urbanism – condemning the commercial engines that powered them. Though never an enthusiastic consumer himself, he maintained a respect for commerce that went back to his childhood in Shanghai – a city built on business. Now, in his mid-seventies, he not only stigmatised that impulse, but did so in apocalyptic terms. Conspicuous consumption, he suggested, was a tyranny, albeit a soft one, and would lead inexorably to a new Dark Age.

Kingdom Come lamented the consumer society's erosion of the core values of Britain, as represented by the eccentrics and seers who had made Brooklands an emblem of pioneering technology. Malcolm Campbell attained near-sainthood on its racing circuit, and generations of aeronauts learned at Britain's first flying school, going on to pilot aircraft manufactured at the nearby Vickers plant. Jim's protagonist, Richard Pearson, is both a failed advertising executive and the son of a former airline pilot. Retiring to Brooklands, his father is shot dead, apparently at random, during a visit to the Metro-Centre. The metaphor is unsubtle but effective.

Richard arrives for the funeral to find Brooklands in the midst of a riot. A car is burning, and businesses run by Pakistanis and Asians are being vandalised. Everywhere he sees a white flag with a red cross, the symbol of St George. Groups of men, oddly disciplined, dressed in variations of the same red and white, are ostensibly helping the police to control the crowds in the streets but, rather, seem to be orchestrating the chaos. They belong to teams formed by the management of the mall. Before the end of the book, two thousand of them, inflamed by the rants of a local ideologue, will have barricaded themselves inside the dome. The police break the siege, but the Metro-Centre, like David Koresh's Waco compound, goes up in flames. As a US officer said of a Vietnam hamlet, 'It became necessary to destroy the village in order to save it.'

Kingdom Come extends the political ideas articulated in *Super-Cannes.* It argues that, if people will abrogate their individuality to the power of advertisers, they'll do the same to a political demagogue. It was an unexpected theory from an inspired publicist who had demonstrated both a flair for practical promotion and, with his *Advertiser's Announcement* series, a respect for advertising as an art. More puzzling still, he shows Richard Pearson, a professional publicist, undergoing a Pauline conversion and offering his skills to the amateur politicians of Brooklands who are fumbling their way towards becoming modern-day incarnations of Josef Goebbels. Pearson suggests that the St George phenomenon illustrates one of the seismic movements that pass periodically through the collective psyche, and which the Nazis and other extremist learned to exploit. In him, we hear the authentic Ballard voice, as masterly at pressing a political point as persuading a woman into bed. It's the voice of a born advertiser, paradoxically preaching a jihad against commerce: the contradiction at the heart of Jim Ballard's life.

CHAPTER FIFTY-FOUR

INNER OUT

Published in 2006, *Kingdom Come* received respectful treatment from reviewers. Nobody rose in horror to denounce a libel of the consumer society. As André Breton had said, it was impossible to shock people any more.

Taking a cue from the vision of the book, HarperCollins's publicity department designed a website for the fictitious Metro-Centre, complete with news of forthcoming meetings of the St George groups and an advertisement for red-crossed T-shirts. Mocked-up posters evoked the campaigns then in use around Britain for Benetton clothing and Silk Cut cigarettes, where one had to stare at the image for a while – the whole point – to understand what was being promoted. Of the Metro-Centre posters, the best is the black and white shot of a young man standing, apparently irresolute, in an empty parking lot. Nearby, a clump of stunted greenery, isolated in the lake of asphalt, stands as shorthand for 'Nature'. Stark white lettering warns 'The Wait is Almost Over'. Not for the first time, Ballard proved prescient. By 2011, 48 per cent of Britons said they would support an anti-immigration English nationalist party if it was not associated with violence and fascist imagery, and would approve policies to make it statutory for all public buildings to fly a patriotic flag – like the red cross of St George.

'The Wait Is Almost Over' also proved an augury for Jim. Early in 2001, Jeremy Reed tried to interest him in a project involving Helmut Newton. He declined, citing a virus – which, he joked, he might have picked up in Soho during signing sessions for *Kingdom Come.* Since contracting the bug, he'd been in and out of hospital, and while he was recovering, the process would take time. The mysterious virus inaugurated a period of declining health for both Jim and Claire. She underwent serious kidney surgery, and was diagnosed with cancer, while Jim was increasingly troubled by persistent pain in his back and ribs that he attributed to arthritis. In June 2006, he learned that cancer, beginning in his prostate, had spread to his bones, and was advanced and inoperable.

Dr Jonathan Waxman of the Cancer Centre at Hammersmith Hospital put him on a drug regime that bought him the time to wind up his life with dignity. Initially, pain management allowed him to live an almost normal life, and, when steroids brought back his appetite, even to dine out at his favourite restaurants such as the Brackenbury or Chez Kristof. Martin Amis recalled,

> my wife and I, together with Will Self and Deborah Orr, had dinner with him and his partner of forty years, Claire Walsh. He revealed in the restaurant that he probably had 'about two years to live'. This was said with instinctive courage, but with all the melancholy to be expected from a man who loved life so passionately.

Early in 2007, and at the urging of Waxman, Jim decided to write the account of his life which he'd blocked for thirty years. The sticking point had always been his parents. Much as he disliked them, he would not have wished to put his feelings into print while they lived. As he told Don Morrison of *Time* magazine, 'Various people have approached me about a biography. But that would require hundreds of hours of interviews about my parents and the like, which I don't necessarily want to consider. I might discover all sorts of horrible things about myself.' He announced his change of heart in a typically wry manner that evaded cruelty through kindness. The latest aspirant had compiled a detailed outline for a biography which HarperCollins submitted for – hopefully – his approval. Jim returned it with lavish praise – and the news that it made the case so effectively for such a book that he'd decided to write one himself.

Miracles of Life, subtitled *Shanghai to Shepperton: An Autobiography*, was published in 2008 by Fourth Estate, a 'boutique' division of HarperCollins. The 'miracles of life', Jim explains, were his children, to whom he dedicated the book – only the second time Jim dedicated anything. Those who knew something of his relationship with his daughters and in particular his son raised their eyebrows, but the news of his imminent demise, contained in an *envoi*, disarmed them. This was not a book to which conventional critical standards could be applied.

With hindsight, however, *Miracles of Life* must be counted a partial failure. Robert McCrum in the *Observer* rightly called it 'disappointing and fascinating'. The long-delayed reminiscences of his parents, though intermittently revealing, are skimpy. He once again rehearses the events of Lunghua, but a succession of mistresses goes unacknowledged. There is some unapologetic padding. A description of jury deliberations and altercations at the 1991 MystFest film festival in Viareggio is lifted verbatim from a 2003 book review. Having kept few records and no diaries, Jim was forced to rely on memory, which he didn't reinforce by showing the manuscript to those who would have corrected simple errors of fact. But Jim was a master of self-promotion, and *Miracles of Life* is above all one of his skilful exercises in image management.

His postscript praises the skill of the medical professionals whose efforts allowed him to keep working. HarperCollins even announced another book, to be based on his dialogues with his oncologist. One report from the Frankfurt Book Fair recounted, 'An envelope arrived [in Hanbury's office], quite out of the blue, a couple of weeks back – Hanbury admits she assumed it was a royalty query. In fact it contained an outline for a new book, working title *Conversations with My Physician*. The physician in question is oncologist Professor Jonathan Waxman of Imperial College, London, who is treating Ballard for prostate cancer. While it is in part a book about cancer, and Ballard's struggle with it, it moves on to broader themes – indeed, the subtitle is The Meaning, if Any, of Life. [Hanbury] is talking to Ballard's long-standing publishers, among them Fourth Estate in the UK.' Once Jim's condition deteriorated, the book was forgotten.

Superficially, Jim appeared as relaxed and optimistic as ever, but the few people close to him knew differently. Mike Moorcock briefly returned to England in early 2007 and the two old friends patched up their feud. On his return to Texas, Jim sent a letter that revealed the true darkness of his thoughts.

> He said that he kept going courtesy of Merck, Pfizer and Smith Kline. He hated chemo; said it was like eating a bad oyster, over and over. His life had become a succession of, in his words, 'hospital car parks, waiting rooms, smiling nurses and friendly doctors whose lips said nothing but whose eyes said everything'.

In 2008, he moved into Claire's flat, which she modified to accommodate his treatment. He'd already stopped watching television and no longer listened to the radio. Concerned at his long periods of silence, Walsh asked what was on his mind. He told her: 'I am thinking about my life.' At the end of the year, increasing pain and exhaustion forced his hospitalisation. He was placed on a morphine drip. The experience exacerbated his lifelong fear of medication, while the presence of so many strangers was deeply disturbing for someone who, for decades, had lived alone. As the drug freed his imagination, the tubes and winking lights of the monitors convinced him he was imprisoned inside an organism that was draining his life.

In February, in growing distress, he was moved back to Shepherd's Bush. Helped by GPs and district nurses, and, in time, by Macmillan nurses, who sat with him through the night, allowing her to rest, Walsh nursed him through March. Even when she wasn't by his side, she slept with a baby monitor by her bed. During his last days, he was only semi-conscious and didn't recognise his surroundings. It had been thought he might be taken back to Shepperton to die, but this idea was abandoned. To expel his last breath there would have imposed inappropriate symmetry on to an asymmetrical life. His condition deteriorated rapidly in the last four days and he no longer knew where he was. He died in his sleep in the early morning of Sunday 19 April 2009. He was seventy-eight years old.

On his last visit to the house, in the summer of 2008, he'd been in too much pain to drive. According to Fay Ballard,

> I hadn't visited Shepperton for many years. I remembered a dried-up orange sitting on the mantelpiece in the nursery. I walked through the door and it was still there. I said, 'Oh my goodness, you still have the orange.' He looked at me and he said, very quietly but seriously, 'It's a lemon.' It must have been there for at least forty years. I don't see the lemon as something eccentric. It's not a relic. It's covered in dust. It hasn't been moved. It's obviously important to him. And it's very beautiful.

As Claire and his daughters gathered up the items he wanted to take back to Shepherd's Bush, Jim looked around the rooms where he'd passed half a century, and which had become so closely associated with him that they seemed an extension of his personality.

In an incredulous voice, he murmured: 'I can't believe I lived in this place so long.'

EPILOGUE

NAKED ON THE FORK

With ample notice of Jim's impending death, a number of newspapers published lengthy obituaries, but his life and achievement proved difficult to assess. To praise the popular *Empire of the Sun* was to neglect contentious works such as *The Atrocity Exhibition* and *Crash*. Worse, to stress his literary accomplishment at the expense of his significance as a spokesman did disservice to both. Most journalists fell back on a summary of his public persona. As Vincent van Gogh became, in popular imagination, the painter who cut off his ear and gave it to a friend, Ballard was celebrated as the inventor of 'inner space' who foretold the death of Princess Di.

The few people who knew Ballard personally were only slightly more successful in summing him up. Most admitted their failure to discern the author of such savage and sinister fiction lurking behind what Martin Amis called the 'robustly rounded and amazingly cheerful, positively sunny suburbanite'. Will Self and Iain Sinclair stressed Jim's ability to appear both ordinary and exceptional, modest and dogmatic, amiable and forbidding. 'I felt an immediate affinity to Ballard the man,' wrote Self, 'one quite as deep and intense as the one I had had to his writing for many years. He was, in person, at once puckish and affable – he had not one scintilla of the affectation or false pride that forms the armature of "great men".'

The same admiration was evident in the outpouring of unashamed devotees such as V. Vale, the San Francisco-based publisher who reissued *The Atrocity Exhibition*, and published collections of Ballard's quotations and interviews. Vale told a panel at the Barcelona conference of 2008,

> As soon as he starts talking and thinking and expressing himself, it's beyond some rational process level. He has such an incredibly detailed and complete philosophy, such an evolved vision of the universe. Unlike most of us, he doesn't have to censor himself or choose his words carefully. It just comes out. Unlike 99 per cent of writers out there, he just tells the truth. How rare is that?

Maggie Hanbury made the official announcement of Jim's death. The funeral would be private, she said, but a memorial would be held on a date to be decided. This took place at Tate Modern on Sunday 15 November 2009 – Jim's seventy-ninth birthday, had he lived. An invitation became London's hottest ticket, with rival guest lists being squabbled over by members of the family. About a hundred people made the cut. Casualties included, it's rumoured, Salman Rushdie, whose *Midnight's Children* had aroused Jim's displeasure. In Rick McGrath's description, 'The area was liquid with light and the format was a simple stage and microphone with flanking video screens. We sat in chairs that fanned in a wide arc along the length of the room.' Bea Ballard introduced the speakers. They included Self and Amis; Amis on video, as were Steven Spielberg and others associated with the film of *Empire of the Sun*. Mike and Linda Moorcock came from Paris and V. Vale from San Francisco. Jim appeared by proxy in a clip from *Shanghai Jim*.

Belying his life of apparent poverty, Jim left a startling £4,019,809. Of this, his son received £100,000, signifying his long estrangement from his father; Claire Walsh £300,000; Fay and Beatrice each got £1.1 million. Inheritance tax was reduced by depositing Ballard's papers in the British Library. It allowed a generous £350,000 rebate on fifteen cartons of manuscripts and other material, mostly dating from after *Empire of the Sun* but including an early version of *Crash*. Though publicised at the time as a treasure trove for scholars, the accumulation was skimpy for so prolific a writer, attesting to the amount incinerated over the years. (Compare, for instance, the eighty-five cartons presented to the Bodleian by John Le Carré the following year, with his voluminous correspondence still to come.) The British Library announced the donation in June 2010, by which time it was also widely known that, a few weeks after the memorial she helped organise, Maggie Hanbury was fired as agent by Bea and Fay, and the estate placed in the hands of the famously proactive Andrew Wylie.

Once the mourning was over, critics attempted to place Ballard in literary perspective and found it a struggle. Except for his relationship to surrealist art, he had few identifiable influences. Those he'd embraced early in his career, such as Ray Bradbury and William Burroughs, had long since been subsumed and transcended. By writing so much and over so long a period, he outlived the traditions and the publishing culture that nurtured him. As Philip Hensher wrote in the *Spectator*:

> Ballard's career would simply not happen in the same way now. His transformations of genre fiction were, in part, made possible by the existence of a market for genre short stories. Science-fiction magazines in the 1950s and 1960s published a remarkable number of stories by what now seem classic writers. Ballard is the last of this distinguished line.

Writers, too, found that, as much as they respected and admired him, he was not a master to whom one could pay the compliment of imitation. His unique and disturbed psychology made him *sui generis*. Any attempt to absorb his influence and apply it to new work degenerated into pastiche. French author Michel Houellebecq was a partial exception. His novels *The Elementary Particles* and *The Possibility of an Island* resonate with Ballard without imitating his style. Their narratives, jumping between the present and the far future, are suffused with such Ballardian characteristics as perverse eroticism, a hatred of the consumer society, and a contempt for politics, religion and sentiment. They lack that quality of the fantastic that Ballard, rarely, possessed, and the ability, shared with the surrealists, in particular Dalí, to regard a barren present and an even more threatening future with a kind of glee. But it was entirely appropriate that the most accomplished of his intellectual children belonged to 'the international menu'.

The final tribute to Jim Ballard – at least at the time of writing – was also the most ambiguous. For *Crash*, a homage mounted by London's Gagosian Gallery in 2010, fifty-two artists filled the east London space with exhibits that putatively evoked his work. Aside from the foreseeable Helmut Newton, Eduardo Paolozzi, two moony Edward Hoppers and a reclining Delvaux nude, these ranged as widely as views of night-time freeways by Dan Holdsworth, a 3.5-metre-wide photograph of a Boeing 747's undercarriage by Adam McEwen, and a Damian Hirst assemblage incorporating the photograph of a car bonnet spattered with the blood of a suicide bomber, accompanied by an installation of surgical instruments. Jim would have appreciated the maquette for Allen Jones's sculpture which dominates the lobby of the Heathrow Hilton, but what would he have made of Christopher Williams's photograph of a girl's foot, caught in the act of pulling on a red sock, or Roger Hirons's dangling bunches of ... is it broccoli? Not to mention Jeff Koons's display of two antique vacuum cleaners. A last dig by the curators at his slapdash housekeeping?

No matter. There could be no 'correct' summation of his career, nor would he have expected one. Jim's skill was to speculate and fantasise, evade and lie. 'Truth' was not a word he regarded with much respect, least of all in describing and explaining his life. In its stead, he deployed the psychopath's reverence for the instant present, for frenzy, for the divine, and for those forces, natural and unnatural, that are forever slipping beyond our control. Reviewing the Gagosian show, Peter Campbell wrote, 'Ballard's sense of something wrong with the world our appetites and ingenuity have created makes ordinary things – suburbs, roads and high-rises – look different, as they might in the lurid glow of an approaching storm.'

*

I knew of Jim Ballard before I ever came to Britain. Ted Carnell published stories by both of us in the mid-sixties, even, occasionally, in the same issues: the high point of my career with Nova Publications may be sharing the cover of *New Worlds* issue No. 140 with 'The Terminal Beach'. That Jim was the superior writer was never in doubt, and when I experimented in his style, Ted published the story but chided my homage. One Ballard, apparently, was enough.

Having collected his books as they were published, I sought Jim out when I arrived in London in 1970. We drifted into an amiable professional relationship, sustained by my bibliophilia. I bought the occasional manuscript or letter of his that came on the market, shelving them next to his scribbled notes to me. These developed into an archive of first editions, proof copies, letters and typescripts which included his outlines for novels such as *Concrete Island* and a typescript of the original unedited version of *Crash*. Jim viewed my collecting with amusement, explaining, to my dismay, that he periodically made a bonfire of such items in a pit in the back garden.

I visited Shepperton occasionally to interview him, in particular for my biography of Steven Spielberg, and observed at first hand the legendary dust and the Delvauxs. He favourably reviewed some of my biographies. It seemed logical that I should write his, but when I proposed it a few times, he declined, citing the trauma of having to examine his relationship with his parents. I subsequently discovered I wasn't the only candidate, and that he refused us all.

I'm glad I didn't write this book when he was alive. It would have taken a stronger will than his to confront the realities of his troubled life. Many of my questions would undoubtedly have drawn the thin-lipped fury of which Mike Moorcock spoke: 'the clam, duct-taped shut'. Asked why he called his novel *Naked Lunch*, William Burroughs growled: 'The title means exactly what the words say: naked lunch, a frozen moment when everyone sees what is on the end of every fork.' Jim fled the reality of such moments, taking refuge in physical isolation and the evasions of art. With him finally at rest, it seems time to ask what that meant in terms of his work and life.

ACKNOWLEDGEMENTS

One of the great pleasures of writing this book was the opportunity to spend many hours with Mike and Linda Moorcock as, despite poor health, Mike generously recalled his memories of the man who, for three decades, was his closest friend. David Pringle, Jim's bibliographer, was unstinting in his assistance. The frequent advice given by Ballard acquaintances to 'Ask David Pringle. He'll know' proved almost invariably correct.

John Harding, archivist of The Leys school, guided me through Ballard's time there, and, with Kelly O'Reilly, gave me access to its records. David Curtis and Biddy Peppin elucidated the history of IRAT and helped untangle the complexities of the *Crashed Cars* exhibition. Sally Potter and Richard John Jones of St Martin's College of Art added additional information. John 'Hoppy' Hopkins loaned his video of the show's private view, and, via Adam Lockhart, authorised its restoration through the Visual Research Centre at the University of Dundee.

Neil Hornick gave me the benefit of his intimate knowledge of the alternative arts scene in the London of the 1960s and access to his archive. He also interviewed Steve Dwoskin on my behalf. Harley Cokeliss made available his correspondence with Ballard over the BBC film of *Crash*. David Thompson drew my attention to numerous obscure items in the BBC archives relating to or involving Ballard.

Malcolm Edwards described his association with Ballard as editor and publisher. Charles Platt supplied illuminating details of his friendship with Jim. John and Judith Clute offered a unique insight into London's science fiction scene of the sixties and seventies, further illuminated by Pete Weston. Simon Sellars's website, www.ballardian.com, was not only a valuable resource but a continuing pleasure and inspiration, as is that maintained by Rick McGrath at www.jgballard.ca

Brigid Marlin's reminiscences of painting Ballard and creating facsimiles of two Delvaux canvases gave an insight into his state of mind. Iain Sinclair was, as always, courteous and insightful in his recollections of his friendship with Ballard. Jeremy Reed, Jonathan Meades, Peter Weston, Brian Aldiss, Rick Gekoski, Don Morrison, Kevin Jackson, Richard Fidczuk, Lee Harding, Rick McGrath, Maxim Jakubowski, Margaret Hanbury and Sir Christopher Frayling were equally obliging. Dr Martin Simpson helped with medical information.

For access to additional documents, letters and other material, I'm indebted to Anne Brichto of the Addyman Bookshop, Hay-on-Wye, and David Aronovitz of the Fine Books Company.

Quotations from Ballard were accessed from the following published sources: 'His Dark Material', *Time*, 28 September 2006, Donald Morrison; 'The Ballard Exhibition', *International Herald Tribune*, 7 August 1981, Richard M. Evans; 'The Ballard of Will Self', *Radio Times*, 2 October 2009, Jane Anderson; 'Free Association. The novelist J. G. Ballard and his daughter Fay talk to Anthony Denselow', *Sunday Times Magazine*, 20 March 1988, Anthony Denselow; '"People seethed with a sort of repressed rage", The Worst of Times. J. G. Ballard Talks to Danny Danziger', *Independent*, 16 December 1991, Danny Danziger; 'Writers' Rooms', *Saturday Guardian*, 10 March 2007, interviewer unattributed; '"When in doubt, quote Ballard"': An Interview with Iain Sinclair', www.Ballardian.com, Tim Chapman; 'Ballard makes a pile out of pile-ups', *Independent on Sunday*, 16 June 1996, Ivan Waterman; 'Crash: J. G. Ballard's artistic legacy', *Guardian*, 13 February 2010, Iain Sinclair; 'The Road to "Crash"', *New Yorker*, 17 March 1997, Tom Shone; 'On a collision course', *Sunday Times*, 11 August 1996, Alex Linklater; 'Censors guilty of hit and run', *Evening Standard*, 19 March 1997, Alexander Walker; 'A movie beyond the bounds of depravity', *Evening Standard*, 8 June 1996, Alexander Walker; 'Weaver of dreams from the stuff of nightmares', *Guardian*, 26 October 1979, Angela Carter; 'Not a Step Beyond Tomorrow', *Time Out*, 2–8 November 1979, Giovanni Dadomo; 'Alien At Home', *Independent Sunday Review*, 15 September 1991, Lynn Barber; 'Believe It Or Not', *New York Review*, 24 October 1991, Robert Towers; 'Riverside Demons', *Observer*, 15 September 1991, Andrew Billen; 'Out of the Shelter', *Sunday Times*, 22 September 1991, Paul Pickering; 'Whatever Became of Jim?', *Mail on Sunday*, 10 April 1988, Jeannette Kupfermann; 'The Film of the Booker',

The Times, 28 November 1987, Chris Peachment; 'Ballard's Worlds', *Observer Magazine*, 2 September 1984, Martin Amis; 'The shopping mall psychopath', *Independent*, 14 September 2000, Thomas Sutcliffe; 'Surrealist seer of suburbia', *The Times*, 13 September 2000, Jason Cowley; 'The surrealist of suburbia', *Telegraph Magazine*, 14 September 1996. Mick Brown: 'Enthusiasm for the mysterious emissaries of pulp: Interview with David Britton', www.ballardian.com, Simon Sellars; 'Driven by Anger. An Interview with Michael Butterworth', www.ballardian.com, Mike Holliday; 'Perverse Technology', *Hard Magazine*, no. 1, 2004, Dan Mitchell and Simon Ford; Interview in *Corridor*, no. 5, 1974, David Britton and Michael Butterworth; 'Angry Old Men. Michael Moorcock on J. G. Ballard', www.ballardian.com, 2007, Mike Holliday; 'Rattling Other People's Cages: The J. G. Ballard Interview', www.ballardian.com, 2006, Simon Sellars; 'News From the Sun' later 'JGB News', issues 1–25, 1981–96, David Pringle, including 'Fact and Fiction in The Kindness of Women', no. 20, 1993; 'Unlucky Jim', *London Review of Books*, 10 October 1991, Julian Symons; 'J. G. Ballard. The Glow of the Prophet', *New York Review of Books*, 9 October 2008, Diane Johnson; 'The Profession of Science Fiction, 26: From Shanghai to Shepperton', *Foundation*, no. 24, 1982, David Pringle; 'Memories of the Sparse Age', www.jgballard.ca, interview by David Pringle and Jim Goddard, 4 January 1975; 'Water Diviner', *Observer*, 13 September 1987, Martin Amis; 'A hack at the Nautico Club', *Independent*, 14 September 1996, Nicholas Wroe; Interview with Sebastian Shakespeare, *Literary Review*, November 2001; 'A horror story from paradise', *Evening Standard*, 8 September 1994, Will Self; 'Riverside Demons', *Observer*, 15 September 1991, Andrew Billen; The Billen Interview, *Guardian*, 7 August 1994, Andrew Billen; 'The Comforts of Madness', *Independent*, 15 September 2006, Marianne Brace; 'From Here to Dystopia', *Telegraph Magazine*, 2 September 2006, Mick Brown; 'A Rebel in Suburbia', *Sunday Telegraph*, 21 September 2003, Emily Bearn; 'The Benign Catastrophist', *Guardian Weekend*, 6 September 2003, Suzie Mackenzie; 'Bard of Boredom', *Time Out*, 17–24 September 2003, Chris Hall; 'The journey from empire to dystopia', *Observer*, 10 February 2008, Robert McCrum; 'The Catastrophist', *The Atlantic*, January/February 2010, Christopher Hitchens; 'Visions of Dystopia', *The Face*, April 1998, Paul Rambali; 'The Art of Fiction no. 85', *The Paris Review*, Winter 1984, Thomas Frick; Interview with Philip Dodd on BBC Radio 4, *Nightwaves*, 7 February

2008; *Desert Island Discs*, BBC Radio 4, 2 February 1992; ‘Nothing is real, everything is fake. Bizarrely, most people like it that way’, www.jgballard.ca, interview with Hans-Ulrich Obrist, 2003; ‘Superhistory’, *London Review of Books*, 6 December, 1990, Patrick Parrinder; ‘Crash and Burn; J. G. Ballard turns the world of genre writing inside out’, *Sci-Fi Universe*, April 1994, Andrew Asch; Appreciation, *New Statesman*, 23 April 2009, John Gray; ‘The Space Age is Over’, *Penthouse* (UK), vol. 14, no. 1, 1979, Chris Evans; ‘A Psychopathic Hymn’: J. G. Ballard’s ‘Crashed Cars’ Exhibition of 1970; *seconds*, no date, Simon Ford (www.slashseconds.org); ‘An Interview with Jannick Storm’, *Speculation*, no. 21, February 1969; ‘“I really would not want to fuck George W. Bush!”: A Conversation with J. G. Ballard’, *Das Science Fiction Jahr 2007*, Werner Fuchs and Sascha Mamczak; ‘Future Perfect. The Crystalline World of J. G. Ballard’, *Street Life*, February 1978, Martin Hayman; ‘The Visitor’, *Hardcore* magazine, 1992, Phil Halper and Lard Iyer; ‘Pictures from an Atrocity Exhibition’ *Sunday Times*, 11 November 1990, John Clute; *Sunday Times Magazine*, 7 March 1999, interviewer unattributed; ‘Seeing him arrive, always smiling, ready for anything, was wonderful’, *Observer Review*, 26 April 2009, Tim Adams; ‘Waiting for Silver Coconuts’, *New Musical Express*, 22 October 1983, Charles Shaar Murray; ‘Strange Fiction’, *Guardian*, 14 June 2008, James Campbell; Interview by Hari Kunzru, 2007, for *Waterstone’s Books Quarterly*, www.harikunzru.com; Interview with Mike Moorcock, Pedro Marques, www.pedromarquesdg.wordpress.com; ‘Spacing Out’, *Times Educational Supplement*, 29 January 1971, Brendan Hennessy; *Transatlantic Review*, no. 39, Spring 1971, Brendan Hennessy; *Books and Bookmen*, April 1971, Douglas Reed; *Studio International*, no. 183, October 1971, discussion with Ballard, Eduardo Paolozzi and Frank Whitford; *The Imagination on Trial*, edited by Alan Burns and Charles Sugnet (Allison & Busby, 1981); ‘Saved by the TV Crew’, *New York Times*, 15 May 1988, Samuel R. Delany; *Memories of J. G. Ballard*, in *Old Leysian Newsletter*, 13, The Leys School, Cambridge, autumn 2009. Barrie Paige.

Extracts are used from the following books:

ABKHAZI, Peggy. *Enemy Subject: Life in a Japanese Internment Camp 1945–45*. Alan Sutton Publishing Company, 1995.

ALDISS, Brian and WINGROVE, David. *The Trillion Year Spree*. Gollancz, London, 1986.

BAUDRILLARD, Jean. *Simulacra and Simulations.* University of Michigan Press, Ann Arbor, 1994.

BESTER, Alfred. *Tiger Tiger* (*The Stars My Destination*). Sidgwick and Jackson, London, 1956.

(CARNELL, E.J.) GODDARD, James. *J.G. Ballard; A Bibliography.* Privately Printed, Lymington, 1970.

CAWTHORN, James. *'Ballard of a Whaler'* from *New Worlds,* January 1967.

GORDON, Richard, *Doctor in the House.* Michael Joseph, London, 1952.

LAING, Adrian. *R.D. Laing. A Life.* HarperCollins, London, 1994.

SINCLAIR, Iain. *Crash. BFI* Publishing, London, 1999.

WOLFE, Bernard. *Limbo.* Random House, New York, 1952.

ZOLINE, Pamela. *The Heat Death of The Universe and Other Stories.* McPherson, Kingston (NY), 1988.

INDEX